Defenders of the Union

Defenders of the Union: A survey of British and Irish unionism since 1801 provides a comprehensive overview of the contentious politics of unionism and the effects it has had on the relationship between Britain and Ireland over the past two centuries. By considering the history of unionism, the Act of Union of 1801, the Anglo-Irish Treaty of 1921 and their aftermath, *Defenders of the Union* provides an essential guide to these historical events and the continuing legacies which they have created.

This book looks at the way the Union has affected Anglo-Irish and Catholic-Protestant relations and also considers its social, cultural and economic effects on Irish and British life.

Key aspects which are discussed include:

- definition of unionism
- establishment of the Union
- defending the Union
- Protestant Churches and opposition to home rule
- unionist literature
- loyalists since 1972
- unionism, Conservatism and the Anglo-Irish Agreement.

D. George Boyce is Professor of Politics at the University of Wales, Swansea. His previous publications include *Nationalism in Ireland* (Routledge, 1995) and *The Irish Question and British Politics 1868–1996* (Macmillan, 1996). **Alan O'Day** is Senior Lecturer in History at the University of North London. His previous publications include *Irish Home Rule 1867–1921* (Manchester University Press, 1998) and *Charles Stewart Parnell* (Dundalgan Press, 1998). **D. George Boyce and Alan O'Day** have also co-edited two books for Routledge, *Parnell in Perspective* (1991) and *The Making of Modern Irish History* (1996).

Defenders of the Union

A survey of British and Irish unionism since 1801

**Edited by D. George Boyce
and Alan O'Day**

London and New York

First published 2001
by Routledge
11 New Fetter Lane, London EC4P 4EE

Simultaneously published in the USA and Canada
by Routledge
29 West 35th Street, New York, NY 10001

Routledge is an imprint of the Taylor & Francis Group

Typeset in Baskerville by
RefineCatch Limited, Bungay, Suffolk
Printed and bound in Great Britain by
St Edmundsbury Press, Bury St Edmunds, Suffolk

British Library Cataloguing in Publication Data
A catalogue record for this book is available from the British Library

Library of Congress Cataloging in Publication Data
Defenders of the Union : a survey of British and Irish unionism since
    1801 / edited by D. George Boyce and Alan O'Day.
        p.   cm.
      Includes bibliographical references and index.
      1. Ireland – Politics and government – 19th century.   2. Unionism (Irish
politics) – History – 19th century.   3. Unionism (Irish politics) – History
– 20th century.   4. Ireland – Politics and government – 20th
century.   5. Ireland – Relations – Great Britain.   6. Great Britain –
Relations – Ireland.   I. Boyce, David George, 1942–   II. O'Day, Alan.
DA950 .D35   2000
941.508 – dc21   00–032168

ISBN 0–415–17421–X (hbk)
ISBN 0–415–17422–8 (pbk)

Contents

Contributors

Arthur Aughey is Senior Lecturer in Politics at the University of Ulster at Jordanstown.

Paul Bew is Professor of Politics at the Queen's University of Belfast.

D. George Boyce is Professor of Politics at the University of Wales, Swansea.

Patrick Buckland is Trustee and Education Adviser to the Warrington Project and is now retired from the Directorship, Institute of Irish Studies, University of Liverpool.

Andrew Gailey is a house master at Eton College.

Gordon Gillespie is Research Officer on an Economic and Social Research Council project sponsored jointly by the University of Ulster and the Queen's University of Belfast.

Alvin Jackson is Professor of Modern Irish History at the Queen's University of Belfast.

Brian Jenkins is Professor of History at Bishops University, Canada.

Greta Jones is Professor of History at the University of Ulster at Jordanstown.

Carla King is Lecturer in History at St Patrick's College, Drumcondra in Dublin.

Alan Megahey is Chaplain of Uppingham School.

Alan O'Day is Senior Lecturer in History at the University of North London.

Alan Parkinson is Senior Lecturer in History and Education at South Bank University, London.

Joseph Spence is Master in College at Eton College.

Norman Vance is Professor of English and Director of the Graduate Research Centre in the Humanities at the University of Sussex.

1   The Union

Introduction

D. George Boyce and Alan O'Day

> The Act of Union has been the aim of so much random invective that its good fruits (for it has borne good no less than evil fruits) are in danger of being forgotten.[1]

Thomas Hobbes reminds us that mankind's basic desire is to find security against each other; Irish history and Anglo-Irish relations bear out the truth of his proposition. In the wake of the United Irishmen's rebellion of 1798 the Act of Union was passed to ensure that there would be no similar challenge to the supremacy of Great Britain. For the Protestant Irishmen who agreed to the Union, the principal attraction was the security it offered against a Catholic majority which bared its sectarian teeth in the rising of 1798. The difference between British and Irish purposes remained at the heart of misunderstanding and mistrust between the two countries down to the present, a point made by Arthur Aughey and Paul Bew in chapters in this book. But what emerged when the Union came into effect on 1 January 1801 was something much more than a mutual security pact; it gave birth to a new state, the United Kingdom of Great Britain and Ireland, though this spelt no change of political regime, no seismic shift in the social order. Yet, if the transition appeared modest, it portended the integration of Ireland into a unified if not necessarily unitary community. Dicey made the point that 'the Union . . . whilst it increases the power of the whole United Kingdom, provides the means of carrying out, and of carrying out with due regard to justice, any reform, innovation, or if you please revolution, required for the prosperity of the Irish people'.[2] On the one hand the Union seemed the last step in the political consolidation of the English state, on the other it represented a brave attempt to absorb a people, the majority different in religion. Ultimately, incorporating all Ireland proved too testing.

As Dicey observed, the Union has not enjoyed an enviable repute. Oliver MacDonagh writes that 'the Act of Union forms the matrix of modern Irish history'.[3] In his estimation, 'it was the pure principle, the very idea, of the Act of Union, and not its substantial clauses, which was at stake'. F.S.L. Lyons states:

> In the unending struggle between those who upheld the Union and those who opposed it, the initiative had habitually rested with the latter. The

business of a conservative, after all, is to conserve, and to Irish and British Conservatives alike a stern, unyielding resistance to change had seemed for most of the nineteenth century the only course open for those who wished to maintain intact the connection between the two countries.[4]

A bit less harshly, R.F. Foster suggests, 'the unionist side tended to brutal truths, and to borrowing the Whig line by depreciating the colonial and elitist nature of the College Green assembly as no great loss: logic demanded a Union as the only alternative to separation. The argument relied on the concept of constitutional union as an integrative force, which experience would disprove'.[5] Alan Ward contends:

> The Act of Union should have simplified the constitutional relationship between Britain and Ireland because the two countries were now governed under a single Crown by a single Parliament. The reality is that the Union failed abysmally as a constitutional device because it was approached in a strange way that did little to eradicate the sense that Ireland was a separate political community.[6]

This apparently near-universal judgement has only recently been balanced by the recognition that protagonists of the Union have usually, thought not always, felt obliged to defend the status quo, the totality of the Union as it actually operated. This is not a logical necessity. To uphold the general framework of the Union does not imply support for every administrative detail or legal aspect of its operation. The chapters in this volume explore aspects of the Union and of Union culture for the past two and a half centuries. The chapters are arranged chronologically around three broad themes – the purposes, establishment and definition of the Union; its modification; and the after-effects and entrenchment.

This was not an amalgamation of equals to be sure, for Great Britain was the dominant partner, but it was something more than neo-colonialism because Ireland received a fair bargain by the norms of the day, and within a relatively short time its people and commerce enjoyed full rights in the new state. Still, during its existence the Union remained unloved by a significant section of the Irish people and misunderstood by many in Great Britain who continued to see it largely in terms of security for themselves. From an early date the Union was challenged by spokesmen for the Catholic majority. This is ironic because the main resistance to the passage of the legislation came at the hands of Protestants in Dublin. The contest spurred an intermittent debate on the nature of the Union itself. Was it a federal compact between equal partners for their common good? Was it merely a pragmatic legislative union or a union of hearts? Was it primarily a defensive arrangement for the protection of the British state and Irish Protestants? There were *ad hoc* responses to such inquiries from time to time when alterations to the Union were either discussed or implemented but until 1921 these were no more than tentative in vital respects and the questions raised by the Union remain open up to the present.

In 1921 the Union was modified by the creation of three jurisdictions – an Irish Free State, Northern Ireland and the remainder of the United Kingdom, something scarcely visualised a generation earlier by any side. The chapters in this volume explore the dialogue about the Union and the changing relationships within it, both relatively neglected topics. While this is relevant to Ireland, it has broader importance for the future of a United Kingdom. Is it a Union state or a unitary state with certain local variations? The creation of assemblies in Scotland and Wales reflects a pragmatic solution to a perceived demand but largely side-steps the problem of the sort of state that should emerge in the twenty-first century.

In Ireland the question of the Union hinged on deep divisions in society springing from distinctions which are not derived from religion alone, but from what it implies – power and the loss of power. This was a long-running battle. The quest for social and political ascendancy, even the establishment of a 'superior' religion and the way of life this exemplified, dates from the arrival of the 'New English' in the sixteenth century, and of the Scots Presbyterians and English who settled in Ulster and elsewhere in the early seventeenth century. Though often divided internally, these immigrants identified themselves with the Protestant or English cause in Ireland. But they never did so unswervingly. George Boyce outlines their conditions and reservations. Central to these was that in the wars of religion of the seventeenth century they had defended themselves by their own swords. In the great crisis of 1912 to 1914 Ulster Protestants showed that this spirit was alive and that reluctantly in the final resort they would brandish their swords again. Irish Protestants' attitude to Great Britain therefore was equivocal and remains so in Ulster, yet they could not but acknowledge that the British connexion was crucial to their survival and victory. This facilitated belief on the part of late eighteenth-century 'patriots' that Ireland under Protestant leadership could stand alone, though within the wider confines of the British Empire. To stand alone, if need be, was articulated once more with the formation in the early 1970s of William Craig's Vanguard. Unease among Protestants about their position and the ultimate intentions of the British state with regard to Ireland have been parts of the Protestant *mentality* for two and a half centuries. Aughey explains how the mix of self-confidence and sense of betrayal boiled over among northern Protestants in the controversy about the Anglo-Irish Agreement, a treaty arranged over their heads by the governments in London and Dublin.

Most of Ireland was not ready for the benefits of French revolutionary ideology – the ending of confessional and political inequalities, the overthrow even of religions, institutions and superstition, specifically embodied in Catholicism. The rebellion of 1798, commemorated in later popular national mythology, seemed to confirm fears that suspicions and hatred were not easily discarded. The sectarian war in Wexford, in particular, fuelled both Protestant and Catholic views of the past. Yet, even in this feverish atmosphere, the Irish Parliament of the late eighteenth century, with all of its limitations and narrowness, assumed a halo for opponents of the Union or conversely was seen as the cause of Irish problems by those who upheld it. 'History' could never be an abstract value-free rendering of the past for it necessarily belonged to and legitimised the stance of each side.[7]

The Union was made between 22 January 1799 and 1 August 1800, coming into effect at the beginning of January 1801. Having put enormous effort into securing passage of the Act of Union, Westminster governments seemed less concerned with its actual workings. This would be a recurrent criticism not only from Irish nationalists but by supporters of the Union. Alan O'Day highlights some Conservatives' concurrence in 1869 that not enough had been done, while Carla King considers Sir Horace Plunkett's critique of the Union and his ideas for improvements. Whatever the objections about the record under the Union, it was a remarkable settlement, with Great Britain making unusual efforts to conciliate the lesser partner. The Act had eight articles, four settling the political basis and the remainder dealing with the unification of the Irish and English Churches, commerce, finance and the law (see Appendix at the end of this book). Ireland was granted 100 representatives in the Westminster House of Commons and 32 representative peers (28 temporal and 4 spiritual) in the House of Lords, thus guaranteeing the country a prominent role in the new state. Unification of the Churches was 'deemed and taken to be an essential and fundamental part of the Union', though one which by the 1840s came under attack and then was modified in 1869. After a period of twenty years the financial and commercial regulations of the two countries were to be harmonised. Contributions to the expenditure of the United Kingdom were set at 15:2, a proportion to be reconsidered after twenty years. The laws in both countries remained in force, subject to such changes as might be made by the United Kingdom Parliament. Unlike the Scottish Union of 1707, these terms were not worked out by the respective parliaments but by the British government and Irish executive, the latter appointed by Westminster. Paradoxically, the Irish Protestant opposition to the Union was too strong to allow equal negotiations. On 2 August 1800 the Irish Parliament met for the final time.[8]

Several aspects of the transaction merit notice. The principal opposition to the Union came from a Protestant Parliament that, throughout its existence, spoke for the Protestant people. This reflected the Protestant concern that the loss of their parliament deprived them of their constitutional protection, the defence both of their own and in their view Ireland's interest, a perspective that characterised northern unionists' demands from 1972 for the restoration of their parliament. That most came to see the Union as essential for their survival and Ireland's welfare reveals not a change in their desires and ambitions but, as Boyce points out, a new perception of how best those desires and ambitions could be secured. But the process of conversion was halting and there remained a residual Protestant tradition that looked back to the Irish parliament with regret, and hoped for its return.[9] Isaac Butt was one notable member of that tradition and his outlook is assessed by Joseph Spence, while Charles Stewart Parnell is another and more famous case, one inspired by familial traditions of resistance to the Act of Union. There were others, too: Thomas Davis, William Smith O'Brien, the members of the Protestant Rule Association are ready illustrations. This residual view among the 'minority' was important as a continuum between the eighteenth century and the present; William Gladstone in 1886 repeatedly propagated the view that, but for British interference, the Protestant patriots of the eighteenth century and Catholic nationalists of his own time would resolve their differences jointly rather than each appealing to London. Such appeals, he believed, had corrupted Irish politics, dividing its people into factions. The home rule measure in 1886 was structured to provide a forum for his own interpretation of the co-operation that previously had been present among Irishmen. This helps explain why he made no special arrangements for the minority and even more so his unwillingness to treat Ulster as a different case. Boyce, Spence, King and the several chapters on Ulster unionism address the conditional nature of the Union in the eyes of many Protestants. This sense of 'differentness' was aggravated by a union conceived for strategic rather than social reasons and British preoccupation with other, usually more important, problems. There was also the lingering sense that the Irish and Ireland were akin to the 'near abroad'.

If Protestants expected the Union to be a bulwark against an aggressive political Catholicism, they were quickly disabused.[10] Admittedly, they retained a grip on the legal apparatus, local and municipal government and land ownership, but each of these in turn came under increasing pressure from Catholic spokesmen who demanded access to and then a 'fair' share of the spoils. Implicitly, the Union promised to be 'fair' but in Ireland the term itself was elusive. 'Fair' could imply rewards linked to merit and loyalty, to equality in the distribution of plums between Protestants and Catholics, or to share bounty in relation to the relative numbers. It required time before Catholics routinely reached the summit and even in 1921 they remained under-represented in some areas of endeavour. During the last decades before 1921 Catholics unquestionably made great headway. Ironically, the settlements of 1921 did not achieve 'fairness' but entrenched Catholic ascendancy in the south and a Protestant one in the north. This vitiated the precept of the Union. Ulster Protestant concern that it would be victimised under home rule was turned on its head; Patrick Buckland casts a wary eye on the extension of Protestant hegemony in the years after 1921, which he attributes to three prime causes – the inexperience of the new leadership of Northern Ireland; grass-roots Protestant sentiment that had to be satisfied by unionist politicians; and a British state that largely ceased to act as a referee between contending factions.

Another irony was that a union designed to give security to Irish Protestants afforded instead a United Kingdom platform for Catholic grievances and a means to moderate the supposed guarantees to Protestants. The Catholic 'offensive' was not long in gestation. William Pitt wanted to take the step of allowing Catholics to sit in Parliament but this was blocked by King George III who insisted that to give his assent to such a measure would violate his coronation oath to defend the Protestant faith and church establishment. The sovereign was not the only one who held such opinions. But this opposition immediately raised a cry among middle-class Catholics for 'emancipation', that is political rights, setting the agenda for a fierce public and parliamentary campaign lasting almost three decades. As Brian Jenkins shows, though, British officials did not meet Irish demands by unrelenting resistance: William Wellesley-Pole, Robert Peel and Henry Goulburn between 1809 and 1827 utilised the powers at their disposal and helped shape enduring policies aimed at sustaining the Union, in part, by appeasing Catholic feeling. Anti-Catholicism was behind the refusal of 'emancipation' but there was a principle at stake as well – the formal role of religion in the state. Repeal of the Test and Corporation acts in 1828 and more certainly Catholic emancipation the following year drove a wedge into the foundations of the confessional state.[11] Benjamin Disraeli attempted a last-minute resuscitation of the confessional ideal, basing opposition to disestablishing the Irish Church in 1869 on the necessity of religion in the life of the community. In the event he lost to a new concept – state impartiality. The Union had ensured the status of the Church of Ireland, uniting it with the English Church, but this was declared void because it stood between the British state and conciliation of Ireland's Catholics.

Disestablishment had implications for the Union. Was this to be a union based on separate laws and institutions to accord with local conditions ('Irish ideas'), which became Gladstone's position by 1886, on the basis that recognition of distinctions would be a source of national strength, or should the state continue on the path to harmonisation of institutions, rights and duties? Because the position of the Church was part of the constitution, religious questions initiated debate on the constitution. Not surprisingly, these disputes revealed differing concepts of the constitution. As discourse about the Union was often a metaphor for the constitution, the debate could never be wholly or perhaps even primarily about Ireland. Because the entire matter concerned principles, tally sheets of benefits and deficits about the Union were inappropriate measures of its utility for either Great Britain or Ireland, though, of course, this did not stop the contestants attempting to establish such a ledger.

British Conservatives held that the Union should be maintained, if not without alteration, at least in major essentials. Though they had opposed legislation for disestablishment, its enactment eased their dilemma. They were no longer in a position of defending the privilege of a small minority but now seized command of the high road, upholding the political Union. Their position received an additional fillip when a succession of land acts mainly sponsored by Conservatives gradually turned a largely Catholic peasantry into owner-occupiers. Just as the case for the Union had ceased being about religious privilege, it also was detached increasingly from Protestant economic advantage. The defence of the Union could be waged on the more solid ground of principle. For classic British unionists there was no dogma of resistance but a deeply held belief in the need to preserve the Union, if necessary at the expense of the security Protestants thought they had purchased in 1800.

British Liberals, too, laid claim to being true defenders of the Union, though by the later Victorian age, in a rhetoric and spirit that accepted Catholic demands and showed no more than limited tenderness to Protestant susceptibilities. What had become a means to secure Protestants' safety became increasingly for Liberals a mechanism to provide a bridge for Catholics to gain a strong, if not dominant, role in Irish life as the formula for Great Britain's security. Gladstone's doctrine that both Catholics and Protestants would be good Irishmen and loyal subjects if they co-operated with each other rather than as at present appealing to London underpinned his home rule scheme just as later it was the linchpin of Conservative thinking on the future of Northern Ireland in the Anglo-Irish Agreement. As the nineteenth century unfolded, Irish Protestants became paranoid about the threat to the Union, or more exactly their notion of the Union which seemed vulnerable not only to Catholic aggression but more ominously at the hands of British politicians. Their worst fears seemed near realisation in 1886 when Gladstone proposed the establishment of a legislative assembly with a responsible executive in Dublin without making special provision for the minority. He thereby triggered the formative question of the generation – the constitutional relationship between Great Britain and Ireland – what constituted a political union, the meaning of British citizenship, whether the voice of national majorities should prevail when this meant that loyal Protestants necessarily would find themselves in a minority, and the legitimacy of governing according to 'Irish ideas'.

Irish and British unionists both had to accept Gladstone's precepts; Alvin Jackson and Carla King trace responses to the threat posed. The contest honed thinking about the constitution, rending the political nation into two – a larger section which declined to accept Gladstone's interpretation and the smaller one prepared to establish devolved government in Dublin, often for pragmatic rather than ideological reasons. Most people, particularly in Ireland, could no longer hedge on this issue. Alan Megahey, Alvin Jackson, Norman Vance and Greta Jones trace the impact of home rule on three groups: Protestant Churches in Ireland, Irish unionists and, very interestingly, the literary and scientific communities. Vance examines the complexity of locating a unionist literature before the home rule crisis and its flourishing thereafter. Jones shows the interconnection between the politics and science. Home rule appeared to threaten the project of modernising science and increasing its share of financial support. A localised culture influenced by Catholic hostility to the modernisation of science and nationalist pressure over academic appointments would undermine another aspect of the Union – a unified scientific elite. Megahey and Jackson treat the impact of home rule on Irish Protestants, dissecting their tactics, but showing as well how these mobilised opinion against home rule and their irritation at the failure of Britain's leaders to understand the parlous situation of Irish unionists. These and other chapters elucidate a union that was always under inspection, one that could not be taken for granted but must be defended repeatedly. In the nineteenth century that defence was successful; the Union's proponents were adept at mustering public support, especially in Great Britain, which they realised was the decisive theatre of action. This contrasts starkly with the malevolent image of unionism since the late 1960s. Alan Parkinson draws a picture of the poor public relations of Ulster unionists, which he attributes to a belief among them in the moral superiority of their position, absence of sophistication in presentation and an inability to elicit sympathetic interest in Great Britain.

It would be inaccurate to see the Union, as nationalist propaganda did with considerable success, as an alien imposition on Ireland. The Union assisted the development of a more complex interaction between Great Britain and Ireland. It worked changes on both sides of the Irish Sea. For Great Britain it enforced, albeit reluctantly at first, responses to the social, economic and political problems in Ireland which frequently had knock-on effects throughout the United Kingdom. In a unified state allowing free movement of people, Irish poverty was routinely transferred to Great Britain, as happened during the Great Famine, when a flood of refugees arrived. Official investigations and legislative reforms reached an unprecedented scale. Hardly an aspect of Irish life remained unexamined as royal commissions and committees of inquiry explored the woes of the country, proposed panaceas and sought to discover the means to reconcile the people to the Union while a small army of private individuals roamed the countryside on their own fact-finding missions, again with the aim of discovering the magic solution to Irish discontent. Modernisation of communication within a unified state made the wretched poverty of small agricultural holdings in remote parts of the west of Ireland as familiar to British minds as the deprivation of London's East End.

These inquisitions resulted in ecclesiastical reform, abolition of tithes, alterations of the land laws, local government reform, creation of a national education system, the erection of new institutions of higher education, mechanisms for dealing with poverty and developments in policing. Ireland's poor received vastly more official attention than did those of Great Britain; Irish farmers had the benefit of legislation withheld from their British counterparts. When the Edwardian social welfare schemes were introduced, Ireland gained disproportionately to England because benefits were not weighted according to relative living costs in different parts of the United Kingdom but distributed equally everywhere. Legacies of these efforts remain in place in both parts of Ireland. Inevitably, debates on Irish problems were taken over and applied to similar situations in the rest of the United Kingdom despite the insistence that Irish remedies would not jump across St George's Channel. Isolation proved a practical impossibility. Yet, the British elite seemed obstinately ignorant of or at least wilfully oblivious to what Irish people felt about themselves and their country, a complaint which Andrew Gailey, Patrick Buckland, Arthur Aughey and Paul Bew see as typical of the contemporary discussion of Northern Ireland. Aughey notes that while defenders of the Union in Northern Ireland subscribe to the idea that the democratic consent of the majority should be durable, British officials take a pragmatic approach, being ready to modify normal constitutional propriety in order to address the problem of internal security.

The very existence of the Union contributed to an evolving set of identities. As George Boyce observes, the Protestants of eighteenth-century Ireland had a dual sense of who they were, but like 'newcomers' before them they increasingly adopted an Irish identity or at least one as the 'British Irish'. In the early stages of the Union Protestants, especially the landed members of the Church of Ireland, enhanced this dual allegiance. There was no contradiction for them between being Irish and British. In their capacity as an educated, sophisticated elite they flourished in the role of leading the Irish nation in the management of the United

Kingdom and Empire, providing leaders for the Church, the army, diplomatic corps, civil service, law, politics and culture. In this they followed the trail blazed in the eighteenth century by Swift, Goldsmith, Sheridan and Burke. It was a brilliant society, some parts with less endearing qualities certainly but one magnificently suited for its post-1801 place in the United Kingdom. But there were other Protestants in Ireland, Presbyterians and Nonconformists (see Alan Megahey's chapter), who were on the periphery, being neither part of a historic elite nor able to make common cause with the other outsiders, Catholics. Some manifested their own discontent in the United Irishmen which precipitated the Act of Union. They were uncertain converts to the Union; though, in time, they became its bedrock, particularly inside post-1886 Ulster unionism which incorporated in a democratic league, merchants, industrialists and labourers in addition to the landed order. Southern unionism, in contrast, was an enclave of well-to-do Protestants, mainly members of the Church of Ireland. The growing devotion to the Union of Ulstermen and women was psychological, religious and economic as well as political. Many gained something valuable from the Union. Their tenacious defence of the Union since 1886 cannot be attributed to 'false consciousness' and in the post-1922 Ireland was viewed by northern Protestants as the only means to avoid the fate of their southern compatriots.[12] The sequence of chapters by Gailey, Buckland, Gillespie, Aughey and Bew shows how pervasive the attachment to the Union became, embracing an active role for women as well as men. Ulster unionism was genuinely a 'people's' movement.

For Catholics, integration was more tenuous. Nevertheless, Daniel O'Connell, the icon of Catholic Ireland, promised that if his co-religionists were treated fairly and the Union made to work, they would be attached firmly to it. O'Connell's prophesy was enshrined in the hopes and policies of British politicians down to 1914 and underscores post-1968 attempts to reconcile the two communities in Northern Ireland. But O'Connell unleashed a force, Catholic nationalism, that temporised about the multiple loyalties that were the nexus of the Union. Few held, as Gladstone did, that there was such a thing as local patriotism which was compatible with imperial patriotism. Whereas Butt talked about Ireland's legitimate interest in the Empire and Parnell pledged that 'your queen will be our queen', John Redmond's deep attachment to the Empire was atypical among Catholics. Catholic nationalism was characterised by a confused rhetoric about allegiance, but its thrust on the ground, especially from the Land War (1879–82) onwards, emphasised an exclusive Irish loyalty. Language peppered with derogatory references to 'West Britons', 'aliens', that is Protestants, 'Ireland for the Irish' and campaigns to dissuade Irish youths from enlisting in the British Army or to boycott royal visitors repudiated dual loyalty indirectly if not explicitly. Eamon de Valera put it more bluntly. At various times he described Ulster Protestants as a 'foreign garrison' and 'not Irish people', 'Are you Irishmen first or Englishmen first?' and if they stood in the way of Ireland's freedom 'we will clear you out of it'; they had a choice 'either to be in Ireland or out of it'.[13] Agitators during the Land War located two enemies – landlords, a metaphor for Protestants, and a Protestant British state. Popular politics requires simplification and in the hothouse environment of the era Britain, the Union and the Empire for ordinary Catholics were villains, the roadblocks to Ireland a nation once again. In a contested situation being for or against 'the Union' was a badge of allegiance, British or Irish.

The defence of the Union was undertaken in many different ways – through the British party system, in halls, clubs, meeting places, in gatherings of churchmen, in the Orange Order, in Parliament, on the streets of Ulster, in the drawing rooms of country houses, in the academic groves of Trinity College and the Queen's College in Belfast, in songs, poetry, literature and history with occasional threats to employ the rifle in the last resort. No moment proved more traumatic to the Union that the prolonged crisis of 1912–21. It exposed the Achilles' heel of the Union, enhanced foreboding among Irish unionists, creating a climate of betrayal and fear among those who stood by the British connexion. This mood is traced in the chapters by Gailey, Jackson, Buckland, Gillespie, Aughey and Bew. Several problems came to the fore during the crisis: the reluctance of the British government to make provision for Protestants, especially those in the north, and the imperative of finding a solution which pushed leaders in London to force Irish unionists into concessions. Ulster unionists found themselves not simply abandoning their southern supporters, something they refused to countenance in 1886, but in the end jettisoning their own in the counties of Donegal, Monaghan and Cavan, parts of historic Ulster. Even then, up to the last minute in 1921 Sir James Craig was confronted by David Lloyd George's attempts to remove the concessions he had made to Ulster unionists in order to reach a settlement with the 'disloyal' representatives of nationalism. It is little wonder that unionists came to distrust London politicians nearly as much as they did Irish nationalists. At this stage Ulster unionists had few sure friends in high places, but one, Andrew Bonar Law, a Canadian-born Scots Presbyterian with close family connexions to the province, was a godsend. Without his support the history of northern unionism might have been different. If British politics ever had a principled rather than a pragmatic unionist, it was Law. The settlement when it came preserved a façade of the Union in the southern provinces and left a new state, Northern Ireland, in the north, thus beginning the modern phase of attempts to affirm, modify and destroy what remains of the Union. How that story will end is a matter for the future but, if the past is a guide, the bones of the Union will continue to be picked over for years to come, perhaps with renewed vigour in the face of revived national sentiment in Scotland and Wales.

NOTES

1 A.V. Dicey, *England's Case against Home Rule* (Reprint and new Introduction, E.J. Feucht-wanger; Richmond, 1973), p. 132.
2 Ibid., p. 138.
3 Oliver MacDonagh, *Ireland: The Union and its Aftermath* (London, 1977), p. 9.
4 F.S.L. Lyons, *Ireland since the Famine* (London, 1976), p. 30.
5 R.F. Foster, *Modern Ireland 1600–1972* (London, 1989), pp. 282–3.

6 Alan J. Ward, *The Irish Constitutional Tradition: Responsible Government and Modern Ireland, 1782–1992* (Washington, DC, 1994), p. 30.

7 Brian Walker, *Dancing to History's Tune: History, Myth and Politics in Ireland* (Belfast, 1996), pp. 57–74.

8 This summary is taken from J.C. Beckett, *The Making of Modern Ireland, 1603–1923* (London, 1966), pp. 280–3.

9 Jacqueline Hill, *From Patriots to Unionists: Dublin Civic Politics and Irish Protestant Patriotism, 1660–1840* (Oxford, 1997), pp. 264–80.

10 Liam Kennedy and David S. Johnson, 'The Union of Ireland and Britain, 1801–1921', in D. George Boyce and Alan O'Day (eds), *The Making of Modern Irish History: Revisionism and the Revisionist Controversy* (London, 1996), p. 65.

11 D. George Boyce, 'Trembling Solicitude: Irish Conservatism, Nationality and Public Opinion, 1833–86', in D. George Boyce, Robert Eccleshall and Vincent Geoghegan (eds), *Political Thought in Ireland since the Seventeenth Century* (London, 1993), pp. 136–7.

12 See R.B. McDowell, *Crisis and Decline: The Fate of Southern Unionists* (Dublin, 1997), chs 6–8.

13 Quoted in John Bowman, *De Valera and the Ulster Question 1917–1973* (Oxford, 1982), p. 32.

Part I

Purposes, establishment and definition of the Union

2 Weary patriots

Ireland and the making of unionism

D. George Boyce

Historians of Irish unionism usually begin their investigations relatively late in time; the period since the first Home Rule Bill (1886) is the focus of attention, with perhaps a backward glance at the Protestant opposition to Daniel O'Connell's agitation for the repeal of the Union in the 1830s and 1840s. The number of books and articles dealing with the unionist struggle against home rule has grown, and shows little sign of abating. But historians of unionism might consider the work of historians of the eighteenth century, who have drawn attention to the central place of religion, and particularly Protestantism, in the making of national identity, or identities, in America, Europe and the British Isles. 'Throughout this period,' two historians have remarked, 'this sense of the fundamental Protestantism of Britain and Ireland was to have far-reaching consequences.'[1] These same historians warn against seeing religion as the main, or only, constituent part of national identity, as providing the sole dynamic force, instead of viewing it as related to other constituent parts, such as race, constitution and language.[2] A further danger lies in adopting a teleological view of religion and identity; local circumstances, historical change, social and economic developments, all play a part in mediating the impact of religion on society. And yet contingency must be balanced by the appreciation of certain traditions of thought that, as Michael Oakeshott reminds us, take their rise from political activity. Practice is prior to doctrine; and so far from a political ideology being 'the quasi-divine parent of political activity, it turns out to be its earthly stepchild'. The search for 'coherence' in political ideologies is an activity of trying to 'alter the world as it affects us into the image we think most favourable to ourselves, the one which will better satisfy our wants': the search by a set of people 'whom chance or choice have brought together' to alter the world so as to suit their needs.[3] This chapter traces the attempt by a set of people in Ireland, the Protestants of Ireland, to change the world in which chance or choice placed them, which is central to the making of Protestantism in Ireland, and to its earthly stepchild, Irish unionism.

I

The political activity and ideas of the people of Ireland, as J.C. Beckett observed in his inaugural lecture in the Queen's University of Belfast in 1963, are shaped by the relationship between the land and the people, by the special conditions of life in Ireland. The stable element in Ireland is the land; the unstable element the people, for the people of Ireland were no homogeneous group, but consisted of various peoples who came to live there and were deeply influenced by the character of the country.[4]

These various layers of settlement gave Ireland its history, and their interaction created its recurring theme of confrontation. One of the most influential layers was the coming of what were in the sixteenth century called the 'New English', in the early eighteenth century the 'English interest', in the later eighteenth century the 'Irish nation', and in the nineteenth century the 'Anglo-Irish'. Another was the influx of settlers, mainly of Lowland Scottish origins, who brought with them their particular brand of Protestantism, the Presbyterian religion. They came to a country that was, and remained, mainly Catholic in religion, and the history of Ireland was shaped subsequently by the conflict between Protestant, Catholic and Dissenter.

These relations altered over time; and, again, it is important not to adopt a teleological view of their history. Some Presbyterians became United Irishmen in the 1790s; and prominent members of the Anglo-Irish community, Isaac Butt and Charles Stewart Parnell, founded and led the nationalist home rule party.

There were other possible pathways for these religiously defined peoples and yet there is a familiarity about their predicament. Art Cosgrove has recently drawn attention to the predicament of an earlier – Catholic – group of Anglo-Irish at the close of the Middle Ages. Their identity was shaped by the special conditions of Ireland, by their self-recognition as the 'English of Ireland'. In 1440 the Anglo-Irish were classified as aliens (as were the Scots). The Anglo-Irish people were, then, regarded as less than English by the English in England. They perceived themselves as different, and were perceived by others as different. Professor Cosgrove sums up the position of the Anglo-Irish thus:

> After three and a half centuries in Ireland they controlled about a quarter of the country; they regarded themselves as having an identity distinct from that of the older native population; while they vociferously protested their loyalty to the crown and their Englishness they were regarded as Irish and described as such in England, sometimes even being confused with the natives from whom they vehemently distinguished themselves. They resented interference from England and particularly the dispatch of English officials to take any leading role in the administration. Nevertheless, some preferred the rule of an Englishman if it was believed that rulers from their own community were becoming too involved with the native population.

'Some of these attitudes', he concludes, 'are as attributable to twentieth-century Ulster unionists, the descendants of the seventeenth-century settlers, as they are to the Anglo-Irish of the early sixteenth century, the heirs to the settlement of the late twelfth and early thirteenth century.' The comparison, he admits, may be 'somewhat strained and, like all analogies, it has obvious limitations. Yet there are sufficient similarities at least to commend the study of the later middle ages in Ireland to present-day Ulster unionists.'[5]

The sixteenth century saw an influx of new settlers, the Protestant 'New English'. Contemporary Irish people are not of course ethnically, let alone racially, pure descendants of seventeenth-century settlers. Intermarriage, the change of religious and therefore political affiliation, renders any such interpretation invalid or at least suspect. And time and changing political exigencies influenced their political choices. In the comparatively quiet year of 1873, for example, Thomas Witherow first published his *Derry and Enniskillen in the Year 1689*, in which is stressed the chivalric nature of the conflict, the absence of massacre, the fact that 'to tolerate human difference of opinion is the spirit that William always aimed to promote'.[6] Yet there arose from the Protestant predicament a body of writing that reflected their particular circumstances. This political tradition originated from the religion of these groups, and their experience of living as Protestants in Ireland, and not ever having the mastery of their own destiny, but living close to the state that possessed or asserted that mastery: England. For the Anglo-Irish of the late Middle Ages the problem was one of political distinction from the mass of the population through cultural differences; for the sixteenth- and seventeenth-century settlers it was one of religion. But for both the problem presented itself in familiar ways.

This minority group, the 'New English', found itself in alliance, briefly, with the recusant or Catholic minority group, then known as the 'Old English'. This reflects the 'Old English' predicament of being conscious both of their English descent and their Irish circumstances. Thus when the Old English recusant Patrick Darcy asked whether the subjects of this kingdom were a 'free people . . . to be governed, only, by the common laws of England, and statutes in force in this kingdome', he based his claim on their 'birth-right and best inheritance'.[7] His idea of an ancient constitution, whereby Ireland should partake fully of the rights of Englishmen and their laws, with new laws made only with the consent of the Irish parliament, was taken up by the Protestant Irishman William Molyneux in his celebrated *Case of Ireland's Being Bound by Acts of Parliament in England* (1698). Molyneux was at pains to point out that the Kingdom of Ireland was indeed annexed to the Crown of England, and he acknowledged that 'we must ever own it our happiness' that this was so. But Ireland possessed her rights too, and enjoyed an original compact with England that she should enjoy the same 'liberties and immunities' as the people of England. Ireland had the right to partake of the liberties conferred on England by Magna Carta. She was not a colony, like Virginia or New England, but an ancient kingdom, endowed with all the liberties of a king and parliament, and courts of justice.[8]

II

Ireland, Molyneux claimed, was mainly peopled by the 'progeny of the English. Britons, that from time to time have come over into this Kingdom'.[9] But, had this been indeed the case – had the 'ancient Irish' been reduced to a 'mere handful' –

then Irish Protestants would have experienced a very different history. Perhaps the ancient Irish were few in number, in racial terms; but the Catholic Irish were not, and this was to exercise a powerful influence over the behaviour of the Protestant minority who gained an uneasy mastery of Ireland in the Williamite wars. The latter were a minority made less secure by their antipathy towards the strongly rooted Presbyterians of Ulster.

The best and most effective exemplar of the Irish Protestant predicament was Jonathan Swift, who was in one sense a displaced Englishman (he hoped to make his career in London) and in another a displaced Irishman (aware, because he had lived in England, of the special local needs of the Irish Protestant). This latter experience made him a fine exponent of the dilemma that the Protestants faced, one that, however, developed certain trends that were not evident in the Anglo-Irish thinking of the later Middle Ages. First, the similarities: Swift wrote for an age when the Church of Ireland was an established, state-supported institution; he had as little time for the pretensions of Ulster Presbyterians as he had for those of Catholics; or even less, for the Catholic was subdued while the Presbyterian was 'an angry cat in full liberty'.[10] But his experience in Ireland brought out both a defensiveness and an assertiveness in his political writings. These were not fully developed; Swift took up his pen according to his pre-occupations at any time. But he revealed certain traits that were characteristic of the Anglo-Irish of the later Middle Ages and early modern age, while adding new ones.

The traditional themes emerged when Swift examined the Anglo-Irish con-nexion. The 'people of Ireland', that is the Protestants, were 'born as free' as the people of England, and yet by crossing the channel they became a 'slave in six hours'. Irish Protestants were dismissed by English governments when trying to impose unjust measures on Ireland as 'the king's subjects of Ireland', a description that implied an inequality between Ireland and England. Thus a loyal man living in Ireland was not regarded as on the same footing as a loyal man living in England.[11] Swift emphasised that he was a loyal man living among loyal men, and that neither he nor his fellow Protestants had any intention of casting off their allegiance to the English crown. But loyalty was not to be confused with dependency: 'a modern term of Art; unknown, as I have heard, to all antient Civilians, and Writers upon Government'. Ireland was, on the contrary, 'called in some Statutes an Imperial Crown, as held only from God; which is as high a style, as any Kingdom is capable of receiving'.[12]

Swift was provoked not only by these English assumptions concerning loyal men in Ireland, but by the fact that

> as to Ireland they know little more that they do of Mexico; further than that it is a country subject to the King of England, full of Boggs, inhabited by wild Irish Papists; who are kept in Awe by mercenary Troops sent from thence; and their general opinion is, that it were better for England if this whole Island were sunk into the Sea: for, they have a Tradition, that every Forty Years there must be a Rebellion in Ireland.[13]

Swift could not, of course, quote the expression of an Englishman and senior government minister more than two centuries later; but he would have recognised the sentiments behind Reginald Maudling's outburst that the north of Ireland was a 'bloody awful country'.[14] This acute sense of English assumptions about subject Ireland, and what Swift regarded as the unpardonable ignorance of England about Ireland, was expressed in his story of the 'injured lady'. Ireland, unlike Scotland, was wooed and then abandoned by England, taken advantage of, and then discarded. Her suitor, England, was always reminding Ireland 'of the vast obligations I lay under to him, in sending me so many of his people for my own good, and to teach me manners . . . that from henceforth he expected his word should be a law to me in all things'.[15]

For Swift, as for many of his contemporaries, there was disappointment that England showed no interest in a project that frequently attracted Irish Protestants: that of a union between England and Ireland on the model of the Scottish Union of 1707. William King, Archbishop of Dublin and ally of Swift, feared that the influx of Scots into the new Parliament of England and Scotland after 1707 would so offend English MPs that they would never risk adding Ulster Presbyterians to their number.[16] Since union was now unlikely, Irish Protestants had to find other means of securing their best interests; and for this they developed the idea that Molyneux had taken from Darcy in the seventeenth century – that of a contract between the two kingdoms: government was by consent of the governed, and if one party, England, broke the contract by placing intolerable burdens on the other, than the contract was deemed to be broken. The idea of contract had another, specifically Protestant appeal: since man without government, and without this contract, lived in barbarism, then it followed that contract and civilisation were inseparable. And an enduring trait of Protestant political thought was one of civility: Protestantism stood for civilisation in Ireland; Catholicism for its opposite. But what was a loyal man to do if this contract were indeed broken or compromised by England? Irish Protestants knew that, as King put it, they and England were all in the same vessel. If England fell, so did Ireland; if England abandoned Ireland, then Irish Protestants would meet a sad fate.[17] Swift was always anxious to insist that Irish Protestants stood by and with their king; they were if anything more loyal to his crown than were the English. Ireland must stay within the imperial framework.[18]

Eighteenth-century Irish Protestants gave these traditional claims another specifically, and enduring, Protestant trait: that of providence. Providence was at work in the world, and the proof of this lay in the survival of Protestantism in the dangerous years of the reign of James II. In 1716 the Bishop of Kilmore preached before both houses of the Irish parliament and the Lords Justices in Christ Church, Dublin, and referred his audience to the need to thank God for prospering Protestant arms and delivering the people out of the hands of their enemies. He compared the Protestants of Ireland to the Children of Israel who praised God when they made their passage through the Red Sea. But, 'should God for the Punishment of our Sins have suffered the *Pretender* to possess the Throne of these Kingdoms: There cannot be formed a Notion of a more miserable

Condition than that to which our Country would have been Reduced'.[19] The Protestants were spared so that they could induct into Ireland values of honesty, civility, even cleanliness: Ireland was not a country of 'Boggs', nor of wild Papists, as Swift angrily declaimed. But to the Protestant need for a political myth – that of contract – was added another dimension: the need to secure Ireland for the civility that only Protestantism could give her, and this could only be done through the Penal Laws, which were destined to keep Irish Catholics in perpetual political subjection. These laws were practical measures, drawn up to meet the specific circumstances of Ireland; and there was some grumbling that England, which was less keen on enacting such laws in Ireland, failed again to comprehend the special circumstances of the Irish Protestant.[20] But practical measures helped create political theory. If such laws were needed (and they were) then it followed that there were indeed wild and barbarous people in Ireland, the Irish Catholics; and it followed therefore that such people, requiring such control, must be the great 'other': potentially dangerous foes. The political elite that governed Ireland must be – for the sake of civility – Protestant, and Anglican at that, for Presbyterians, though not of course in the same category as Catholics, were likely to set their sights on the mastery of certain areas of Ireland in which they were numerically strong. Yet Presbyterians too shared notions of the Catholic Irish lack of civility. So the idea of Providential intervention, saving Ireland from the superstitious Catholic masses, became firmly embedded in Protestant and Presbyterian thinking, even while the two faiths were deeply at odds on theological and political grounds.

   This produced what might be called violent mood swings in Irish Protestants; providential thinking invites apocalyptic attitudes. This was reflected in Swift's old age, which is not always studied by historians, entranced with the high period of his writings. Swift, his biographer writes, was in the end silenced by despair induced not by his own personality, but by the condition of Ireland.[21] But before the silence came the despair born of a bleak vision of Ireland's political and economic condition. Swift could have lived happily in England, perhaps more happily than in Ireland. He was always very conscious of his English forebears. But by the middle of the eighteenth century this feeling had changed:

> the great Men in Power sent hither from the other Side were by no means upon the same Foot with his Majesty's other Subjects of Ireland. They had no common Ligament to bind them with us; they suffered not with our Sufferings, and if it were possible for us to have any Cause of Rejoycing, they could not rejoyce with us.[22]

These were prophetic and indeed tragic words, for they revealed Swift's acknowledgement of the great danger to the loyal man: that men of power were of a different stamp, with different perceptions to those of the loyal men of Ireland.

   It might be expected that such a distinction, such a fundamental difference in outlook, might change the Protestant perceptions of where their best interests lay – and to some extent it did. By the end of the eighteenth century, and under the influence of the American and French revolutions, the Protestants of Ireland, Anglican and Dissenter, reoriented their politics and, led by Henry Grattan and the more radical Theobald Wolfe Tone, they asserted a new and more self-consciously Irish political identity. Grattan called (or is alleged to have called) the spirit of Swift to his side when he made his famous declaration of 'independence' in 1782;[23] Tone believed that he could offer Protestant leadership – enlightened and progressive – even to Catholics. Grattan hoped to defend the rights of Ireland in a still subordinate Irish parliament, endowed with modest legislative powers; Tone sought complete separation.[24] But it was perhaps another Protestant Irishman (though one with Catholic family affinities) who best expressed the problem of the Protestants of Ireland, even though he strongly supported the admission of Catholics to full political rights.

Edmund Burke was not primarily interested in Irish affairs, but he felt under an obligation to attend to the affairs of his native land, and his special position – as an Irishman who made a successful career in England – enabled him to act as a kind of teacher to both nations. He was devoted to maintaining Ireland in the Empire, which he believed was indispensable to her peace and prosperity. Burke was no advocate of formal union between the two countries; but he believed that while Ireland, '*constitutionally*, is independent [i.e. was a sister kingdom to England]; politically, she never can be so. It is a struggle against nature'.[25] He believed that, if matters came to a crisis, then political union might be necessary; but for the moment the British control of the Irish parliament would suffice. Burke insisted that 'as a member of the empire, an Irishman has every privilege of a natural-born Englishman, in every part of it, in every occupation, and in every branch of commerce'. But he admitted that the Catholics of Ireland did suffer a grievance which, however, he warned, must not be attached to the 'groundless pretence' of separation.[26] The United Irishmen were in his sights, as the men who wanted to pull together all sorts of discontents 'in order to produce all kinds of disorders'. Catholics depended for their religion and their 'solid advantages which, even under the present restrictions, they are entitled to' on their 'connection with this kingdom'.[27] They must not turn the 'objects of their relief into a national quarrel'.[28]

But Burke knew that the happy connexion between England and Ireland, on which so much rested, could not be secured by formal constitutional means alone. The crux of the matter was, as Swift earlier admitted, that the men from over the sea must feel affinity with the men of Ireland. Burke wrote in 1796 that 'I cannot conceive how a man can be a genuine Englishman, without at the same time being a true Irishman, though fortune should have made his birth on this side the water'.[29] And this was the question that posed itself for the Protestants of Ireland when what Burke saw as the disastrous policies of the United Irishmen obliged England to force through a union with Ireland in 1799–1800. Would the man born in England also be a true Irishman? The problem was compounded by the fact that the Irish Protestants would shortly be pushed aside from their late eighteenth-century claim to be the 'Irish nation', with the Catholic asserting himself as the 'true Irishman'. The idea of the Protestant religion as the foundation of English identity and constitutional and political genius was unshaken. But there was the less happy reflection that, while Protestantism was an essential part of English identity, it was not the only part; and Protestantism in England was itself divided between Anglicanism and various Dissenting groups. Scotland, for her part, enjoyed a Presbyterian establishment. If Protestantism invited unity, it also beckoned diversity. Moreover, English policy towards Dissenters in Ireland in the first half of the eighteenth century, and towards Catholicism in the second, revealed that reasons of state could easily overcome religious affiliation between England and Ireland.[30] It was, in England's eyes, politic to seek to remove disabilities from Protestant Dissenters in Ireland after 1689–90, much to Anglican alarm. It was politic in time of dangerous rebellion in America and revolution in France to relieve Catholic disabilities, and even to endeavour (however unsuccessfully) to link Catholic emancipation with the Act of Union in 1799–1800. English, British or imperial interests might propel the major partner in the United Kingdom to modify the hold that the Protestants of Ireland still had on political power which exercised in the law, local government, the Church and the police force. And the story of the Union bore this out, with the British government obliged to make concession after concession to Catholic demands, ranging from Catholic emancipation in 1829, to reform of the tithe system (by which the Anglican Church maintained its economic self-sufficiency), to municipal reform, disestablishment of the Church of Ireland, land reform and, finally, home rule for Ireland.

III

The Union, therefore, created unionists as the Protestants of Ireland sought to combine their Irishness with a full commitment to, and membership of, the British nation. But the Union, though an event of profound significance for all the people of Ireland, must not obscure the continuities of Irish Protestant ideas. Patriots of the late eighteenth century contained at least some of the seeds of unionism within them. If Protestants no longer spoke of the rights of the kingdom of Ireland, they still held to the contract theory on which it was based: the theory that loyal men enjoyed a special contract with England which, if once broken, freed them from blind political obedience. But they also knew, as did the Protestants of the early eighteenth century, that rebellion, if this was what it came to, could be a disaster. They could only push matters so far. They also believed, as did the eighteenth-century Patriots, and United Irish leaders, that Protestantism, and Presbyterianism, stood for the best elements in Ireland: civil and religious liberty, economic progress, freedom, civil rights for all – providing these could be carefully controlled, measured and vetted by the Protestants of Ireland. But now these great benefits could best be secured, not by parliamentary reform, but by a firm and loyal adherence to the crown, the Union and the Protestant constitution. When these were in danger, an apocalyptic mood could reassert itself, and the workings of Providence be recalled.

These traits emerged, or re-emerged, in Ireland after the first two decades of the Union, which saw the recovery of Catholic politics after the 1798 rebellion. In July 1834 the *Dublin University Magazine*, the organ of Irish Toryism, wrote anxiously of the emigration of Protestants from Ireland. The Protestant population, it reminded the British government, 'are all on the side of England, and of property, and of law'.

> They have never forgotten that they are the descendants of the original English and Scottish settlers, inheriting their names, their language, their habits, and their religion, and they are, therefore, in all their feelings and interests, attached to British connections; they are ever recognised as loyal to the crown, and obedient to the laws, so much so as to have their excessive loyalty often cast in their teeth as a crime, by their enemies.

The *DUM* contrasted the Protestant 'peasantry' with the Catholics, who all too often bid for farms against the Protestants, and succeeded because they offered to pay a 'Popish price'; that is, a greater rent. The Catholic was able to do so because 'The Protestant requires decent clothing, good feeding, and a certain portion of education for his family. He cultivates cleanliness in his house and person, and displays an independence of mind and conduct in all things'. All these required some expenditure, and the Protestant took this into account when offering his price, whereas the Catholic 'merely calculates whether he shall be able to make the rent', for he was less particular about 'everything that savours of external decency and comfort'. Moreover, Irish 'turbulence' had met with English concession, and thus many Protestants resolved to leave Ireland, seeing that England only slighted, neglected and injured them. The 'lower orders of Protestants', in particular, felt betrayed and sacrificed to their antagonists.[31]

In 1834 a great Protestant demonstration was organised at Hillsborough, County Down, to call for Protestant unity in the face of the O'Connellite threat. A leading Presbyterian minister, Dr Henry Cooke, who, his biographer claimed, was 'an ardent advocate of liberty, civil and religious', but a man who distinguished between 'real liberty' and 'the licence of anarchy',[32] pondered on whether to join a meeting called by luminaries and representatives of the Anglican faith. His attitude was watched by the 'whole Protestant community' with 'intense interest', because 'a large number of the Presbyterian clergy looked upon the meeting with no friendly eye'. They regarded it as possibly a demonstration for Tory politics and 'High Church ascendancy'.[33] But Cooke saw where his duty lay. He soon repudiated any objection to a clergyman involving himself in politics: a minister must interfere in politics, when politics interfered with religion. 'I pity the faithless watchman who sees the enemy coming in like a flood, and will not blow the trumpet and rouse the sleeping garrison'.[34] Never was Protestantism in greater danger than at this hour. Common Protestantism had asserted itself in the past: before a critic would 'condemn me for uniting in defence of our general and common Protestantism, ask himself would he condemn our Presbyterian forefathers for uniting in a similar defence within the walls of Derry, or at the passes of Enniskillen?'[35]

Cooke spoke in apocalyptic terms of the danger of division: the dying father demonstrated this to his sons by giving them a quiver of arrows, first one by one, then tied together, showing that the strongest son could not break the combined arrows. The great fault of Protestants was that they trusted in princes and men's sons, not in the living God. Common faith and common danger caused all to unite for protection of their consciences and their liberties. Cooke's biographer acknowledged that not all Presbyterian clergy were pleased with his stand at Hillsborough,[36] but the distinction between Anglican and Dissenter was in any event lessened by the evangelical movement of the nineteenth century, which rendered Irish Anglicanism, never very 'high', into a more fundamentalist mode. The 'new Reformation', as one anonymous writer called it in 1854, made inroads into Irish Catholicism in certain parts of the country. The result was that another trait central to the Protestant self-concept was made manifest: the bringing of civility to the Catholic through evangelical crusade. The moral character of the convert was improved; 'they were distinguished for cleanliness and decency of appearance'. The children never begged. They ceased from theft and petty crime. They did not drink.[37]

Irish Protestantism was not yet a unified political entity despite Cooke's efforts at Hillsborough; nor were all Protestants the sober, law-abiding citizens that their myth described. Indeed, in their search for influence over the British government, Protestants, and especially members of the Orange Order, sometimes went too far, and damaged their own cause. The order, founded in 1795 in County Armagh, soon spread over Ireland, directed from 1797 by a grand lodge, to defend the lives and property of Protestants, to support the Protestant constitution, and 'to maintain the Protestant ascendancy for which our ancestors fought and conquered'.[38] The order sought to unite Protestants of all classes, stations and shades of opinion. They opposed what they called 'undue concessions' to the Catholics, and they declared it as fundamental that there should be Protestant harmony:

> Let not the poor man hate the rich,
> Nor rich on poor look down,
> But each join each true Protestant
> For God and for the Crown.[39]

In 1835 a government inquiry acknowledged the high precepts of morality, but decreed that Orangemen frequently acted at variance with them. Orangemen in Dublin in 1822 demonstrated against the Viceroy, the Marquis of Wellington, at the Theatre Royal, for failing to support the 'glorious memory'; the result was that the administration banned the dressing of the statue of William III in Dublin, and in 1825 the Orange Order was suppressed (only to return in 1828). Not surprisingly, O'Connell spoke gratifyingly of the fact that 'if we had hired out large numbers of Orangemen, they would not have done our business half so well'.[40] The select committee inquiring into the order in 1835 elicited the fact that Orangemen marched through towns playing party tunes 'which have been productive of annoyance'.[41]

This was not how the Order saw itself; it was as sure that it stood as much for liberty and freedom as did any Protestant patriot of the eighteenth century. One of their symbols was the tree of liberty, an orange tree, brought to Ireland by William III, and said to have almost been destroyed by the rebels in 1798:

The tree that I planted to root up they thought, Which tree at the Boyne with my own blood I bought; Then rise, my true sons, make them welter in gore, And hang up their leaders, that they ne'er shall rise more.[42]

Orange symbols were taken from the Bible, especially from the book of Exodus:

From whence came you? – From the House of Bondage – Whither do you go? – to the Promised Land. – How do you expect to get there? – By the benefit of a password.

The password was then MIGDOL – the place where the Israelites first encamped, and, according to one authority, the idea was 'a contrast between the people of the true religion, supposed to be under persecution, and those of a worse religion'.[43] Biblical images told the story of danger, wanderings in darkness, and then the coming to the Light. In the early twentieth century an Orange songsheet contained the lines:

Dark deeds of devilry trouble our land
Satan and popery walk hand in hand.[44]

But the Orange Order knew that in the end it would prevail, because

The winter blew severely, and the soil did not agree,
And it blew the branches fairly off our darling Orange tree.
Now winter it is past and gone, and summer fair and clear,
Our Orange tree is budding in the springtime of the year.[45]

Then charge high your glasses, ran the 'Tree of Liberty' song, 'and drink our Great Cause, our blest Constitution, our King, and our Laws'.[46]

At times the order proved embarrassing to leaders of the Protestant cause. But, as W.H. Crawford remarks, 'since the Protestants were not united in a single Church only Orangeism was able to provide a vehicle for a united Protestant leadership'.[47] Orangeism was not synonymous with Protestantism; but in apocalyptic times – and the nineteenth century saw an uncomfortably growing incidence of apocalyptic times for Protestantism in Ireland – it was central to the Protestant defence against Catholic power. In April 1835 the *Dublin University Magazine* asked the question, 'What is an Orangeman?', and answered in a long article explaining the origins of the order, its commitment to religious and civil liberties, its loyalty to the crown. It protested that, if the authorities wished the order to dwindle, then it should remove the causes of its existence, rather than try to suppress it. The order drew its strength from the fact that it had 'become the interest of British statesmen to associate with their foes', and the order still saw the necessity to resist aggression and defend, if necessary, their properties and their lives.[48] But, asked the *DUM* a few months later (echoing Swift), 'Who ever expected knowledge of Ireland from an Englishman? They know more of Siberia or Caffreland than they do of their next door neighbour.'[49] A 'Great Protestant Demonstration' at Hillsborough on 30 October 1867 to protest against the disestablishment of the Church of Ireland, and therefore against the conspiracy to annul 'the fundamental article of the Union compact',[50] was one supported by the descendants 'of those who, by their resolution and determination in 1834, successfully defended our valued institutions'. Presbyterian and Protestant were urged again to unite,[51] behind a 'Protestant constitution, a Protestant Crown, and a Protestant Church'.[52] These were under attack from 'the Ultramontanists of Ireland and the Radicals of England';[53] and this raised the question of how England could be trusted not to betray her own people. Civil and religious freedom must be defended, and 'barbarism and superstition' defeated. England must be made to understand the grounds for this defence.[54]

But what if England did not understand? British anti-Catholicism had, by the end of the nineteenth century, lost its vigour.[55] The Orange Order had an answer, one that was formulated during the crisis over the third Home Rule Bill in 1912:

> The men of Ulster won't have it, I say they're quite right.
> If the Home Rule Bill's passed, they're determined to fight.
> We've been true to Old England, the land of the brave,
> But we'll never submit to be treated like slaves.[56]

In other words, the Orangeman did not see why a loyal man should be a free citizen in England, but become a slave in six hours by crossing the channel.

The religious character of unionism was strengthened in this pre-war struggle against home rule, not least because the confessional basis of Irish nationalism had not lessened since 1886, and indeed seemed to have come more to the fore, as evidenced by the Protestant fears over the Vatican's *ne temere* decree of 1908, which insisted that children of a 'mixed marriage' be brought up as Catholics, and by incidents such as a Catholic attack upon a party of Protestant schoolchildren returning from an excursion in Castledawson, County Londonderry on 29 June 1912.[57]

This analysis might seem too wide-ranging, including in its discussion Protestant Anglican and Presbyterian, and lumping together what has been called an 'Anglo-Irish tradition' with the narrower aspirations of Ulster unionism.[58] And Protestant society was diverse and even divided, with landlord and tenant, employer and worker, skilled working man and unskilled working man, urban and rural, all under the common name of Protestant. These objections can be met in part at least. It is easy to overemphasise the distinctions between Anglo-Irish (or southern Irish Protestant and unionist) and Ulster unionist. It may well have been that there is a discernible 'Anglo-Irish tradition', with its wider form of unionism and its emphasis on Britain and the Empire, unlike the narrower, more sectarian unionism of the north. Certainly the north was different: it was distinct from the rest of Ireland not by its solid Protestant character but, on the contrary, by its special problems as a region in which Protestant and Catholic lived in inextricable proximity, and yet dwelt in separate political worlds. But it is possible to exaggerate the difference: all Protestants feared their nationalist and Catholic enemies (with a very few exceptions). Southern Irish Protestant rhetoric, whether defending tithes or the established Church against the Liberals in 1868, sounded the same note of warning: that the enemy was at the gate, and freedom and true religion were compromised.

Second, it is misleading to characterise the northern brand of unionism as essentially based on a Presbyterian culture, or depict the state of Northern Ireland, established in 1921, as in some sense a Presbyterian triumph, a victory for a certain 'ethnic' group. There is no evidence to suggest that this was so, or that Presbyterians saw this as their state. Indeed, the Orange Order, central to Ulster unionism, included many Anglicans in its ranks, and was not altogether popular with Presbyterians. Furthermore, although Presbyterians were the larger denomination in Ulster, and then Northern Ireland, there was also a substantial Anglican population.[59] It is true that the diversity of Protestant society was a barrier to unity, and it is not argued here that there is such a thing as a 'Protestant mind', handed down unchanged throughout the ages. Presbyterians nursed their grievances too; in February 1880 the *Witness* demanded, 'How long will Presbyterians endure these things [the denial of their religious liberties and demand for places of "position"]? We have as good a right to our privileges as they [the Catholics]'. But the foundations of loyalism were already laid. The *Witness* declared that Presbyterians had 'always been loyal subjects', and that their Church had been 'more loyal in times of trial to the houses of Orange and Hanover' than the Church of Ireland.[60] And in time of trial the Protestants could see themselves as one community, draw upon its myths and historical episodes, and draw too upon the fact that liberty and ascendancy were not incompatible – that, on the contrary, they were essentially linked under the Protestant faith. If this was to defend a 'Protestant ascendancy', then so be it. But that ascendancy was not one exclusively of economic privilege. There were poor Protestants as well as poor Catholics. Protestants differed from Catholics mainly in their disproportionate representation in the landed class, the magistrates and the higher ranks of the police force. But these were, as one historian has called them, 'small differences' in economic terms.[61] And they did not prevent Presbyterian tenant farmers and Anglican landlords settling their differences and combining against the common foe.

The ascendancy was one of attitude, and drew strength from the tradition that Protestantism stood for progressive values, for civil liberty, for prosperity. As Beckett noted, there existed in Ireland a strong sense of Protestant superiority; this was not only felt by landlords, who lived in the large houses and county towns, or by Protestants who ran the most flourishing businesses. Lower still 'the

Protestant workman commonly regarded himself, and was sometimes regarded by others, as marked off from his Catholic mates by superior cleanliness, honesty and industry'. For even the most well-disposed Protestants, the Catholic remained external to themselves, 'the friendly Protestant's conception of good and amiable Catholics',[62] a view which found a modern, if unconscious, reflection in the Northern Ireland Prime Minister Terence O'Neill's claim in 1969 that 'it is fright-fully hard to explain to a Protestant that if you give Roman Catholics a good job and a good house, they will live like Protestants because they will see neighbours with cars and television sets and want to live like them'.[63] The *Northern Whig* asserted on 12 April 1886 that Parnellism stood for 'intimidation . . . the oppres-sion of minorities . . . by unscrupulous majorities'. The question of 'loyal and Liberal Ulster', it declared later the same year, was a vital one and not subject to compromise.[64] Home rule would 'inevitably increase the poverty and pauperism of Ireland, and flood the labour market of manufacturing Ulster, and of English and Scotch industrial centres, with hosts of Irish unemployed'. Home rule would 'reduce Ireland below the status of a colony' and inflict upon her 'the unconsti-tutional and unbearable injustice of taxation without representation'.[65] Thus spoke the organ of Ulster liberal thinking; and its words were no different from those of southern, or any other, unionism. Nor from those of Isaac Butt when, in his Conservative days, he warned against municipal reform in 1840, which would bring in its wake tyranny, the triumph of Catholicism, disorder and a Popish ascendancy.[66]

Certain other themes emerged as the Protestant minority drew up its battle lines, with, at bottom, its proposition: why should they consent to become a minority in a Catholic state, when they could insist that Irish Catholics remained a minority in a Protestant one? After partition, the point remained the same: why should Ulster unionists consent to become a minority in a Catholic (united Ire-land) state, when they could ensure that Ulster Catholics remained a minority in an Ulster Protestant (and wider British Protestant) state? These campaigns drew upon the traditions established in the early modern age, even upon those of the late medieval colony: a fear of treachery on England's part; a resentment of high-handedness; the constant anxiety over betrayal, which southern unionists expressed in their opposition to home rule between 1886 and 1914, when they did not expect the English people to allow any minister or government to barter away, for the venal votes of the representatives of Irish disaffection, the property, liber-ties and lives of the loyalists of Ireland – men whose only offence was that they had been friends of England through evil report and good report, and had stead-fastly endeavoured to maintain the unity of the British empire.[67]

The Presbyterian *Witness* noted in 1912 that, whereas the United States gov-ernment went to war to save their union in 1861, the British government 'do not fight; they surrender', and thus sacrificed their loyal friends in Ireland. The Ballymoney *Free Press* put this down to what it called 'the decadence of England'.[68] Carson feared betrayals in 1913 as he contemplated British unionists' attraction towards federal schemes.[69] But he sensed that, as Swift's biographer Irvin Ehren-preis put it, 'Without British backing Swift's class could not survive. With it, they could only survive'.[70] The southern Protestants failed to retain British backing in 1921 and they did not survive. But the Ulster unionists were not so easily put aside.

IV

The first two decades of the Northern Ireland state saw, therefore, not the end of the struggle against Catholic assertion, but its entering another phase. Northern Ireland was not a confessional state, in the sense that eighteenth-century Anglicans had sought to maintain Ireland as a confessional state, for there was no longer an establishment to support it and uphold its legal and political foundation. But the Protestant monopoly of political power was as important as it had been for Anglicans in the eighteenth century; and now that Presbyterians were subsumed under the common names of Protestant and unionist, the unofficial establishment was forged. The Protestants of Ireland in the 1830s and the Protestants of Ulster after 1921 were, as R.B. McDowell puts it, 'political frontiersmen, regarding their religion and their politics as different aspects of the same cause'.[71] And, like their forebears, they retained a (perhaps well-founded) suspicion of England. In 1834 at a meeting of Protestants in Dublin, the Revd Mortimer O'Sullivan welcomed 'the cordial friendship of our brethren in England', but warned Irish Protestants that, while 'you should be benefited by the exertions of your friends, you must be true to yourselves. Your cause has been blackened by foul misrepresentations'.[72] The Earl of Roden in 1834 noted that the enemies of Protestantism said that the Orange Institution was 'calculated to excite bad feelings, and to provoke tumult and aggression'. But the Orange Institution 'replies – by the tranquillity of Ulster'. The first Prime Minister of Northern Ireland, Sir James Craig, though at first reluctant to embrace an Orange identity, by the 1930s would have been comfortable with Roden's words that 'never did there exist in Ireland a body of comparatively recent institution, to whom the County owes so deep obligation as to the loyal ... Orange Society'.[73] The Orangemen 'do more – they say, we saved the country in the hour of its sorest peril'.[74]

But there was, still, even after 1921, the danger of the lukewarm nature of English support for her fellow citizens. This predicament faced all minorities in Ireland, from the time that they began to work out how best to cope with the fact that they were indeed a minority in Ireland, and dependent on support from across the channel. This had provoked eighteenth-century Irish patriots, such as Swift and William King. Now it provoked twentieth-century Ulster unionists, in their not too dissimilar predicament. In his *Ulster Was Right* (1934) Henry Maxwell described the opening of the Stormont parliament building as having 'constituted the final harvesting of the long-tended promise': the establishment of Northern Ireland. But in the dozen years since the foundations of the state 'much had happened to impair the confidence of the Ulster people in the durability of the original charter, and even, it must be said, in the good faith of English politicians'. The bond of Union was to the Ulster people 'the breath of their living'. Between the English people and the Ulster people there existed 'a sympathy of race and sentiment' which was 'deep and abiding'. Ulster needed British protection and was jealous of all that tended to weaken her connections with the mother country: 'She is dependent upon Great Britain for her very existence, and her dependence is manifest'. But, he added (echoing his Protestant forebears), 'Great Britain is none the less dependent upon Ulster by reason of the fact that her dependence is impalpable, and therefore easily denied by those who wish her ill'. Ulster fought battles against the Empire's foes 'often without assistance and without recognition'. This was why an event such as the Prince of Wales's opening of Stormont was 'greatly treasured'; such events were symbolic and they gave Ulster strength and credence. And with Ulster's strength and credence 'the welfare of Ireland as a whole is fostered'.[75]

But the nagging doubt remained: did those of the British who lived 'across the water' appreciate the Ulster unionist predicament? Maxwell quoted from a newspaper interview given by Carson: in the 'vast British electorate there is a large percentage of young people who naturally have little or no knowledge of the difficulties and dangers that Ulster men and women had to overcome ten or more years ago'. The Ulster people 'regard themselves as a branch of the British oak. Cut off the branch, and not only will the branch itself wither, but the tree will be left mutilated and weakened'. Maxwell believed that any attempt to intimidate Ulster would be resisted by the British people; but younger generations were fast growing up who were ignorant of the events that led to the founding of Northern Ireland and the Irish Free State. 'Unless they are conversant with the essential facts in that unhappy history they cannot be in a position to give Ulster the full support and sympathy to which she is most surely entitled'. Englishmen were 'too willing to shut their eyes to hostility'.[76]

Maxwell claimed that he wrote his book to educate the British people and to explain to them that the enemies of Great Britain always struck through Ireland, and could always count on the help of the Catholic Church in Ireland and abroad. Under the 'cloak of British indifference, the enemies of our interests have worked too long and too easily for our embarrassment in Ireland, and not the least of the difficulties and dangers which the indomitable determination and courage of Ulster have overcome has been the apathy shown by her relations in the face of her bitter suffering'. Ulster as much as England would like to forget 'but neither can afford the luxury'. As an outpost of Great Britain, the 'imperial Province' of Northern Ireland had her enemies both within and without her gates. But 'with the help and hand of Great Britain, she will emerge triumphant in the end, to be the great bulwark of the English creed which she has ever aspired to be, but, behold "he that guardeth Israel must neither slumber nor sleep"'.[77]

The *Dublin University Magazine* expressed this Protestant dilemma as long ago as 1842; let no one despise the Protestant who might be attracted to the nationalist cause, because, while 'security for Protestantism in Ireland is not separable from the British connection', yet it was the British who threatened to tear that connexion asunder.[78] The watchmen must be ever watchful, the weary patriots must not rest; but the Second World War, and then the Cold War which followed, seemed to ensure that the unionist desire for security would be fulfilled: Ulster was indeed an 'imperial outpost'. But the anxiety showed through. In the general election of February 1949, which the Northern Ireland Prime Minister Basil Brooke called to demonstrate unionist solidarity in the face of Eire's renewed claims for the reunification of Ireland, one unionist candidate claimed that, if Northern Ireland were invaded, the King's soldiers should support the King's men.[79] The response of the Labour government, not in sending the King's soldiers, but in passing the Ireland Act to secure that the Northern Ireland state would continue to exist as long as its parliament so willed it, seemed to mark the final settlement of unionist fears that had remained the same as they had done for Irish Protestants since the seventeenth century: that the contractual relationship between England and Irish Protestants be secured and maintained; that England should not betray her friends across the sea; that at the same time English interference in the affairs of Northern Irish Protestants be kept at bay; but that the connexion with Britain be secured and continued.

V

These issues were to resurface even more acutely in the late 1960s, and the thirty years of troubles that followed. But it might be useful at this stage to pause and ask why, if indeed British and English identity was based on Protestantism, Irish Protestants never felt secure that their British identity would be appreciated and supported by Britons on the other side of the water.

Protestantism did indeed become ineluctably associated with Britishness and Englishness in the sixteenth and seventeenth centuries, and this lasted into the early years of the twentieth century at least. But this followed, rather than preceded, strong national identities that were forged in the Middle Ages. The English knew who they were long before the Reformation added Protestantism to their self-assurance and suspicion of foreigners. Protestantism, through the accident of Tudor dynastic need, reinforced a strong sense of Englishness. But the old idea that there were in the archipelago four nations, England, Ireland, Scotland and Wales, preceded this, and even the success of the Reformation in Wales (particularly) and Scotland could not eradicate these older national identities, however spurious they might be: and certainly Scottish identity, thanks to the long and continuous history of its kingship, was far from shaky or spurious. The position in Ireland was more complex, not least because of the various layers of settlement there; but the medieval historian R.R. Davies has argued that

> In the case of Britain and Ireland the centuries from the eleventh, or perhaps more correctly the tenth, to the fourteenth were a key period in shaping the nomenclature of the peoples of these islands in a form which, regardless – or indeed because of – its ambiguities and simplifications was to last long into the future.[80]

Ireland was regarded as a distinct *nation*, whatever the fate of the Reformation there; the fact that it failed only made the distinction more acute, for now

Catholicism became associated with Irishness. In the eighteenth century Irish Protestants, a minority in the kingdom, wrested the claim to be the Irish nation from the Catholics; but they were, despite their Protestantism, still seen by England as a quasi-separate people at least: as Protestant, certainly, but still as Irish. Irish Protestants were caught in a dilemma of their own making. They began by calling themselves the 'English in Ireland', or the 'English interest'; by the end of the eighteenth century they referred to themselves as the 'Irish people'. They distinguished themselves from the English, and yet they could not escape the dangerous admission, made by Wolfe Tone even as he sought to create a united Irish nation, that Catholics were 'the Irish, properly so called'.[81] In 1807 a Protestant pamphleteer put the case that the peculiarity of the Irish situation was 'that the Catholics of Ireland look upon themselves as the original and legal proprietor of the island; the rightful and inherent possessors of the soil; that the Protestants have forcibly intruded upon the country; and have transferred the property and influence from the Catholics to a Protestant Supremacy'.[82]

Protestantism could not unite the British nation, for no such nation was ever created. The English kept their own myths, though Irish Protestants were permitted to borrow into it through such events as the Glorious Revolution and the siege of Derry. But a reading of Whig historians, especially G.M. Trevelyan, reveals how differently that revolution was seen in England and in Ireland. Whereas an Orange gentleman declared that the purpose of Orange processions was to 'commemorate great national events, such as the establishment of the British Constitution by the Bill of Rights in 1688',[83] the Trevelyan version of the consequences of this victory for Ireland was not one with which an Orangeman would have agreed. In his *The English Revolution, 1688–1689*, published in 1938, Trevelyan contrasted the revolution settlement in England and Ireland. In England it established constitutional government; in Ireland it was 'imposed by the sword'.[84] The Scottish revolution, by contrast, was 'made by the Scots themselves ... It was not dictated from Whitehall or Westminster'.[85] In Ireland the revolution rested 'on force alone ... Our ancestors, Whig and Tory alike, understood little of realities in Ireland, and thought it a light matter to convert, or at least to hold down, a whole nation by force'.[86] 'The reconquest, which meant slavery for Ireland, meant freedom and safety for England.'[87] The revolution settlement in Ireland remained unaltered until 1782, and 'was, as we have seen, one of the worst settlements ever made ... it was exactly the opposite in spirit of the revolution settlement in England, for it represented the mere spirit of conquest and arbitrary power.'[88]

Common Protestantism – and given the differences within Protestantism it was not all that common – could not obliterate the contours of the past, erase ideas of nationality already formed, and incorporate Irish Protestants into the English/British nation. As England experienced growing secularism after the First World War, it would be even harder to base the Union upon the idea of a common Protestantism, or to see Northern Irish Protestants as in any sense integral to the English/British nation – especially as the English tended to equate Britishness simply with Englishness anyway.

VI

When Brian Faulkner appeared on the balcony of the Stormont building after the British decision to suspend the Northern Ireland parliament he spoke, not Swift's words, but his sentiments: Ulster would not be treated as a 'coconut colony'.[89] The idea of contract, on which William Molyneux based his case for the kingdom of Ireland's Protestant inhabitants, entered the debate with a surprisingly apt freshness – apt, that is, in Irish but not in English perception. William's namesake, James Molyneux, wrote in March 1994 that

> The post-election [British] Government will be forced to establish a clear understanding of the Union and then underpin it with constitutional arrangements which demonstrate that the citizens of Ulster are, like their colleagues in England, Scotland and Wales, citizens of the United Kingdom with identical rights and obligations.[90]

Swift's sense of marginality expressed in his 'Injured Lady' essay was expressed in an editorial in the *Ulster Unionist* in March 1994: 'the British Government's assertion that they have "no selfish, strategic or economic interest in Northern Ireland" comes perilously close to making unionists feel like unwanted lodgers'.[91] This resentment was most eloquently and tragically expressed by the Ulster Unionist MP, Harold McCusker, in the aftermath of the signing of the Anglo-Irish Agreement in November 1985. Describing his feelings when he managed to get from a policeman at Hillsborough a copy of the agreement, he spoke of his desolation 'because as I stood in the cold outside Hillsborough Castle everything that I held turned to ashes in my mouth'. The House of Commons, he insisted, should be above party: 'It has a responsibility to cherish all the children of the nation . . . [I] thought I belonged to that nation, and I thought that the House had an obligation to cherish me as it cherished the rest.' But now he must tell his own children that they were not able to put their trust in the House; better to tell them that than let them spend the rest of their lives 'knowing that they are now some sort of semi-British citizens'. But, at the end, Protestant pride was not dead. McCusker dismissed threats that unionist opposition might result in the turning off of the 'taps' of British subsidy to Northern Ireland: 'I do not want money to be offered to me to buy my acquiescence . . . we are a proud people'.[92]

The Democratic Unionist response to British policy in Ireland after 1972 was similar. William McCrea in the same debate protested that the British government 'have decided that the unionists of Northern Ireland are a liability, instead of desiring them to be in the family'.[93] The principle of consent and the self-determination of the people of Northern Ireland had to be established.[94] Government was being carried on in a 'colonial fashion' from London.[95] 'The Dagger of Treachery strikes at the heart of Ulster'.[96] How could the Union be safe, demanded the Democratic Unionists, 'when the British government itself has been guilty of the most dastardly and cowardly betrayal since the days of Lord Carson?'[97]

In a policy document, 'What's the British Government up to?', published in 1994, the *Democratic Unionist* reminded its followers that Carson's fight for the Union was of as crucial importance then as now: 'They knew that the British connection was an essential safeguard for the practice of their religion and their freedom to pursue their way of life.' It quoted Norman Lamont as saying that the people of Northern Ireland cannot be coerced; and that the government of Northern Ireland should be put on a comparable basis with the rest of the United Kingdom, and 'not run as if it were a colony waiting to be handed over to the government of a foreign power'.[98]

These statements, though set in a very different context, have a historical resonance. As Richard English remarks, 'Authors who have explored the nineteenth century have found that the roots of the unionist tradition are older and sturdier than nationalists were traditionally disposed to admit'.[99] The *Dublin University Magazine* spoke for succeeding generations of unionists when it complained bitterly in September 1843 that England, having taken over the responsibility for governing Ireland directly, having made solemn promises and engagements, obtained from the Protestants their consent to protect their rights. And now that the enemies of Protestants

> have proved themselves truce-breakers and false, England is called on, not to withdraw from them powers which they had dishonestly obtained, but to imitate their bad example, by betraying friends who have confided in her, and who have loyally defended her interests and honour [*sic*] through all vicissitudes. Such is the expedient by which a great nation is advised to relieve itself from an embarrassment.[100]

These sentiments stretch back not only to the early nineteenth century, when a Catholic ascendancy first seemed a real possibility, but to the early eighteenth century, when Irish patriots attempted to assert their rights, and the rights of Ireland, and yet maintain the British connexion. They find a location in the work of Swift, with his demand that Irish Protestants be treated as equal and fellow Britons.

This is not to deny or ignore what Toby Barnard has called the 'variousness' of Irish Protestant history;[101] but ideologies are an abridgement, a necessary simplification of history. At times of political anxiety, crisis or trauma, actors articulate the ideology, and the audience understands and responds to what is being represented on the stage. The most significant contemporary example is the claim of the local Portadown Orange lodge to march down the Garvaghy Road. This first confrontation, in the summer of 1995, seemed to act as a kind of rallying point, a line in the sand, for the defenders of the Union.[102]

Irish Protestants, to use Oakeshott's words, sought to alter the world so as to suit their needs. This explains the eclectic character of their political thought: from Lockean contract principles to providential deliverance; from rights as British citizens to rights to self-determination; from defending the rights of the Irish parliament to defending the Union with Britain whole and entire; from being

British to being anti-British; from feeling Irish to feeling anti-Irish; from a Protestant parliament for a Protestant people to a pluralist parliament for a pluralist people. This does not render their ideas any the less valid or authentic; Irish nationalism too has proved itself a protean ideology. The siege of Derry, as Ian McBride has shown, could take on different meanings according to circumstance, or could be taken as meaning 'what it always meant', even when time and circumstance rendered it different. Unionists can call upon a tradition of thought, arising from the Protestant predicament in Ireland, that has a greater depth and richness than is usually supposed. Irish Protestant life and thought (like that of other groups) have been shaped by geopolitics: by the influence of the land on the people. Art Cosgrove rightly commends the study of late medieval Irish history to unionists. The result might surprise unionists. But as Thomas Hobbes pointed out, in a phrase that applies appropriately to both these minority groups in Ireland, who were resolved to maintain the English connexion, 'The cause which moveth a man to become subject to another is the fear of not otherwise preserving himself'.[103]

NOTES

1 Tony Claydon and Ian McBride (eds), *Protestantism and National Identity: Britain and Ireland, c.1650–c.1850* (Cambridge, 1998), p. 3.
2 Ibid., pp. 12–15.
3 W.H. Greenleaf, *Oakeshott's Philosophical Politics* (London, 1966), pp. 42–3, 75.
4 J.C. Beckett, 'The study of Irish history' (1963), reprinted in *Confrontations* (London, 1972), pp. 11–25, esp. pp. 23–5.
5 Art Cosgrove, 'The writing of Irish medieval history', *Irish Historical Studies*, 27, 106 (November 1990), pp. 97–111, at pp. 110–11.
6 Thomas Witherow, *Derry and Enniskillen in the Year 1689: The Story of Some Famous Battlefields in Ulster* (1873; 4th edition, Belfast, 1913), pp. 363–4, 369, 370–1.
7 D. George Boyce, *Nationalism in Ireland* (3rd edition, London, 1995), p. 77.
8 Ibid., pp. 102–4.
9 Ibid., p. 105.
10 Revd Richard Mant, *History of the Church of Ireland* (London, 1840), II, p. 122.
11 Herbert Davis (ed.), *The Prose Works of Jonathan Swift*, Vol. 10, *The Drapier's Letters and Other Works, 1724–1725* (Oxford, 1941), p. 31.
12 Ibid., pp. 39, 61–2.
13 Ibid., p. 103.
14 Paul Bew and Gordon Gillespie, *Northern Ireland: A Chronology of the Troubles, 1968–1993* (Dublin, 1993), p. 28.
15 Boyce, *Nationalism in Ireland*, pp. 106–7.
16 R.H. Murray, *Revolutionary Ireland and its Settlement* (London, 1911), p. 336. William King to Mr McCausland, 14 October 1708, Trinity College Dublin, King MSS, 2531/4.
17 William King to Mr Jenkins, January (?) 1711, Trinity College Dublin, King MSS, 750/11/1/380.
18 Davis, *Prose Works of Jonathan Swift*, 10, p. 62.
19 *A Sermon Preach'd before their Excellencies the Lords Justices of Ireland and both Houses of Parliament; at Christ's Church, Dublin, on Thursday June the 7th, 1716. Being the Day appointed for a Publick Thanksgiving, Etc. By Timothy, Lord Bishop of Kilmore and Ardagh* (Dublin, 1716), pp. 6–8, 13. See also, among many examples, *A Sermon Preached before the Honourable House of Commons, at St Andrew's Church, Dublin, May XXIX, 1709. By D. Prat, D.D., Senior Fellow of*

Trinity College Dublin. Chaplain to his Grace the Duke of Ormonde, and to the Honourable House of Commons (Dublin, 1709), and *A Sermon to bring to Remembrance God's wonderful Mercies at the Boyne; preach'd on the second day of July, 1699. At St Nicholas Within, Dublin, by John Stearne, D. D.* (Dublin, 1699). See also Toby Barnard, 'The Uses of 23 October 1641 and Irish Protestant Celebrations', *English Historical Review*, 106 (1991), pp. 889–920, at pp. 891, 908–9.

20　William King to the Bishop of Bangor, 8 February 1708, Trinity College Dublin, King MSS, 2531/45.

21　Joseph McMinn, 'A weary patriot: Swift and the formation of an Anglo-Irish identity', *Eighteenth Century Ireland* (1987), 2, pp. 103–13, at p. 111.

22　Ibid., p. 112.

23　For which see Gerard O'Brien, 'The Grattan Mystique', *Eighteenth Century Ireland*, 1 (1986), pp. 177–94.

24　J.C. Beckett, *The Anglo-Irish Tradition* (London, 1976), pp. 54–5, 58–9.

25　Edmund Burke, *Letters, Speeches and Tracts on Irish Affairs, collected and edited by Matthew Arnold* (London, 1881), p. 406.

26　Ibid., p. 405.

27　Ibid., pp. 406–7.

28　Ibid., p. 409.

29　Ibid., p. 412.

30　For a general discussion of reasons of state in eighteenth-century Europe see Jeremy Black, 'Confessional state or elect nation? Religion and identity in eighteenth-century England', in Claydon and McBride, *Protestantism and National Identity*, pp. 53–74, esp. pp. 64–72.

31　*Dublin University Magazine*, July 1834, pp. 1–12.

32　J.L. Porter, *The Life and Times of Henry Cooke, D.D., LL.D.* (London, 1871), pp. 263–4.

33　Ibid., p. 269.

34　Ibid., p. 272.

35　Ibid., p. 273. For a discussion of the shifts of mood in Irish Presbyterianism see David Hempton, *Religion and Political Culture in Britain and Ireland. From the Glorious Revolution to the Decline of Empire* (Cambridge, 1996), pp. 94–101.

36　Porter, *Henry Cooke*, pp. 275–8. For successful efforts to close the gap between Anglicans and Presbyterians before 1914 see Alvin Jackson, 'Unionist politics and Protestant society in Edwardian Ulster', *Historical Journal*, 33, 4 (1990), pp. 839–66, at pp. 864–5.

37　Anon., *The Protestant in Ireland in 1853* (London, 1854), pp. 99–106.

38　G.D. Zimmermann, *Irish Political Street Ballads and Rebel Songs* (Geneva, 1966), p. 295.

39　Ibid., p. 296.

40　J. Hill, *From Patriots to Unionists: Dublin Civic Politics and Irish Protestant Patriotism, 1660–1840* (Oxford, 1997), pp. 327–9.

41　Zimmermann, *Irish Political Street Ballads*, p. 297.

42　Ibid., p. 303.

43　Ibid., p. 302.

44　Ibid., p. 298.

45　Ibid., p. 304.

46　Ibid., p. 311.

47　W.H. Crawford, 'A look at the past', in James McLoone (ed.), *The British–Irish Connection* (Galway, 1985), pp. 1–10, at p. 8.

48　*Dublin University Magazine*, April 1835, pp. 471–90.

49　Ibid., December 1835, p. 682.

50　*The Great Protestant Demonstration at Hillsborough: October 30, 1867. Authentic Report* (Belfast, 1867), p. 5.

51　Ibid., p. 20.

52　Ibid., p. 22. Presbyterian opinion was divided on the disestablishment issue, but there was a significant degree of support for the established Church in its campaign. See *Report of a Meeting of Presbyterians of Belfast, Ulster Hall, 29 April 1869*, where the attendance, some 10,000 to 15,000 in number, was told that the Protestant Church was 'all one family', and the Revd Hugh Hanna urged the meeting to 'protest, in the name of heaven and with all your hearts, against Mr Gladstone's project of national apostasy from the Protestant faith'. He recalled the common Protestant cause at Derry's walls. The Revd Henry Henderson of Hollywood warned Presbyterians that they must support the Church of Ireland in its time of trial for the sake of 'common Protestantism' (Public Record Office of Northern Ireland, T277I/7). But for a contrary view, see W.D. Killen, *Why Should Prelacy Dominate in Ireland?* (Belfast, 1868), esp. pp. 1, 6–7.

53 *The Great Protestant Demonstration*, p. 25.
54 Ibid., p. 56.
55 D. Hempton and M. Hill, *Evangelical Protestantism in Ulster Society, 1740–1890* (London, 1992), pp. 160–87.
56 Zimmermann, *Irish Political Street Ballads*, p. 319.
57 Paul Bew, *Ideology and the Irish Question* (Oxford, 1994), pp. 31–4, 56–8.
58 The most persuasive exponent of this view is Beckett, *The Anglo-Irish Tradition, passim*, esp. p. 90.
59 In 1861 the numbers in the province of Ulster were: 50.5 per cent Catholic; 20.4 per cent Church of Ireland; 26.3 per cent Presbyterian. In 1926 in the six counties of Northern Ireland the proportions were: 35.5 per cent Catholic; 27.0 per cent Church of Ireland; 31.3 per cent Presbyterian (Ruth Dudley Edwards, *An Atlas of Irish History* (London, 1973), p. 129.
60 *Witness*, 13 February 1880.
61 D.H. Akenson, *Small Differences: Irish Catholics and Irish Protestants, 1815–1922* (Kingston and Montreal, 1988), *passim*.
62 Beckett, *The Anglo-Irish Tradition*, pp. 119, 141–2.
63 Caroline Kennedy-Pipe, *The Origins of the Present Troubles in Northern Ireland* (London, 1997), p. 35. For a nineteenth-century example see the southern unionist claim that the so-called 'English garrison' in Ireland provided an 'oasis of culture, of uprightness and of fair dealing', and that without them Ireland would be 'smothered in an atmosphere of superstition, greed and chicanery' (Patrick Buckland, 'Carson, Craig and the partition of Ireland, 1912–21', in Peter Collins (ed.), *Nationalism and Unionism: Conflict in Ireland, 1885–1921* (Belfast, 1994), pp. 75–89 at p. 80). Irish Presbyterians shared this view. See Thomas Croskery, *Irish Presbyterianism: Its History, Character, Influence and Present Position* (Dublin, 1884), p. 23: 'The Presbyterians found Ulster a morass and have made it a garden.'
64 *Northern Whig*, 15 July 1886.
65 Ibid., 28 June 1886.
66 *Speech by Isaac Butt at the Great Protestant meeting in Dublin, on Thursday 13 February 1840* (London, 1840), pp. 2, 15–16.
67 Patrick Buckland, *Irish Unionism One: The Anglo-Irish and the New Ireland, 1885–1922* (Dublin, 1972), p. 11. For more examples see D.W. Miller, *Queen's Rebels: Ulster Loyalism in Historical Perspective* (Dublin, 1978), pp. 91–2. For an example of contract theory see Alvin Jackson, *Colonel Edward Saunderson* (Oxford, 1995), pp. 114–18.
68 Bew, *Ideology and the Irish Question*, p. 46.
69 Alvin Jackson, *The Ulster Party: Irish Unionists in the House of Commons, 1884–1911* (Oxford, 1989), p. 315.
70 Joseph McMinn, 'A weary patriot', p. 110.
71 R.B. McDowell, *Public Opinion and Government Policy in Ireland, 1801–1845* (London 1952), p. 110.
72 *Case of the Protestants of Ireland Stated in addresses delivered in Dublin, Liverpool, Bristol and Bath, in the year 1834, by the Reverend Mortimer O'Sullivan* (London, 1836), p. 1.
73 Quoted in Ibid., p. 33.
74 Quoted in Ibid., p. 34. For a strong defence of Orangeism and its identification with the state see *Northern Whig*, 13 July 1933, where the order was described as 'the nucleus around which the Unionists of the Province gathered, when danger or submission in a Nationalist and Roman Catholic dominated Ireland threatened'.

75 Henry Maxwell, *Ulster Was Right* (London, 1934), pp. 8–9.

76 Ibid., pp. 13–14.

77 Ibid., pp. 15–16.

78 *Dublin University Magazine*, July 1843, p. 109.

79 *Belfast Newsletter*, 24 February 1949.

80 R.R. Davies, 'The peoples of Britain and Ireland, 1100–1400, II. Names, boundaries and regnal solidarities', *Transactions of the Royal Historical Society*, 6th series, V (1995), pp. 1–20, at p. 20. See also his articles in *TRHS*, IV (1994); VI (1996) and VII (1997). For a series of essays on that topic see Brendan Bradshaw and John Morrill (eds), *The British Problem, c. 1534–1707: State Formation in the Atlantic Archipelago* (London, 1996), esp. pp. 5–9, 18. See also Ralph A. Griffiths, *'This Royal Throne of Kings, This Sceptr'd Isle': The English Realm and Nation in the Later Middle Ages* (Swansea, 1983), *passim*, esp. pp. 24–5, for examples of thirteenth-century stereotypes of 'wild Irish' (and wild Welsh).

81 Boyce, *Nationalism in Ireland*, p. 128.

82 Edward Brynn, *The Church of Ireland in the Age of Catholic Emancipation* (New York, 1982), p. 440.

83 Miller, *Queen's Rebels*, p. 62.

84 G.M. Trevelyan, *The English Revolution, 1688–1689* (London, 1938), p. 205.

85 Ibid., p. 215.

86 Ibid., p. 227.

87 Ibid., p. 228.

88 Ibid., p. 239. See also the great Whig historian Macaulay's qualification of the Glorious Revolution in its Irish context (Ian McBride, *The Siege of Derry in Ulster Protestant Mythology* (Dublin, 1997), pp. 60–2).

89 Brian Faulkner, *Memoirs of a Statesman*, ed. John Houston (London, 1978), p. 157.

90 *Ulster Unionist*, 12, March 1994, p. 3.

91 Ibid., p. 5.

92 *Parliamentary Debates*, 6th series, 87 (27 November 1985), cc. 912–18.

93 Ibid., c. 957.

94 Democratic Unionist Party press release, 20 May 1996.

95 Ibid., 1 February 1993.

96 Ibid., 19 April 1995.

97 Ibid., n.d. (August 1994).

98 Democratic Unionist Party policy document, pp. 12, 14.

99 Richard English, 'The Unionists', in John Wilson Foster, *The Idea of the Union: Statements and Critiques in Support of the Union* (Vancouver, 1995), pp. 42–5, at p. 43.

100 *Dublin University Magazine*, September 1843, p. 359.

101 Toby Barnard, 'Crises of Identity among Irish Protestants, 1641–1685', *Past and Present*, 127 (1990), pp. 39–83, at p. 83. But Barnard also refers to the way in which events such as 1641 and 1691 'were swiftly incorporated into the continuum of Irish history' (Barnard, 'Uses of 23 October 1641', *English Historical Review*, 106 (1991), p. 894).

102 See *Case of the Protestants of Ireland, Stated*, p. 56, for an earlier example of the question of parades, when Mortimer O'Sullivan defended the rights of Orangemen to march. O'Connell, he noted, protested about the 'threats' of the Orange Order. But, O'Sullivan maintained, the problem was that 'every concession rendered the Roman Catholics more impatient – every display of Protestant principles became an annoyance in the same degree in which there was a hope that it might be presented, and as soon as government was found willing to yield a ready ear to complaint, complaint was prepared to occupy it'.

103 G.P. Gooch, *Political Thought in England from Bacon to Halifax* (London, 1937), p. 37.

Quotations from the William King MSS are given with kind permission of the Librarian, Trinity College Dublin.

3 The Chief Secretary

Brian Jenkins

Late in his lengthy political career, and long after the declaration of his mission to pacify Ireland, William Gladstone privately assailed the Union as an ill-considered British imposition which he would have resisted had he been an Irishman living at the turn of the nineteenth century. Of course, this assertion was far from inconvenient at a time when he was anxious to elevate above the level of political expediency his own belated advocacy of a very modest portion of political autonomy for Ireland. But the commitment, in the fourth quarter of the century, of one of the two great political parties, or at least its greater part, to the cause of 'home rule' reflected the inability of the Union's defenders since 1801 to render it impregnable. Not that they had failed for want of trying, persuaded as most of them had been that the connexion was vital for Ireland and essential for Britain's security and the integrity of the Empire.[1]

A quarter of a century before Gladstone made his private admission, Lord Acton wrote that 'A State which is incompetent to satisfy different races condemns itself; a State which labours to neutralise, to absorb, or to expel them, destroys its own vitality; a State which does not include them is destitute of the chief basis of self-government.' This stricture might have been interpreted as a succinct summary of the Union's failings, but they were not Acton's target. He viewed the British and Austrian empires as 'substantially the most perfect' states, arguing that they had managed to include 'various distinct nationalities without oppressing them'. Within five years Fenianism was bedevilling Britain, Ireland and Canada, while Austria was obliged to concede the dual monarchy to Hungary. Both events were later to contribute in however misinterpreted a fashion to the philosophical underpinnings of Sinn Féin.[2]

In the minds of some historians, and especially those impressed with Ireland's exceptionalism even as part of the United Kingdom, a belief lingers that Wales and Scotland had been 'easily assimilated' into the British state. Instead, the Union effected with Scotland in 1707 had been incomplete, and the compromises and concessions which were a feature of this constitutional settlement provided some clue to the problems which the promoters and defenders of the later union were to encounter and ultimately fail to resolve. On the other hand, the apparent success of the British nation by the end of the eighteenth century offered them the encouragement, perhaps even the assurance, that history was on their side.[3]

Union with Scotland simplified the means by which England controlled the northern kingdom, both economically and politically. After 1707, in addition to a single monarchy, the enlarged British state possessed a single parliament and a single central administration. However, that Parliament usually legislated separately for a Scotland which retained distinctive local institutions, not least a different legal system and a different national Church. In short, this was no truly unitary state and might even have been considered an anomalous one. Within it there remained three historic nations whose peoples spoke three different languages, and these were overlaid by innumerable and often mutually unintelligible regional dialects. Such multi-ethnicity frequently found mutually antipathetic expression. The complications notwithstanding, Great Britain successfully weathered the early disillusionment of Scottish unionists, and survived two Scottish rebellions within the first four decades of its existence. By the century's end, the Union was generally considered to be a vindication of far-sighted statesmanship. Scotland's finances had been stabilised, industrial development and urbanisation were under way, and agriculture was being modernised. More than this, 'a growing sense of Britishness' was in evidence. It originated in a common Protestantism, a common struggle against France, and a common pride in, and common profiting from, a vastly enlarged empire.[4]

However reassuring the evolution of the Union with Scotland, and the sense of British identity, advocates of much the same arrangement with Ireland were confronted by a number of peculiar complications and challenges which threatened to make far more difficult its defence once it had been effected. England, Wales and Scotland were contiguous, but Britain and Ireland were separated by the sea, as Robert Peel reminded the Commons in 1817. England, Wales and Scotland shared a common Protestantism, however distinctive their respective versions of the Reformed faith, whereas the people of Ireland remained overwhelmingly Catholic. And the decision to unite the Church of England and that of Ireland's Protestant ascendancy in the articles of Union merely placed at the centre of the new state the additional anomaly of an establishment which represented a mere fraction of the Irish population and was regarded as anathema by fully three-quarters of it. At the same time a strident anti-Catholicism continued to enjoy a broad popular appeal in Britain. If Protestantism 'was the foundation that made the invention of Great Britain possible', it was all too likely under these circumstances to be the rock on which the United Kingdom foundered.[5]

In Ireland, a bitter sectarianism was forced – fed by the savage rebellion of 1798 and its brutal repression. Religious antagonism served to complicate, in a way not often to be found in Britain, the relationship between owners and occupiers of the land. The former were predominantly Protestant while the latter were largely Catholic. Nor were landlords' nerves calmed by the emergence of a class of 'underground gentry' who claimed descent from the old, dispossessed Catholic proprietors. Their sense of insecurity was heightened by the all too frequent eruptions of agrarian violence. These disturbances prompted contemporaries to compare unfavourably the 'turbulent and ignorant' Irish with the peaceable and instructed Scottish peasants. Moreover, there were elements, Defenders and

Ribbonmen among them, who were politically subversive as well as socially disruptive. And Ireland's reputation, whether truly deserved or not, was for exceptional lawlessness and disloyalty. Peel deplored 'the wretched depravity and sanguinary disposition' of the Irish lower orders. Yet much of the violence could be attributed to a breadth and depth of poverty which was exceptional, as contemporaries recognised. However, discontent was all the more alarming there given the recent rebellion and relatively higher degree of popular political activity following the extension of the parliamentary franchise to Irish Catholics on the same terms which governed its exercise by Protestants. In short, Scotland and Ireland 'were distinguished by differing levels of social tension and polarisation'. More than this, the general causes of violence were present in Ireland to a singular degree – the economic pressure of want; social and political aspirations; and religious differences.[6]

The motive power of Union was essentially the same in both cases – British security. The argument has been made that it was the increasing strength, not weakness, of the Irish state in the late eighteenth century, 'and the threat that this appeared to pose to imperial unity, that prompted British ministers to urge its absorption into the greater British state'. Certainly distrust even suspicion of Anglo-Irish nationalism had played its part in strengthening unionist sentiment in London from the middle of the eighteenth century. Pitt made no bones of the fact that his fundamental purpose was to 'add to the strength and power of the empire', but his concern was primarily with the external threat. Ireland 'is the point to which our enemy has chiefly directed his attention', he later reminded the Commons, 'and, therefore, we are the more bound to take care that this point, the most important in the British empire, should be preserved from hostile aggression and secret machinations'. The 'internal treason' which had erupted so bloodily with the rebellion in 1798 'ingrafted jacobinism on those diseases which necessarily grew out of the state and condition of Ireland'. Consequently, for the Union to succeed, the island needed to be rescued from those 'great and deplorable evils' which were rooted 'in the situation of the country itself – in the present character, manners and habits of its inhabitants – in their want of intelligence, or, in other words, their ignorance – in the unavoidable separation between certain classes – in the state of property – in its religious distinctions – in the rancour which bigotry engenders and superstition rears and cherishes'. Echoing Adam Smith, he declared that closer 'connection and intercourse with Great Britain' through an 'impartial legislature' would be the means of channelling to Ireland, as it had to Scotland, the English capital fundamental to the promised economic development. The resultant increase in national wealth, the infusion of 'English manners and industry', the fostering of those middle classes who united 'the highest and the lowest orders of the community without a chasm in any part of the system', would ultimately 'improve the temper and manners, as well as the understanding of the people of Ireland', and thus promote also 'internal tranquillity'. In short, the Empire was to be made 'more powerful and more secure, by making Ireland more free and more happy'.[7]

If anything was clear after a decade of union, it was that Ireland remained far from happy. Francis Plowden opened his history of the new relationship with the ironic understatement that it 'has not realised the flattering prospects which the British Minister held out to the Irish people as inducements to adopt the measure'. Sir Jonah Barrington served up much the same opinion in his published memoirs. The *Dublin Evening Post* observed that a union which 'was to have given freedom to the Catholic, and extension to our commerce', had produced neither benefit. Instead, 'our artisans are existing on public charity; our manufacturers and shopkeepers are bankrupt; our exports consist of more than two millions sterling to absentees [and] Our imports are principally of that very raw material manufactured by English hands'. Ireland had been injured and insulted, the newspaper concluded, and reduced to a form of 'colonial servitude'.[8]

These were but three in an army of critics who sooner or later assailed the Union for failing to establish 'religious equality'. Pitt had wished to liberate Ireland from 'the blind zeal and phrenzy of religious prejudices'. Yet his personal commitment to Catholic emancipation was more tactical than principled, and the certainty that its inclusion in the Union would further complicate the already formidable task of persuading the Protestant ascendancy to agree to the abolition of its parliament caused him to temporise. However, before many Catholics, he had successfully dangled the bait of relief just as soon as Ireland's Protestant minority gained in confidence and security as part of the United Kingdom's sectarian majority. And many leading Catholics signed on to the Union out of fear of the French and in the belief that it would pave the way to prompt emancipation. Indeed, Pitt mused aloud that generally more attractive concessions were in prospect, such as the eventual relief of the overwhelmingly Catholic Irish lower orders 'from the pressure of tithes, "together with" effectual and adequate provision' for their clergy. Not that these were ever more than qualified half-promises. Emancipation would only be introduced 'when the conduct of the Catholics shall be such as to make it safe for the government to admit them to the participation of the privileges granted to those of the established religion, and when the temper of the times shall be favourable to such a measure'. Here was an elastic excuse for delay, and Pitt immediately availed himself of it, given the precarious mental health of a monarch who blamed his illness on the agitation of this issue.[9]

The task of defending the unpopular Union fell to the leaders of an executive government whose very survival in Dublin Castle further illustrated Ireland's incomplete integration into the enlarged United Kingdom. She retained her own Privy Council, her own distinct legal structure, her own Treasury and Chancellor of the Exchequer, and boasted more than a score of administrative departments. In this sense the Union preserved as much of the historic Irish nation as that of 1707 had of the Scottish, and thereby 'either created or perpetuated forces' which were likely eventually to work for its modification or repeal. In the cautionary words of Peel, Ireland 'is a country separated by nature from that to which she is united by law; a country having once had an independent existence – having within twenty years had an independent legislature – having still her separate courts of justice, and distinct departments of executive government'. Lording it over this small empire was a viceroy whose office dated back seven centuries, but with the Union his chief secretary had an opportunity to emerge from his shadow and ultimately become the more important figure in all but pomp. For in addition to supervising the Irish administration, he travelled to London for the parliamentary year. He was expected to pilot legislation through the Commons, answer questions, and explain as well as defend policy. As a result, he necessarily consulted with, and was consulted by, the most senior ministers of government, not least the Prime Minister and the Home Secretary. In the opinion of one perceptive contemporary observer of the Irish scene, this office demanded a man of 'first-rate virtues and talents – a man of enlarged mind, and enlightened views; one who, looking forward to the future, can profit from the past; who is able to plan as well as to execute, and who, possessing sufficient penetration to discover the latent sources of national prosperity, has zeal and activity to turn them to advantage'.[10]

Few, if any, of these qualities were quickly on display. Although the prime ministerial instructions to the first post-Union chief secretary included an assurance 'That the scene was great, and the business would be to render the Union a real Union', there followed a string of short-lived tenures, eight within the first decade. These early holders of 'this arduous and important office' lacked the interest, the will, the stamina or the health to make much of an impact on Ireland or her problems and thus strengthen the Union. But three men, William Wellesley-Pole (1809–12), Robert Peel (1812–18) and Henry Goulburn (1821–7) eventually provided stability and continuity, utilised the previously dormant powers of their position, and helped to shape enduring policies which were intended to sustain the Union.[11]

All three were subsequently embraced by the sweeping criticism of one Irish peer who protested that they 'came over from England totally ignorant of the country [they were] to govern' and saw 'no person from whom to collect information but the clerks of the Castle or the needy expectants who endeavour to recommend themselves by misrepresenting the people'. Yet the first of them was an Irishman, and not one of them was as naive or as credulous as this critic alleged. Two of them brought considerable administrative experience to the office, and the third was already marked as something of a political prodigy. Nor were they blind to the complexities of the Union's periphery. Wellesley-Pole had initially opposed this constitutional arrangement because of his concern that a distant parliament in London might be less disposed to adopt the stern measures which he had considered necessary to protect the people from rebels.[12]

The second of Ireland's most illustrious contemporary family of brothers, William Wellesley had lengthened his name on succeeding to the Queen's County estates of his cousin William Pole. He was more than twenty years older than both Peel and Goulburn, and no doubt considered himself socially a cut above them. His origins were aristocratic, however recent the ennoblement, while Peel was the son of an industrial magnate and Goulburn the heir of a West Indian planter who had married the daughter of a minor lord. Wellesley-Pole was also abrasive, arrogant and inexhaustibly ambitious, for his brothers as well as for himself. Peel did not want for ambition, but was more discreet in its pursuit. Equally, he exhibited a natural reserve and a more becoming self-assurance, founded as it was on his widely acknowledged intellectual brilliance and forensic powers. Goulburn was admired for his many personal virtues, intelligence, hard work and administrative efficiency. He shunned the limelight.[13]

No matter the generational gulf, or the national, social and personality differences, which separated Wellesley-Pole from his two longer-serving successors as Chief Secretary, there did exist an ideological affinity between these men. The older man's career reached its apogee, while those of Peel and Goulburn were launched as members of the Perceval administration. They all subscribed to a form of Pittite Toryism, being heavily influenced by the French Revolution and the prolonged war against France. They treasured the balance of the constitution, and also treasured the established Church as a bulwark of the state and of social stability; they considered large property holders the nation's natural governors, regarded the rule of law as the first essential for the enjoyment of liberty, and were fearful of the turbulent mob. They had witnessed the explosion of the 'military–fiscal state' and its progressive centralisation, but subscribed to the emergent orthodoxy which advocated a reversal of state growth whenever that became possible, and the avoidance of state intervention in the economy. They all took pride in the phenomenal expansion of the British Empire, on which Tories boasted the sun now never set. It had been in India that Richard and Arthur Wellesley had each made his mark, and excited not a little controversy, while Peel and Goulburn both served apprenticeships at the Colonial Office before moving to Dublin.[14]

What were their views of the Irish problem? They regarded the Union 'an inviolable compact'. They believed that their essential task was to determine 'by what course of policy shall we best promote the interests of the empire at large?' All three rejected Catholic emancipation, at least while in their Irish office, although they were all ultimately to change their tunes if not minds on this most sensitive of issues. They were agreed that toleration of the faith of the majority but maintenance of that of the minority as the established Church was the more likely course 'to preserve, inviolate, the Union between the two countries'. That minority had held Ireland 'fast to the British connexion', Goulburn later claimed. But the overwhelming preponderance of Catholics in Ireland made that country an anomaly within the anomalous United Kingdom, and all three men operated on the basis of the island's exceptionalism. Thus Wellesley-Pole feared that the cabinet in London would govern this 'anomalous country . . . upon General Principles which do not apply to her most particular cases'. Of course, these very principles, one newspaper later remarked, had been held sound when applied to England 'and every other civilised country'. In much the same frame of mind, Peel complained that 'an honest Englishman . . . knows about as much of the state of Ireland as he does the state of Kamchatka'. Goulburn likened the island to the somewhat less remote but dark continent of Africa. He warned the Commons that 'if gentlemen imagined that what was the rule in England, could be uniformly applied to Ireland, or that the difference of habits and situation of the people did not require a separate mode of conducting the affairs of each, they would grievously err'. Lord Liverpool, who succeeded Perceval as Prime Minister, agreed with them. Ireland was a political phenomenon, he wearily observed, 'not influenced by the same feelings as appear to affect mankind in other countries'.[15]

The three were as one in successfully elevating their roles in the government of Ireland. Although Wellesley-Pole was appointed to serve an assertive and activist viceroy, his own powerful connections in London, his local influence in Ireland and his impulsive nature often saw him pay little more than lip-service to the Duke of Richmond's supremacy. In the words of one of his critics, he was 'the great actor' in the Irish business. Peel, on succeeding him, initially moved cautiously, for the well-established Richmond expected the proprieties to be observed. Hence his irritation that he had not been consulted before Peel's appointment. Moreover, unlike Wellesley-Pole, Peel did not hold the office of Irish Chancellor of the Exchequer along with the chief secretaryship. However, after but a few months there, he concluded that a highly centralised regime was essential 'in a country situated and governed as this is'. The authority of the Viceroy 'ought to be paramount over everything in Ireland', he argued, but this increasingly meant, especially when Richmond was succeeded by the easy-going Whitworth and he in time by the ineffectual Talbot, that 'the Chief Secretary [is] the channel through which the power and patronage in Ireland must flow'. For the distribution of patronage was in Peel's opinion a vital means not only of managing Irish Members of Parliament but of maintaining and manufacturing loyalty to the Union.[16]

Richard Wellesley, on his appointment as Lord Lieutenant late in 1821, had ambitions to be the master of the whole machine of government and he spoke of not being 'clerk-ridden'. This dismissive allusion to his chief secretary notwithstanding, Wellesley's appointment had been delayed until the cabinet found in Goulburn a secretary who would compensate for the new viceroy's widely recognised defects of character and administrative deficiencies. Before long, the Viceroy succumbed to hypochondria and poetic vanity and sank, after an initial burst of diligence, into an all too familiar comatose state with respect to his more demanding public duties. Goulburn, meanwhile, secure in the knowledge that his closest political friend and greatest personal admirer, Peel, was at the Home Office, and that a devoted under-secretary in Dublin would keep a watchful eye on developments there while he was absent in London, acquired almost by default effective control of Irish business.[17]

The second decade of the nineteenth century found important sectors of the British economy, and the textile, wool and hosiery trades in particular, struggling with the consequences of Napoleon's Continental System and an American embargo. Compounding the misery were a rash of bank failures. Then, a poor harvest drove up the price of food even as artisans were thrown out of employment. The story was not a great deal different in Ireland, but there the contrast between the sustained and seemingly spectacular economic expansion of the late eighteenth century and the current distress provided old enemies, those who had identified prosperity with an Irish parliament, with a fresh opportunity to assail the new constitutional arrangement as the principal source of Ireland's troubles. Yet under the terms of union Irish industries had been granted a substantial if temporary measure of tariff protection, despite the best efforts of its then Irish opponents to seek allies among British textile and woollen interests by playing upon their commercial jealousy of Irish competitors. Peel's father, as a spokesman of the cotton industry, had patriotically declared that the national interest took precedence over commercial considerations.[18]

But Irish prospects of continued industrial expansion, and economic diversification, had been far less rosy by 1800 than native optimists naturally allowed. Ireland lacked readily utilisable sources of power, and even though her population was now expanding significantly it failed to increase correspondingly the domestic market for manufactures. All too many of these people were trapped in the ranks of the rural poor. However, the vulnerability of the economy had long been masked by a wartime prosperity as British demand for Irish foodstuffs increased, along with prices. The lion's share of the profits were garnered in Ireland as in Britain by large landowners, in the form of inflated rentals; nevertheless, they were also helping to create, if undetected by most contemporary observers, new members of the Irish middle class in the shape of substantial Catholic farmers. Not that these were the bricks of the bridge which Pitt had wished to see constructed across the chasm dividing wealth from poverty. Indeed, the fact that many of them were tempted to grasp the even easier profits to be made by subdividing and subletting lands they held on long leases served only to deepen the subsistence stratum and thus further 'unbalance the social structure of rural Ireland'.[19]

Equally unexpected and discouraging was the collapse of Ireland's finances following the Union, for her contribution to the expenses of the United Kingdom had been calculated in 1800 with care and with a desire for equity. However, the ongoing and heavy expenses of war, and the failure to extend to Ireland any form of income tax, saw ever higher indirect taxation. Before long, revenues from this source could no longer keep pace with expenditures and the Irish Exchequer was compelled to borrow heavily. The debt quadrupled in little more than a decade, and by 1815 all but a fraction of annual revenues were being applied to its servicing. The end of the French wars found Ireland 'effectively bankrupt'. Here was a crisis which nourished the corrosive suspicion that Ireland's interests had as a result of the Union been subordinated and sacrificed to those of Britain.[20]

Wellesley-Pole took office against a background of ominous discontent with the Union among the Protestant commercial and artisan classes of Dublin who had been expected to be among its firmest supporters but had in truth been prominent among the defenders of the Irish parliament. The *Dublin Evening Post* complained in April of that year that more attention was paid in London to an English Turnpike Bill than any subject 'of perhaps vital importance to the interest and prosperity of Ireland'. There was an explosion of criticism the following year when John Foster, then the Irish Chancellor of the Exchequer, but in 1799 a bitter opponent of union, introduced a budget which sought to raise an additional £350,000 in taxes. He did not aid his cause by speaking of Ireland's 'growing prosperity' or by proposing a higher duty on newspaper advertisements. The demoralising frequency of mercantile failures, which amounted to an eightfold increase in bankruptcies during the first six months of 1810, as compared with the first six months of the last year before the 'accursed Union', were widely advertised, as were the tight money policy pursued by banks and the 'decaying revenue and increasing debt'. Elements of the press applauded the summoning of public meetings to petition for repeal of the Union, and in its reply to the charge of disloyalty for agitating this issue in the midst of Britain's life or death struggle with France, the *Dublin Evening Post* observed: 'We never received a particle of power or privilege from the *generosity*, nothing whatever from the *liberality* of England.' All concessions, such as the restoration of a measure of legislative independence in 1782, had been 'wrung from her capitulating fears' at a time of external danger.[21]

In his reports to London, Wellesley-Pole emphasised the seriousness of an economic crisis in which 'hundreds' of its victims in the textile and woollen trades of Dublin were represented 'to be actually starving'. He stressed the extent to which these unfortunates had earned favourable consideration of their plight by their 'wonderful moderation' in the face of such adversity. 'The temper of this affected body has given me a better opinion of the state of the public mind than I had before,' he added. Citing pre-Union precedents, he proposed that the Bank of Ireland extend loans to manufacturers on security of their stockpiles of goods, and with 'particular attention' to the protection or promotion of employment. This objective might be achieved if demand was stimulated as a result of more confident manufacturers extending longer terms of credit to middlemen, who would then have more time to dispose of goods to shopkeepers. And it was with the same end in view that Wellesley-Pole opened a public subscription to create a fund from which to pay a 5% bounty to merchants who purchased goods from Irish manufacturers.[22]

There was, however, in the opinion of the Chief Secretary, an even more 'effectual Relief that could be afforded to a great Body of Manufacturers of Ireland', and that was the revival of 'the order of 1775, which directs all Colonels of Regiments on the Irish Establishment to take care that all the accoutrements and appointments as well as clothing, with which their respective corps are to be supplied, be from time to time provided, and made in Ireland'. The Union had cancelled this order, and even the superior reputation of Irish clothing had failed to prevent this trade being cornered by British suppliers. To offset 'the growing distrust and jealousy of England', there was an 'absolute necessity' to grant every possible advantage to Irish manufacturers. 'It is of the first importance to shew the people here that you are alive to their Interests,' Wellesley-Pole wrote insistently, 'and to remove from them every just cause of complaint'.[23]

The fervour with which he pleaded his case reflected not only the depth of the crisis but Wellesley-Pole's awareness of Ireland's English problem. The proposed loan to manufacturers had already been heavily criticised by cabinet ministers. 'If once begun, where are you to stop,' Harrowby had asked, 'and do not the recent failures in England afford a prospect of our being called upon to adopt a similar measure here?' Would they not be assuming responsibility for providing employment to workmen? Fortunately, Chief Secretary and Viceroy pre-empted the opposition by announcing the loan before the official response came from

London. But resistance to the proposed clothing order was swifter and sharper. Ministers were not prepared to restrict the entry into Ireland of cheaper English cloth, nor to revise the entire system for clothing the military. Already a transfer from the English establishment to Ireland was regarded as a grievance by regimental commanders, because it did involve a certain loss of income. Hence the cabinet's reminder to Wellesley-Pole 'of those general Principles of Freedom of Trade which are now known and acknowledged to be indispensable to its prosperity'. In response, he scornfully but vainly protested that general principles ought not to apply to Ireland. The essential task, he repeatedly but unavailingly explained, was to convince the people of Dublin, by an 'overt act', that it was not the Union which had robbed them of the valuable business of clothing the troops, and thus 'remove one false ground against the Union and against the British connection'.[24]

Ironically, the shoe was soon to be on the other foot. Legislation introduced to relieve tenants in England of any obligation to pay their rents in gold did not extend to Ireland. This was peculiarly unfortunate, Wellesley-Pole pointed out, for the practice was common in parts of his island but had been threatened in only a single instance in England. Moreover, the constant inflation in the value of gold guineas merely added to the burdens of the tenantry and exposed them to the sharp practice of some land agents. Significantly, several of those Irish landowners who were in the habit of collecting their rents in gold were in the vanguard of those calling on the government to exempt Ireland from the legislation. Now it was the Chief Secretary's turn to protest a form of exceptionalism. 'I much dread the impression that may be made here by the Imperial Parliament's passing a law which will at once relieve all the tenantry of Great Britain from every apprehension of the grievance, while it will leave Ireland to suffer under the grievance, and liable to having it increased'. Another nine months were to pass, however, before he succeeded in having the protection extended to Irish tenants.[25]

Despite the seeming insensitivity of the Perceval cabinet to Ireland's peculiarity and problems, Wellesley-Pole eventually managed to dampen down the anti-Union sentiment, at least within the Dublin Corporation. He had been unnerved by the failure of any of the aldermen to warn him in July 1810 that they intended to submit to the pressure exerted by the Commons of that institution for a committee to draft a petition of grievances. He reported to the Home Secretary

> It is difficult for any person, not conversant with the Irish character, or with the peculiar features of the mass of the Corporation of Dublin to comprehend the motives which can have induced the most respectable part of the City, and, amongst them, those who wish best to the connection with England, and who are most alive to the dangers of rebellion, and to the intentions and desires of the people of the Country not being Protestants, to take a part which the slightest Reflection must shew them can only tend to increase the difficulties of Government, and to abet and encourage the spirit of anarchy and Insurrection, the very first consequences of which must be their own destruction.

Here was a line or argument which the 'Castle influence' now assiduously advanced, and to some effect.[26]

Although an aggregate meeting of Dublin's guilds at the Exchange on 18 September 1810, to press for repeal of the Union, attracted so much attention that all of the routes to the meeting place were 'crowded to suffocation' by early morning, the sheriff in the capital, and gentry elsewhere, were prevailed upon not to summon similar meetings of local citizenry. And at the quarterly meeting of the Corporation on 19 October, the aldermen employed a procedural device to prevent discussion of the petition of grievances. When the Commons then decided to debate the issue, the Mayor dissolved the assembly, effectively silencing them for three months until fresh elections to the Commons were held. These would be 'attended to', the Chief Secretary promised meaningfully. Yet he remained far from sanguine. There was such a want of confidence, and of respect for the government, so little public spirit among its supporters, he warned, 'that altogether the machine is in so disordered a state that one almost shudders to think of it'.[27]

The repeal movement soon subsided, however, largely as a result of the success of the loans to troubled industries and a disinclination to intensify a constitutional crisis caused by another failure of the King's health and the passage of a Regency Bill. But the stifling of anti-Union sentiment within the Dublin Corporation did not herald any significant improvement in the sorry condition of the capital's woollen and textile industries. Soon after Peel's arrival in 1812, manufacturers were again appealing for government assistance and complaining of the 'bitter effects' of the Union. The new chief secretary was obliged to resort to essentially the same strategy as his predecessor, extending credit to the beleaguered industrialists through the Bank of Ireland. For in London ministerial opposition to any more generous scheme of government assistance remained rooted in the fear that it would excite demands for equal treatment from hard-pressed British manufacturers. The executive did succeed, however, in vetoing a proposal of the Board of Trade to remove a duty on foreign linens. If that industry was one of the island's few successes, there could be no disputing the continuing agricultural dominance of the economy. Wellesley-Pole had drawn the attention of the House of Commons in March 1812 to Ireland's ever larger share of the British cereals market. Not surprisingly, therefore, Peel accepted the argument of those Irishmen who lobbied for the protection of that market from foreign suppliers. And while a new Corn Law could not be passed until the British agrarian interest had been 'converted', the young Chief Secretary was convinced that it would be 'of the greatest service' to the smaller island. He believed 'that Ireland on account of the fertility of soil & cheapness of labour and other natural advantages can ensure a regular supply of corn to England'. With Ireland's legion of smaller farmers in mind, the tariff was amended in order to provide them with an even larger share of the British market for their butter. The success of these strategies was evident in the ever increasing tonnage of trade clearing Irish ports, which helped to offset the decline in prices. Moreover, the consolidation of the two Exchequers, in 1817, together with debts and revenues, went some way towards lightening the crushing burden of debt under which Ireland now laboured.[28]

Even a guaranteed British market for Irish foodstuffs could not rescue an economy in desperate need of diversification. Instead, this form of assistance eventually multiplied the problems arising out of an excessive dependence on the land at a time of rapidly expanding population. Because of the absence there of the safety net which had been erected in England, the swelling ranks of the rural poor were peculiarly vulnerable, as indeed were thinner ranks of urban distressed. 'We have not in Ireland the Poor Rates to resort to', Wellesley-Pole had reminded the Home Office in 1810, 'and we can therefore only look to private subscriptions, and if they fail, it must be for consideration whether Government shall advance money for the maintenance of the Poor'.[29]

The fact that grinding poverty and recurrent food shortages appeared to be advancing in lock-step with a rapidly growing population was inevitably interpreted as confirmation of the gloomy Malthusian analysis of Ireland's plight. One widely touted remedial measure for overpopulation was state-assisted emigration to the colonies, and both Peel and Goulburn experimented with schemes. However, they were more interested in peopling the Empire than in rescuing Irish paupers and hoped that the mere possibility of free transportation to Canada would serve to 'induce the lower orders to adopt a more peaceable line of conduct'. Furthermore, their interest diminished in the face of the evidence that a large proportion of the voluntary emigrants came from the Protestant side of the sectarian divide. Where was the advantage in helping to remove from Ireland those usually identified with loyal support of the Union?[30]

The launching of private subscriptions in Britain to relieve acute as distinct from chronic distress in Ireland was another means of impressing upon the Irish that they were now West Britons. Substantial sums were contributed in 1822, for example, in the name of policy, patriotism and humanity. 'Read the extracts from the Irish papers, and then refuse or hesitate any longer if you can', the *Cambrian* declared. Surprisingly, having documented the fundraising across the length and breadth of the principality, it added: 'there is hardly a town in England of any magnitude where subscriptions have not commenced'. Yet, in the absence of a system of parochial poor relief, a greater responsibility belonged to the central government to uphold in Ireland the 'principle of benevolence'. Thus the Prince Regent's bounty was extended to distressed operatives in the Irish capital, as it had been to the poor of Spitalfields, London, although Peel concluded that 'a much less sum would be sufficient as the Donation for Dublin'.[31]

Peel and Goulburn were confronted by peculiarly severe crises in 1817 and 1822, respectively, when the potato crop failed in areas of Ireland. Both responded cautiously and conservatively, and one reason in Peel's case was his interpretation of Irish exceptionalism. As distinct from Britain, he reasoned that in Ireland distress would rather tend to diminish than to increase lawlessness. Goulburn, for his part, as an evangelical, believed that to inform the poor that any earthly power could emancipate them from want and dependence was tantamount to impugning the 'dispensations of Providence'. Moreover, both men subscribed to the emerging orthodoxy of political economy, with its aversion to state interference. Self-help was the only solution for chronic poverty. No government could 'provide food for the whole population of any country', Goulburn remarked on one occasion, and he cautioned Members of Parliament that to embark on any general system of relief was to commit the state to vast expense. His Christian duty to help the weak and alleviate distress was always qualified by the availability of the means to do so.[32]

Peel established a model for the delivery of public assistance in Ireland, and it was one Goulburn dutifully adapted in 1822. By that time, of course, Peel was at the Home Office. First, there was to be an accurate assessment made of the extent and state of distress. Second, in its response the government was 'to excite the least attention possible', lest private charity be halted and the notion fostered that England was 'about to undertake the subsistence of Ireland'. However, wherever people were 'actually starving' or were 'without the hope of relief from other quarters', all considerations of 'general policy and principle' were to be put aside and food provided to them at government expense. Corn was to be quietly purchased abroad or from Irish distillers, duties suspended on imported rice and Indian corn, seed potatoes and biscuit discreetly distributed, and the oats rations of cavalry regiments strictly limited. To supervise the system, to investigate conditions, and to decide on requests for assistance, a central relief commission entirely free of the taint of sectarianism was established at the Castle. In the first instance, advances were to be made to assist local subscriptions and aid given at the lowest possible price to those areas where local proprietors were shouldering their responsibilities. Agents were dispatched to places with neither resident gentry nor local means, to provide relief there as cheaply as possible. This might either be through soup shops or through the employment of people on a wide and imaginative variety of public works. Here the guiding principle was that 'the more employment and less gratuitous relief' given the better.[33]

Peel hoped that the Union would be strengthened by the fact that the government had been brought 'into contact with the public through the medium of kind offices'. There seemed every reason to believe that the Irish would not bite its succouring hand. Yet the extraordinary lengths to which the executive went to disguise the extent of its intervention, the premature discontinuance of relief in some instances and the rhetoric of political economy did serve unfortunately to create a countervailing impression of hard-heartedness. A rueful Goulburn admitted at the height of the 1822 crisis that he was supposed to be 'the most inhuman and unfeeling of men' because he refused to give 'an assurance that the Government of Ireland will feed all the people'. On the other side of the Irish Sea, there were soon complaints from those who claimed to be liberal in their response to the Irish problem that the charitable aid sent from Britain had 'in many instances been infamously jobbed'.[34]

However progressive the relief policies pioneered by Peel, at least in the context of the times, neither they nor the overwhelmingly agricultural economy made much of a dent in the island's chronic poverty. The release in 1823 of a parliamentary 'Report on the Condition of the Poor in Ireland' prompted one incredulous British newspaper to observe that in County Clare more than 26,000 persons had been 'supported at an expense of *not quite one penny per diem*'. Indeed, an aristocratic witness had testified that some of the labourers employed by the 'better sort' of farmers were worse off than slaves in the West Indies. From all of this the committee concluded that 'the employment of the people of Ireland, and the improvement of their moral condition [was] essentially necessary' for peace and tranquillity and for the 'general interests of the United Kingdom'.[35]

Chronic unrest appeared to be a permanent feature of rural Ireland, as secret agrarian societies were spawned amid the poverty and associated peasant griev-ances. Overtaxation, sectarian injustice, the tithe and access to a subsistence plot of land were all factors in a seemingly endless succession of disturbances. It was not merely the frequency and extent of the disorders but their savagery which alarmed the Castle. However conservative the participants' immediate objectives, the established order and ultimately perhaps even the Union were being chal-lenged. Certainly the Ribbonmen, whose greater urban bias did not prevent their name being indiscriminately applied to unconnected agrarian societies, appeared to be the lineal descendants of the Defenders who had provided much of the rebel rank and file in 1798.[36]

On the eve of Wellesley-Pole's appointment outrages were being reported from Waterford, Tipperary and Kerry. However, the monthly returns of the General Officers and Yeomanry Brigade Majors indicated that the rest of the country was more 'tranquil' than for some time past. So, in the spring of 1810, Wellesley-Pole announced that the government intended to repeal the most draconian provisions of the Insurrection Act which had been passed in 1807 to facilitate the suppres-sion of disorders, even though they would have expired, anyway, in a few months. 'No lover of the constitution could ... wish to see such a law upon the statute-book, unless the circumstances of the times rendered it indispensably necessary', he declared in the Commons. Within a few weeks he was anxiously scanning reports of large bodies of armed men, organised as Shanavests or Caravats, fighting pitched battles at Tipperary fairs. There was no comparison to be drawn between the rowdyism common at Scottish and English fairs and the 'sanguinary and preconcerted conflicts' which disgraced those in Ireland, Peel later explained to Parliament.[37]

Wellesley-Pole may have come quickly to regret his bravado in repealing the Insurrection Act, for by the end of the year the activities of the 'disaffected' embraced fifteen of Ireland's counties. Yet the 'positive enactment' of repeal made any immediate attempt to revive the act too politically embarrassing to contemplate. Instead, he appealed for troop reinforcements and a change in the senior command of the army which was led by two martyrs to gout. Unless measures were promptly instituted, he cautioned the Home Secretary in mid-summer 1810, 'the preservation of Ireland to Great Britain becomes every day more hopeless'.[38]

From the dates of their respective appointments, Peel and Goulburn were also confronted by 'lawlessness and disturbances'. They sought to meet the challenge without excessive dependence upon the military. Although neither man was inclined to exaggerate the political significance of the 'atrocities', both overcame their own constitutional qualms and secured renewals of the Insurrection Act, supplemented by the suspension of habeas corpus. In Goulburn's opinion severity was absolutely necessary 'otherwise men would be taught to believe either that mere Whiteboyism . . . is not a capital crime or that the Government are afraid to punish with severity'. More constructively, they experimented successfully with the organisation of an effective police force. Peel's Peace Preservation Force was a flying squadron, but Goulburn created an armed, national, regular force of some 4,000 men. The police were to be assisted by stipendiary magistrates in the event that the local resident gentry failed to shoulder its responsibilities. Every county of Ireland was now assured of effective policing.[39]

If the first duty of the state was to suppress lawlessness, the second was to root out the causes of evil. Wellesley-Pole, Peel and to a lesser extent Goulburn viewed elements of the Irish press as a disruptive force subversive of the Union. Nor was this surprising, given the boast of the *Dublin Evening Post*: 'The Press of Ireland survived the wreck of her independence; in the spirit of that freedom she had lost, it lived to console her for the crimes of a corrupt Parliament, to cheer her in misfortune, and to illume the path which might again lead to liberty'. The 'villainy' of the press, its 'most foul and personal abuse', and its encouragement of 'licentiousness and disaffection' were recurring themes of Wellesley-Pole's correspondence with the Home Secretary. In response, he subsidised a 'Castle press' which received early intelligence of military developments in the French war in an effort to boost circulation, and enjoyed free distribution around the country. The *Evening Post* complained that the favoured newspapers were distributed to its subscribers under the usual cover of the *Post* but from which it had been withheld. At other times, the Chief Secretary hounded his tormentors with indictments for seditious libel.[40]

Peel proved to be even more determined and thorough than his predecessor in his efforts to manufacture press friends and curb 'factious prints'. 'I am most friendly to Prosecutions', he privately admitted. By hauling newspaper publishers before the courts for printing the 'inflammatory speeches' of Daniel O'Connell and his colleagues in the movement for Catholic emancipation, he saw a means of driving a wedge between agitators and their publicists. His relentless legal pursuit of John Magee, the Protestant proprietor of the highly critical and all too popular *Evening Post*, did serve ultimately to humiliate O'Connell when a chastened publisher deserted to the ranks of the Castle press. But there was a price to be paid for this and similar successes. Many Catholics interpreted them as proof of the government's hostility to them as a body, which conclusion did not strengthen their attachment to the Union. Moreover, when Goulburn relaxed the system of press management, for he had neither the funds to sustain friends nor the will or time to intimidate enemies, Catholic organs of opposition were revived and emboldened. And O'Connell regarded them as vital instruments of mass propaganda.[41]

The third duty of the state, once the lawless had been suppressed and the causes of evil uprooted, was to 'determine the real grounds of complaint' and seek proper remedies. 'We must repel force by force', Peel observed on one occasion, 'but the more we can soothe the better for the future at any rate'. A series of remedial measures was implemented in an effort to halt if not reverse Catholic alienation from the Union. Integral to the slow and gradual progress of conservative reform was elementary education, which it was hoped would rescue the Irish lower orders from their 'ignorance' while it improved their character and thus made them less likely to be 'so easily misled'. Perhaps influenced by the example of Scotland, Wellesley-Pole thought it would be possible to produce these worthwhile results by obliging the clergy of the established Church to set up in all of Ireland's more than 2,000 parishes the schools for which the law already provided. The objection to this solution in an overwhelmingly Catholic nation was obvious, so Peel opted for a measure of public support for the Kildare Place Society. Although founded in 1811 to establish schools divested of sectarian distinctions, Catholic suspicions of its proselytism were not long suppressed. When a parliamentary commission later recommended to Goulburn the creation of a government board to supervise schools, and the 'doctrinally neutral' instruction of their pupils, he would agree only to experiment with a new system while maintaining the old. He was responding to Protestant criticisms of the proposals, and to his conviction that the Catholic hierarchy would never be content until they had denominational schools under their 'complete controul'. Not that Catholic suspicions of the Kildare Place schools were entirely unfounded. Goulburn, for one, privately mused

> that if you educate the people of Ireland on Christian principles you work effectually for the overthrow of the Roman Catholic persuasion. It cannot stand against the light of the Gospel. If however you attempt directly to convert them you arouse every feeling of the parents against you and I am anxious therefore on all occasions to disclaim any proselytizing or direct attempt at conversion.[42]

If sectarianism inevitably intruded into the debate on education, it had long bedevilled the largely Protestant administration of justice and local government. However, steps were now taken to appease Catholics on this score. The appointment of sheriffs was to be purified, the conduct of sub-sheriffs more carefully monitored, while petty sessions increasingly replaced hearings before individual magistrates, the incompetent and invisible were weeded out of the magistracy, and Catholic lawyers appointed to the important position of assistant barrister of quarter sessions. Also, half of the initial appointments to Goulburn's constabulary were earmarked for Catholics.[43]

A far more serious grievance of Catholics was the tithe, and it was not simply a matter of the apparent injustice of charging them for the support of the established Church, but the unpredictability of the levy from year to year and its greater punishment of the most industrious of them. Wellesley-Pole had evaded the issue, insisting that tithes in Ireland were 'a mere flea-bite' compared to those in England. He laid the problem at the door of extortionate middlemen who extracted high rents from tenants who did not realise that they were responsible for payment of the tax. Citing the 'many diversities' in different parts of the country, he protested 'that it would be most difficult to frame any general system that would embrace them all'. Peel also pleaded the complexity of this issue, remarking that any equitable arrangement from the standpoint of the clergy would surely prove injurious to those who paid the levy. By 1822 the problem could no longer be ignored, however, for in some areas of Ireland resistance to the tithe was not only violent but had reduced many clergy to a state of penury. Significantly, Goulburn's response was dictated by his conviction that the great majority of Irishmen were grimly determined to 'defraud' the Church of her due. His principal concern was to defend her from 'plunder', not to lighten the burdens on Catholic occupiers of the land. Consequently, although his Composition Bill did eventually rationalise and reduce the tax in approximately half of the parishes of Ireland, it did not remove the grievance.[44]

There was a similar ambivalence in the executive's response to the persistent complaints that Orangemen were the source of much of the bigotry and thus sectarian tension in Ireland. Peel and Goulburn were alive to the 'possible danger' of an organisation controlled 'by any other authority than that of the Government', and both drew the line at behaviour 'meant to irritate and insult others' and give a 'just cause of complaint'. On the other hand, neither wished to alienate a body so vocal in its loyalty to the British connexion or give Protestants the impression that they wished to 'depress' them and 'elevate' Catholics. Nor had Peel any desire to promote the unity of Ireland's lower orders. That would only result, he reasoned, in the 'adoption by the [minority] Protestants of the Principles of the Catholics', and in his and Goulburn's minds these included hostility to the Union. 'While their principles respectively remain the same, I hope they will always be disunited', he privately admitted. The 'great art is to keep them so and yet or rather not at war with each other'. This proved to be a difficult art to master and the Orangemen embarrassing allies. A transparently reluctant Goulburn was eventually obliged to introduce a bill, in 1823, to suppress them. Not that this measure earned the then Chief Secretary any credit with the dominant figure in the campaign to secure Catholic emancipation.[45]

The campaigns for emancipation merely highlighted the most glaring of Irish anomalies. 'In other countries the church establishment followed the creed of the population', Prime Minister Liverpool observed in 1817, 'but in Ireland the church and the property are on one side, and the great mass of the population on the other'. However, in his Assize Sermon at York several years earlier, one member of the established clergy had ironically noted that the English usually regarded the Irish 'as objects of pity, or of condemnation', except when they were seen in the van of the victorious British soldiery on European battlefields. In short, resistance to emancipation implied a certain lack of appreciation of the 'patriotic dead'. The Revd Francis Wrangham had then asked a pointed question: 'Why will we forbear to confer as a favour, what soon may be wrested from us as a right?' He might have added that the Union had only been carried with the tacit support of Catholics who had been assured that emancipation would not long be delayed in a United Kingdom. Equally, would not this concession enhance the influence of the gentry, especially the Catholic gentry, over a turbulent peasantry and bind them ever more closely to the British connexion? 'So long as the

Catholics are treated as a degraded caste, and unjustly deprived of their rights', warned the *Edinburgh Review*, 'so long will there be disaffection and rancour brooding in their minds, which misguided ambition or instinctive turbulence may easily direct to purposes of danger'. Why then would intelligent men committed to the defence of the Union resist Catholic relief?[46]

In his answer to this question, Lord Liverpool gave voice in 1817 to the widely held opinions that once put on a completely equal footing with Protestants in Ireland, Catholics would soon demand disestablishment; that they would next seek to establish their ascendancy over Protestants and exclude them from offices; and that the opening of Parliament to Catholics and other dissenters would eventually make impossible the maintenance of an exclusively Protestant crown. In short, concession would undermine the foundations of a constitution under which Britons had 'so long enjoyed security and happiness'. Liverpool's position was a crowded one, occupied as it was by many who proclaimed themselves friends of religious toleration. 'Unless . . . we are prepared to go to the alarming length of a total subversion of our Church Establishment in Ireland, to endanger all the vested property in that Kingdom, and entirely remodel our Glorious Constitution', the *Cambrian* declared, 'we cannot but say, that it is our duty earnestly to petition against Catholic Emancipation'. Similarly, while accepting that Catholics should enjoy full liberty of conscience and 'partake, to a certain extent, of the benefits which the civil constitution of the country affords', the *Chester Chronicle* drew the line at 'them sitting in St Stephen's Chapel'. So long as they acknowledged the Spiritual Supremacy of a 'foreign earthly potentate' but declined to state what that supremacy meant, and so long as they failed to give voluntarily that security which the Pope had conceded to 'every despotic Sovereign in Europe', then in the opinion of Peel they ought not to be admitted to Parliament.[47]

Behind the charge of divided allegiance, and suspicions that for reasons of personal ambition O'Connell and other agitators deliberately inflamed Catholic opinion against the government by harping upon 'supposed grievances', there certainly lurked a powerful sectarian enmity. Evangelical churchmen, such as Goulburn, despised the Roman Church. They assailed it for denying the true Bible and hence the Word of God to the laity. Goulburn also complained that Catholics, by an astute incremental strategy, had secured an ever larger share of the rights of full citizenship. Their full emancipation, he feared, would jeopardise the establishment and confirm the dominant position in Ireland of a well-disciplined and secretive priesthood. After all, even 'the first Roman Catholics' were no more than the priests' 'puppets'.[48]

Peel, Goulburn and Wellesley-Pole subscribed to the opinion that Ireland's Protestants were contending for their religion, their property, their existence and the survival of the Union. Writing to the Home Secretary on the last day of 1811, Wellesley-Pole detailed what he understood to be the true ambitions of Ireland's Catholics. They sought, he warned, a proportionate share, or 80%, of all offices, civil, military and political in Ireland; of Irish seats in both Houses of Parliament, and of Irish peerages; of corporate offices and privileges; of religious establishments. Indeed, just a few weeks before he was to make his own journey down a Damascan road, he informed the Commons that he had not as yet seen any plan for extending additional privileges to Catholics 'which afforded even a plausible hope' that they could be granted 'with a due regard for the safety of the establishments in church and state'.[49]

For all three men, their opposition to emancipation was most deeply rooted in the conviction, which the form of agitation all too frequently served only to strengthen, that the ultimate ambition of Catholics was disunion. It was an association of causes which the popular *Dublin Evening Post* did its best to foster, before being brought to heel by Peel. 'The Catholic should feel that his Emancipation can only be attained through the "Emancipation of his country"', the newspaper proclaimed in 1810. Here was confirmation of Wellesley-Pole's analysis of the Catholic meeting held several months earlier. 'There is scarcely a topick which can be worked against the constitution, and in favour of separation from England, and from the Protestant Government, that has not been introduced', he had warned.[50]

Further complicating the situation was the obvious weakness of the Castle government. They had little or no support 'out of doors', Wellesley-Pole grumbled. He estimated that all but ten of Ireland's counties were dominated by a Catholic interest, and charged that the parliamentary representation was 'so in the hands of Catholic freeholders' that exclusively Protestant Members of Parliament were inclined to put discretion before loyalty on the issue of emancipation. Such concerns made Wellesley-Pole, and subsequently Peel and Goulburn, peculiarly sensitive to any agitation which appeared to reflect 'a thorough contempt for the legitimate Government', perhaps even an attempt to establish a parallel administrative structure. As one ascendancy liberal remarked, 'the very insignificance of the Irish Government makes it impossible for them to exist with a rival that would overshadow them'. Thus the Catholic Committee conducted itself in 1811 in a highly provocative manner. It operated within the shadow of the Castle, adopted procedures all too reminiscent of those of the House of Commons, and eventually organised a form of election of delegates from the country. Castle anxiety grew with the decisions to make Catholic prelates, peers, baronets and peers' sons component parts of the committee. In short, it threatened to 'comprise in its members all the Rank, Learning, Religious Enthusiasm, Talents, Property, Ambition and I may add Treason among the Catholic Body'. Moreover, the addition of the priests would 'infallibly bring all the lower people and middling sorts' into the fold.[51]

Defending the eventual suppression of the committee, and the launching of prosecutions of those who staged elections, or sought to be elected, Wellesley-Pole stoutly denied that he was seeking to interfere with the constitutional right of petition. He insisted 'that greater forbearance and lenity is shewn to Catholics than we should have thought necessary to any other body of the King's subjects'. Also, he sought to maintain contact with the more 'moderate' Catholic elements, and hoped that by firm action he would strengthen their position even as he was giving heart to 'Loyal People'. To more skittish ministers in London, he repeated his

earlier warning: 'you cannot agree to let this Convention meet without molest-
ation unless you are prepared to allow the Frame of Government to be dissolved
and the Country to be thrown into the utmost confusion and disorder'. However,
after an initial setback in the trials of persons prosecuted for their prominence in
the election of delegates, the executive did secure a conviction in February 1812
and then immediately dropped the other cases lest another jury weaken through
an acquittal the symbolic effect of this victory.[52]

The holding of the line against full Catholic emancipation was not eased,
Wellesley-Pole advised the cabinet, by the supposed sympathy of the Prince
Regent with relief. Another problem was the defection of Irish Protestant Members of Parliament, Protestant peers and Protestant gentry. Attributing their
behaviour to fear or 'supineness', he cited the presence of prominent Protestants,
among them the son of the commander of the military forces in Ireland, at a
dinner of the 'Friends of Religious Liberty' as additional proof 'of the absence of
all fair support to the Irish Government upon most vital points'. However, such
demonstrations of Protestant sympathy, and the assassination of Spencer Perceval, were soon to serve as the pegs on which he could hang his own conversion.[53]

Following a period of political jockeying, Lord Liverpool succeeded the murdered Prime Minister at the head of an administration founded upon the pragmatic and evasive principle of cabinet neutrality with respect to emancipation.
Wellesley-Pole did not join the new government. Influenced by his eldest brother,
and as a member of the Wellesley–Canning faction in the Commons, both of
whose principals advocated Catholic relief, he did an about-face on the issue
much to the incredulity of his former colleagues at Dublin Castle. Moreover, he
sought deliberately to embarrass his young successor as Chief Secretary. 'We have
the Catholics of Ireland unanimous, we have a great proportion of the Protestants
of Ireland for the question, and we have a cabinet divided and not prepared to
submit any measure to parliament upon it', he declared during a debate in 1813,
before ridiculing Peel as a political novice who seemed 'to think the most effectual
way of making the people quiet and happy [is] to clap on a perpetual blister, to
draw the bad humours of the country together, and to keep them in a state of
continued irritation'.[54]

Neither Peel nor other leading members of the Irish executive were yet prepared to compromise with the growing sentiment in Parliament in favour of
concession. After all, they could still claim that they were more representative of
popular opinion, and they still accepted that suspicious analysis of Catholic ambitions which had earlier shaped Wellesley-Pole's conduct. They feared the destruction of the Protestant ascendancy and the separation of Ireland from Britain.
Equally, the Catholic Board, which orchestrated the renewed agitation in Ireland,
appeared to be no less a challenger to constitutional authority than the suppressed
committee. Peel argued the expediency of putting an end to all bodies 'which
whether delegated or not, or assuming to be representative or not', still profess 'to
be of a permanent nature' and are thus 'inconsistent with the existence of a
regular Government'. And a significant erosion of support in the Commons for a
Relief Bill introduced by Henry Grattan in 1813, as it made its way from second

reading to third, was attributed to 'the intemperance manifested in the proceedings of the Catholic Board, and the high hand with which they carried their impudent resolutions'. Already the victim of internal differences, the board was suppressed in 1814 under the provisions of the Convention Act.[55]

When he arrived in Ireland late in 1821, Goulburn found himself thrust into a situation potentially even more embarrassing than that of Peel almost a decade earlier. He was Chief Secretary to the eldest Wellesley, whom O'Connell greeted as the 'harbinger' of emancipation. Also, the current parliamentary champion of that cause was appointed Attorney General of Ireland. However, yet again, the form of the agitation, as much as its substance, excited alarm beyond the ranks of those who, like Goulburn, still believed that the 'protestant interest' was the only true support both of the government and of the British connexion. O'Connell's Catholic Association was a formidable and intimidating mass organisation, embracing as it did a large section of the priesthood, whose influence Goulburn was not one to underestimate, and attracting the support of a number of noblemen and gentlemen. But his apprehensions were rooted less in the association's numbers, members or funds, and more in the 'progressive tendency' of its 'measures of organisation'; more specifically, in its increasing ability to address itself, through agents, 'to most parts of the country, and directing simultaneously to one object the great mass of the people'. In short, it aped and assumed 'the Authority of Parliament'. So, in 1825, Goulburn piloted legislation through the Commons outlawing the association. Not that he expected the artful O'Connell long to be hamstrung by the Unlawful Societies Bill. The New Association was no less objectionable than its predecessor. 'No country can be satisfactory to the Government in which a power exists stronger than that of the Government, independent of the Government, and in which that power can at any moment direct against the Government a mass of poor, ignorant, unemployed and discontented population', the Chief Secretary admitted in October 1826. That such a mass existed might well have been interpreted as an unfavourable judgement of the Union. Within three years, as senior ministers in the Wellington administration, Peel and Goulburn were required to make a virtue of necessity and guide Catholic emancipation on to the statute-book.[56]

Emancipation, politically unavoidable though it was by 1829, represented a severe reverse for those who had based their resistance to this concession on its threat to the Union. That it would pacify the Irish countryside had never seemed likely. 'An interest in its success cannot be entertained by the lower classes of the people of Ireland', one English provincial newspaper observed in 1813, 'because it is not likely they could ever profit from its enactment'. That it would long appease the powerful Catholic clergy seemed equally unlikely, for only disestablishment could satisfy their demand for religious equality. 'Take away this supremacy of the Protestant Church and we shall be all equal before the law', one pro-Union Catholic bishop privately insisted more than a generation later during the Fenian crisis. However, a score of Limerick parish clergy, led by the Dean, had already prescribed a more radical therapy for Ireland. They insisted that an 'English Parliament' could never understand the island's need for 'the most exceptional legislation' or satisfy the people's yearnings for nationality. Concede to Ireland her own parliament, they declared in December 1867, and her 'federal amity' would be a tower of strength to Britain.[57]

The conviction to which Peel and Goulburn had long held until expediency dictated concession, that emancipation was merely a stalking horse for separation, appeared to be fully vindicated by O'Connell's launching, soon after its enactment, of a repeal movement. Of course, those who had long resisted the measure contributed significantly to the identification of Irish nationalism almost exclusively with Catholicism. This identity was yet another Irish anomaly, at least within the context of European national movements. But then, the passage of Catholic emancipation had not modified the 'Protestant worldview' of the great majority of Britons, tens of thousands of whom petitioned against this measure of relief.[58]

There had been great good sense in Edward Wakefield's warning in 1812 that so long as Ireland was administered like some 'distant province', national spirit, jealousy and prejudice would thrive there. However, historians have been far more reluctant than their colleagues in other related disciplines to view Ireland through the lens of neo-colonialism. Yet the Union was effected during a war of dramatic imperial expansion which altered attitudes towards empire and helped inculcate into the British a stronger sense of their civilising mission. They considered the Irish not merely as different but as less civilised than themselves. Hence the taste for likening conditions on the island to Kamchatka and Africa. The retention of the viceregal structure, the demand for a more highly centralised administration, the dispatch first of Peel and later of Goulburn to Dublin, direct in both cases from the Colonial Office, even their policies of kicks and kisses, encouraged and reflected an imperial mindset among these early defenders of the Union. They had a natural tendency to view Ireland more as part of the Empire than as a truly integrated and equal member of the United Kingdom. Similarly, one of Gladstone's recent biographers has suggested that his initial efforts to pacify Ireland, following the general election of 1868, were partially vitiated by the 'colonial spirit' in which he approached the task.[59]

Forty years earlier Peel had sought to contradict accusations that the problems of Ireland had been frequently studied and just as often ignored by the imperial Parliament, that she had been treated with an 'unsalutary' neglect, and had been discriminated against with respect to public investment. Instead, one contemporary investigator documented an impressive list of grants in aid of economic development or to finance employment on public works. Indeed, her experience during the early nineteenth century was consistent with one modern theorist's analysis of the initial advantages which accrue to a 'backward' territory incorporated into a larger, more advanced empire – 'a minimal economic "infrastructure", some development, and some education'. Additionally, Ireland's widely acknowledged exceptionalism had served to excuse an unusual measure of state activity at times of grave social crisis, as in 1816–17 and 1822. In short, the Union could be defended as beneficial to Ireland. But its encouragement of economic progress, the experiments with rudimentary welfare policies and publicly funded primary education were always less apparent than the widespread and seemingly endemic poverty and rural violence which fed on each other and nourished national resentment. Moreover, had the Union's benefits been more widely advertised and recognised, they would still have been unable to provide an unstormable bulwark against a sense of national distinctiveness and identity which was being assiduously promoted among the literate, by newspapers and a 'patriotic antiquarianism', and reinforced among the Catholic lower orders by teachers in hedge schools. Implicitly or explicitly anti-English, such agents reminded Catholic Irishmen, in particular, of their membership of an historic state. Their religion served much the same purpose, especially when politicised so brilliantly by O'Connell. And this sense of national distinctiveness survived the efforts of those defenders of the Union who had assumed that it would be both possible and beneficial to absorb this 'backward' and 'inferior' people into the larger British nationality.[60]

NOTES

1 R.F. Foster, 'History and the Irish Question', *Transactions of the Royal Historical Society*, 5th series, 33 (1983), p. 181.

2 Lord Acton, *The History of Freedom and Other Essays*, reprint edn (New York, 1967), pp. 298, 278.

3 Kevin Whelan, *The Tree of Liberty: Radicalism, Catholicism and the Construction of Irish Identity 1760–1830* (South Bend, 1996), p. 99; Brian P. Levack, *The Formation of the British State: England, Scotland, and the Union 1603–1707* (Oxford, 1987).

4 T.W. Moody (ed.), *Nationality and the Pursuit of National Independence* (Belfast, 1978), pp. 75–6, 93–4; Levack, *Formation of the British State*, pp. vi, 13, 65–6, 103, 113, 172; for the diversity of England and Britain see Keith Robbins, *Nineteenth-century Britain; Integration and Diversity* (Oxford, 1988); E.W. MacFarland, *Ireland and Scotland in the Age of Revolution: Planting the Green Bough* (Edinburgh, 1994), pp. 33, 36–9: Linda Colley, *Britons: Forging the Nation 1707–1837* (New Haven, 1992), p. 6.

5 Colley, *Britons*, pp. 23, 54; MacFarland, *Ireland and Scotland*, p. 37.

6 Whelan, *Tree of Liberty*, pp. 33, 3; Peel to Sidmouth, 1 November 1816, HO 100/191; MacFarland, *Ireland and Scotland*, pp. 40, 31, 35, 39; T.A. Critchley, *The Conquest of Violence: Order and Liberty in Britain* (New York, 1970), p. 5.

7 Thomas Bartlett, 'From Irish state to British Empire: reflections on state-building in Ireland, 1690–1830', *Etudes Irlandaises*, 20, n.s. (1995), p. 25; James Kelly, 'The origins of the Act of Union: an examination of unionist opinion in Britain and Ireland, 1650–1800', *Irish Historical Studies*, 30 (1987), p. 249; Colley, *Britons*; W.S. Hathaway (ed.), *Speeches of William Pitt in the House of Commons* (London, 1806), III, p. 363; IV, p. 369; III, pp. 354–61, 382, 396, 471.

8 Francis Plowden, *The History of Ireland from its Union with Great Britain in January, 1801, to October 1810* (Dublin, 1811), III, p. 49; *The Cambrian*, 20 January 1810; *Dublin Evening Post*, 13 September 1810.

9 *Montreal Gazette*, 12 March 1867; *Pitt's Speeches*, III, pp. 354, 379–81; John Ehrman, *The Younger Pitt: The Consuming Struggle* (Palo Alto, 1996), pp. 175ff; for the ongoing debate on the sincerity of Pitt's support for Catholic emancipation see Richard Willis, 'William Pitt's resignation in 1801: re-examination and documents', *Bulletin of Historical Research*, 44 (1971), pp. 239–57, and Charles John Fedorak, 'Catholic emancipation and the

resignation of William Pitt in 1801', *Albion*, 24 (1992), pp. 49–64; J.S. Connolly, 'The Catholic Question', in W.E. Vaughan (ed.), *Ireland under the Union*, I, *1801–70* (Oxford: 1989), p. 28.

10 Brian Jenkins, *Era of Emancipation: British Government of Ireland 1812–1830* (Montreal and Kingston, 1988), pp. 54–5; Levack, *Foundation of the British State*, p. 22; *Parliamentary Debates [PD]*, 1st series, 36, c. 412; Edward Wakefield, *An Account of Ireland Statistical and Political* (London, 1813), II, pp. 328–9.

11 Michael MacDonagh, *The Viceroy's Postbag* (London, 1904), p. 4; *Bee-Hive*, 2 December 1865.

12 Cloncurry to Holland, 18 June 1822, BL Add. Ms. 51573; *The Wellesley Papers* (London, 1914), I, pp. 86–7.

13 Iris Butler, *The Eldest Brother* (London, 1973), p. 85; Jenkins, *Era of Emancipation*, pp. 57, 167, 169; see also Brian Jenkins, *Henry Goulburn 1784–1856: A Political Biography* (Montreal, Kingston and Liverpool, 1996).

14 Wellesley-Pole to Richard Wellesley, 19 October 1806, BL Add Ms. 37309; Jenkins, *Era of Emancipation*, pp. 61–2; Jenkins, *Goulburn*, pp. 19–23, 65–7; Lawrence James, *Rise and Fall of the British Empire* (New York, 1994), pp. 132–3.

15 *PD*, 36, c. 412; Wellesley-Pole to Delaney, 24 January 1810, BL Add Ms. 40221; Jenkins, *Goulburn*, pp. 133, 135, 145; Wellesley-Pole to Ryder, 23 July 1810, HO 100/158; *Toronto Globe*, 13 May 1867; Peel to Whitworth, 29 February 1816, BL Add Ms. 40290; *PD*, 2nd series, 9, c. 1283; Liverpool to Peel, 28 January 1816, BL Add Ms. 40181.

16 Brian MacDermot (ed.), *The Catholic Question in Ireland and England 1798–1822: The Papers of Denys Scully* (Dublin, 1988), p. 295; Peel to Richmond, 16 July 1813, Richmond Papers, 71, National Library of Ireland; Peel to Liverpool, 20 October 1813, BL Add Ms. 40285; Charles Stuart Parker (ed.), *Sir Robert Peel from his Private Papers*, reprint edn, 3 vols (New York, 1970), I, p. 112; see also Robert Shipkey, 'Sir Robert Peel's Irish policy, 1812–1846', Ph.D., Harvard University, 1985.

17 Jenkins, *Goulburn*, pp. 131, 135, 183; Jenkins, *Era of Emancipation*, p. 169.

18 Jenkins, *Era of Emancipation*, p. 19; D. George Boyce and Alan O'Day (eds), *The Making of Modern Irish History: Revisionism and the Revisionist Controversy* (London and New York, 1996), p. 20; G.C. Bolton, 'Some British reactions to the Irish Act of Union', *Economic History Review*, 2nd series, 18 (1965), pp. 367–75.

19 Jenkins, *Era of Emancipation*, pp. 22–6; Colley, *Britons*, p. 158; Whelan, *Tree of Liberty*, p. 52; J.S. Connolly, 'Eighteenth Century Ireland', in Boyce and O'Day, *Making of Modern Irish History*, p. 22.

20 Liam Kennedy and David S. Johnson, 'The Union of Ireland and Britain, 1801–1821', in Boyce and O'Day, *Making of Modern Irish History*, pp. 43–4; Jenkins, *Era of Emancipation*, p. 25; McFarland, *Ireland and Scotland in the Age of Revolution*, p. 242.

21 J.S. Connolly, 'Aftermath and Adjustment', in Vaughan, *Ireland under the Union*, I, p. 22; *Saunders's Newsletter*, 5, 29 June, 2 July, 19, 27 September 1810; *Dublin Evening Post*, 15 April 1809, 3, 7, 10, 14, 31 July, 25 August 1810.

22 Wellesley-Pole to Ryder, 5, 16 July 1810, Harrowby Mss., XCV, Sandon Hall, Staffordshire; Wellesley-Pole to Ryder, 10, 17 July 1810, Home Office (HO)100/158, Public Record Office (PRO), London; Wellesley-Pole to John Patrick *et al.*, 11 July 1810, HO 100/157.

23 Wellesley-Pole to Ryder, 5, 14, 16 July 1810, Harrowby Mss., XCV.

24 Wellesley-Pole to Ryder, 16 July 1810; Harrowby memorandum, 8 July 1810; Mulgrave memorandum, 10 July 1810; Ryder minute on Wellesley-Pole to Ryder, 5 July 1810, Harrowby Mss., XCV; Wellesley-Pole to Ryder, 23 July 1810, HO 100/158.

25 Wellesley-Pole to Ryder, 10 July 1811, Harrowby Mss., XCVIII; Ryder to Wellesley-Pole, 12, 13 July 1811, Harrowby Mss., 1235a; Wellesley-Pole to Ryder, 15 July 1811, Harrowby Mss., XCVIII; *PD*, 1st series, 22, c. 3.

26 Wellesley-Pole to Ryder, 26 July 1810, HO 100/158; *Dublin Evening Post*, 14, 18 August 1810.

27 *The Cambrian*, 28 September 1810; *Dublin Evening Post*, 14 August 1810; Wellesley-Pole to Ryder, 28 October 1810, Harrowby Mss., XCVI; Wellesley-Pole to Ryder, 26 July 1810, HO 100/158.

28 Jacqueline Hill, *From Patriots to Unionists: Dublin Civic Politics and Irish Protestant Patriotism 1660–1840* (Oxford, 1997), p. 269; Jenkins, *Era of Emancipation*, pp. 83–4, 112–13; Peel to Gregory, 20 July 1814, BL Add Ms. 40287; *PD*, 1st series, 22, c. 3; Peel to Whitworth, 23 February 1815, Whitworth Papers, U269/0225/11, Centre for Kentish Studies, Maidstone; Kennedy and Johnson, 'The Union of Ireland and Britain, 1801–1821', in Boyce and O'Day (eds), *Making of Modern Irish History*, pp. 38, 44.

29 Kennedy and Johnson, 'The Union of Ireland and Britain', in Boyce and O'Day, *Making of Modern Irish History*, p. 39; J.S. Connolly, 'Unionist Government, 1812–23', in Vaughan, *Ireland under the Union*, I, p. 61; Wellesley-Pole to Ryder, 10 July 1810, HO 100/158.

30 Jenkins, *Era of Emancipation*, pp. 126–7, 136, 259; Goulburn to Peel, 15 November 1823, BL Add Ms. 40329; Jenkins, *Goulburn*, p. 128.

31 *The Cambrian*, 24 May, 7, 14 June 1822; Jenkins, *Era of Emancipation*, p. 128; Peel to Sidmouth, 5 December 1816, HO 100/191.

32 Parker, *Peel*, I, p. 235; Jenkins, *Goulburn*, p. 150; Goulburn to Wellesley, 15 June 1822, BL Add Ms. 37299; *PD*, 2nd series, 7, c. 148.

33 Peel to Whitworth, 13 June 1817, BL Add Ms. 40293; Peel to Whitworth, n.d. [March 1817], 8 March 1817, BL Add Ms. 40292; Peel to Whitworth, 9 June 1817, BL Add Ms. 40293; Jenkins, *Era of Emancipation*, p. 131; Goulburn to Wellesley, 2, 15, 16 April, 19 June 1822, BL Add Ms. 37299.

34 Jenkins, *Era of Emancipation*, p. 132; Peel to Sidmouth, 21 July 1817, HO 100/192; Goulburn to Gregory, 18 June 1822, Gregory Papers, Emory University; Buckingham to Wynn, 8 October 1822, Coed y Maen Mss., National Library of Wales.

35 *The Cambrian*, 8 November 1823.

36 Jenkins, *Era of Emancipation*, pp. 29–36; Oliver Macdonagh, *States of Mind: A Study of Anglo-Irish Conflict 1780–1980* (London, 1983), pp. 71–2; Connolly, 'Aftermath and Adjustment', in Vaughan, *Ireland under the Union*, I, pp. 18–20.

37 Saxton to Beckett, 12 April 1809, HO 100/153; *PD*, 1st series, 17, c. 203; *Speeches of Sir Robert Peel*, I, p. 34.

38 For the extent of disturbances at the end of 1810 see HO 100/163; Wellesley-Pole to Ryder, 15 February 1811, Harrowby Mss. XCVII; Peel to Gregory, 23 November 1813, Gregory Papers; Wellesley-Pole to Ryder, 23 July 1810, Harrowby Mss. XCV.

39 *PD*, 1st series, 28, cc. 163, 646–9; Peel to Goulburn, 6 November [1822], Goulburn Papers, Acc 304/36, Surrey Record Office; Goulburn to Wellesley, 28 February 1822, BL Add Ms. 37298; Peel to Whitworth, 2 December 1813, U269/0225/3.

40 *PD*, 2nd series, 6, c. 1479; *Dublin Evening Post*, 19 June, 7 August 1810; Wellesley-Pole to Ryder, 14 July 1810, Harrowby Mss. XCV; Wellesley-Pole to Ryder, 23 July 1810, HO 100/158; Wellesley-Pole to Ryder, 6 August 1810, Harrowby Mss. XCVI; Wellesley-Pole to Ryder, 10 February 1811, Harrowby Mss. XCVII.

41 Peel to Whitworth, 1 February 1817, BL Add Ms. 40292; Peel to Sidmouth, 21 October 1813, HO 100/173; *PD*, 1st series, 28, c. 167; Shipkey, 'Peel's Irish Policy', p. 54; Oliver MacDonagh, *The Hereditary Bondsman: Daniel O'Connell, 1775–1828* (London, 1988), pp. 117ff; Jenkins, *Era of Emancipation*, pp. 94, 206.

42 *PD*, 2nd series, 6, c. 1479; Peel to Whitworth, 13 June 1817, BL Add Ms. 40293; *PD*, 1st series, 31, cc. 877–9, 20, c. 149; Levack, *Formation of the British State*, p. 211; Parker, *Peel*, I, pp. 89–90; Jenkins, *Era of Emancipation*, pp. 115, 136; Jenkins, *Goulburn*, p. 169; H. Goulburn to J. Goulburn, 31 March 1824, Acc 304/67.

43 Jenkins, *Era of Emancipation*, p. 123; Jenkins, *Goulburn*, pp. 158–9.

44 *PD*, 1st series, 20, c. 581, 23, c. 728, 16, cc. 674–5; Peel to Liverpool, 30 March 1816, BL Add Ms. 40290; Jenkins, *Goulburn*, p. 148; Jenkins, *Era of Emancipation*, pp. 185, 201–4.

45 Plowden, *History of Ireland*, III, p. 711; *Dublin Evening Post*, 15 April 1809; Peel to Whitworth, 23 July, 16 June 1814, U269/0225; Jenkins, *Era of Emancipation*, p. 188; Jenkins, *Goulburn*, p. 157.

46 *PD*, 1st series, 36, c. 650; *Saunders's Newsletter*, 23 January 1810; Colley, *Britons*, p. 327; Bartlett, *Etudes Irlandaises*, 20, pp. 33–4; Jenkins, *Era of Emancipation*, p. 43; *Edinburgh Review*, 43 (1826), p. 163.

47 *PD*, 1st series, 36, cc. 650–1; *The Cambrian*, 17 May 1822; *Chester Chronicle*, 23 May 1813; Peel to Richmond, 21 May 1813, BL Add Ms. 40282; Peel to Whitworth, 7 May 1814, U269/0225; Peel to Richmond, 2 March 1813, BL Add Ms. 40281.

48 Peel to Richmond, 27 February 1813, BL Add Ms. 40281; Peel to Whitworth, 7 May 1814, U269/0225; Jenkins, *Era of Emancipation*, pp. 167, 43; Goulburn to Peel, 13 September 1826, BL Add Ms. 40332.

49 Redesdale to Perceval, 23 October 1803, BL Add Ms. 49188; Peel to Richmond, 21 May 1813, BL Add Ms. 40283; Wellesley-Pole to Ryder, 31 December 1811, HO 100/165; *PD*, 1st series, 21, c. 593.

50 *Dublin Evening Post*, 8 November 1810; Wellesley-Pole to Ryder, 16, 23 July 1810, Harrowby Mss. XCV.

51 Wellesley-Pole to Ryder, 31 December 1811, HO 100/165; Wellesley-Pole to Ryder, 23 July 1810, Harrowby XCV; MacDermot, *Papers of Denys Scully*, p. 301; Ryder to Prince Regent, 15 February 1811, Harrowby Mss. XCVII; Wellesley-Pole to Ryder, 20 July 1811, Harrowby Mss. XCVIII; Wellesley-Pole to Ryder, 6 September 1811, HO 100/164.

52 *PD*, 1st series, 19, c. 280; Wellesley-Pole to Ryder, 21 February 1811, Harrowby Mss. XCVII; Wellesley-Pole to Ryder, 4 March 1811, Harrowby Mss. 1235a; Wellesley-Pole to Ryder, 10 July 1811, Harrowby Mss. XCVIII; Wellesley-Pole to Ryder, 12 February 1811, Harrowby Mss. XCVII; Wellesley-Pole to Ryder, 20 July 1811, Harrowby Mss. XCVIII; Richmond to Ryder, 2 February 1812, HO 11/166.

53 Wellesley-Pole to Ryder, 31, 21 December 1811, HO 100/165.

54 Lytton Strachey and Roger Fulford (eds), *The Greville Memoirs 1814–1860* (London), I, p. 91; *Wellesley Papers*, 2, pp. 96–7; Richmond to Peel, 16 April 1813, BL Add Ms. 49187; *PD*, 1st series, 23, c. 672; 24, cc. 894, 897.

55 Richmond to Peel, 6 May 1813, Richmond Papers, 69, NLI; Whitworth to Sidmouth, 5 May 1814, HO 100/178; Peel to Whitworth, 11 April 1814, U269/0225/4; Peel to Sidmouth, 23 May 1815, BL Add Ms. 40289; *Chester Chronicle*, 23 May 1813; MacDonagh, *O'Connell*, I, p. 128.

56 Maurice O'Connell (ed.), *The Correspondence of Daniel O'Connell* (Dublin, 1972–81), II, p. 347; Jenkins, *Era of Emancipation*, p. 237; Jenkins, *Goulburn*, pp. 163–5; Goulburn to Peel, 27 October 1824, Acc 304/35; Goulburn to Peel, 10 October 1826, HO 100/216.

57 *Chester Chronicle*, 23 May 1813; Moriarty to Monsell, 2 March 1868, Gladstone Papers, BL Add Ms. 44152; 'Limerick Declaration' reprinted in *Montreal Gazette*, 17 January 1868.

58 E.J. Hobsbawm, *Nations and Nationalism since 1780: Programme, Myth, Reality* (Cambridge, 1990), p. 69; Colley, *Britons*, pp. 368, 328–31.

59 Wakefield, *Account of Ireland*, II, pp. 325–7; Marilyn Silverman and P.H. Gulliver (eds), *Approaching the Past: Historical Anthropology through Irish Case Studies* (New York, 1992), pp. 297–8; Roy Jenkins, *Gladstone* (London, 1995), p. 319.

60 J.W. Croker, *Commentaries on National Policy and Ireland* (Dublin, 1831), pp. 55–60; Jenkins, *Era of Emancipation*, pp. 177, 301; Kennedy and Johnson, 'The Union of Ireland and Britain', in Boyce and O'Day, *Making of Modern Irish History*, p. 62; Ernest Gellner, *Thought and Change* (Chicago, 1964), p. 176; Foster, *Transactions of the Royal Historical Society*, 5th series, 33, pp. 173–4, 176–7; James Hunter, 'The Gaelic connection: the Highlands, Ireland and nationalism, 1873–1922', *Scottish Historical Review*, 54–6 (1975–7), p. 181; Hobsbawm, *Nations and Nationalism*, pp. 68, 34.

4   Isaac Butt, Irish nationality and the conditional defence of the Union, 1833–70

Joseph Spence

Isaac Butt, born in the glebe-house at Glenfin, County Donegal in 1813, remains one of the more enigmatic figures of modern Irish history. Making sense of the story of how the leading young defender of the privileges of Protestant ascendancy and Orange exclusivity in the 1830s became the 'father of home rule' in 1870 has never been easy. Is Butt's story one of a sudden transformation from Orangeman to ecumenical nationalist, is it a story of the evolution of a patriot, or is there an underlying consistency in Butt's political and cultural outlook between 1833 and the 1870s? Potential biographers have occasionally appeared on the promontory, but most of them, having offered lightning sketches of one or two aspects of his career, have moved on to other projects rather than complete a comprehensive survey of his life.[1]

There are, of course, references to the prominent role Butt played in Irish politics in the late 1860s and early 1870s in most surveys of Irish nationalism, but his career is seldom afforded close attention here either.[2] Most historians have accepted the traditional reading of Butt as a late convert to the conservative nationalism of home rule, whose limited political vision was almost immediately consigned to the dustbin of Irish history by more committed and radical patriots. However, the neglect of Butt also owes something to the fact that his rakish personal life made it difficult for either constitutional nationalists or constructive unionists to turn him into the plaster saint they sought for their pantheons of Irish heroes.

A reckless, warm-hearted man with a melancholy streak (most clearly detectable in his fiction[3]), Butt seems to have spent most of the time that he did not give over to politics or the law flirting with debt and women. He knew the inside of the Marshalsea and fathered a number of illegitimate children (and was once caught *in flagrante* with the Young Ireland poetess 'Speranza', later the mother of Oscar Wilde[4]). In the Butt archives there are clues as to the difficult state of his private life – cryptic notes and cheques made out for various women friends – which read like something out of a pseudo-Victorian novel.[5]

Butt knew himself a sinner, but he was no hypocrite, and he refused to leave any sanitised memoirs for posterity. It should be added, therefore, that Butt's own sense of unworthiness, as a leader of public opinion in Ireland, both as a unionist in the 1830s and 1840s and as a nationalist in the 1870s, has also played a part in confining him to the shadowy waters of historical research. The late Terence de Vere White, who wrote what remains the only full-scale biography of Butt, made sense of his subject by offering the thesis that his early 'road of excess' (Orange bigotry and personal immorality) led eventually to 'the palace of wisdom' (a rational promotion of home rule and an acceptance of the Victorian familial ideal). That version of events makes for a compelling narrative, but it necessitates an underplaying of Butt's early national feeling and it demands the choosing of a moment or more extended period of 'conversion' to nationalism which this chapter will suggest never occurred.

Thirty-five years ago, in his work on the early home rule party, David Thornley analysed the tortuous path of what he called Isaac Butt's 'imperial nationalism'.[6] He revealed Butt as a parliamentary leader who found it necessary to dissent from the body of his party, on policies and (more often) tactics, with increasing regularity, until overthrown by Charles Stuart Parnell at the end of 1877. This chapter reveals that Butt's early political and intellectual career was scarcely less anguished, for it will be suggested that he was often as ambivalent in his defence of the Union in the 1830s and 1840s as he was later to be uneasy with the aggressive promotion of home rule. However, what is also revealed is that, for all his political insecurity, Butt was consistent in his promotion of the cause of Irish 'nationality' and never believed that a political commitment to the defence of the 1801 parliamentary settlement rested illogically with that.

Butt, like Charles Boyton, Samuel Ferguson and Charles Lever (who also deserve further attention from Irish historians), believed that his vision could be unionist, imperialist and national, without contradiction.[7] This vision led him to play a part in the promotion of a sense of Anglo-Irish nationhood from the mid-1830s; five years ahead of Thomas Davis and Young Ireland, for whom he was more of an inspiration than has previously been recognised. As Thornley analysed Butt the 'imperial nationalist' of the 1870s, so this chapter attempts to understand the mindset of Butt the national unionist, through an exploration of the political, journalistic, historical, economic and literary writings of the first two decades of his public life. The chapter concludes with an endnote that reveals that, between 1833 and 1870, Butt's political language and outlook changed rather less than has generally been imagined.

I

At Trinity College Dublin, in 1833, the twenty-year-old Isaac Butt, a promising student of the classics with a penchant for political controversy, was already regarded as the rising hope of stern, unbending Irish Toryism. He was to become, within a couple of years, the acknowledged leader of a pack of radical Irish Tories determined to salvage something for Protestant Ireland from the wreckage of Catholic emancipation. Many older Irish Tories believed that Catholic relief in 1829 and parliamentary reform in 1832 had destroyed any possibility of a political culture based on the eighteenth-century ideal of Protestant ascendancy. Butt believed that resurrecting the myth of the Protestant Nation could prevent the further encroachment into Irish government of a misplaced Benthamite reformism and, by uniting Irish Protestants of all classes, act as a bulwark against O'Connell's emergent Catholic nationalism.

Faith in Protestant ascendancy, and the need to defend the Union, for the sake of Irish Protestant and imperial security, led Butt and others to launch the *Dublin University Magazine (DUM)* in January 1833. Never a university journal, in the narrow sense of the term, the magazine was to be the chief organ of Irish Toryism for more than thirty years. It promoted the idea that a national feeling for Ireland – for her distinctive cultural heritage – was compatible with unionism. It quickly attracted a loyal readership in Ireland and throughout the Empire (albeit for its literature rather than its politics) and caught the attention of some influential English politicians. The young Gladstone submitted political articles to the *DUM* in 1834, but successive 'able papers' were returned for alteration.[8] While what remains of these articles in manuscript form makes it difficult to determine what it was that the editors of the *DUM* found wanting in Gladstone's political analyses,[9] the need for the English Conservative to alter his work for the Irish Tory market neatly symbolises differences between the two creeds which were to recur.

A lack of 'unity of purpose' between the Irish Tories and the Conservative leadership, newly ensconced at the Carlton Club, was soon exposed. In 1835, offended by recurrent criticisms of his Irish policies, most notably those – often by Butt himself – which demanded that he bestir himself more energetically in defence of the Irish Corporations and the Irish Church,[10] Peel asked that his subscription to the *DUM* be terminated.[11] In his reply, Butt, now the magazine's editor, warned Peel that only the *DUM* could reconcile the mass of Irish Tories to Peelite Conservatism.[12] Implicit here was a belief that only the radical Irish Tory could see the gulf between 'English Theories and Irish Facts',[13] distinguish between the desires of the constituents of Tamworth and the demands of those of Tyrone, and counter the flawed understanding of Ireland evident among politicians of all parties at Westminster.

Toryism remained a force in Irish politics after 1832 – capable of winning 40 or more of Ireland's 105 seats at Westminster into the 1860s – because of its ability to build upon 'reserves of social and religious cohesiveness'.[14] Irish Tory recognition of the need to appeal to men of all classes led to the formation of the Irish Protestant Conservative Society (IPCS) in February 1832. Its members understood the art of what their ablest spokesman, the Revd Charles Boyton, Butt's tutor at Trinity College Dublin, called the politics of 'publicity'.[15] It was Boyton who taught Butt how to appeal to the various constituencies of Protestant Ireland: to political Protestants and loyal Conservatives; to local prejudices, imperial pride and national feeling for Ireland. He sought an Irish Party 'independent of Wellington and opposed to Whiggery' and sometimes flirted with the idea of an Orange–Repealer union.[16] Boyton's loyalty to the Union was, in some ways, conditional. Respecting the antiquity of the British constitution, he regarded the Union as an experiment, the results of which were still being analysed. This was a position Butt was to inherit from Boyton, and one that, it will be argued, informed his politics hereafter. For both men, some form of political connexion with Britain was desired, but to impose on them their class's later (that is, post-1886) commitment to the Union *per se* would be misleading.

Both Boyton and Butt were fascinated by O'Connell. Boyton taught Butt to admire O'Connell's ability to debate with 'the public mind of Ireland' and sought to direct Irish Tory attention away from the culture of resignation which had been breeding since the Union and exacerbated by the measures of 1829 and 1832. He promoted the establishment of the IPCS as an 'open association' (unlike the Orange Order) to address the failure of Irish commerce and manufacturing, the ignominy of the appointment of Englishmen to fill places in Irish departments and the decay of Dublin since 1800. Boyton was no soothing Tory apologist. He blamed the state of Ireland on Protestant dereliction of duty, as much as on Popery, Whiggery and demagogy, and abhorred, equally, absenteeism and the tendency of resident Irish Protestants 'to cling to England in helpless imbecility'.[17]

The IPCS soon attracted the attention of O'Connell. However, although he tempered his radicalism in his quest for an alliance with Boyton, O'Connell's assurances were insufficient for the Irish Tories.[18] They recognised repeal of the Union as 'a senseless but not uncaptivating cry', but determined that it was traitorous 'to inflame national passions at the expense of imperial interests'.[19] Butt was to employ very similar language some thirty years later, in establishing the Home Government Association – to petition for a Federal Union, combining the nations of the United Kingdom into 'one great Imperial State'[20] – and in quelling the nationalistic and obstructionist ardour of his Home Rule Party.[21]

Admitting that they were obliged to decline an O'Connellite alliance in the 1830s, the Irish Tories had to ensure that O'Connell did not convert the Protestant merchant class to repeal. One potent weapon used by the Irish Tories in the Dublin Corporation was to associate their unionist cause with a Protestant Patriot tradition, dating back to the 1740s.[22] The IPCS strove to prevent repeal ideas capturing the poorer Protestants, by infiltrating societies like the Aldermen of Skinners' Alley (of which Boyton and Butt were honorary members) and by preaching a gospel of the duty of landlords (through attacks on absenteeism).[23]

Irish Toryism lost something of its potential for social radicalism with Boyton's withdrawal from public life in 1836. In 1844 *The Nation* lamented that his death had left a gap in Irish Tory ranks that would not be filled 'unless his nationality as well as his humanity descend upon Mr Butt'.[24] In fact, Butt had already assumed Boyton's mantle in the Irish Metropolitan Conservative Society (IMCS). At its inaugural meeting, in November 1836, the duty of members to identify themselves with Ireland was stressed by the Secretary, R.W. Nash, who ventured:

> Our Protestant ancestors contented themselves with preserving the constitution, enforcing the laws, and maintaining a connexion with England. They omitted to improve their estates and disregarded the . . . welfare of those who dwelt on them; they affected to think themselves English instead of raising their native country to a moral rank in which they might be proud to own themselves her sons . . . You are an Irish Society, formed for the political and religious improvement of your native land [and] for the promotion of

everything connected with her agriculture, manufactures and commercial interests.

When Butt spoke he declared, reviving one of Boyton's favourite phrases, that he would give 'an impulse to the Protestant mind of Ireland'. He called, in similarly Boytonian manner, for independent Irish Tory action and no more trusting to British sympathy.[25] Whether distrust of Britain would have led the ICMS to consider adopting an anti-unionist position publicly is uncertain, but we do know, from the novelist Sheridan Le Fanu's gossipy note of 1840, about a 'hot debate' at a private meeting of the society at which some members spoke 'vehemently in favour of an open declaration for repeal and none spoke directly against it'.[26] However, as Le Fanu's biographer neatly puts it, to some extent, all the Irish Tories were doing here, in their secret conclave, was celebrating an atavistic dream of ascendancy and expressing their 'longings for an eighteenth-century solution to a nineteenth-century crisis'.[27]

After 1840, the Irish Tories and the repealers also debated Irish issues in the reformed Dublin Corporation, which both treated as a surrogate parliament. In February 1843 O'Connell, the Lord Mayor, and Alderman Butt, as a sort of Tory spokesman on national issues, engaged in a well-publicised debate on the repeal question. O'Connell praised the 1782 settlement, argued that repeal would extend Irish prosperity and promised that it would not lead to Catholic ascendancy. In his reply Butt criticised O'Connell for rooting his Irish nationality in rights that had English origins. He purported not to understand how O'Connell could call the 1782 constitution a final settlement, while Irish laws were still passed under the Great Seal of England.

In the course of his own speech on the repeal issue Butt offered what has been called the clearest statement of the Irish unionist position ever made:[28]

> I am quite willing to discuss this question as an Irishman. I am not – I cannot be indifferent to the prosperity of the British Empire . . . I believe with Pitt that no one can speak as a true Englishman who does not speak as a true Irishman; or as a true Irishman who does not speak as a true Englishman. I am satisfied that we have all a much greater stake in the strength and in the prosperity of the Empire at large, than we have in any petty and separate interest of any of its component parts.

The implication was clear. Whatever was threatened in the private meetings of the IMCS, Butt still stood for national unionism as preferable to repeal because the Union represented a state in which, he believed, Ireland could have a healthy and positive – and hopefully a mutually beneficial – say in imperial affairs.

Later in the same speech Butt offered another challenge to O'Connellism. He purported to understand calls for the separation of England and Ireland, but not for simple repeal. He stood with Wolfe Tone, a man 'as sincerely attached to the honour of his country as any', in believing that Grattan had not made Ireland 'A Nation Once Again' by winning the limited independence the Irish parliament had attained in 1782, but had been duped into accepting a measure which had kept her 'a paltry, pitiful province'.[29]

Winning the debate on repeal within the Dublin Corporation, as he was bound to do, O'Connell could afford to be magnanimous about his opponent. He let it be known that he had liked the national focus of Butt's opposition and declared that the young Orangeman was 'in his inmost soul an Irishman', and that 'we will have him struggling with us for Ireland yet'. More purposefully perhaps, he also admitted that he understood that the association of the policy of repeal with land and franchise reform, and with disestablishment of the Church of Ireland, was preventing some people (like Butt?) from supporting his national agitation. He could only retaliate: 'We are not Chartists', revealing his own social conservatism, and declare that repeal was sufficient, while all the rest without that was not.[30]

In September 1844 there was a further expression of Irish Tory national feeling in the Dublin Corporation, in a debate on Henry Maunsell's motion that an imperial parliament should be held in Dublin once every three years. Supported by Butt, Maunsell discussed the feasibility of an 'ambulatory parliament', and called for Irish 'political unanimity', which had never existed because

> The craft of English politicians has divided the people of Ireland into two armies of hostile functionaries and under the conventional names of Whig and Tory, we have been hallooed to battle to our own great loss, but to the party gain, sometimes of a Sir Robert Peel – sometimes of a Lord John Russell . . . [L]et us break the spell that has so long bound us to the tails of the English Whigs or the English Tories. Let us give one unanimous voice for old Ireland.[31]

No vote was taken, however, and the debate was something of a put-up job, to hint at the possibility of Irish Tory repealism. Butt and Maunsell played their national games in their surrogate parliament, but, caught between O'Connell and Peel, they had only a minor role in the real political drama of the early 1840s and no more than a walk-on part after 1846.

While a good deal of historical and literary reflection on the nature of Irishness continued among a minority of Irish Protestants into the later 1840s, the political expression of Irish Tory national feeling in the famine era was restricted to the limited involvement of a few individuals in a few curious inter-party societies. In late 1847 Samuel Ferguson, the poet and antiquarian, who had written many political and literary pieces for the *DUM*, was conspicuous (and Butt a silent witness) in an Irish Council, whose membership was drawn from a great spectrum of Irish political opinions, from the Conservative to the more radical elements of Young Ireland. The members of this council met occasionally to debate the major Irish issues of the day, of which the most divisive was probably tenant-right rather than the Union. When John Mitchel stated at one meeting of the council that he read into the doctrine of tenant-right a justification for the transfer of property, it was Ferguson who countered that it was an idea rooted in the Ulster custom and, as such, an unspoken contract subsisting where landlord–tenant relations were good and understood to exist for the security of each party.[32]

At the only meeting of a Protestant Repeal Association, in May 1848, Samuel Ferguson defined repeal as 'the great principle of self-government to counter the anti-national and servile spirit in the land'.[33] Within two months, however, the rising of a former Irish Tory, William Smith O'Brien, had created a situation in which a Protestant Repeal Association had no place. Ferguson quit politics and Butt was left to question the justice of the Union in his courtroom defences of Smith O'Brien and Thomas Francis Meagher (who saw his advocate as 'the Curran of 1848'[34]). The core of that defence was that Young Ireland's argument was directed against the Union as a failed experiment and not against the Queen and British connexion, and that no patriot could be satisfied with the state of Ireland. The failed legislative union needed amending to facilitate the creation of a true emotional union of the English and Irish people. Butt contended, for

> I do not see that the Queen, Lords and Commons of Ireland sitting in Dublin would be in any way inconsistent with our Union with England in feeling and interest or that the restoration of the ancient constitution of Ireland should create anything but good feeling between the countries.[35]

However, for all the rhetoric, Butt did not capture the attention of the whole Irish people with the idea of the emotional union of England and Ireland until he led the 'Protestant day-trip to home rule' in 1870.[36] A parliamentary day-trip that may have been, but the Protestant unionist mind was not necessarily anti-national in orientation before that date, as the exploration of Butt's early political rhetoric has begun to suggest, and as an examination of his contribution to Irish history, political economy and literature will further reveal.

II

Isaac Butt imbibed the lessons of Irish history from historians and antiquarians of the early nineteenth century, of whom the most influential was probably the Revd George Miller. Between 1816 and 1828, Miller published a long series of *Lectures on the Philosophy of Modern History*, which owed something to Kant, Voltaire and Herder, but more to Holy Writ. The lectures were originally delivered at Trinity College Dublin between November 1800 and 1811 and encompassed, albeit tellingly hidden in a universal history, an Irish Tory history of Ireland. Miller's universal historical concern in 1800 was to discover why God had allowed such a catastrophe as the French Revolution. He studied history as a subject possessing 'the unity of a moral drama' over thirteen centuries, but the history of Ireland formed an increasing part of the universal story. It was the Union of 1800 which emerged as the event to end an era rather than the revolution of 1789 and, of course, in Ireland it was. Indeed, one historian has described Miller's eleven-year course of eighty-four long lectures as 'no more than a massive pamphlet upon a single point of altered political views regarding the union'.[37]

Miller's message was that the Act of Union was providential and would promote the cause of Irish nationality within an imperial framework. (When the Irish Tories needed reassuring of this, in 1832, with the passage of the Reform Bill, and in 1849, in the wake of the famine and Young Ireland's rebellion, Miller's history was republished.) Miller would make even greater claims for the Union and declared that he read from the result at Waterloo a divine declaration that the United Kingdom of Great Britain and Ireland would be preserved as 'an instrument of good to a recovering world'. Implicit in Miller's philosophy was the belief that union between nations was natural and a state towards which the world was progressing. Thus the divine justification for the Act of 1801.[38]

Irish Tory justifications of the Union and reflections on Irishness were also disseminated in the 1830s and 1840s by a number of biographers who shared a belief that their work was, as one of them put it, 'more national than personal'.[39] As editor of the *DUM*, Butt himself supervised the publication of a long running series of biographies published as the 'Gallery of Illustrious Irishmen', which claimed many eighteenth-century leaders of Irish public opinion as progenitors of nineteenth-century Irish Toryism. Thus Swift, Grattan, Flood, Lord Charlemont, Sheridan and John Philpot Curran were claimed for the Irish Tory succession along with more obvious 'conservatives', Burke, Berkeley, Goldsmith and Lord Clare. These ascendancy heroes performed four distinctive functions in the national unionist rhetoric of Butt and the Irish Tories. Molyneux, Swift and Berkeley were celebrated as the writers who first voiced Ireland's grievances in the half-century after 1688, while Goldsmith, Sheridan and Burke, whose distinctive Irish role was less evident, were lauded as the intellectual gems of Protestant Ireland, as voices of Irish genius heard and admired throughout the world and, thereby, in some way, as men whose careers excused the harsher aspects of Protestant ascendancy. Third, there were the great statesmen – Grattan, Flood and Charlemont – who were remembered for having institutionalised the battle for the redress of Irish grievances and who personified the Irish nation of 1782. Finally, the Irish Tories added a figure who did not feature in the nationalist canon of patriotism – John Fitzgibbon, Earl of Clare. According to the nationalists, in effecting the Union, Fitzgibbon betrayed his nation; according to the Irish Tories, in seeing the necessity of the Union he adapted the cause of the Irish nation and saved it. The picture the Irish Tories sought to provide, therefore, was one of an Irish nation which grew from the Protestant ascendancy, and of an ascendancy that sacrificed itself for the cause of nationality – but whose sacrifice was misinterpreted.

Introducing his 'Gallery', Butt stated that in the illustrious lives of men like Swift, Grattan and Lord Clare there was to be found a rare cause for Irish 'national pride', adding in the characteristically defensive manner with which he was to preface all his Irish fiction:

> To Ireland we consecrate this part of our work. There are those who stigmatize our politics as anti-national, and would fain have it believed that we do not care for our country. Our politics may be wrong ... but God is our witness that we have no desire but to see Ireland as she ought to be.

Butt went beyond this rhetoric, however, and cautioned that the mere sentimental appreciation of past greatness was not patriotism:

> An allusion to the 'emerald island' at a public meeting will draw thunders of applause but in that tribute to sentiment, our nationality too often effervesces . . . the Scotchman cultivates his thistle in his garden; the Irishman wears his shamrock till it withers on his bosom or he drowns it in his bowl.[40]

However, the limits of the 'nationality' of the Irish Tories were revealed in their failure to produce a history of Ireland. It was an admission of their partial understanding of Irish life that they sought to glorify ascendancy heroes rather than understand the life of the native people or countenance their alternative pantheon of heroes. However many hidden histories of Ireland are found in their antiquarianism or in their pseudo-universal histories, it was to reveal an intellectual descent from the Protestant nation that the Irish Tories wrote of Ireland's past, not to seek to understand other Irish traditions. A generation later the greatest Irish historian of the century also did this. As W.E.H. Lecky wrote his *Leaders of Public Opinion in Ireland*, in Italy in 1860, Butt was completing a history of Italy in which he reflected: 'In no country perhaps, save one, have the traditions and memories of the past taken equal hold upon the hearts and imaginations of the people'. If Butt did not write a history of Ireland, therefore, he nevertheless offered a surrogate history in his work on Italy.[41]

Of course, the history-mindedness of the Irish is widely acknowledged and Irish politics has invariably involved a utilisation of a real or imagined past.[42] However, Irish Tories sometimes supplemented their arguments from history with lessons learned from other disciplines. In the eighteenth century there developed in Ireland what might be called a tradition of applied political economy which can be traced through a succession of writers from Swift and Berkeley to Mountifort Longfield and Butt. These last two, the Irish Tories who first held the Whately Chair of Political Economy at Trinity College Dublin, founded in 1832, discussed in academic guise, more freely than they were to do elsewhere, the economic questions of their day: absenteeism, the state of the poor and the extent to which laissez-faire doctrines could be applied to the specific case of Ireland. Longfield and Butt endowed Irish political economy with a sense that all economic reasoning had to be based on observation, with an understanding that analogy was not argument and with an appreciation of subjective factors and inductive and historical reasoning.[43]

Butt succeeded Longfield as Whately Professor in 1836, at the age of twenty-three. He was unique among early economists in professing to find the roots of his discipline not in Adam Smith, but in the thought of an Irish precursor. Attacking 'artificial materialism', Butt regarded Berkeley's economic thought as his source. The Irish Tory's concern was, therefore, he stated, with the welfare rather than the wealth of nations. He held that Irish political economy had to have as its primary object 'to correct a habit of carelessness in the public mind' – again, Butt had adopted the language of Boyton – so that economic issues could be 'redeemed from the province of passion and declamation'. Butt may have directed the 'public mind' towards such issues, but he did not thereby depoliticise them. Indeed, in Ireland's case, he stated, the economist's inquiries had to come into contact with the moralist's and the politician's: to shrink from this was to deprive political economy of its dignity and value.[44]

In *Protection to Home Industry*, delivered at Trinity College Dublin in 1840, but not published until 1846, Butt stated that any restriction upon free trade was '*prima facie*' an evil, but added that – from his reading of scripture, Berkeley, Burke and Longfield – he saw that national prosperity lay in the promotion of an economic system which would fulfil the first duty of civil society: 'to secure to all within the country the means of earning by their labour a comfortable independence'. That rule, he argued, excused protective duties in Ireland where they acted as a 'national poor law'. Butt's concern was with the distribution of wealth which, he stressed, was as important to a national economy as wealth production. He distinguished between monetary value and 'national value-in-use' – and the nation with which he was concerned was Ireland. 'How deeply the condition of too many of our peasantry reproves the unprofitableness of our politics', he reflected, before asking his readers to reflect upon a problem identified in Berkeley's *Querist* (1735–7), which had yet found no solution: 'What binders us Irish from exerting ourselves, using our hands and brains; doing something or other, man, woman, and child, like the other inhabitants of the earth?'[45]

By 1846 Young Ireland had provided a climate in which these thoughts, which Butt had delivered in a Trinity lecture hall in 1840, could be pronounced publicly. John Mitchel read Butt's lectures as repeal essays, seeing them as continuing a tradition of Irish political economy that had begun with Swift and Berkeley. Butt was held to be the only modern economist to appreciate Swift's view that there could be no such thing as surplus produce in a country until its own people had been fed and one of the few to understand Berkeley's view of the evils of absenteeism.[46]

Butt pronounced even more forthrightly on the state of the Irish economy in his pamphlet *A Voice for Ireland – Famine in the Land* in April 1847. His thesis, however, was one which he developed from an idea he had first forwarded a decade previously: that Ireland still needed an effective Poor Law (the 1837 Irish Poor Law Amendment Act he had always portrayed as a piece of 'forced legislation', designed to salve English consciences[47]) and he identified the absence of such a law as the source of England's 'moral crime' in Ireland. In his potted history of the famine, one can trace the course of the growth of his national despair for Ireland under the Union: disgust that the famine was rendered a party question in England, anger at the English Conservatives complacent belief that the crisis was the invention of agitators and his belief that Ireland was paying for Whig adherence 'not to the doctrines of political economy, but to an utterly mistaken application of them'. A telling contrast was drawn between the manner in which the British Parliament had met and an Irish parliament would have met the crisis. Butt condemned those who talked of Ireland being a drain upon 'the English treasury' and added that a little more treating of Ireland as a conquered country 'and he would be a bold man who would promise many years continuance of the Union'.

Threats whispered earlier were now voiced openly. The death of O'Connell in 1847 had, he believed, encouraged Irish politicians to think they had come to the end of a fending era. Already, Butt held, Irishmen of all classes had determined upon 'a Grand Inquest' of British government and the gentry had formed an Irish Council, at which were propounded federalist, if not repealer, sentiments.[48]

The famine had certainly radicalised Butt's view of Anglo-Irish economic relations and his most nationalistic economic statement was delivered in a public letter to Lord Roden in April 1849. Roden, a leading Orangeman and evangelical, was prominent among Ulster landlords opposed to a new tax upon Irish land which, it was suspected, was to be taken from the rich poor law unions to pay for those where pauperism prevented a tax being levied. Their fear was that Ulster would be taxed into the devastated state of Connaught. Butt attacked the way in which Ulster made the matter of this tax, the rate-in-aid, its own and counselled against provincialism. Seeing the new tax as 'the crisis of the poor law of 1837', Butt felt that once again English consciences were being salved by action taken without regard to Irish needs and he called for united Irish opposition and an Irish Board of Trade and Plantations (to be presided over by a cabinet minister, preferably an Irishman), and suggested emigration schemes. But what was most needed, he added, was for a man of Roden's standing to proclaim that, whether under a united or a separate legislature, Irishmen demanded justice for their nation as part of that great confederacy the United Kingdom. He went further:

> And, after all, we feel that, let acts of parliament declare what they will, Antrim and Cork ARE parts of the same nation; Mayo and Kent are NOT . . . [A]fter half a century's experience of the Union, we still feel that Ireland is a separate country. Those who have spoken of the English exchequer, and proposed an Irish national rate-in-aid, have unequivocally proclaimed their conviction that it is so.[49]

Butt noted that a recent meeting between the Prime Minister and the Irish MPs had established the principle that Ireland, notwithstanding the Union, had sometimes to be treated as a separate state. That meeting he read as 'the momentary reconstruction' of an Irish legislature. He concluded that such 'involuntary recognitions of the essential character of Ireland's separate Nationality' perhaps foreshadowed a time when the domestic affairs of Ireland would be handed over to Irish management.[50] This was a time for which Butt called on his countrymen to prepare and about which he was curious and excited. Such curiosity ultimately killed the parliamentary unionist in him.

III

In its first issue the *DUM* had called for 'the repeal of the literary union'[51] and this call was echoed in subsequent reflections on Irish literature. In 1837 Butt saw a clear relationship between the political and literary state of Ireland. He complained that English encumbrances had hindered Irish literature for centuries and argued that this was so because unceasing party strife was read as evidence of the backwardness of Ireland and ensured that no Englishman saw the integrity of the Irish struggle. He bemoaned the absence of a market for literature in Ireland and stated that only 'national feeling' had kept the *DUM* from moving to London. Its very existence, therefore, was a source of hope for Irish literature and culture. He set down as its aims: to encourage native learning; to give Ireland a civilised reputation in foreign countries; to give a 'home direction' to the absentee; to attract capital to Ireland; to awaken its publishing trade. The last objective had national significance, for Butt held that a native press could supply the place that a legislature had once had as a nursery of talents.[52]

Given that it was while he edited the *DUM* that William Carleton, James Clarence Mangan, Charles Lever and Sheridan Le Fanu made their first contributions, Isaac Butt is one of the great hidden patrons of Irish literature. However, he also wrote Irish fiction himself, stories heavy with melancholy and an urge to moralise. After some attempts at propagandist peasant fiction,[53] he began writing about an Ireland he knew far more immediately: that microcosm of ascendancy society, Trinity College Dublin. *Chapters of College Romance*, which appeared between 1834 and 1837, promised Scott-like attention to the 'romance of truth'. In fact, the tales evinced an Irish Tory's sectarian fears. 'The Bribed Scholar', a representative 'Chapter', told of a young man who voted for Catholic relief to secure a loan needed to save his father from ruin, having once declared the measure a 'national sin'. The scholar had convinced himself that sectarianism had brought ruin on his family and that his only way of atonement was to support emancipation. His father accepted no such argument, countering that for over a century the Crawfords had suffered in 'the Protestant cause':

> down from your great-grandfather that was killed at the battle of the Boyne to your uncle that the rebels murdered at Gorey. Little did I think that a son of mine would bring disgrace upon our house. Arthur Crawford, ye are an apostate – Arthur Crawford, ye are no son of mine.[54]

Butt reminded Protestants of an historical debt, but he hesitated to develop the theme, being aware of the innate ambivalence of any argument from history. His most stinging attacks were delivered at fashionable Whiggery and lazy latitudinarianism, and delivered most tellingly through a utilisation of the Faust legend, which a number of his Irish Tory contemporaries also employed.[55]

The Irish Tory Faust stories revealed the insecurity of the Irish Protestant under the Union: a people caught between two worlds, one dying (Protestant ascendancy) while the other was struggling to be born (Irish democracy and separatism). Butt's utilisation of the Faust legend in the *College Romance* entitled 'The Murdered Fellow' (1835) owed a particular debt to Charles Maturin's *Melmoth the Wanderer* (1820), itself a narrative of Anglo-Irish displacement after the Union. In both tales the narrative is drawn from a family manuscript, which provides the intimation of hereditary sin. In Butt's tale the major character is the student Wallis, one who entered Trinity not having learned what Butt called, in a phrase revealing the depth of Irish Tory pessimism, 'the philosophy of experience

. . . to distrust all in whom we have no special reason to place confidence'. At Trinity, Wallis fell in with the atheist Browne, a Whig, who 'in the pride of human reason . . . dared to pry into the deep things that reason cannot comprehend'. It was Browne who drove Wallis to commit murder. Wallis escaped suspicion but, in his subsequent life, never escaped a sense that Browne was stalking him. Like Maturin's Wanderer, he went abroad and plunged deeper into sin, but returned to Ireland to witness the death of a relative and spent his later life as a resident Irish landlord, in a bid for expiation. He became the idol of his tenants, but still felt the presence of 'the Evil One' whose 'damned howl' – heard upon Wallis's violent death – echoed Melmoth's 'demonical laugh'.[56] Butt's Faustian tale further evinced an Irish Tory's fear of the Whiggification of Dublin. In 'The Murdered Fellow' he stated that he wrote an historical tale to prevent 'the spiteful [gratifying] their malevolence, by making to living characters a personal application of what I say'. Yet he added that his most malicious characters held high places in Dublin society in the 1830s. As we shall see, historical fiction was often the most politically potent of all forms of Irish literature.

The authorship of the novel *Irish Life in the Castle, the Courts and the Country*, published anonymously in Dublin in 1840, has also been attributed to Butt and internal evidence would suggest that he did write the book. It was a panoramic novel, which owed a debt to Maria Edgeworth and particularly to John Banim's *The Anglo-Irish in the Nineteenth-century* (1828). The latter was a commentary on Dublin society and an adjacent plea for Catholic relief, which followed the year after its publication, but the imminent passage of which seemed as assured in its pages as had the Union in the preface of *Castle Rackrent*. *The Anglo-Irish* brought Irish society fiction back to Dublin. In *The Absentee* and *Ennui* Edgeworth had exposed the vices of London society to which the Irish gentry were particularly susceptible and led her characters to a purer provincial Ireland where, she intimated, their duties lay. She contrasted an artificial 'society' with a natural 'community'. What Banim did in 1828 was to express some of the liveliness of post-Union Dublin society.

Twelve years later, in another flawed novel of great scope, Butt analysed Dublin society more severely. *Irish Life* opened with a characteristically defensive testament: 'Nationality has been his object; and if . . . any remarks may appear to bear too severely upon any particular class, body or profession, the author begs most respectfully to disclaim any feelings of an acrimonious nature.'[57] In view of his attacks on the suffocation of Dublin society by mercantile interests in the novel, it may be that Butt's apology was directed specifically to members of the old Dublin Corporation which he was in the same year to defend, impressively, at the bar of the House of Lords. A brief reflection on some of Isaac Butt's known activities in 1840 reveals neatly the ambivalence of the nationally minded Irish Protestant's position. Growing disillusioned with the meagre fruits of the Union, he was tentatively debating the possibility of Protestant repeal in the IMCS, promoting economic nationalism at Trinity and reflecting on the nature of Irishness in his fiction. However, fearful of throwing off any of the habiliments of Protestant ascendancy, he was also defending the old Corporation as a fortress for the protection of the Union.[58] Butt's strenuously ecumenical novel was perhaps his personal antidote to his contemporaneous defence of Protestant exclusivity in municipal government. Unsurprisingly, the novel, like its author, veered between idealism and pessimism.

Butt admitted in *Irish Life* that one could walk the 'fashionable beat' and convince oneself that Dublin was more like a capital than any other city of the Empire. However, he revealed Dublin in all its manifestations, and the presence of 'broad brass plates' in its once aristocratic squares and the mock grandeur of Dublin Castle were aspects of its life to which Butt drew attention. (The brass plate and the sham-court also featured in William Makepeace Thackeray's reflections on Dublin in his *Irish Sketch Book* of 1843 and it may be that Butt's ideas found their way into that work which was intermittently superior, in its understanding of the nuances of Irish life, to the majority of Victorian records of Ireland.[59]) There was no point upon which Banim, in *The Anglo-Irish*, and Butt more closely agreed than in their criticisms of the artificiality of the Irish court. However, their perspectives differed. For Banim, 'the racket-court [of the] vice-king and deputy-queen' was at the root of the problem and it was intimated that once it was reformed – once Catholics were able to share its fruits – Irish society would be purified. For Butt, however, Dublin Castle betrayed a decadence which infected every aspect of Irish life. 'Castle Protestants' and 'Castle Catholics' were found among those 'officially titled' aristocrats he castigated, but particular scorn was reserved for the fact that 'O'Connell and his dirty tail' patronised the viceregal levees.[60] On one level, this exposed Butt's sectarianism, but it also revealed him as a dissenter from Dublin fashion, while O'Connell was the conformist. Thus the nationally minded Tory was portrayed as more truly national than the self-seeking demagogue.

Where Banim and Butt most clearly diverged was in their conclusions. Banim had intimated that there was a new greatness in Dublin, in the form of O'Connell. But when he gave his hero, Gerald Clangore, a one-way ticket out of Dublin, romantic nationalism supplanted practical polities. His odyssey had led him from an artificial London, through a vibrant Dublin to rural Ireland, where Banim concluded his duty lay. The provincial spirit instilled by Maria Edgeworth continued to pervade and the hero ended the novel poised to become a good resident landlord. *The Anglo-Irish* was the work of a liberal Catholic optimist. Conversely, the Ireland Butt portrayed in *Irish Life* had not benefited from the Union and nor had Catholic relief brought it peace. His hero O'Donnell sought, hopelessly, for a moral-force movement, undisturbed by fanaticism or bigotry. O'Donnell was, one might imagine, a Thomas Davis figure, but in 1840, in that character bearing the name of his maternal ancestors, Butt projected himself. O'Donnell echoed a number of Butt's beliefs: notably that Ireland needed to manage her own trade and look more critically at the reasons for 'her mendicant merchants, her unfrequented customs'-house, her bankrupt shopkeepers [and] her pauperized gentry'. Butt had O'Donnell lament that he found in Dublin 'a universally pauperized community ... whose crouching humility disgusts', and had him conclude bitterly: 'Compare them with the extravagance, the insolence and the presumption of the English officials that grind them to the dirt, and reflect that you too are an Irishman.' Speaking through O'Donnell, Butt professed to see the Irish following a 'spurious patriotism' which led only to the 'false lights that glimmer on the deadly promontory of English intrigue and domination'. The keynote of his analysis was that the promise of the Union had not been met: England still governed Ireland on divide-and-rule principles, fit for the subjugation of a colony, but not for a people with whom they were meant to exist in 'co-citizenship'.[61] Already he was haunting himself with the idea that only a federal settlement could bring that state of affairs into being.

Irish Life was the converse reflection of *The Anglo-Irish*. In Banim's novel an Anglicised Irishman arrived accidentally in his native land and emerged as a good landlord, having thrown off his Anglo-Irish theories. Thus the confident Catholic on the eve of emancipation. In Butt's novel an Irishman of good birth rebelled against the degenerating English element in Irish life, but grew so disgusted with Irish politics that he could no longer contemplate living in Ireland. Thus Butt's pessimism. Yet despite the antithetical conclusions, the authors had been led to them by a critique of the same elements of Irish life: the Irish imitation of English ways, English misgovernment, absenteeism and the farce of the viceregal court.

Other analogies and allegories are revealed in a study of that most present-minded body of work, Irish historical fiction, and Butt also wrote an historical novel. A century before Stephen Dedalus muttered 'History is a nightmare from which I am trying to awake', Irish writers began to quarry the Irish past and play out the conflicts contained within it in fictional form. They all sought to write an Irish *Waverley*. But whereas Walter Scott ensured that Clio was in some degree anaesthetised, the Irish ancestral memory was fiercer than that of the Scots or the English. A century after the wars of 1688–91 an obligation to seventeenth-century familial and national tradition remained intense, as Butt had revealed in 'The Bribed Scholar'. By the 1790s the past had been elided into the Irish mind and politicians began to refer to seventeenth- or even twelfth-century history as English statesmen did to the reports of select committees. Consequently, the historical novel became an adjunct of political commentary. Hence the particular popularity of the genre at times of political crisis: in the mid-1820s writers sought to illuminate by reference to past pledges and Catholic constancy the justice of the call for emancipation; from the 1830s, Irish Tories sought from the past some justification for a broad definition of Irish nationality to disturb the growing belief that only a Catholic could be a true Hibernian.[62]

Pre-empting criticism that his historical novel was disguised politics, Butt purported to offer in *The Gap of Barnesmore* in 1848, 'something to mitigate the bitterness of present animosities'.[63] This was too sanguine a hope. The Irish novels of 1800 to 1850 were described by Yeats as written in a 'fiery shorthand', which offered a code for political statements.[64] Of no single work would this label seem more fitting than Butt's tale of Ulster politics in 1688–9. The heroes of the novel were the Oakleys who, like Butt's own family, had married into the O'Donnells and who were as proud of their descent from the Kings of Tyrconnell as they were of their English ancestry.

Proving adept at blending the public and private elements of his tale, Butt drew his heroine's suitors in such a way as to be able to portray the class from which each came. The O'Donnell represented the ancient Irish chieftainry; he was brave and honourable, but wrong-headed and without a place in modern Ireland (very like the Highlander Fergus MacIver in relation to post-Culloden Scotland in Scott's *Waverley*). Carroll represented new Catholic Ireland: born into insecurity, but brought up to believe that he had a right to the land, he was brutal, dishonourable and self-seeking. Spencer was a southern Protestant: brave, kindly and generous, but ultimately limited in his understanding of the people. Ellen Oakley's other suitor was Hamilton, the King's Sheriff. While Spencer was bewildered by the complexities of Irish life, Hamilton was united with Ellen in 'conscious sympathy' for all the people they found themselves among. In the juxtaposing of Hamilton and Spencer, Butt made a claim for the Protestant Ulsterman as he to whom Ireland had to look for salvation. It was Hamilton too who had the subtlety to be able to distinguish between the government of the Viceroy and the majesty of King James. Butt sought, thereby, to defuse the notion that Protestant Ulster had 'revolted' in 1688–9 while also evoking the clannishness of Irish life, concluding the novel with two marriages which united ten families. However, any thought that this made the novel an ecumenical tract needs qualification. Butt did not admit the possibility of Catholic and Protestant union. Having one character become a Protestant before her marriage, the ceremonies which could have united the two Irelands, only brought together four Ulster Protestants. The men of other traditions, O'Donnell and Spencer, did not marry.

Butt always declared that he wrote fiction with an ecumenical purpose, but a sense of Protestant superiority and an admission of sectarian ancestral guilt were prevalent features of his tales. Gavan Duffy read Butt's historical novel as work inspired by Thomas Davis and, therefore, in some way, a Young Ireland tract.[65] In fact, it was nothing of the kind. If in 1840 writing fiction had allowed Butt a release of national feeling, at a time when he was publicly engaged in the defence of Protestant exclusivity, by 1848 it provided him with an opportunity to weigh the nationalist rhetoric he was soon to employ in defence of Young Ireland and offer a critique of it. Unlike Scott's *Waverley*, which ensured that it offered a sense of resolution to the vexed question of Scottish identity under the Union of 1707, Butt found it difficult to offer hope to Ireland of a union of the native Irish and Anglo-Irish. As he had one Fr Meehan declare, in Berkelian mode: 'All over the world races coalesce; the land of their birth unites them. [Why] is Ireland different from every other country upon earth? The Saxon has forgotten the curfew; the Norman has become English. In Ireland only, the natives and the aliens refuse to blend'. When Anglo-Irish Spencer retorted that many 'colonists' were deeply attached to Ireland, still Butt refused to allow the celebration of an ecumenical spirit. Instead, he acknowleged the limitations of the national vision of his own people: 'Yes, you are in one sense attached to Ireland, but by Ireland you mean yourselves. You look upon yourselves as the Irish Nation; you look upon Ireland as the Council of Ten looked upon Venice; you would be patriots, while you were permitted to trample upon the Irish'.[66]

At the moment when some Irishmen were hoping to identify him as an ecumenical nationalist, Butt was writing more critically and realistically about the state of Ireland than he had ever done, and resisting their appeals. It was as if he saw romantic Ireland as already dead and gone, and with Thomas Davis in the grave. However, Butt continued to write on various aspects of Irish public life throughout the 1850s and 1860s,[67] and, in 1870, he posited his ideas in a political form to attract support for a federal solution to the Irish question from both uneasy unionists – hurt into national politics by the disestablishment of the Church of Ireland – and some of the more amenable Fenians, whose public advocate he had been as President of the Amnesty Association in 1869.

IV

In November 1833 Samuel Ferguson, who challenged Butt in the range of his national interests, wrote 'A Dialogue between the head and the heart of an Irish Protestant', which, like Butt's own writings, revealed the extent of Irish Tory national feeling.[68] The trouble was that Ferguson's and Butt's purported dialogues were read by other Irishmen as monologues and, as such, as no substitute for dialogue with Catholic Ireland. The Irish Tories, in a state of Irish Protestant paralysis, disdained to show sufficient respect for other traditions of Irishness and, thereby, lost the right to be leaders of public opinion. Ferguson admitted as much when he wrote that the position of the Anglo-Irish in Ireland remained insecure because 'their intelligence has not embraced a thorough knowledge of the genius and disposition of their Catholic fellow citizens'.[69]

As Samuel Ferguson failed Ireland on the intellectual plane, so Isaac Butt, having also striven to be something of an 'Irish Matthew Arnold',[70] ultimately failed his nation on the political plane. John Butler Yeats, who idolised Butt as his son William did Parnell,[71] suggested that had he been less of a statesman he could have become 'the idol of Irishmen frenzied with hatred' who were waiting for a Parnell. William O'Brien thought Butt the only man of genius he had known, apart from Gladstone, but believed that when Butt stigmatised Parnellism as 'the policy of exasperation' he hit upon the precise quality which his own politics lacked, but which recommended Parnell to the mass of the Irish people and impressed English opponents.[72] Butt's philosophy of Irish Toryism encompassed a policy of nationality, but it never understood why the Irish believed they had to exasperate England into concessions. It can be suggested, therefore, that Butt only ran a sideshow in the history of Irish nationalism. However, the contribution he made to the creation of a sense of critical ecumenical Irishness in the generation before the famine was not without influence.

The most obvious legacy of pre-famine Irish Toryism was that 'imperial nationalism' with which Butt endowed the early home rule movement. Butt went to Westminster in 1852 and spent his early years as an MP in shady speculation and shadier liaisons, but by 1870 he offered an Ireland which was at last ready for (and was soon to outpace) his ideas, the experience of one who had spent four decades setting out for the Irish people Berkelian queries as to the best foundation for Anglo-Irish relations.[73] However, he did not thereby suddenly become a nationalist. An examination of the pamphlet literature he produced at this time, declaring his political creed and what he understood by 'home government for Ireland', reveals that there had been little change, semantically or politically, from the young don who defended 'home industry' for Ireland in the 1840s. As this chapter has sought to suggest, those who seek to identify a point on Butt's Damascan road as the moment of conversion to the cause of Irish nationalism may be surprised to read in the pamphlets, essays, speeches, lectures and stories Butt wrote between 1833 and 1848 statements which he was able to repeat almost verbatim as 'the father of home rule' in the 1870s.

It was 'equally essential' to the safety of England and to the happiness of Ireland that Irish self-government be restored, wrote Butt in a preface to his *Irish Federalism* in 1870. He had no difficulty declaring, in this home rule manifesto, that he still sought to 'preserve the unity and integrity of the empire'[74] and he was to offer the same security to 'British connexion' four years later when he first introduced a home rule motion in the Commons.[75] It is revealing that Butt did not call himself a nationalist in 1870, but asked whether those who did accept that nomenclature would despise a federal solution. He did not think they would:

> I have more confidence in the sagacity and sober-mindedness of 'Irish Nationalists' than to believe this. I have satisfied myself that in a federal Union, Ireland would exercise a greater influence than she did do, or ever could do, under the Constitution of 1782. I propose that Constitution perfected by a Federal Union with England. This ought to have been done in 1800. Instead of this the Irish Constitution was destroyed.[76]

In the third edition of *Irish Federalism*, a couple of months later, Butt was to sound an even more conservative note, asserting that his object was not to stimulate the desire for national independence but to point out how it was possible 'to realize that independence without breaking up the unity of the empire, interfering with the monarchy, or endangering the rights or liberties of any class of Irishman'.[77]

Some of Butt's readers believed, initially, that his tract was tactically conservative rather than conservative in essence, but it became increasingly clear, as the 1870s progressed, that he saw the *modification* of the Union as necessary for the good of the Irish people and for the safety of the Empire equally. That is, the modification of the Union was necessary because the 1801 experiment had failed as an imperial measure on two counts: it had failed to consolidate the security of the Empire and it failed to allow Irishmen a share in the benefits of imperialism. The Union had been carried when England had been engaged in war with France. With the peace of Europe again uncertain, with the rise of Prussia, Butt suggested that there were lessons to be learned from recent European history. That is, as defeat at Sadowa had led Vienna to realise the potential benefits of bringing Hungary into confederation with Austria, so after the Fenian atrocities and in the light of shifts in the European balance of power, England needed to be encouraged as to the benefits of a federal union with Ireland. That Ireland's leader understood the European and imperial dimensions of the Irish question would, he believed, encourage Westminster to look favourably on his cause.

Discussing the status of the Irish parliament before the Union, Butt again repeated his statements of the 1830s and 1840s: he still held that Ireland had not been, between 1782 and 1800, an independent or sovereign state. The King of England had then acted, with regard to Ireland, on the advice of the English Privy Council and through ministers responsible only to the English Parliament, while Ireland had had no voice in 'the external affairs of the Empire'. Trade too had been dependent upon England, and restrainable, for the English Parliament had possessed the same power of legislating against the importation of Irish products as they would have had against those of Holland.[78] The Union of 1801 had promised to offer Ireland more security than this, but there was an even better solution in what he was to call for with the introduction of home rule at Westminster in 1874: a new Anglo-Irish compact, carried not by 'fraud and coercion', as the Union had been, but with the positive sanction of the Irish people.[79] If Ireland's railways, post office, public works, courts, corporations, education, and commerce and manufactures were brought under home government, then she would, for the first time, enjoy the benefits of government 'attentive to Irish interests' and 'in harmony with Irish feeling' because it would be carried on by ministers of the crown brought into daily contact with representatives of the Irish people. Only such a constitutional relationship between the two sister nations could ensure that Ireland was not governed in a manner to salve English consciences rather than to address directly Irish grievances in their own right: 'Let us have a National Parliament in which Irishmen will learn to manage their own affairs [and] in which national sentiment will find its expression . . . In the teachings of such a parliament we would learn the lessons of national dignity and mutual self-respect'. Much of this any nationalist could approve, but when Butt turned to other issues, his markedly imperial and conservative orientation resurfaced. Countering the fears of those who thought that an Irish Commons would lead to an era of 'democratic violence', he replied that such fears were 'visionary' because:

> There is no people on earth less disposed to democracy than the Irish. The real danger of democracy or revolutionary violence is far more with the English people. The time may not be far distant when a separate Irish parliament might be, in the best sense of the word, the Conservative element in the British Confederation.

Butt was always a constitutional idealist rather than a practical nationalist. He was a party leader who professed that he was above party politics. One specific hope he had of the restoration of an Irish parliament was that the 'Irish Vote' at Westminster would never again be abused for mere party purposes, as it had been so often since 1832. Seven years before the Home Rule Party began to fissure over the issue of obstruction, he denounced 'the illegitimate action of the Irish element in the House of Commons to exercise a decisive effect on the course of politics'.[80]

Such a stance was to lead to the shuffling off of the party of Butt from what was to become, after the 1880 election, incontrovertibly, the party of Parnell. As the latter's historian had it, Butt and his party of gentlemen, believing as they did in 'the persuasive powers of human reason' and in 'the virtues of enlightened oligarchy' were 'more sensitive to the tone of the House at Westminster than to the feelings of [their] constituents in Ireland'. Parnell, by contrast, was 'indifferent to what was thought of him in Westminster, provided that he could secure and retain the confidence of the Irish', and emerged as the leader of the splinter group of 1877 which 'prided itself on its [obstructionist] activity and its contempt for English institutions'.[81]

For all Butt's respect for British constitutional tradition, however, the failure of the Union was directly addressed in *Irish Federalism* when Butt ventured that all the scheme of 1801 had done was to create a race of Irish emigrants hostile to England. That seventy years of union with the richest country in Europe had left Ireland still 'the most wretched', he averred, recalled to his mind Edmund Spenser's prophecy that Ireland's 'fatall destiny' was to be a secret scourge to England. Such prophetic reflection led him to reveal that the role of Providence in history was accepted as confidently in 1870 as it had been when George Miller had written his covert Irish Tory history of Ireland – under the guise of a philosophical analysis of the progress of unity in world history – sixty years earlier. 'I do not envy the man', wrote Butt, 'who can study history [as] the records of detached human actions and who does not see that over [it] there presides an over-ruling power that moulds and fashions the life of nations to some particular purpose'.[82]

As in his Irish fiction, where Butt had often veered between Tory pessimism and nationalist idealism, so at the end of his major party-political pamphlet, having argued rationally for a conservative constitutional adjustment in Anglo-Irish relations, he gave way to romantic assertions of nationhood. Butt voiced great pride in the idea that Ireland had once been a land of saints and scholars and he celebrated the legends of Ireland – notably that of St Brendan and the Irish discovery of America – as 'the instincts of the nation – the presentiments of the future lying deep in the national heart'; that is, as intimations that Ireland had a special destiny. The diffusion of the Irish across the world, he held, led him to share with nine-tenths of Irishmen a belief that: 'The Providence that has watched over the Irish people has designed and is fitting them for some high and noble end'; for some great positive purpose rather than to be the scourge of England – although that threat would remain, he added, falling from the visionary to the critical again, if England continued to promote religious and political dissension among Irishmen for its own sole benefit. For he did not doubt that: 'It was England that made the peoples of Ireland her garrison, upholding them in return in an ascendancy which made the political position of Protestantism odious, not because it was Protestant, but because it was anti-Irish'. Thus the various reflections offered by Butt in his survey of why Ireland was fit for and needed self-government 'to do full justice to our national life'.[83]

This chapter has examined Isaac Butt's use of political and historical rhetoric, political economy and politicised fiction to create a sense of Ireland as a nation under the Union in the 1830s and 1840s. It has sought to reveal that any attempt to pinpoint when Butt 'became a nationalist' can be offset by evidence of earlier emanations of national feeling: the defender of the Fenians of 1868 was no more trenchant in his criticism of the failings of the Union than Young Ireland's advocate of 1848; the author of *Irish Federalism* in 1870 argued the case of Irish nationhood no more plainly than the economist who addressed Lord Roden in 1849. Nor did the old man who returned to Trinity College to address the 'Hist' (the famous College Historical Society) in 1879 associate himself with the perfecting of Grattan's heritage any more resolutely than had the prodigy who, as President of the Society in 1834, had declared it to be the duty of its members to draw together Ireland's youth, regardless of their politics, to train them to benefit their nation:

> I will not believe that better days are not in store for my unhappy, but still my loved, my native land . . . I see food for Ireland. An orator shall yet arise whose voice shall teach her people wisdom and whose efforts shall procure for him the epithet of the father of his country . . . [T]he time will come when faction shall flee away and dissension shall be forgotten, when Ireland's orators and Ireland's statesmen shall only seek their country's good; when the law shall be respected and yet liberty maintained.[84]

Isaac Butt had, from 1833, sought to promote the cause of Irish literature and politics within Britain and to invent a tradition of nationally minded Irish Tory avatars to challenge O'Connell's conception of Irish nationality. In this, he predated the writers of *The Nation* and gave them a national vein to work. The latter's success, under Thomas Davis, was in more confidently and widely disseminating ideas which Butt had already suggested in the Irish Metropolitan Conservative Society, had sent to the big houses and glebe-houses of Ireland through the *DUM* and had shared with the scions of the ascendancy in his economic lectures at Trinity. Thomas Davis extended, but he did not create the national spirit of pre-famine Ireland; he has to share the credit with that uncertain national unionist, Isaac Butt, who had never set the *ne plus ultra* to his vision of the imperial progress of Ireland, and who never would.[85]

NOTES

1 The most interesting of recent short reflections is W.J. McCormack, 'Isaac Butt and the inner failure of Protestant home rule', in Ciaran Brady (ed.), *Worsted in the Game: Losers in Irish History* (Dublin, 1989), pp. 121–31.
2 See, however, D. George Boyce, *Nationalism in Ireland* (London, 1982), pp. 192–9, for a very useful brief analysis. Butt is also carefully treated by F.S.L. Lyons, *Ireland since the Famine* (London, 1973), pp. 147–58.
3 T.P. O'Connor, *Memoirs of an Old Parliamentarian* (London, 1929), 2 vols, who saw Butt's pursuit of pleasure as 'but the misnomer for the flight from despair', thought his early

fiction had 'a vein of the morbid melancholy of Alfred de Musset' (quoted in Terence de Vere White, *The Road of Excess* (Dublin, 1946), p. 25).

4 W.M. Murphy, *Prodigal Father: The Life of John Butler Yeats* (Cornell, 1979), pp. 31, 551n.

5 See National Library of Ireland Ms. 8701 (letters to Butt and cheques made out by him, c. 1868–77) and NLI Ms. 830 (John Butler Yeats's reminiscences, 16 April 1913: on Butt's secret family in Drumcondra).

6 David Thornley, *Isaac Butt and Home Rule* (London, 1964), p. 20.

7 See R.F. Foster, 'Varieties of Irishness: cultures and anarchy in Ireland', in *Paddy & Mr Punch: Connections in Irish and English History* (Harmondsworth, 1993), pp. 26–7. The case of Butt, Lever and Ferguson as nationally minded conservatives (and descendants of Burke) is discussed by D. George Boyce, 'Trembling solicitude: Irish conservatism, nationality and public opinion, 1833–86', in D. George Boyce, R. Eccleshall and V. Geoghegan (eds), *Political Thought in Ireland since the Seventeenth Century* (London, 1993), pp. 124–45.

8 Charles Stuart Stanford, first editor of the *Dublin University Magazine*, to W.E. Gladstone, 21 February, 19 May, 23 August 1834, and Butt, having taken over as editor, to Gladstone, 22 September 1834, in the Gladstone Papers, British Library Add. Mss. 44354, fols. 26, 34, 54, 56. See also my 'Nationality and Irish Toryism: the case of the *Dublin University Magazine*, 1833–52', *Journal of Newspaper and Periodical History*, 4 (Autumn 1988), pp. 2–17.

9 Article intended for the *DUM*, May 1834, Gladstone Papers, Add. Ms. 44681, fol. 12.

10 See [Butt], 'Corporation Reform', *DUM*, 6 (August 1835), pp. 118–24, and 'The Irish Church Abolition Bill', *DUM*, 6 (August 1835), pp. 125–40.

11 Sir Robert Peel to Messrs Simpkin Marshall, publishers, 23 October [1835]. Transcript in the bookseller Andrew Jones's *Catalogue 87/3* (privately printed, Oxford, 1987), pp. 27–8.

12 Butt to Peel, 11 and 28 December 1835, in the Peel Papers, BL Add. Mss. 40421, fols. 95, 131.

13 *DUM*, 6 (December 1835), p. 682.

14 K.T. Hoppen, *Elections, Politics and Society in Ireland, 1832–1885* (Oxford, 1985), p. 278.

15 Charles Boyton to Baron Farnham, 29 February 1832, NLI Farnham Papers Ms. 18609 (4).

16 Boyton to Farnham, 14 and 15 December 1830 and [December 1830/January 1831], Farnham Papers, Ms. 18609 (2, 4).

17 Boyton to Farnham, 29 February 1832, ibid., Ms. 18609 (4), and Charles Boyton, *Speech at the Protestant Conservative Society . . . 10 July 1832* (Dublin, 1832).

18 Daniel O'Connell to P.V. Fitzpatrick [February 1833] and O'Connell to Remmy Sheehan, editor of the Tory *Dublin Evening Mail*, March 1833 and 16 July 1834, in M.R. O'Connell (ed.), *The Correspondence of Daniel O'Connell* (Dublin, 1975), V.

19 *DUM*, 1 (April, 1833), p. 459, and 2 (December 1833), p. 606.

20 Address of the Home Government Association, Dublin, November 1870. Roy Foster has highlighted the connexions between the Irish Tories of the 1830s and the early HGA in 'Parnell and his people: the ascendancy and home rule', in *Paddy & Mr Punch*, pp. 62–77.

21 As late as 1875 Butt would still be counselling his MPs that their duty was to make 'honest and intelligent Englishmen realise to themselves the deficiencies of their Irish government' (*The Nation*, 29 May 1875). On Butt's imperialism, see Thornley, *Isaac Butt*, pp. 380–1.

22 See Jacqueline Hill, *From Patriots to Unionists: Dublin Civic Politics and Irish Protestant Patriotism, 1660–1840* (Oxford, 1997), pp. 376–83.

23 See the Ledger of the Members of the Antient and Loyal Society of the Aldermen of Skinners' Alley [c. 1800–60] and the Minutes of the Aldermen of Skinners' Alley, 4 December 1842, Royal Irish Academy MS 23/H/51–52.

24 *The Nation*, 24 March 1844.

25 *Report . . . of the Irish Metropolitan Conservative Society* (Dublin, 1836), pp. 4–12, 37–41.

26 Sheridan Le Fanu to his mother [August 1840], NLI Le Fanu papers, n. 2,976.

27 W.J. McCormack, *Sheridan Le Fanu and Victorian Ireland* (Oxford, 1980), p. 85.

28 De Vere White, *Road of Excess*, p. 67.

29 Butt, *Speech delivered on 28th February 1843 on Repeal of the Union* (Dublin, 1843).

30 *The Nation*, 11 March 1843.

31 *The Warder*, 28 September 1844.

32 *Dublin Evening Mail*, 29 September and 5 November 1847.

33 The *Warder*, 13 March 1848. See also Lady [Mary] Ferguson, *Sir Samuel Ferguson in the Ireland of his Day* (London, 1893), pp. 207–8.

34 See the dedicatory inscription from T.F. Meagher (3 June 1849) in Butt's copy of Thomas Davis's edition of *The Speeches of John Philpot Curran* (Dublin, 1845) now in the British Library at shelf-mark 12301.L.20.

35 Quoted in de Vere White, *The Road of Excess*, pp. 118–20.

36 Hoppen, *Elections, Politics and Society*, p. 327.

37 Donal MacCartney, 'The writing of history in Ireland, 1800–1830', *Irish Historical Studies*, 10 (September 1957), p. 352.

38 George Miller, *Lectures on the Philosophy of Modern History* (Dublin, 1816), I, Preface, pp. vii, xiii. For a philosophical context, see the discussion of Kant's *Perpetual Peace* (1795) in Murray Forsyth, *Unions of States: The Theory and Practice of Confederation* (Leicester, 1981), pp. 95–104.

39 James Prior, *Life of Goldsmith* (London, 1837), I, Preface. See also James Wills, *Lives of Illustrious and Distinguished Irishmen* (Dublin, 1839–47), 6 vols, comprising 2,500 pages of political, literary and ecclesiastical biography, mainly focusing on the characters who played their part in the evolution of the Irish Nation from 1760–1800.

40 *DUM*, 7 (January 1836), pp. 26–30.

41 Isaac Butt, *History of Italy* (London, 1860), p. 11.

42 See Oliver MacDonagh, *States of Mind: A Study of Anglo-Irish Conflict, 1780–1980* (London, 1983), p.14, and Foster, 'History and the Irish question', in *Paddy & Mr Punch*, pp. 1–20.

43 See R.D.C. Black, 'The Irish dissenters and nineteenth-century political economy', in A.E. Murphy (ed.), *Economists and the Irish Economy* (Dublin, 1984), pp. 120–37. See also T.A. Boylan and T.P. Foley, *Political Economy and Colonial Ireland* (London, 1992), especially pp. 1–43.

44 Isaac Butt, *An Introductory Lecture on Political Economy* (Dublin, 1837), *passim*.

45 Isaac Butt, *Protection to Home Industry* (Dublin, 1846), p. 108. Recent research suggests that Butt's 'highly selective set of tariffs' would have made only a modest impact on the Irish economy, see Liam Kennedy and David S. Johnson, 'The Union of Ireland and Britain', in D. George Boyce and Alan O'Day (eds), *The Making of Modern Irish History: Revisionism and the Revisionist Controversy* (London, 1996), p. 49.

46 John Mitchel, *Irish Political Economy* (Dublin, 1847), pp. 9, 35.

47 This was a view Butt first expressed in *The Poor Law Bill for Ireland Examined* (London, 1837).

48 This pamphlet first appeared as an article in the *DUM*, 29 (April 1847), pp. 501–40.

49 Isaac Butt, *The Rate in Aid: A Letter to the Earl of Roden* (Dublin, 1849), pp. 65–8, *passim*.

50 Ibid., advertisement, 10 April 1849.

51 'Writers on Irish character', *DUM*, 1 (January 1833), p. 41

52 [Isaac Butt], 'The present state of literature in Ireland', *DUM*, 9 (March 1837), pp. 365–76.

53 'Perils of the Irish Poor', *DUM*, 1 (January 1833), pp. 73–86, and 'Village Annals', *DUM*, 1 (February–March 1833), pp. 174–84, 304–17 have been suggested as early tales by Butt.

54 'The Bribed Scholar', *DUM*, 8 (October 1836), pp. 435–47.

55 See, for example, J.C. Mangan, 'The Man in the Cloak', *DUM*, 12 (November 1838), pp. 552–68.

56 'The Murdered Fellow', *DUM*, 5 (March 1835), pp. 332–52. See also my 'The great angelic sin: the Faust legend in Irish literature, 1800–1900', *Bullán: An Irish Studies Journal*, 1 (Autumn 1994), pp. 47–58.

57 [Isaac Butt], *Irish Life in the Castle, the Courts and the Country* (London, 1840), I, pp. vi–vii. In spite of the grandiose title, it should be noted that Butt's novel did not really survey Irish life outside the capital.

58 See Isaac Butt, *Speech delivered at the bar of the House of Lords on the Municipal Corporation Reform Bill* (London, 1840).

59 *Irish Life*, pp. 28–9, 71–2. Compare these pages with W.M. Thackeray, *Irish Sketch Book of 1842* (London, 1990 edition), pp. 363–4. Butt was chosen by Charles Lever as Thackeray's guide around Dublin in 1842, Lever suggesting that he was 'in a question of "cram" equal to anything from the Siege of Troy to Donnybrook Fair'; quoted in W.J. Fitzpatrick, *The Life of Charles Lever* (London, 1884), p. 185.

60 John Banim, *The Anglo-Irish in the Nineteenth-century* (London, 1828), I, pp. 225–6; *Irish Life*, I, pp. 86–8, 119; II, pp. 242–3. Other Irish Tory novels of the period also examined the sham-court and/or the faded greatness of Dublin; see, for example, Sheridan Le Fanu, *The Cock and the Anchor* (Dublin, 1845) and W.H. Maxwell, *O'Hara, or 1798* (London, 1825).

61 *Irish Life*, I, pp. 170–1 and III, pp. 243–9.

62 For a fuller analysis of this subject, see my 'Allegories for a Protestant nation: Irish Tory historical fiction, 1820–1850', *Religion and Literature*, 28 (Summer–Autumn 1996), pp. 59–78.

63 Isaac Butt, *The Gap of Barnesmore* (London, 1848), I, pp. 5–12.

64 W.B. Yeats to Fr Matthew Russell, 1889; quoted in Thomas Flanagan, *The Irish Novelists, 1800–1850* (New York, 1959), p. vii.

65 Charles Gavan Duffy, *Young Ireland* (London, 1880), pp. 501–2.

66 Butt, *Gap of Barnesmore*, III, pp. 16–20.

67 See, for example Isaac Butt, *National Education for Ireland* (Dublin, 1854); *Land Tenure in Ireland: A Plea for the Celtic Race* (Dublin, 1866); and *The Irish People and the Irish Land* (Dublin, 1867).

68 Samuel Ferguson, 'A Dialogue between the head and the heart of an Irish Protestant', *DUM*, 2 (November 1833), pp. 586–93.

69 *DUM*, 3 (April 1834), p. 457.

70 Terry Eagleton, *Heathcliff and the Great Hunger: Studies in Irish Culture* (London, 1995), p. 237.

71 Malcolm Brown, *The Politics of Irish Literature: From Thomas Davis to W.B. Yeats* (London, 1972), pp. 230–39, suggests Butt was the ideal Yeatsian politician and traces lines of continuity from Butt to W.B. Yeats: 'Isaac Butt's political ideal was proto-Yeatsian. He deplored rancour, party strife, and loose-lipped demagogues. His code of conduct was pure but futile, and he was quickly overwhelmed in the parliamentary jungle' (p. 239). For an exploration of the roots of Yeatsian politics and its broader cultural impact, see Edward Said, *Culture and Imperialism* (London, 1993), pp. 265–88.

72 John Butler Yeats's (16 April 1913) and William O'Brien's responses to Frank MacDonagh's requests for reminiscences for a proposed life of Butt, c. 1913, NLI Ms. 830.

73 See Butt, *The Irish Querist* (Dublin, 1867), his version of Berkeley's Irish tract *The Querist* (1735–7). See also his lecture *Berkeley* (Dublin, 1860).

74 Advertisement to the first edition of Butt's *Irish Federalism: Home Government for Ireland* (Dublin, 1870), 15 August 1870, p. v. *Irish Federalism* was one of a number of Butt's Irish tracts to be read by Gladstone; see H.C.G. Matthew (ed.), *The Gladstone Diaries* (Oxford, 1986), IX, p. 95 (6 January 1876).

75 *Parliamentary Debates [PD]*, 3rd series, 220 (30 June 1874), c. 700.

76 Advertisement to the first edition of *Irish Federalism*, p. v.

77 Advertisement to the third edition of *Irish Federalism* (Dublin, 1870), 2 November 1870, p. ix. In the body of the text he coolly asserted: 'I know that the best and wisest of Irish Nationalists believe with me that Ireland ought, by all possible means, to maintain her connexion with England' (p. 45).

78 *Irish Federalism*, pp. 24–6.

79 *PD*, 220 (30 June 1874), c. 700.

80 *Irish Federalism*, pp. 37–9, 47–8.

81 Conor Cruise O'Brien, *Parnell and his Party, 1880–90* (Oxford, 1957), pp. 4, 21, 23.

82 *Irish Federalism*, p. 57.

83 Ibid., pp. 42–3, 57–9, 62–5.

84 See Butt's 'Address to the College Historical Society', 1834, NLI Ms. 13,151.

85 A short version of this chapter appeared as 'Isaac Butt, nationality and Irish Toryism, 1833–52', *Bullán: An Irish Studies Journal*, 2 (Summer 1995), pp. 45–60. My thanks to Ray Ryan for allowing its reappearance here. For an analysis of the political and intellectual context within which Butt wrote, see my thesis, 'The philosophy of Irish Toryism, 1833–1852: a study of reactions to Liberal reformism in Ireland in the generation between the first Reform Act and the famine', University of London, Ph.D., 1991.

5 Defending the Union

Parliamentary opinions, 1869 and 1886[1]

Alan O'Day

> What is the essence of the Union; that is the question. It is impossible to determine what is and what is not the repeal of the Union, until you settle what is the essence of the Union. Well, I define the essence of the Union to be this – that before the Act of Union there were two independent, separate, co-ordinated Parliaments; after the Act of Union there was but one. A supreme statutory authority of the Imperial Parliament over Great Britain, Scotland, and Ireland as one United Kingdom was established by the Act of Union. That supreme statutory authority it is not asked, so far as I am aware, and certainly it is not intended, in the slightest degree to impair.
>
> (W.E. Gladstone's introduction of the Government of Ireland Bill, 1886)[2]

> I do not care whether Ireland is one or two nations; at any rate, she is not a foreign nation but an integral part of the British Empire . . . We know that the seat of Irish Government must be somewhere and we prefer that it should be here, where the scales of justice can be held evenly.
>
> (A.W. Hall, 1886)[3]

Introduction

When introducing the Home Rule Bill in 1886 Gladstone defended the continued existence of the Union in terms of the formal powers to be devolved to an assembly in Dublin. This delegated authority would not breach the Act of Union, he pleaded. As seen in the extract above, Gladstone viewed the Union in terms of a statutory conferment which invested supreme authority in the Imperial Parliament. What Parliament made, it could alter. 'While I think it is right to modify the Union in some particulars, we are not about to propose its repeal', he pronounced.[4] Gladstone was careful to point out that what was given to Ireland could not be denied to Scotland should people there demand the same treatment.[5] Many, indeed the majority of the House of Commons and the electorate, were not persuaded by Gladstone's vision of the Union in 1886, though by 1921 the essence of his reasoning was adopted by a Conservative-dominated coalition administration.[6] In contrast, Gladstone's opponents in 1869 and more especially in 1886 saw the Union as an integrative link. Gathorne Hardy in 1869 held that the Union was not just a structural link through the crown and by a Westminster Parliament invested with a theoretically ultimate authority, but implied equality of treatment and the congruence of the modes of governance for the United Kingdom as a whole. He protested:

> Mr O'Connell and others use to say – 'Give us like institutions'; but now the demand is – 'Give us unlike institutions; let Ireland be governed on Irish principles' and you are endeavouring to make a severance of this Imperial realm, and to put Ireland on a different footing from England[7]

In 1886 the Marquess of Hartington underlined this interpretation:

> if the kingdoms are to be made a United Kingdom, the people of this country will never tolerate any marked or real inequality between the institutions of the Three Kingdoms, and that they will demand that perhaps not identical, but practical, equality of institutions shall be conceded to Ireland.[8]

'One Throne, one law, and one Parliament' was E.W. Beckett's succinct declamation in 1886.[9]

It is often suggested that the first home rule incident gave British Conservatives a compelling ideology – to defend the Union. This cause, it is alleged, diminished during the war of 1914 to 1918; then in 1921 a Conservative-dominated coalition broke the Union for three-quarters of Ireland. Still, a sticking point in the negotiations over the treaty in autumn 1921 was David Lloyd George's refusal to grant a republic: the link of the crown must be retained for southern Ireland. The Irish Free State would be granted virtually full autonomy in domestic matters but foreign relations remained the preserve of the imperial government, the right to appeal to the Privy Council was retained and some other topics were reserved to Westminster. Ireland received limited sovereignty and something of the Union thereby was incorporated in the Anglo-Irish Treaty, but this was not the Union as it was understood before 1886. During the home rule debates in 1886 the Attorney-General, Sir Charles Russell, defined the Act of Union in terms anticipating later events. After claiming that he could find no satisfactory definition of the Act, Russell suggested, 'no doubt, under the bill, this [Westminster] Parliament ceases to legislate for all purposes for all parts of the United Kingdom; but it continues to be the paramount authority for all purposes, the sole authority for Imperial purposes residing in the permanent authority of the Parliament of the United Kingdom'.[10] The treaty was a species of union reflective of the shifting relationship between Great Britain and the old 'white' dependencies.

Recently, it has been argued that the concept of employing the Union as a touch-stone of Conservatism can be dated to the last year of Benjamin Disraeli's life.[11] This same author subsequently suggests that after 1868 Disraeli's interest in Irish affairs declined; it was only in 1886 that 'Ireland became part of the Conservatives' domestic political ideology through the defence of the Union, a development which was as much the product of Gladstone's political dynamism

as had been the defeat of Disraeli's church politics in 1868'.[12] This surely exaggerates the position; references to the Union continued to pepper Conservative
rhetoric in the years between 1868 and 1886 but certainly its maintenance took
on an urgency after 1886 if only because then the Anglo-Irish bond seemed on
the verge of severance. Expanding upon views enunciated by Gathorne Hardy
and Hartington, A.V. Dicey formulated the classic case for its defence in 1886,
insisting that it was an obligation and perhaps even a burden:

> whatever be the difficulties (and they are many) of maintaining the Union,
> not in form only but in reality, the policy is favoured no less by the current of
> English history, than by the tendencies of modern civilisation. It preserves the
> unity of the State which is essential to the authority of England and to the
> maintenance of the Empire. It provides, as matters now stand, the only
> means of giving legal protection to a large body of loyal British subjects. It is
> the refusal not only to abdicate legitimate power, but (what is of far more
> consequence) to renounce the fulfilment of imperative duties. Nor does
> Union imply uniformity. Unity of Government – equality of rights – diversity
> of institutions, – these are the watchwords for all Unionists. To attain these
> objects may be beyond our power, and the limit to power is the limit to
> responsibility. Still, whatever may be the difficulties, or even the disadvan-
> tages, of maintaining the Union, it undoubtedly has in its favour not only all
> the recommendations which must belong to a policy of rational conserva-
> tism, but also these two decisive advantages – that it does sustain the strength
> of the United Kingdom, and that it does not call for any dereliction of duty.[13]

The analyses which currently reflect scholarly thinking generally minimise earlier affirmations of the Union, and, perhaps more importantly, treat the Union as
static and institutional. Dicey, in contrast, viewed the Union as a vibrant organ-
ism. This investigation examines perceptions of the Union and what various
public figures believed they were defending. It suggests that those who adopted
Gladstonian home rule in 1886 tended to adopt a moral view of the Union,
judging it by its supposed utility while opponents typically saw it as an organic
connexion, though one open to modification. Ironically, because the centre-right
in British politics held to an interpretation of Ireland as an integral portion of the
United Kingdom, it was better adapted to advocate constructive remedies than
the centre-left which increasingly pictured the Emerald Isle as different, even
'foreign'.

Absorption of Ireland into the Union caused an upheaval in Great Britain for it
introduced a substantial enclave of Catholics into a Protestant, and in 1801,
confessional state. This challenge to national identity spurred the search for a
viable new ethos based on a multinational, religiously tolerant and pluralistic
community. The literature on nationalism tends to emphasise the rise of nascent
or emergent 'communities' with the demand for a distinctive 'national state' cor-
responding to the 'nation'. Nationalism, thus, is pitted against the rival claims of
the currently dominant state. However, the defence of the Union demonstrates

that dominant states faced with emergent 'nations' within their own boundaries strive to reinvent themselves by much the same process. As the Union was the cornerstone of a state based on the incorporation of the whole of the British Isles, notions about its legitimacy, utility and content were vital to the formulation of a new 'nationality' – British – not merely English, Welsh, Scottish or Irish. Four issues ran through in the Irish controversy in the nineteenth century – responses to the Protestant ecclesiastical establishment; political legitimacy based on numbers; the nature of citizenship; and whether Irish Catholics could be integrated into the fabric of the community. These were not questions admitting to simple answers and their outcome was vital to establishing whether a unified culture or a multi-national, religiously diverse pluralist community should be the goal. The Union was an important ingredient in the debate.

The parliamentary discussions on the Irish Church Bill in 1869 and the Government of Ireland Bill in 1886 illuminate and amplify the problems of identity, centring on conceptions of the Union. Although in 1869 only the confessional link in the Act of Union was openly challenged, the wider question of what constituted a United Kingdom and the Union was taken up implicitly; in 1886 under the impact of a direct threat to the Union these points were raised explicitly. Though there was a parallel public discussion, the key themes were articulated during parliamentary debates. In the later Victorian era Parliament, particularly the House of Commons, had an exceptional place in political culture. Walter Bagehot's contemporary *The English Constitution* pointed out that the House of Commons was the 'efficient' part of the constitution, the cockpit of responsible government with five major functions, of which three – expressing of the mind of the nation 'on all matters which come before it'; teaching the country 'what it does not know'; and informing the sovereign people of complaints and grievances – lay at the heart of the debates of 1869 and 1886.[14] During the discussion of the proposed home rule measure Gladstone employed the forum of Westminster as a school room. Speakers on the Church Bill in 1869 sought to express the mind of the nation 'on all matters which come before it' and inform the sovereign people of complaints and grievances about the ecclesiastical establishment in Ireland. As Lord Henry Scott observed, 'true, it was not possible for the opponents of the Bill to defeat it by a numerical majority; but it was nevertheless their duty, both as a party and as men holding conscientious views on the subject, to strive to have the country well informed upon the whole matter'.[15]

The Union of Great Britain and Ireland came into effect on 1 January 1801. Its birth was a matter of dispute and almost immediately there were calls, periodically reiterated, for its repeal. Daniel O'Connell in the 1840s mounted a popular movement for repeal, but the Union's existence was not seriously imperilled before 1886. Essential features of the Act of Union were:

1   the two kingdoms were 'for ever, be united into one kingdom';
2   that succession to the crown would be 'settled, according to the existing laws, and to the terms of Union between England and Scotland'; the 'United

Kingdom [would] be represented in one and the same Parliament' in which Ireland would have a specified number of seats in both houses;

3   the unification of the Churches of Ireland and England; and
4   that His Majesty's subjects for economic intercourse 'be entitled to the same privileges, and be on the same footing'.[16]

Since its creation the Union was an unloved stepchild. For this there are many reasons – the supposed corrupt means resorted to for its passage, disappointment with the effects and an Irish patriotic challenge which, if nothing else, scored heavily in the historical debate.[17] This stereotypical patriotic Irish view of the Union was aired in 1869 by a member for Dublin, Sergeant Dowse:

> The bulk of the Irish people were no parties to it. It was made behind the backs of the Irish Catholics and Nonconformists. The Protestant Anglicans confined within the walls of their privileges made the treaty, and their descendants insisted that the Irish nation should be bound by what had been done although they were never consulted in regard to it. But the treaty had, since the Union, been subjected to the revision of Parliament.[18]

Nor was this vilification restricted to Irish members. During the debates in 1869, the Quaker John Bright, President of the Board of Trade, identified the policy behind the Act of Union as 'wise' but stated 'the mode by which it was brought about was one of unexampled corruption and wrong'. 'I am for Union as much as any Gentleman on that side of the House, but I am for a real Union', Bright proclaimed.[19]

Liberals did not have a monopoly on this perspective. The Conservative, Sir Stafford Northcote, accepted that:

> the Roman Catholic population of Ireland were in every sense of the word a down-trodden people. They were excluded, not only from political privileges and right, not only from a share in the representation of the country, and even from the right of voting for representatives; but they were even excluded from the liberal professions, from every social privilege, and from the ordinary rights of citizens in regard to the tenure of land.[20]

However, the situation had been transformed: 'the Roman Catholics are now admitted to an equality with Protestants in all matters affecting their political and social position'. Yet, Northcote recognised, 'there is no defence whatever to be made for the conduct which this country pursued towards Ireland for a very long series of years . . . I will yield to no man in the desire to act fairly and even liberally toward Ireland. We owe her, I think, great reparation for great and long continued wrong'.[21] Northcote's viewpoint was a precursor to what was later labelled 'constructive unionism'.

The Irish Church Bill, 1869

The late 1860s ushered in an extended era when Irish controversies were at the centre of British politics and the Church Bill foreshadowed this obsession. John Morley in 1868 pinpointed why Ireland should assume a position which it had not had since the 1820s, 'underneath the surface of this, and wrapped up in it, are nearly all the controversies of principle which will agitate the political atmosphere of our time'.[22] Surprisingly, despite its recognised significance, the Church Act usually receives brief notice. Morley, who gives it more attention than most subsequent commentators, nevertheless states 'the details are no longer of concern, and only broader aspects survive'. In this he is followed by J.L. Hammond, who observes merely that 'it is unnecessary to relate in detail the negotiations that ended in the passing of the Bill, or to discuss the particular degree of credit due to the different actors'.[23] Richard Shannon devotes little more than a page to the episode in the second volume of his biography of Gladstone, though he identifies it as his 'great legislative centrepiece'.[24] This legislation was a crucial moment in Gladstone's career, exemplifying two key principles: an attack upon the entrenched privileges of the few at the expense of the many and the link between Church and state. Existing commentary focuses on the technicalities of the legislation for dismantling the legal status of the Church of Ireland, political arguments for disestablishment, manoeuvres to gain passage, and the adaptation of the Church to voluntary status.[25] The parliamentary discussions raged over details of the measure, the role of religion in society, threats to property rights and similar concerns. Only a small portion of speeches pertained directly to the status of the Union, though many assumptions about it were encapsulated in these discussions.

Disestablishment had been fiercely debated for a generation. For 1868 the *Annual Register* recorded:

> It may, indeed, almost be said that the entire political interest of the present session was concentrated on the question of the Irish Church, and as soon as the existence of the Parliament came to an end the scene of the controversy was merely shifted, and the issue transferred from the benches of the House of Commons to the hustings of the three kingdoms.[26]

Although Ireland was not the sole matter before the much enlarged electorate, Gladstone advocated that by 'the removal of this Establishment I see the discharge of a debt of civil justice, the disappearance of a national, almost a world-wide reproach, a condition indispensable to the success of every effort to secure the peace and contentment of that country'.[27] Three hundred and eighty-two Liberals, including sixty-five from Ireland, were returned; Conservatives were in a minority with 276 seats. A change in the status of the Irish Church was inevitable, a fact which invited MPs to stake out positions and to articulate an ideology of the Union. The Church Bill pertained to Article 5 of the Act of Union:

[T]he Churches of England and Ireland, as now by law established, be united into one Protestant Episcopal Church, to be called *The United Church of England and Ireland,* and that the doctrine, worship, discipline and government of the said United Church shall be, and shall remain in full force for ever, as the same are now by law established for the Church of England; and that the continuance and preservation of the said United Church, as the Established Church of England and Ireland, shall be deemed and taken to be an essential and fundamental part of the union.[28]

The Queen's Speech at the opening of Parliament in 1869 promised 'the constant aim to promote the welfare of religion through its principles of equal justice, to secure the action of the undivided feeling and opinion of Ireland on the side of loyalty and law, to efface the memory of former contentions, and to cherish the sympathies of an affectionate people'.[29] Disestablishment was promoted by Liberals as a limited incursion into the Act of Union, justified by the need to conciliate the majority of people in Ireland to the remaining and more crucial parts of the Union. A bill was introduced by Gladstone in the House of Commons and read for the first time on 1 March; the second reading was moved on 18 March and debated on the 19th and 22nd, passing this phase on 23 March; the committee stage opened on 15 April, continuing on 16, 19, 22 and 29 April, then on 3, 4, 6, 7 May, being reported on the last date; on 12 May the bill as amended was considered; it was recommitted and considered on 28 May; then carried the third reading on 31 May.[30] It was enacted on 26 July, coming to force on 1 January 1871. This Irish Church measure, Donald Akenson observes, 'as an exercise in legislative draftsmanship . . . was an impressive, political document'; Colin Matthew notes that it was a technically complex proposal.[31] Gladstone devised the measure almost entirely on his own, as he would do again with the Government of Ireland Bill in 1886. Its main features were ending the established position of the Church of Ireland; separating it legally from the Church of England; disendowing the Church; making arrangements for the transfer of its assets to a new ecclesiastical body; creation of an interim agency to facilitate the transition between the eras of establishment and disestablishment; providing compensation for lost interests; conversion of annual grants to a once and for all sum for Catholic and Presbyterian theological training; and sequestration of surplus church revenues along with their application to the general welfare.[32] The scheme was warmly welcomed by Catholics who saw the establishment as an affront, by Irish Presbyterians who also resented the status of the Church of Ireland, by Nonconformists in Great Britain who desired to end all confessional establishments and by the great mass of Liberal supporters who identified the Irish Church with wealth and privilege.

Advocates of disestablishment developed several themes: that the Church as the personification of ascendancy stood in the path of reconciling all Irish people to the Union, it was an anomaly, that real union rested on bonds of sympathy. Their attitude was shaped by a utilitarian and relativist outlook. This bill was, as Gladstone observed, the first major alteration of the Act of Union:

The act of Union has been altered on other occasions, though never for so grave a cause as this; but we shall confidently contend that while we are altering this particular provision of the Act of Union, we are confirming its general purport and substance, and labouring to the best of our humble ability to give it those roots which unfortunately it has never yet adequately struck in the heart and affections of the people.[33]

Its chief deficiency was that only 11 to 13 per cent of the people in Ireland belonged to it. The Solicitor General, Sir John Duke Coleridge, summed it up as the Church of a 'miserable minority of the population and cannot place its interest against the interest of the great majority of the people'.[34] The Chancellor of the Exchequer, Robert Lowe, propounded the argument, saying 'you may have lost the support of a small clique, but you will have conciliated the nation'.[35] Then he observed,

> the State Church in Ireland is not the national Church, and the national Church is not the State Church . . . We should look upon the whole subject, not from a legal or sentimental point of view but from the most elevated point of view which we can take – that is, as a matter of justice and conscience.

Sir Roundall Palmer, though, a critic of disendowment but not of disestablishment, made an interjection which Shannon notes 'centred dangerously around the implications of Irish Church disestablishment for the Union'.[36] He admitted there was 'a real crisis in Ireland . . . and I cannot but think we are called upon more than at any previous period, deeply to consider the causes of this evil, and discover, if we can, a remedy for these causes', proposing, 'we must approach the question of any political privilege given to the Church by considering whether the privilege is for the public good'. Palmer, then, contended,

> The duty of civil government is to govern all and every part of the country committed to its charge with impartiality and justice and with regard to those interests which it belongs to human laws to protect. National religion, as I understand it, is not any profession, embodied in laws, or forms and ceremonies, made by those who are at the head of the Government; but it is the religion of the people who constitute the nation.

The case for revising the Union was that 'adjustments of institutions to the necessities of civil government, as time went on simply tended to make the Government a more true and faithful representative of the social conditions and actual state of the people', while, as he alleged, 'the exclusion of any classes of persons from their fair share of political power, on the ground that they do not belong to a dominant Church is no longer recognised as being good either for the State or for the Church'.[37]

Sir Henry Lytton Bulwer reaffirmed the need to amend the Union, stating 'we do not intend to violate or repeal this Act [of Union]. We intend to alter it'.[38] This was essential because 'Ireland has altered'. He proceeded to give an account of the main ingredients of the changed circumstances, pointing out that it was not simply that the Church of Ireland commanded only minority allegiance but that the admission of Catholics to political citizenship spelled a need to end the current position. Accordingly, Bulwer argued,

> when this Act was passed only Protestants had political power in Ireland. At this time Protestants and Catholics exercised political power on equal terms. The political Ireland of today is not the political Ireland of seventy years ago and therefore, wishing our political Union with Ireland to be a political reality and not a political fiction, we change our arrangements with Ireland to suit the change which has occurred in Irish affairs.

Bulwer also contrasted the present situation with that when the Church was given legal status, emphasising the modern principle of state impartiality to all religions in Ireland:

> The Protestant Church was one of the instruments they employed to obtain this ascendancy. It was easy for philosophers and historians to say that the State might at that time have taken up an independent position between religious parties. The State itself was then a religious party; and as long as it had been itself a religious party it was quite rational, and for its interests expedient, to pay and maintain a religious party Establishment. But now that the State, amid an entire change of circumstances, has ceased to be exclusively Protestant, it can no longer exclusively pay and patronise a Prot-estant priesthood. The Irish Church I say, is, and ever has been the shadow and servant of the State, and must follow the policy of the State, which was formerly to favour one religion and is now to be impartial to all religions.[39]

Earl Granville in the House of Lords simply declared, 'the Irish Church is a great anomaly, [in] that it has not fulfilled the position which it was intended to fill, and that it is a great injustice to the people of Ireland'.[40]

Conservatives determined to resist the bill but most granted that the Act of Union could be altered. Disraeli concentrated on the essential linkage between religion and the state which he maintained the bill would break. Yet, he raised crucial points about the character of the Union. In his estimation it was vital in order to give Ireland suitably effective administration, to train the Irish over what necessarily would be an extended period into practices essential to sound govern-ment, while the disorderly state of Ireland was evidence of the need to uphold the present connexion. It was his contention that,

> the Government of Ireland is not a strong Government: its sanctions are less valid than those of the Government of England. It has not the historic basis which the English Government has. It has not the tradition which the English Government rests upon. It does not depend upon the vast accumulation of

manners and customs which in England are really more powerful than laws and statutes. The Government of Ireland is only comparatively strong from its connection with England; and the reason the Government of Ireland is a weak Government is that a considerable portion of the inhabitants of Ireland are disorderly and discontented.[41]

Northcote denied that there was any 'new policy' or a 'more cordial and friendly tone which England adopts', pointing out, 'for a great many years and throughout the political life-time of all the public men of the present day, we have been steadily pursuing a course towards Ireland which was intended to have, and which has had, the effect of very much improving relations between the two countries'.[42] He objected that the proposed measure would interrupt the continuity of an approach to bring about the better condition of Ireland and its relations with Great Britain, calling for

> the continuance of the policy on which this country has been acting for the last thirty or forty years – tentatively no doubt – slowly and imperfectly, perhaps, but at the same time with very satisfactory results. Those results are, of course, not yet completely satisfactory . . . [and] require a long course of just and considerable legislation.

Perhaps most pertinently, Northcote insisted that in a United Kingdom

> England is not for the English, nor Ireland for the Irish [because] anything which tends to bring about such a result, and to close up the sympathy of the two countries for one another, and to diminish the influence when the one ought to have on the other, will be bad for both.

The Earl of Harrowby in the House of Lords conceded: 'I cannot say that the Act of Union is in itself for ever an insuperable bar to all change – I do not believe that any act of legislation can tie up all posterity'.[43]

Less compromising Conservatives defended the Union as an agreement etched in stone. Sir George Jenkinson maintained, 'the whole Act of Union must be retained intact, or repealed'.[44] John Vance declared, 'it was a solemn compact between the two nations. The Parliament of one of the countries was defunct, and therefore it was impossible that the Parliament of the other could ever take the Act into re-consideration, as to do so would be a breach of faith and a violation of national rights'.[45] Lord Claud Hamilton, son of the Duke of Abercorn, was even more adamant, rejecting the concept of an evolving union. He saw 'it as a grave constitutional question – as an invasion of the rights and privileges which their ancestors had enjoyed for centuries, and which they were just entitled to hand down to their descendants – and as a policy which, if carried out, would in all probability be fatal to the Union of the United Kingdom'. In his opinion,

> it was a mistake to suppose we could repudiate the obligation imposed upon us by the Act of Union. We were not justified in stigmatising it as a mere Act

of Parliament; it was no such thing; it was a solemn arrangement made between two independent Parliaments representing two distinct kingdoms, and the Union of the Churches was one of its essential conditions. Without that the Parliament of Ireland would not have passed it; and, it were said that the Irish Parliament did not represent Ireland and that therefore it was incompetent to unite the Churches, it was also incompetent to pass the Act of Union; but if the two Parliaments were competent to effect the Union, we were bound by the terms which they agreed to. If they were in existence, they could undo their own act; but by solemn compact they refused to future Parliaments the power to rescind the Act of Union, and they explicitly and solemnly declared no such power should exist.[46]

Harrowby accepted that the Act of Union was open to some change but claimed 'at the same time, this is a very peculiar Act – it is a treaty between two nations'.[47] He felt that it 'gives the Protestants of Ireland some claim to regard the Act of Union not as a common Act of Parliament'. This strict interpretation of the act did not represent the views of the majority of Conservatives. Moreover, Gladstone dismissed the argument, pointing out that the Act legitimately could be altered because this proposed course had been endorsed 'at the election . . . with the large majority of her representatives which she sent here to support the policy of Her Majesty's Government with respect to the Church Establishment'.[48]

If there was an air of unreality in the discussion, there was none the less a serious attempt by both Liberals and Conservatives to place the Union in context, to consider its future and to find a means to build the bond between the two countries. In the end the theme emerged that the terms of the Act required modification from time to time in order to meet the objectives of the original compact, but the legislative connexion must be maintained. Most politicians looked upon the Union as something more than a mere institutional link between Great Britain and Ireland; it was not simply a legislative connexion but was intended to tie all aspects of the community into a single harmonious relationship. It was admitted that this had not been achieved to date, but the goal remained desirable and obtainable.

Neither Ireland nor the question of the Union fell into abeyance between the passage of the Church Act and 1886. The Land Act of 1870, the rise of a home rule movement, the Land War and the power of a national party under Charles Stewart Parnell's leadership kept the problem in front of the public. Isaac Butt, in particular, floated a federal plan that anticipated Gladstone's proposal in 1886. Politicians gave thought to the future of the Anglo-Irish connexion before 1885 but it was only from that time that the Union seemed in danger.

The Government of Ireland Bill, 1886

Home rule did not elicit the consensus that existed for changing the status of the Irish Church and it implied a much larger amendment of the Act of Union. The general election in late autumn had not been conducted in Great Britain specifically on the issue and its outcome had left Liberals with just eighty-six seats more than Conservatives. Parnell's party, with eighty-six members, could sustain Gladstone but was not able to keep a Conservative administration in office. Gladstone was appointed Prime Minister for the third time on 1 February on the restricted pledge 'to examine whether it is or is not practicable to comply with the desire . . . for the establishment . . . of a legislative body, to sit in Dublin and to deal with Irish as distinguished from imperial affairs'.[49] A number of former Liberal ministers did not join his government because of their objections to taking up the self-government claim. Other important Liberals, including Sir William Harcourt, the Chancellor of the Exchequer, and the Earl of Rosebery, the Foreign Secretary, were known to lack enthusiasm for Irish self-government. Gladstone faced a daunting task to convert his own followers, the House of Commons and the country to a large scheme. Defenders of the Legislative Union had more at stake than verbal pyrotechnics. Well aware of opposition from all quarters, Gladstone drafted the bill with minimal consultation; the cabinet was not allowed to see an outline of the proposal until 13 March. When Harcourt finally saw it on 7 March he called Gladstone a 'criminal lunatic'.[50] On 15 March Chamberlain and Trevelyan tendered their resignations, though these were not put into effect until after the cabinet meeting of 26 March described by Harcourt as 'by far the most disagreeable [he had] ever seen'.[51] Parnell was not privy to the bill's provisions until two days before its introduction on 8 April. Parliamentary debate only proceeded after the bill was introduced and prior discussion was hampered because 'no-one knows what the Ministerial scheme in its latest development is to be'.[52] Many suspected that in the final analysis it would constitute some advanced plan of local self-government, a concept enjoying wide bi-partisan backing.

Throughout this period, however, there was a lively public discussion on the principles of self-government. During the parliamentary discussions after the bill's introduction the Liberal position was plagued by inconsistencies in interpretations of the Union, a tendency to slide between maintaining that it would remain in effect through the crown and the supremacy of the Imperial Parliament and an almost metaphysical notion of Union. Also, they used the terms Empire and United Kingdom loosely. Conservatives, if not always consistent, had a simpler burden.

On 8 April in a chamber 'crammed to suffocation from floor to ceiling' Gladstone spoke for three hours and twenty-five minutes introducing the Government of Ireland Bill.[53] During his statement he outlined his notion of the Union. Gladstone referred to it as a legislative union which he proposed to replace with a bond of mutual sympathy. In order to give effect to his object he proposed to create a legislative assembly of two orders with a responsible executive in Dublin. This body would have virtual autonomy over domestic matters, excepting those areas specifically reserved to the Imperial Parliament – 'everything which is not excepted is confessed'.[54] These exclusions fell under three main headings: the powers of the crown, defence, foreign and colonial affairs. Ireland's representation in the two Houses of Parliament at Westminster would cease. Gladstone sought to promote his plan on the basis that it would strengthen the Union by creating the goodwill of Ireland's people which 'conduces to the real unity of this great, noble, and world-wide Empire'.[55] According to the Prime Minister, the 'law is discredited in Ireland, and discredited in Ireland upon this ground especially – that it comes to the people of that country with a foreign aspect and in a foreign garb'.[56] Subsequently, when confronted by criticism that the law was 'foreign', he retracted this, in part, saying, ' "foreign garb' does not refer to good laws but to operations of the criminal law'.[57] Still, Gladstone argued that in major ways Ireland's people differed fundamentally from those in Great Britain. He specified in his introductory speech, 'there is something more in this world occasionally required than even the passing of good laws'. Gladstone professed:

> It is sometimes requisite not only that good laws should be passed, but also that they should be passed by the proper persons. The passing of many good laws is not enough in cases where the strong permanent instincts of the people, their distinctive marks of character, the situation and history of the country require not only that these laws should be good, but that they should proceed from a congenial and native source, and besides being good laws should be their own laws.[58]

'The principle that I am laying down,' Gladstone added carefully, 'I am not laying down exceptionally for Ireland'. It could be applied to Scotland. In his estimation 'there is such a thing as local patriotism which, in itself is not bad, but good . . . but it does not follow that because his local patriotism is keen, he is incapable of Imperial patriotism'.[59] He defended the plan as a recognition of the distinctive and permanent character of Ireland and as the expressed democratic demand of its people.

His analysis was refined further on 13 April when Gladstone sought to meet certain criticisms. He argued that it was 'a question of humanity, of justice and of a desire to make atonement for a long – a too long – series of former, and not yet wholly forgotten, wrongs'.[60] Additionally, Gladstone rejected 'the justice of the principle that self-government in Ireland is necessarily to be limited by the wishes of England and Scotland for themselves'. He wanted to 'lay our hold on the hearts of the people, and which aim at no force and no repression, but at an Union far closer and more durable than that which now exists on the Statute Book'. Then on 10 May the Prime Minister reiterated that autonomy and imperial unity were compatible, though he confessed that the bill 'constitutes a most important modification of that Act [of Union]'.[61] A Liberal, W.S. Shirley, quickly expatiated on a concept of the Union now seen principally as the 'unity and integrity of the Empire'.[62] Glancing backwards, he pointed out, 'in all those great debates, in which Pitt and Fox took part, no one ever expressed a doubt that the unity and the integrity of the Empire existed, notwithstanding the fact that Ireland had then a separate Parliament'. Privately, the Earl of Kimberley thought it was less common interest that held the Union together than the continued power of Great Britain for 'with Army and Foreign Affairs in the hands of the

Imperial Government, the essential unity of the Empire is not lost; not to mention the Customs and other points reserved'.[63] Morley, the Chief Secretary, developed two lines of argument. First, he maintained that the Union was safe because

> the whole of the Prerogative of the Crown would remain absolutely intact; that the veto, therefore will remain subject to no more limitation than exists either in the case of a colony or any other political relations. With reference to the power of Parliament, of course, the power of Parliament is absolutely illimitable.[64]

Second, he suggested that the removal of Ireland's representatives from Parliament was essential because:

> The exasperation that has been produced by the unfortunate historical relations between Great Britain and Ireland has brought about a state of feeling which has alienated the sympathies of the Irish, and diverted their interests from the topics that interest us. They do not look at Imperial topics and interests from the same point of view as we do; they do not assist us in the manner in which it is essential that counsellors in this Parliament should at least endeavour to do. If our adjustment is successful, if, after some years of experiment the result is what we desire and expect, it may then be possible enough that our successors may invite Irish Representatives back again.[65]

In Morley's opinion Irishmen were so alienated that at present it was not appropriate for them to partake in the decisions about the imperial realm. Sir Charles Russell, the Attorney General, contributed to an emergent Liberal redefinition of the Union. According to him, the crucial test was whether the 'United Parliament' which he characterised as only an 'experiment' had fulfilled its obligations:

> I also agree that if this Act had answered its purpose, or had half answered its purpose – if it had been found to bring peace to the country, strength to the Empire and real Union among the people, then I say let no man dare to put his hand upon it.[66]

But, he alleged, 'the results certainly cannot be shown to be satisfactory'. His view was that the Union was maintained for 'the supremacy of the Crown, and of the Imperial Parliament in matters which are Imperial'. Russell contended that the real essence of the Union was 'existence under one Kingship, and under one paramount authority'. He countered suggestions that the removal of Ireland's representation from Westminster was undesirable, echoing Morley's opinion that the Irish were so 'alienated' that they could not participate effectively in vast imperial concerns. According to him, 'so far as the questions of peace and war go, Ireland has never felt that the Irish Members had any effective or controlling voice'. On 10 May Gladstone endorsed this opinion, pointing out 'foreign affairs

. . . do not stand exactly the same relationship to Ireland as they do to England and Scotland'.[67]

Other Liberals amplified the dominant themes in favour of creating a legislative assembly in Dublin. Thomas Burt, for instance, wished to retain Ireland's parliamentary representation at Westminster as 'a visible and outward tie between England and Ireland' but at present there was no real union. A real union, he believed, 'was only possible on a moral basis. It was only possible by winning the affection, the trust, the confidence, and the goodwill of the people that had to be brought under Government'.[68] In supporting home rule Burt 'took his side in favour of a thorough and complete Union between the two countries'. Samuel Whitbread maintained 'there is something I fear even more than obstruction – namely, the assistance which Irish Members would lend to our legislation'.[69] Elaborating that Ireland's representatives were 'foreign', he foresaw a 'compact body of votes thrown from one side or the other, without regard to the subject under consideration, but merely with a view to the interests of the Irish Party at the moment'. Edward Russell simply denounced the 'fetish of a discredited Union, and a system which had produced every ill which diabolical ingenuity could produce'.[70]

In the resumed debate after the Easter recess, Sir Henry Campbell-Bannerman, recently Chief Secretary for Ireland, upheld the contention that national susceptibilities had to be satisfied, asserting, 'there is and has been this popular feeling in Ireland extending gradually and steadily against our rule . . . whatever you do you must satisfy the national sentiment of Ireland'.[71] B. Coleridge sought to deflate the idea that legislative separation meant the end of the Union by the emphatic plea, 'we have but one Monarchy, one Army, and one Navy, one National Debt . . . You can hardly say that that means disintegration of the Empire.' He held a relativist position for the 'laws of countries should be the product of the circumstances, characteristics, and the habits of the people who live in them, and no laws which have not that indigenous quality will be guarded or respected'.[72]

Liberal speakers continued to address the key themes, many casting doubt on the Union or redefining what might constitute a satisfactory connexion. Much of this comment was directed to the imperative of recognising the distinctiveness of an Ireland which could never be accommodated within the current legislative union. J.E. Thorold Rogers, for instance, maintained, 'the greatest blunder that Pitt ever made was the Union between Great Britain and Ireland'.[73] James Bryce argued that Westminster could not satisfy Ireland's wants because the Irish were only a small minority in the House of Commons:

> It is idle to think of legislating satisfactorily for Ireland in a House in which the Irish Members constitute a small minority out of sympathy with the majority – a House chief composed of Members who have never been in Ireland and have no direct personal knowledge of Irish conditions and Irish sentiment – a House whose acts and votes are checked and nullified by another and an irresponsible House, in which there is not a single Representative of Irish national feeling.[74]

Henry Labourchere insisted, 'we had endeavoured to force down the throats of the Irish people our system of law, because we considered that it must be good for them as it was good for us. What was one man's meat was another man's poison'.[75] The Secretary to the Treasury, H.H. Flower, intoned, 'he was a unionist; but he was not a believer in a Union which united the Parliaments while dividing the people, but rather in one which, while it might divide the Parliaments, would unite the nations'; the Under-Secretary of State for the Colonies, Osborne Morgan, believed they 'would be laying the foundations of a real Union – not an Act of Parliament Union – not a parchment Union – but a moral Union, a Union of heart and soul between two Sister Nations'.[76]

Liberals, including Gladstone, were not consistent by any means as to what they meant by the Union or would wish to defend. Most claimed to be against separation and for the Union but wanted a connexion that was renegotiated, more in moral than in institutional terms. Most Liberals argued that the proposed plan provided adequate limits on Ireland's autonomy so as to preserve imperial unity. As progression of the debates showed, however, Liberal ideas about the Union were in flux and a few decried it altogether.

Gladstone's opponents quickly seized the initiative in the parliamentary arena. Irish and dissident Liberals led the way in the early going. An Irish MP, E. Macnaughton, wondered 'what was it, if it was not Repeal of the Union. What was left out?' He objected that 'there was no voice that it could have in the affairs of England, and it could not have a voice in the affairs of the Empire as a whole'.[77] William Johnson, representing South Belfast, protested that the scheme was 'an open, unmistakable abandonment of the Union'.[78] David Plunket, MP for the University of Dublin, noted,

> the right hon. Gentleman said – 'Why should not a man be a patriot in Ireland, and take an interest also in Imperial affairs?' Certainly, that is my view of patriotism. But the right hon. Gentleman would exclude Members of the Irish Parliament from all opportunity of exercising patriotism by preventing the Irish Parliament from having any opportunity of taking any part at all in Imperial affairs.[79]

Chamberlain examined several aspects of the proposal, advocating, in particular, that some form of wider imperial federation might be the appropriate answer. One of his arguments against the current scheme which resonated widely was that the 'proposal seems to me to be inconsistent . . . as a cardinal principle of our English Constitution – namely, that taxation and representation should go together'.[80]

Hartington, in an especially telling speech, was 'still convinced that, in the interest of both countries, the Legislative Union with Ireland should be maintained'. He proceeded,

> The words 'United Kingdom' have some meaning distinct from the words 'British Empire'. The British Empire must endure, though, separate

Legislatures were conferred, not only upon Ireland, but upon England, Scotland, and Wales. But the United Kingdom is the creation of a particular Act – the Act of Union . . . What was the distinguishing feature of the Act of Union? It was the creation of one sovereign Legislature, which was to be henceforth the sole Legislative Body for the Kingdoms of Great Britain and Ireland.[81]

A short time afterwards, he continued,

It would be an error to suppose that the unity of the Empire is maintained if it presents a united front in foreign policy, if it is represented by a united Navy and a united Army. As far as external matters go, and as far as our relations with other states and nations are concerned, we may be able to preserve the semblance of unity after this bill is passed; but as far as our internal position goes, I say that with the passing of this bill the unity of the Empire will have disappeared. We may have not only different laws in Ireland from those which prevail in England and Scotland; but laws founded on totally different principles, and administered in a totally different spirit.[82]

G.J. Goschen explained, 'our interests, English, Scotch and Irish are all interlaced in a manner, totally different from what is the case between Britain and the Colonies . . . You cannot treat Ireland differently from England and Scotland without involving yourself in innumerable anomalies and injustices'.[83] The former Liberal Attorney General, Sir Henry James contested the core of the home rule case:

The unity of the Empire . . . [means] the unity of Great Britain and Ireland . . . Unity, by virtue alone of one Crown being paramount over the Three Kingdoms, is substantially no unity . . . The real unity of a kingdom must depend upon the unity of its laws. I do not mean by that that there must be an identity of laws . . . But what I mean is that there must be a power which can make identical laws for a kingdom supposed to be united. It is not the identity of manufacture; it is the identity of the manufacturing power that makes the unity of a kingdom. Therefore, when we speak of the unity of the Empire, as applied to the United Kingdom, that unity is not maintained by virtue of there being the one Crown paramount over England and Ireland. There was that junction before the Act of Union, yet Great Britain and Ireland did not form the United Kingdom. The real Union of the Empire, as it now exists, was effected by the junction of the two Parliaments. There was no United Kingdom of Great Britain and Ireland before the Act of Union.[84]

A.R.D. Elliot, another dissident Liberal, interposed, believing that shedding Ireland would weaken the position of the United Kingdom abroad. He did not believe that if Ireland were refused home rule it would be a source of weakness. 'I know that we have had trouble and I know that we may have it again,' he stated, 'but after all, Irishmen have shared many dangers with us, and I am convinced will do so again'.[85]

Conservatives, too, increasingly entered the fray. An Irishman sitting for a Liverpool constituency rejected Gladstone's designation of the Irish being 'foreign', insisting

> it was I think, most unfortunately that the right hon. Gentleman should apply the word 'foreign' either to England or Ireland. I have been brought up in the belief that I am no foreigner in England, and I have not been treated as if I were.[86]

Hicks Beach interjected,

> when all other countries in the world are consolidating their resources, when our most remote Colonies are endeavouring to draw together in closer Union with the Mother Country, we should be asked to take the first step in splitting up the very kernel around which our great Empire is formed, and dividing, for legislative and administrate purpose the two islands that have been so closely associated hitherto. That is a step backward in the history of this country.[87]

Unlike Morley and some other Liberal speakers he did not resent the attention Irish MPs gave to the business of the House of Commons. 'Irish Members are to be absolutely deprived of all that in which certainly they have hitherto a very intelligent and powerful interest, and to which, I must say, they have quite as much right as the inhabitants of any other part of the United Kingdom'.[88] Sir Richard Assheton Cross insisted,

> what we contend for is the supremacy and the sovereignty of the Imperial Parliament. Why we want to retain the Irish Members within the walls of this House is that without them we shall cease to be an Imperial Parliament. It would be the Imperial Parliament of Great Britain, but it would not be the Imperial Parliament of the three United Kingdoms. Some confusion has arisen from talking about the unity of the Empire; what we want is to maintain the unity of the three Kingdoms, and thus secure the freedom of the Empire, and if we once let Ireland go these objects are destroyed.[89]

In contrast to 1869 the opponents of home rule found themselves in possession of a good if not always consistent line of argument. Many of the points lodged, of course, were a crude denunciation of the Irish party and National League. Yet, they were able to express a vision of an Ireland integral to the future of the nation, an Irish people who were capable of being part of a greater British Empire.

Conclusion

Political ideology is usually the product of a crisis. This axiom applies to the controversies over the Church and home rule. In the late 1860s there was still some indecision about what constituted the Union and the debates in 1869 were an increment in giving it a firmer definition. Nearly everyone concurred that its maintenance was desirable and the vast majority accepted that the Union had to move with the times. Thus, it was seen as possible by most MPs to change the status of the Irish Church without undermining the Union. Conservatives, like Liberals, professed a deeply held desire to remedy Irish grievances. It could be said, of course, that there was some insincerity on the part of Gladstone's opponents, though the main difference lay not over the principle of relieving grievances but of classifying what was a legitimate grievance. In any event Conservatives in 1869 were reduced to fighting a rearguard action and Liberals held the high ground, viewing the disestablishment of the Church as a cornerstone in the quest to complete the integration of Ireland into a genuine United Kingdom. Disestablishment allowed Conservatives to continue the process of disengagement from the confessional state and to embrace a diverse though political unified community.

In 1886 the position was very different and opponents of home rule were well aware that they had a golden opportunity of thwarting Gladstone's plan. Concerns about the nature of the Union raised in 1869 were articulated fully and ideas about its composition evolved during the controversy. However, the importance of the incident which held portents for the future was that the scheme's proponents were not only vague and inconsistent about what they believed to be the essence of the Union, but that many were forced into advocating home rule on the basis that Ireland was distinctive and the Irish in some ways 'foreign'. In 1869 Conservatives warned that adapting institutions to reflect the 'Irish ideas' of Ireland's majority opened the path to viewing all Irish people as 'marginal Britons'.[90] What was sometimes no more than implicit in 1869 was very explicit in the debates of 1886. If the people of Ireland should make their own laws, the incentive to construct Westminster-concocted remedies was correspondingly less for Liberals. The Gladstonian response to the fragmentation of the Union was that true unity must be based on moral principles, that the ultimate supremacy of the Imperial Parliament and the common crown ensured that the connexion between the countries would persist. Gladstone himself tended to elide the notions of a moral and institutional union while many supporters of home rule fudged distinctions between the Empire and the United Kingdom. To the extent that Liberals refined what they meant by the Union during the home rule debates, this was forced upon them especially by dissident Liberals. From differing perspectives, Trevelyan, Chamberlain, Hartington, James and Goschen were effective critics of the scheme.

Opponents of home rule were not of a single mind about the Union. They claimed to be eager to remedy any real grievances and most advocated the grant of fairly wide local self-government. Some, like Chamberlain, were ready to countenance federalisation of the Empire or at least of the whole United Kingdom.[91] But the opposition were clear that real union was not just a moral principle or a common crown, but contained the kernel of a paramount legislative body that sought to equalise conditions so far as practicable throughout the three kingdoms. Irish representation at Westminster, as Hicks Beach observed, was necessary to this unity. Moreover, the challenge of home rule enforced an increasing recognition of the differences within the whole community, some of which required separate treatment, but that an organic fabric must be woven from the various peoples of the three kingdoms. If Liberals were prepared to admit the existence of nationality, opponents of home rule increasingly emphasised the necessity of harmonisation across the national territory, adumbrating the polarisation of views in contemporary Britain about the future direction of the European Union.

NOTES

1 I wish to acknowledge assistance in preparation of this chapter by Miles Bradbury, John Broad, George Boyce, Barbara Gauntt, Donald and Shirley Ginter, Sheridan Gilley, Terry Gourvish, David Howell, Michael Hurst, Margaret Mullally, Andrew O'Day, Colonel Helen E. O'Day, Roland Quinault, Geneviève Schauinger, Charles Thomas, F.M.L. Thompson and Gabrielle Ward-Smith.
2 *Parliamentary Debates [PD]*, 3rd series, 304 (8 April 1886), c. 1049.
3 Ibid., 305 (17 May 1886), cc. 1236, 1240.
4 Ibid., 304 (8 April 1886), c. 1049.
5 Ibid., c. 1081.
6 Alan O'Day, *Irish Home Rule 1867–1921* (Manchester, 1998), pp. 295, 303, 308.
7 *PD*, 194 (23 March 1869), c. 2072.
8 Ibid., 304 (9 April 1886), cc. 1251–2.
9 Ibid., 306 (18 May 1886), c. 374.
10 Ibid., 304 (12 April 1886), c. 1354.
11 Allen Warren, 'Disraeli, the Conservatives and the government of Ireland: Part 1, 1837–1881', *Parliamentary History*, 18 (1999), pp. 45–6.
12 Allen Warren, 'Disraeli, the Conservatives and the Government of Ireland: Part 2, 1868–1881', *Parliamentary History*, 18 (1999), p. 167.
13 A.V. Dicey, *England's Case against Home Rule*, new intro. E.J. Feuchtwanger (Richmond, 1973), p. 283.
14 Walter Bagehot, *The English Constitution* (17th edn; London, 1985), pp. 150–82.
15 *PD*, 195 (15 April 1869), c. 923.
16 See Appendix.
17 Liam Kennedy and David S. Johnson, 'The Union of Ireland and Britain, 1801–1921' in D. George Boyce and Alan O'Day (eds), *The Making of Modern Irish History: Revisionism and the Revisionist Controversy* (London, 1996), pp. 36–44.
18 *PD*, 194 (22 March 1869), c. 1958.
19 Ibid. (19 March 1869), c. 1886, 1887.
20 Ibid., c. 1869.
21 Ibid., cc. 1871, 1876.
22 John Morley, 'Old Parties and New Policy', *Fortnightly Review*, 4, new series (1 September 1868), p. 327.
23 J.L. Hammond, *Gladstone and the Irish Nation* (new impression; London, 1964), p. 90.
24 Richard Shannon, *Gladstone: Heroic Minister 1865–1898* (London, 1999), p. 65.

25 See, P.M.H. Bell, *Disestablishment in Ireland and Wales* (London, 1969), pp. 112–57; E.R. Norman, *The Catholic Church and Ireland in the Age of Rebellion 1859–1873* (London, 1965), pp. 353–84; Donald Harman Akenson, *The Church of Ireland: Ecclesiastical Reform and Revolution, 1800–1885* (London and New Haven, 1971), pp. 226–321; R.B. McDowell, *The Church of Ireland 1869–1969* (London, 1975), pp. 26–50; John D. Fair, *British Inter-party Conferences: A Study of the Procedure of Conciliation in British Politics, 1867–1921* (Oxford, 1980), pp. 17–34; J.P. Parry, *Democracy and Religion: Gladstone and the Liberal Party 1867–1875* (Cambridge, 1986), pp. 280–8.

26 *Annual Register* (1868), pp. 44–5.

27 Quoted in Bell, *Disestablishment*, p. 84.

28 See Appendix.

29 *PD*, 194 (16 February 1869), c. 416.

30 Akenson, *Church of Ireland*, pp. 260–1.

31 Ibid., p. 265; H.C.G. Matthew, *Gladstone 1809–1898* (Oxford, 1997), p. 194.

32 *PD*, 194 (1 March 1869), c. 416.

33 Ibid. (19 March 1869), c. 1944.

34 Ibid. (22 March 1869), c. 1982.

35 Ibid., cc. 1989, 1990.

36 Shannon, *Gladstone*, p. 66.

37 *PD*, 194 (22 March 1869), cc. 1907, 1909, 1910. For a comment on his speech see Nancy E. Johnson (ed.), *The Diary of Gathorne Hardy, Later Lord Cranbrook, 1886–1892: Political Selections* (Oxford, 1981), p. 92. See also Angus Hawkins and John Powell (eds), *The Journal of John Wodehouse, First Earl of Kimberley for 1862–1902* (London, 1997), pp. 23–40.

38 *PD*, 194 (23 March 1869), c. 2020.

39 Ibid., c. 2021.

40 Ibid., 196 (14 June 1869), c. 1635.

41 Ibid., 194 (1 March 1869), c. 1671.

42 Ibid., c. 1864, 1872–3, 1874.

43 Ibid., 196 (14 June 1869), c. 1669.

44 Ibid., 194 (18 March 1869), c. 1708.

45 Ibid. (22 March 1869), c. 1966.

46 Ibid., cc. 1973, 1974.

47 Ibid., 196 (14 June 1869), cc. 1669–70.

48 Ibid., 195 (15 April 1869), c. 930.

49 Quoted in John Morley, *The Life of William Ewart Gladstone* (London, 1903), III, p. 292.

50 Lewis Harcourt's Journal, 8 March 1886, Harcourt Papers, Bodleian Library, Oxford, Ms. 377.

51 Ibid., 26 March 1886.

52 Derby diaries, 7 April 1886, quoted in John Vincent (ed.), *The Later Derby Diaries: Home Rule, Liberal Unionism and Aristocratic Life in Late Victorian England* (Bristol, 1981), p. 66.

53 Harcourt's Journal, 8 April 1886. Discussions of the bill can be found in Alan O'Day, *Parnell and the First Home Rule Episode, 1884–87* (Dublin, 1986), pp. 178–200 with the measure reprinted, pp. 234–51, and James Loughlin, *Gladstone, Home Rule and the Ulster Question, 1882–93* (Dublin, 1986), pp. 53–94.

54 *PD*, 304 (8 April 1886), cc. 1065.

55 Ibid., c. 1044.

56 Ibid., c. 1042.

57 Ibid. (13 April 1886), c. 1535.

58 Ibid. (8 April 1886), c. 1080.

59 Ibid., cc. 1081, 1082.

60 Ibid. (13 April 1886), cc. 1545, 1547.

61 Ibid., 305 (10 May 1886), c. 582.

62 Ibid., 304 (8 April 1886), c. 1794.

63 John Powell (ed.), *Liberal by Principle: The Politics of John Wodehouse 1st Earl of Kimberley, 1843–1902* (London, 1996), pp. 184–5.
64 *PD*, 304 (9 April 1886), c. 1261.
65 Ibid., c. 1277.
66 Ibid. (12 April 1886), cc. 1348, 1349, 1353, 1357.
67 Ibid., 305 (10 May 1886), c. 590.
68 Ibid., 304 (12 April 1886), c. 1369.
69 Ibid., cc. 1400, 1402.
70 Ibid. (13 April 1886), 1494.
71 Ibid., 305 (13 May 1886), c. 938.
72 Ibid., c. 1020.
73 Ibid. (17 May 1886), c. 1192.
74 Ibid., c. 1227.
75 Ibid. (18 May 1886), c. 1333.
76 Ibid., 306 (31 May 1886), cc. 523, 1040.
77 Ibid., 304 (8 April 1886), c. 1091.
78 Ibid. (9 April 1886), c. 1227.
79 Ibid. (8 April 1886), c. 1138.
80 Ibid., c. 1191. See J.L. Garvin, *The Life of Joseph Chamberlain* (London, 1932), II, pp. 203–4 and Richard Jay, *Joseph Chamberlain: A Political Study* (Oxford, 1981), pp. 137–9.
81 *PD*, 304 (9 April 1886), c. 1243. See, Bernard Holland, *The Life of Spencer Compton, Eighth Duke of Devonshire* (London, 1911), II, pp. 141–7 and Patrick Jackson, *The Last of the Whigs: A Political Biography of Lord Hartington Later Eighth Duke of Devonshire (1833–1908)* (Rutherford, Madison and Teaneck, 1994), pp. 226–9.
82 *PD*, 305 (10 May 1886), cc. 615–16.
83 Ibid., 304 (13 April 1886), c. 1466.
84 Ibid., 305 (13 May 1886), cc. 915, 916.
85 Ibid. (18 May 1886), cc. 1384–5.
86 Ibid., 304 (12 April 1886), c. 1409.
87 Ibid. (13 April 1886), cc. 1518–19.
88 Ibid., c. 1525.
89 Ibid., 305 (13 May 1886), c. 1174.
90 See D. George Boyce, 'The marginal Britons: the Irish', in Robert Colls and Philip Dodd (eds), *Englishness: Politics and Culture 1880–1920* (London, 1986), pp. 230–53.
91 See John Kendle, *Ireland and the Federal Solution: The Debate over the United Kingdom Constitution, 1870–1921* (Montreal and Kingston, 1989), pp. 32–56.

Part II

Modification of the Union

6 Irish unionism, 1870–1922

Alvin Jackson

The history of unionism in Ireland is one of simplification, retreat and retrench-
ment. Through much of the nineteenth century unionism – defined very broadly
as a belief in the constitutional connexion between Britain and Ireland – was the
normative condition of Irish politics. Unionism was a luxuriant intellectual and
cultural growth which entwined itself around mainstream Liberal and Tory politics, and pollinated even those more popular movements which have been seen
exclusively within the history of nationalist development and progression:
O'Connellite repeal and Parnellite home rule were, stripped of their patriotic
ebullience, campaigns for a more workable relationship with Britain – for a more
refined union – rather than for absolute separation.

Even when the definition is tightened, and when unionism is seen in a more
conventional light (as the movement upholding the Act of Union), its ideological
grip upon a wide and diverse section of Irish society, whether northern or southern, was still astonishing. Unionism linked southern landed capital with the world
of northern Presbyterian embourgeoisement: it bound commercial magnates
with Orange labourers. Unionism commanded a working-class constituency in
nineteenth century Dublin no less than in Belfast: it ruled in the southern suburbs
of the national capital (Rathmines returned a Unionist to the Commons as late as
1918) no less than in the southern suburbs of its northern rival. Unionism linked
financial with intellectual muscle: the movement found unembarrassed advocates
among the luminaries of both Trinity College Dublin and Queen's College Belfast – this, moreover, at a time when – as the *Northern Whig* remarked in 1914 –
there were 'giants among the professors'.[1] And yet this luxuriant diversity was
swiftly pruned down to a northern core, very largely middle class in its leadership,
and unadorned by the intellectual foliage of its mid- and late Victorian predecessor: the stolid and – for the most part – undifferentiated bourgeois ministers seated
around James Craig's cabinet table were merely the remnants of a once more
varied and sophisticated political culture. In an island where for the most part this
vibrancy is remembered only through fossilised remains, and where unionism is
seen as alien and marginal, it is instructive to recount, not just the processes of
retreat, but the extent to which the movement (or at least its governing idea) once
occupied a central role within Irish political life.

The issue of definition has already been broached. Cast in institutional terms, unionism was essentially an amalgam of Irish Toryism, Orangeism and the Church of Ireland. Defined in social terms, unionism was essentially an amalgam of the Irish landed interest with the northern Presbyterian bourgeoisie: if nationalism drew strength from Catholic embourgeoisement in the nineteenth century, then there was a parallel northern Protestant development. There was of course much more to unionism than these several building blocks, and in particular with the passage of time new forces, new organisations and a new equilibrium emerged within the movement; but these three institutions and two social groupings were arguably the key constituents of the unionist conglomerate, at least so far as the mid- to late Victorian period was concerned.

Of the three institutions, perhaps the single most significant was the Irish Conservative Party. Irish Toryism supplied much of the organisational infrastructure around which unionism was constructed; and it supplied trained advocates to the loyalist cause. Conservatism was the unsung success story of mid-Victorian politics, profiting from the tightly regulated electorate created under the Irish Franchise Act (1850) and from a well-regimented party organisation (as evidenced by the Central Conservative Society, created in 1853); indeed, as K.T. Hoppen has observed, the modernisation of Conservative organisation in Ireland occurred well ahead of similar initiatives within the English or Scots parties.[2] Nor was this Conservative success exclusively a northern phenomenon; on the contrary, throughout the country a combination of a disproportionately Protestant electorate, landed influence and a well-oiled organisational machine ensured regular Tory victories in such unlikely (from the late nineteenth-century perspective) territory as County Sligo. Moreover, although the cause suffered a succession of legislative reverses – the disestablishment of the Church of Ireland in 1869 (of which more later), the passage of the Ballot Act in 1872 and the Corrupt and Illegal Practices Act in 1883 – there were compensations. Unlike the Liberals, who remained tied to the farming and textile interests (and even then only in an incomplete fashion), the Tories attracted new talent both among the young and from new and influential professional and commercial interests; an army of young lawyers, fired with righteousness, fought the battle for loyalty in the revision courts of the 1850s and 1860s. In addition a rich populist tradition upheld the values of the cause in Ulster and other parts of the island; William Johnston of Ballykilbeg, elected as an independent MP for Belfast in 1868, was soon accommodated within Conservatism and articulated a populist sectarianism which was identifiable elsewhere (such as in the fulminations of the Revd Tresham Gregg, the hero of Dublin working-class Protestants).[3] The challenge supplied by Johnston, and by the home rule and Liberal parties in the 1870s, kept up the need for organisational revision, and this was especially marked in the north, where, in 1880, the year of the great Liberal revival, an Ulster Constitutional Union was founded – and where, in 1883, the year of the home rule 'invasion' of Ulster, an Ulster Constitutional Club opened its doors to the Belfast commercial elite. Both would soon prove to be organisational pivots for the Ulster unionist movement.[4]

Conservatism was a predominant influence within emergent unionism, in an ideological as well as an institutional sense. But it would be wrong to dismiss the impact of Irish Liberalism, even though it is conventionally assumed that nationalism annexed the vestigial Liberal tradition. Certainly the home rule movement acquired Liberal parliamentary constituencies, most spectacularly at the general election of 1874 when some fifty-six Liberal seats fell to supporters of Isaac Butt; but the moribund party rallied in Ulster in 1880, revived momentarily by the oxygen of the land crisis, only to fall victim to the home rule issue in 1885–6.[5] Still, if the Home Rule Party inherited Liberal seats, as well as the favour of Catholic voters, then unionism inherited both many Liberal activists and some of the ideological trappings of the effectively defunct party; a meeting of Ulster Liberals, held on 19 March 1886, declared its support for the Union, and from this there grew an uneasy alliance with Conservatism. What this meant was, not so much a massive electoral accession, but rather the (highly tentative) recruitment of Presbyterian leaders and activists as well as some popular farming support. It introduced a measure of social reformism into unionism, in particular with regard to landed issues, but it also heightened tensions within the movement over policy and patronage. The enlistment of the Liberal unionists also tended to dilute the strongly Orange flavour of the unionist alliance, since many of the most influential of the new recruits, while no great friends to Catholicism, were at the same time intensely suspicious of all forms of religious chauvinism.

It would also be quite wrong, however, to interpret the broad Liberal unionist tradition as exclusively enlightened. On the contrary, Liberal unionism embraced not only a social radicalism (as articulated most passionately by T.W. Russell), but a sterner Whig tradition which mixed a passionate sense of Irishness with an unflinching respect for the revolutionary settlement of 1688, as well as a boundless faith in the powers and abilities of the landed elite. Edward Saunderson, the first leader of the Irish Unionist Parliamentary Party (1886–1906) – indeed, arguably the first leader of Irish unionism – seemed to be the epitome of Orange Toryism, but in reality he had migrated from a long-standing family tradition of Whiggery (he had sat as a Liberal MP for Cavan between 1865 and 1874) and had joined the Orange Order only in 1882, when he was forty-five.[6] This ideological journey was much shorter than might be supposed.

Saunderson was a passionate Anglican, and indeed the Church of Ireland represented another key element within the unionist compound. Perhaps the greatest, and certainly the most direct, contribution of the Church of Ireland to the evolution of organised unionism came, paradoxically, through its defeat and humiliation in 1868–9 over disestablishment. This was W.E. Gladstone's initiative, and it was simultaneously the keystone of a broader project promising 'justice' for Ireland, as well as part of a highly astute electoral strategy; as R.V. Comerford has wryly observed, 'Gladstone had a well publicised and sincere conscience about such matters [as the Church of Ireland] but his conscience never ran ahead of his pragmatic political practice'.[7] The measure offered little to substantiate the more lurid Tory fears: there was in fact no sweeping expropriation (except in a strict technical sense, and in the rhetoric of the measure's opponents); nor did the Irish Church Act announce (as many Catholics and some Presbyterians fondly hoped) the demise of the Church of Ireland. Indeed, though the Act is conventionally seen as a measure of democratisation which heralded the unravelling of the Union, there is a strong case to be made for exactly the reverse proposition. At the very least disestablishment 'can with equal justice be seen as a new beginning for the Union'.[8] .

In some respects the Irish Church Act acted, not as a spanner in the works of the Union, but rather as a mechanical refinement which prepared the constitutional jalopy for future mileage. The termination of the establishment, though supported by many Presbyterians, removed a source of division between the two main Irish Protestant traditions, and therefore prepared the way for the inclusivist 'Protestant' identity which underlay the early successes of unionism. Disestablishment bolstered unionism in even more direct and tangible ways: the cause of the threatened Church stimulated the creation of several protest organisations – the Central Protestant Defence Association, the Ulster Protestant Defence Association – which in a modest form looked forward to the organisational spree of 1885–6. In addition many of the most prominent defenders of the establishment (the fourth Earl of Erne, Viscount Crichton, Lord Claud Hamilton) would soon move into the last ditch of the Union; many of these advocates of Church and Union shared a social base in the landed elite of the 'outer' counties of Ulster (Tyrone, Fermanagh, Cavan), and were disproportionately significant in formulating the ideological first principles of Irish unionism.[9] Disestablishment underpinned the evangelical identity of these men, and taught them the limits of what British politics might deliver for their cause.

One of the key resources in Protestant society exploited by territorial dynasties such as the Hamiltons, the Crichtons or (eventually) the Saundersons was the Orange Order. Even though many Irish loyalists in the mid-1880s (such as Saunderson) sought to promote a non-sectarian unionism, in reality the organisational foundation supplied by Orangeism seemed to be both crucial for future growth and a barrier to wider Catholic participation. This tension between the ideal of a secular unionism and the utility of Orange organisation has characterised the movement since its origins in the early and mid-1880s. At this time the order provided the only credible basis for loyalist opposition to both the Land League and the National League, since the alternatives (such as the Ulster Constitutional Union) were party based, regional or simply too weak. Orangeism served to unite members of the Church of Ireland with the increasing number of Presbyterians who saw the order as being a necessary, if sometimes unlovely, remedy to the greater evil of an expansionist Catholicism. Although dissolved in 1836, the order was reconstituted in 1846 with the Earl of Enniskillen (another of the South Ulster populist magnates) as Grand Master. In general, however, the reputation of the order for rowdiness and its alleged association with the Duke of Cumberland's Ruritanian ambitions towards the English throne meant that, with one or two prominent exceptions, the gentry held aloof from enrolment. One of the exceptions who demonstrates this rule is William Johnston of Ballykilbeg, the owner of a small and encumbered estate in Lecale, County Down. Johnston's efforts to overthrow the Party Processions Act (1850) won him a short spell in Downpatrick jail (in March–April 1868), massive popular favour (he was returned as an independent MP for Belfast in November 1868) and the utter contempt of his landed peers. The social appeal of the order was thus, despite its wide confessional and geographical spread, highly limited, at least until the challenge of the Land League helped the northern gentry to overcome their squeamishness.

The significance of the Orange Order in terms of the ideological and institutional groundwork for unionism can hardly be overstated. When, in 1879–80, the Land League began to make inroads into Ulster, and even among Protestant farmers, it was the order which supplied the predominant loyalist response: in the autumn of 1880 a series of Orange counter-demonstrations was held, designed to coincide with Land League meetings, and to proclaim the order's faith in the necessity for reform.[10] This articulation of a cross-class identity of interest would soon emerge as a fundamental tenet of the unionist creed. Moreover, the Orange campaign against the Land League brought to the forefront numerous landed leaders (E.M. Archdale, Viscount Castlereagh, Viscount Crichton, Lord Hill-Trevor, Somerset Maxwell, Edward Saunderson) who lent the order both an enhanced social respectability and high-political connexions and experience (Lord Crichton, for example, as has been mentioned, had been a leader of the campaign to save the Church of Ireland from disestablishment). Again, when the Land League was replaced by the National League in October 1882, it was the Orange Order which governed and supplied the northern response. Timothy Healy's 'invasion' of Ulster was met by Orange counter-demonstrations, including one controversial affair at Rosslea, County Fermanagh, on 16 October 1883 when an Orange leader, Lord Rossmore, seemed bent on a violent confrontation with the leaguers. The first efforts at popular unionist organisation, in 1885–6, were certainly influenced by the new Orange leaders and their inclusivist social message, but the organisational roots of the Irish Loyal and Patriotic Union (May 1885) or the Loyal Irish Union (August 1885) extended far beyond Orangeism. On the other hand, it was a coterie of Orange MPs, and pre-eminently Edward Saunderson, who successfully agitated for the creation of a distinct Irish Unionist Parliamentary Party in January–February 1886. Several of the originators of this new party had been associated either with the Orange campaign against the leagues, or with the struggle against disestablishment.

So far an emphasis has been placed on the social and institutional origins of unionism, at least within the twenty or so years before the first Home Rule Bill. The following thirty or so years – from the defeat of the Home Rule Bill on 8 June 1886 through to the eve of the Battle of the Somme, 1 July 1916 – may be regarded as the apogee of the unionist movement, at least in so far as it successfully maintained its central objective, and sustained a form of organisational unity and harmony. For this period the central interpretative theme is unquestionably the localisation of the movement, a motor force which was fuelled by several interconnected but subsidiary developments. The defining relationships of the period serve to illustrate the importance of the drift towards a more localised unionism: the relationship between landed and middle-class power within the movement; the changing bond between Ulster and southern unionism and between Ulster unionism and British Toryism; the changing balance between the parliamentary and militant traditions within the movement. The unravelling of these different themes helps to unveil not merely the logic of the partition settlement of 1920–1, but the pattern of later unionist failures within the confines of that settlement.

One of the keystones of unionism, as has been argued, was the alliance between landed and commercial capital. Between the mid-1880s, when the institutions of unionism were laid down, and 1914 the balance of social forces within the leadership of the movement was decisively altered; indeed, the balance of power between land, commerce and the professions shifted within Ireland and Britain as a whole. In 1885–6 Irish landed politicians were of great importance to the formation of independent loyalist bodies both within and beyond the House of Commons: the Irish Loyal and Patriotic Union and its northern counterpart the Ulster Loyalist Union (January 1886) were each largely the result of landed initiative, while the Irish Unionist Parliamentary Party was predominantly landed in the 1880s, as were its progenitors (Saunderson, Lord Claud Hamilton). This is not to deny the significance of business leaders or commercial capital even at this formative stage: various Belfast magnates – J.P. Corry (Mid-Armagh), William Ewart (North Belfast), H.L. Mulholland (North Derry) – had already infiltrated the ranks of the parliamentary party with the general election of 1886. But even with massive urban demonstrations of unionist conviction, such as Lord Randolph Churchill's visit to Belfast on 22 February 1886, or the great Ulster Convention of 17 June 1892, landlords played a significant part: the committee of senior unionists who guided the convention into existence was still predominantly landed, and was chaired by Lord Arthur Hill, the uncle of one of the greatest Irish proprietors of the age, the sixth Marquess of Downshire.[11] Irish squires such as Saunderson had a remarkable influence over sections of the Conservative leadership throughout the 1890s, and in particular over Lord Salisbury, the party leader: Saunderson and his allies acted as a brake upon the reformist initiatives of constructive unionist ideologues like Gerald Balfour and Sir Horace Plunkett.[12] Irish landlordism continued to lurk within all the upper ranks of British politics: at the cabinet level (St John Brodrick, the eighth Duke of Devonshire, Lord George Hamilton, the fifth Marquess of Lansdowne were all both ministers and Irish proprietors), within the Lords (where there were 144 peers with Irish interests in the home rule era) and within the House of Commons (where there was a more variable but – as late as the 1890s – still substantial Irish landed interest).[13]

But the overall drift within unionist politics, as indeed more broadly, was towards landed decline. The landed command of the parliamentary party very swiftly collapsed after 1900, having held relatively steady throughout the 1890s: by the general election of 1918 only one landed proprietor was returned to the House of Commons in the Irish unionist cause. The new representative institutions of Ulster unionism which were emerging after 1904, though they retained a landed presence, were principally agencies for the commercial and professional interests of the Belfast middle classes. The Ulster Unionist Council, which was created in 1904–5, was in some ways a rejection of the landlord-dominated and high-political focus of late Victorian unionism; and while it gave a representation to landlords – about a third of the UUC standing committee were proprietors in 1910 – this was always a minority representation.[14] The leadership of Ulster unionism at the time of the third Home Rule Bill contained landed elements (the Londonderry and Abercorn families remained prominent) but again as a marginal and in some ways merely a symbolic phenomenon. In the 'outer' areas of Ulster landlords like Basil Brooke (Fermanagh) or Lord Farnham and Oliver Nugent (Cavan) retained a primacy, active in recruitment to the Ulster Volunteer Force (January 1913) and sometimes to the Ulster Special Constabulary (1920). It might be speculated that just as the landed proprietors of these counties were disproportionately significant forces in the origins of organised unionism, so their ascendancy was preserved longer here than elsewhere. It might be further conjectured that the serious nature of the challenge to loyalist culture in southern and western Ulster invoked a social conservatism and a continued acceptance of deference, which were more marked than in areas with a more complete unionist dominance.

These shifts within the social typology of the unionist command have an importance beyond the obvious: they are linked to the issue of regional differentiation within the unionism movement, as well as to the question of the relationship between unionism and British politics. Unionism began as a movement which encompassed the entire island of Ireland, albeit in a highly uneven manner. In some ways southern unionism educated its northern partners: perhaps the earliest example of effective Liberal–Tory co-operation on the issue of the Union occurred in Rathmines in March 1885, well in advance of similar developments within Ulster.[15] Also, the first effective unionist missionary organisation was created in Dublin, in May 1885, in the shape of the Irish Loyal and Patriotic Union. Ulster unionists, though very much alive to the challenge of Parnellism, were much slower in giving organisational shape to their apprehensions. Indeed, it is tempting to broaden this point and to question whether Dublin unionism might in fact have been, for all its cussedness and occasional regression, intellectually more vibrant and more active than its Belfast counterpart.

The richness of Dublin unionist culture is easy to overlook, given its defeat and reinvention within independent Ireland, but the interlayering of different social classes and networks, of churches and clubs, was (even allowing for the relatively small size of the community) impressive in its complexity. A small working-class loyalist community defied the norms of propertied Protestantism as well as of the political mainstream. But there was also a Pooteresque world of clerks and shopkeepers who lived in the primly respectable townships south of the capital, and whose existence might easily be forgotten were it not for the evidence of church records and the admission books of Orange lodges.[16] This was also the caste into which Sean O'Casey was born. Indeed, O'Casey, though clearly unique in terms of his literary gifts, might conceivably serve as an illustration of the forces of political and social accommodation and upward mobility which helped to dissipate this community.[17] Harder to miss is Dublin's unionist bourgeoisie, whose eastward longings are perpetuated in the street names of Blackrock, Dalkey and Dun Laoghaire: many commercial and professional figures spent their days in the city, only to retreat to Rathmines or Rathgar or (for the more prosperous) to a coastal villa in the evening (Edward Carson's father, for example, had lived in Rathgar while pursuing his work as an architect in the city centre). At the top of the pyramid were the haut bourgeoisie – figures such as Sir Maurice Dockrell of Monkstown (who represented Rathmines in the House of Commons between 1918 and 1922) and Andrew Jameson of Howth, a director of the Bank of Ireland and chairman of John Jameson Ltd. Also in this august sphere were *déclassé* squires such as Plunkett of Foxrock (MP for South Dublin between 1892 and 1900) and Bryan Ricco Cooper of 'Khyber Pass' villa, Dalkey, and Markree, Sligo (who represented South Dublin both as a unionist MP in 1910 and later as a deputy within Dáil Éireann).[18]

Even if one were to examine only the world of Dublin Toryism, a scarcely less complex picture might emerge: a world which united the self-regarding sophisti-cates of Trinity College with the rougher trade of the Dublin City and County Workingmen's Club; a world which combined the urbane if treacherous circle around Lord Justice Fitzgibbon at Howth with the Orange readership of Lindsay Crawford's paper the *Irish Protestant*. Dublin Conservative organisation had always been luxuriant, and a succession of initiatives from the Irish Protestant Conserva-tive Society (1831) through the Metropolitan Conservative Society (1836) and the Central Conservative Society (1853) underlined the vitality of the party's strat-egists; indeed, as Hoppen has observed, 'the first great centre of organised work-ing class Protestantism was Dublin, not Belfast'.[19] Trinity College supplied an intellectual force to these partisan impulses, with its long tradition of Conservative thought (represented variously in the careers of such very different Tories as Gerald Fitzgibbon, Edward Gibson (Lord Ashbourne), William Johnston and William Moore and in the work and thought of a renegade Orangeman like Isaac Butt or a lifelong nationalist like John Redmond).[20] Trinity provided a home to two of the greatest Conservative thinkers of the time, the historian W.E.H. Lecky (strictly speaking a Liberal unionist) and the literary critic Edward Dowden; both men were also prominent advocates of the Union.

Outside Dublin and Ulster, the pattern of unionist activity grew rather more faint. The focus of unionism in many localities was inevitably the big house, together with the networks of aristocrats and squireens who dominated rural Protestant society in the south and west. Some farming communities, in west Cork and in the northern midlands, contained Protestants and unionists, but these tended to be politically and socially vulnerable (both were targeted by the IRA during the Anglo-Irish War).[21] There were some signs of unionist life elsewhere, but the evidence was often ambiguous: Galway City, for example, returned a Unionist MP to the Commons in 1900 in the shape of a popular Catholic gentle-man, Michael Morris; but when Morris inherited the family peerage in the follow-ing year, the pleasing aberration of a loyalist Galway was rectified. In other major towns there were small unionist electorates, but these were rarely given a chance of declaring their faith: in no-hope divisions like Cork City or Limerick City the electoral battle was generally left to rival nationalists, even though there were sizeable unionist minorities in both boroughs. Cork unionists last fielded a candidate in 1891, when – despite the crisis within Parnellism, and despite the blessing of having a candidate named Patrick Sarsfield – the party amassed only 1,100 votes in a poll of just under 7,000.[22]

In some ways the apparent strengths of southern unionism – its cultural diversity, as well as its metropolitan vitality – acted instead as a cancer which accelerated the demise of the movement, and the surrender of initiative to the north. For diversity implied difference, and vitality brought with it the energy to pursue differences into sometimes disastrous divisions. One of the best examples of this comes with the Dublin elections of 1900, when two moderate Unionist MPs – Plunkett in South County Dublin and J.H.M. Campbell in St Stephen's Green – were ousted, very largely because of the actions of die-hard unionists. Right to the end of its existence southern unionism displayed this tension between an accommodationist strategy, represented in the 1890s by Plunkett and after 1917 by Lord Midleton, and the hard-line irreconcilables, represented in the 1890s by the group around Lord Ardilaun, and after 1918–19 by John Walsh and the vestigial Irish Unionist Alliance. These divisions were self-wounding in 1900, but – as will become clear – by the final years of the Union they were nothing less than suicidal. It is sometimes argued that the marginalisation of southern unionism after 1920 occurred because of northern self-interest, but the internal state of the southern movement also provides clues and explanations.[23]

There were at least three strong centrifugal forces pulling apart an all-Ireland unionism. First, as has been argued, the rather fragile condition of southern unionism in itself militated against a settled, uniform movement. In some ways it is an oversimplification to see Ulster unionism and southern unionism in binary terms, given the highly complicated regional political relationships within the movement, but it is none the less true that, while some branches of southern unionism maintained friendly links with Belfast, the increasingly fragmented condition of the movement meant that Ulster unionists, like the British or indeed Sinn Féin, tended to discount its credibility and importance. But there were other aspects of this disintegration. The decline of Irish landlordism, which has already been chronicled, was also by implication the decline of southern unionism, given the very strong landed nature of the community outside of Dublin. The financial and physical retreat of this class helped to exacerbate tensions between an embattled landed lobby and an often more conciliatory urban unionism; at a more fundamental level this retreat ultimately robbed unionism of financial and intellectual capital.

But an equally complex problem for southern unionists lay with the gradual popularisation and localisation of the movement in the north. The heyday of parliamentary unionism – roughly the twenty years between 1886 and 1905 – permitted southerners to exercise a disproportionate influence over their northern counterparts, since southern unionism possessed exaggerated parliamentary and financial resources. But, with the defeat of the second Home Rule Bill in 1893, this parliamentary focus was being challenged within the north by various interest groups who argued in unison that the rather disengaged unionism of the 1880s and 1890s was no longer adequate for the needs of the movement. This case was presented by labour candidates and by populist sectarians in Belfast, by farmers under the leadership of the wayward but brilliant T.W. Russell, and – briefly, between 1898 and 1900 – by dissident Presbyterians in eastern Ulster. Each of these groupings had a distinct sectional case, but they all were united by the conviction that the Irish unionist parliamentary leadership was failing to represent its broad constituency. By far the most serious of these challengers was Russell, who cobbled together an alliance of thrusting farmers, Presbyterian malcontents and some tactically minded Catholics, and who – behind the call for compulsory land purchase – captured the unionist constituencies of East Down (February 1902) and North Fermanagh (March 1903), and came within 850 votes of seizing South Antrim (traditionally one of the safest unionist seats in Ireland) in February 1903.[24]

These challenges, and in particular Russellism, were occurring at a time when the parliamentary influence of unionism was apparently exhausted, and when ambitious Tory chief secretaries like Gerald Balfour and George Wyndham were pursuing their revisionist course unworried by the burden of loyalist dissent; indeed, it seemed that Wyndham was reinterpreting unionism as a devolutionist creed, a philosophical contortion which unnerved even his front-bench allies.[25] This combination of local and parliamentary humiliation forced the Ulster unionist leadership into a series of strategic initiatives, of which the most important was the creation of a popular representative forum in Belfast, the Ulster Unionist Council (March 1905). The UUC provided some (highly limited) representation to southern unionists, but it was in practice a co-ordinating mechanism for the north rather than for Ireland as a whole. Communication between Ulster unionism and Dublin did not abruptly cease in the aftermath of the UUC and, indeed, the leaders of the movement – Walter Long (1906–10) and Carson (1910–21) – for long remained bound to southern unionism, at least through family and constituency ties. Moreover, co-operation continued at other levels of the loyalist hierarchy (in the Orange Order, for example, or the Joint Committee of the Unionist Associations of Ireland). But, while it would be wrong to portray the creation of the UUC as effecting an immediate, dramatic change in the relationship between the two unionisms, it would be equally misleading to ignore the importance of this development. For Ulster unionism had taken a hesitant, but still vital step towards the creation of a distinctive northern movement and it might well be contended further that the UUC represented not merely an eye-catching regional initiative, but a prototype for the unionist parliament which came into being in 1921, and which governed Northern Ireland for fifty-one years. At the very least the UUC, and the parallel constituency reforms of the mid- and late Edwardian period, helped lay the groundwork for the mass mobilisation of Ulster unionism which occurred in 1912–14. Viewed in this light, the UUC represented the institutionalisation of a growing chasm within Irish unionism.

If, given the vestiges of co-operation which remained in the later Edwardian period, there remained any doubt about the regional unity of unionism, then this was further dispelled between 1911 and 1914, when the movement once again went to war against home rule. By the time of the third Home Rule Bill unionism was to all intents and purposes an Ulster phenomenon: southerners still played a prominent role (Carson and Campbell are obvious examples of this) but only within the context of the northern movement. Thus, some of the most famous images of unionist resistance to home rule portray southern leaders (such as at the signing of the Covenant at Belfast City Hall in September 1912), but they are invariably acting as advocates for, or adjuncts to, the northern cause. Southern unionism resorted to the low-key agitation which had been apparently successful in the past (county meetings, invitations to English voters to see Irish 'realities', evangelism in Britain); there were also isolated examples of efforts to mimic the more militant tendency within Ulster unionism. Kingstown and District Unionist Club attempted in a half-hearted manner to emulate the military discipline of their northern counterparts by organising drilling practice; but these bourgeois rebels proved themselves to be more bourgeois than rebellious, continually fretting about the possible repercussions of their action, and soon abandoning their thoughts of military glory in favour of a relatively cushioned ringside seat for the Irish revolution.[26]

The indecision of the Kingstown loyalists reflected the broader condition of southern unionism. There is a discernible pattern in southern unionist action, which to some extent is also perceptible within the more recent convolutions of Ulster unionism. Southern unionists were divided throughout most of the home rule era, but often it was the most rigidly conservative elements which were the most vocal, or the most conspicuous, elements of the broad partnership. This combination of stridency and division coupled with the very severe external challenges which the movement continually confronted meant that there was a predictable sequence to southern unionist politics: tough-minded, even reactionary, protest was often followed by an astonishingly swift, and even gratuitous, collapse. Many southern unionist leaders advocated a hard-line resistance to the third Home Rule Bill, and many associated themselves with the Ulsterised unionism of the time, believing that this held the key to a successful campaign, and that a revitalised Union, rather than partition, would be the prize. Nevertheless, as Carson and the Liberals edged towards a deal on the exclusion from home rule of the six north-eastern counties, so the strain on the southern unionists grew. Already by the autumn of 1913 there was a degree of frustration and hostility between the southern leadership and Carson, who privately complained that the southerners had not been 'prepared to run any risks . . . it is very difficult to ascertain what the South and West want us to do as they only talk in generalities'.[27] The crystallisation of the Ulster unionist case into a demand for the permanent exclusion of the six counties was complete by the spring of 1914, and effectively reduced southern unionists to the role of anxious bystanders.

The final years of the movement, which may now be conveniently dealt with, were also characterised by this overlayering of division, anger and a cancerous demoralisation. Rocked by the looming threat of partition, and educated in a tradition of political entrenchment, southern unionists oscillated between an affectionate embrace of Redmondism at the outbreak of the war, when the nationalist leader promised support for the British war effort, and the sabotaging of the Lloyd George negotiations of May–July 1916 – a pyrrhic victory which helped to destroy Redmond, and which bought five more years of Union at the cost of effective political marginalisation. Southern unionists attempted to broker a deal with the Redmondites through the Irish Convention (July 1917–April 1918) but the result – while embodying an historic reconciliation – was marred by rank-and-file opposition within both traditions, and was in any case overshadowed by the conscription crisis and by Sinn Féin's growing strength. Subsequent divisions within southern unionism, institutionalised by the split between the Irish Unionist Alliance, led after 1919 by John Walsh, and Midleton's Anti-Partition League, effectively immobilised the movement. Midleton had some minor influence over the details of the Government of Ireland Act (1920), and was a useful go-between for the government and Sinn Féin in the weeks preceding the truce of July 1921; again, he and his followers had some slight input into the shaping of the Irish Free State Constitution Act (1922).[28]

But in truth southern unionism was already dead by 1919, certainly in an institutional sense – broken by the strength of its opponents and by the constraints of its own traditions. The smallness and heterogeneity of the movement had made for cultural interest, even sophistication, but had been at the same time an immense political burden. The relative wealth of the community had offered some compensation, and had acted as a life-support machine for relations with the north and the Union as a whole. But the retreat of landlordism, and the relative diminution of landed capital, had ultimately served to flick the switch on this support mechanism. The devastation visited on the community by the First World War, and to a lesser extent by the 'Tan' and civil wars, have traditionally been seen as crucial factors in the marginalisation of southern unionism, but there is a counter-argument which, while acknowledging the reality of this devastation, highlights broader contexts. W.E. Vaughan was doubtless coat-trailing in claiming that 'the loss of [gentry] sons during the First World War was the mere speeding up of what usually happened on the hunting-field', but his core conviction that 'the gentry's depletion after 1914 was to some extent a continuation of what had always happened to landed families' has to be taken seriously.[29] In more narrowly political and strategic terms it is difficult to resist the suspicion that a divided leadership, peopled by arrogant liberals and blinkered reactionaries, did little to negotiate terms for its people; certainly internal differences invariably defied reso-lution, producing schism and weakness. Midleton, by no means incapable or immoderate, refused to disarm opposition within the IUA to his strategies, and preferred to leave the alliance in 1919 in order to form the APL, a body which he also eventually left – in 1922 over a disagreement concerning the Free State senate. A prevailing tendency within the movement to use its waning strength to garrison untenable positions brought inevitable failure and demoralisation. Southern unionism failed as dramatically as it did partly because its political culture did not develop in step with its social retreat.

The overwhelmingly northern nature of unionism in 1911–14 had undoubt-edly speeded the southerners along this path towards isolation and defensiveness, division and defeat. The gradual democratisation of Irish politics, the relative decline of the landed interest and the concomitant strengthening of the business and professional classes all facilitated the rise of Ulster unionism within the broader Irish alliance. As has been chronicled, the mounting challenges supplied by local politics in the north, as well as the mounting frustrations of parliamentary life, encouraged the belated but sweeping elaboration of Ulster unionist organisation. A luxuriant northern popular political culture both reflected and encouraged the mass mobilisation of the Ulster Protestant community behind the cause of Union. In addition, by 1910 – probably for the first time – a systematic policy of militancy was being planned in conjunction with more conventional constitutional strategies by the unionist leadership.

Before the issue of militancy is considered, one particularly striking aspect of this mass mobilisation in the north demands attention – namely, the growing involvement of northern women within the institutions of unionism. The role of women within the propagation of unionism has often either been overlooked or – where it has received attention – judged merely within a formal and institutional context. The importance of women in promoting loyalist and unionist conviction within the home and the role of voluntary and recreational organisations in consolidating women's unionism have received only the slightest scholarly attention. Some early women unionists, primarily Isabella Tod, who founded the North of Ireland Women's Suffrage Committee in 1872, and who organised a women's protest against the first Home Rule Bill, have fared rather better (Tod has been the subject of at least two biographical essays).[30] Some unionist men who were sympathetic to women's political concerns have also been studied (though, as with William Johnston of Ballykilbeg, rarely from the standpoint of their feminism). All this is to say that women's unionism before 1912 was significant, even if in scholarly terms it remains submerged beneath apparently more considerable issues. The third home rule crisis, however, coinciding as it did with the crescendo of suffragist activity throughout the United Kingdom, brought an empowerment of unionist women: women created for themselves, or were given, wider opportunities than before for involvement in unionist politics, while the formally dismissive unionist high command was forced to reconsider its patriarchal attitudes. The most significant expressions of this new women's unionism came with the Ulster Women's Unionist Council, created in 1911, and the women's Covenant, signed (as with the men's Covenant) *en masse* in September 1912.[31] There were, however, other significant developments: a Unionist Women's Franchise Association flourished at this time, claiming just under 800 members in 1913; and Carson (himself an anti-suffragist) declared that women would be enfranchised by the Ulster Provisional Government (the executive which was to be established by the unionists in the event of home rule).[32] Deprived of a formal role within high politics, some women (notably Theresa Lady Londonderry) contrived to carve out an individual role and influence in defiance of conventional restraints.

Ulster unionist militancy in 1912–14, to which women contributed so extensively, was rooted in a variety of shifting political relationships. First the militancy was in part an expression of the looser bond with the south, since southern unionists – for all their bluster – tended, as a vulnerable minority and as property-owners (for the most part), to shy away from threat or violence; the heroes of Kingstown Unionist Club were the exception which illustrates the broader rule. Second, Ulster unionist militancy was an expression of a deeply flawed relationship with British Conservatism, a relationship which had come close to divorce under the chief secretaryship of Wyndham (1900–5) and which had scarcely undergone any significant improvement since Wyndham's resignation in March 1905. Lastly, this militancy reflected increased fear of both home rule and 'Rome rule', partly because of worsening sectarian relations in the later Edwardian era, and partly because – with the threatened emasculation of the House of Lords – the nationalist millennium looked to be at hand.

Evidence of Ulster unionist militancy is discernible as early as November 1910, when the UUC established a secret defence committee with a view to approaching foreign arms dealers.[33] By mid-December 1910 sample weapons were already before the committee, while in March 1911 substantial sums of money were voted for the purpose of large-scale acquisitions. These early efforts towards an armed response were much less conspicuous than later initiatives such as the creation of the Ulster Volunteer Force (formally launched in January 1913) or the Larne gun-running (of 24–5 April 1914). But they were an essential starting point for this subsequent activity. In addition they illustrate the extent to which Ulster unionist militancy was not simply a response to the enactment of the Parliament Bill and the threat of the third Home Rule Bill, but predated both these measures, and reflected instead a series of more complicated political relationships and attitudes.

Nevertheless, the most famous aspects of Ulster unionist militancy were unquestionably the formalisation of the popular paramilitary craze which swept unionist Ulster in 1911–12 into the Ulster Volunteer Force. This body was organised along the lines of the British Army, with local platoons and battalions, and a county regimental structure: its structure reflected not only the experiences of many of its Irish officers and men in the service of the crown, but the influence of the numerous English officers who were recruited to the Ulster unionist cause, including the commander, General Sir George Richardson, and Captain Wilfrid Spender. The UVF expanded very rapidly and by late 1913 was claiming a membership of 100,000; the true total may have fallen somewhat short of this boast, but probably not by much. The purpose of the UVF was in reality more complex than appearances might have suggested: it has sometimes (and persuasively) been argued that the creation of the force reflected the desire of unionist political leaders to exercise greater control over the militants within their movement.[34]

The complexity of the unionist leadership's attitudes towards the UVF and the broader issue of militancy is underlined by an examination of the issue of arms. The forces impelling the unionists towards a civil conflict should not be under-estimated: a disproportionately large number of the unionist leaders had been inured to violence in the South African War, while parliamentary politics – even under the late Conservative government – had held out ever weakening attractions. There were thus many hawks in the loyalist aviary, but this is very far from saying that there was a consistent or homogeneous policy of militancy. On the contrary, while there were relatively uncomplicated belligerents like Fred Crawford represented in (or on the margins of) the high command of the movement, there were also those like Lord Londonderry, or even Carson, who associated themselves with militant defiance while privately expressing qualms or seeking to apply moderation. It is probably accurate to see popular unionist militancy as a kind of Frankenstein's monster, called into life by Carson and Craig, but threatening to defy the authority of its creators. Certainly Carson blessed unionist militancy through his speeches and through his presence at various martial displays; but in private he advised against pushing the make-believe aggression of the UVF into the realm of reality. On at least two occasions – in December 1912 and May 1913 – Carson argued against the general arming of the Volunteers; and it was only comparatively late in the crisis – on 20–1 January 1914 – that he finally succumbed to the pressure of the hawks, and indeed to the logic of his own strategies, by accepting the need for a major gun-running coup.[35] This was the hesitant beginning of the Buchanesque adventure which culminated in the landing of some 25,000 rifles and 3 million rounds of ammunition at Larne and other Ulster seaside towns on the night of 24–5 April 1914.

Larne not only failed to solve the military problems of the UVF (indeed, to judge it in narrowly military terms would probably be a mistake); in some ways it also rendered a political solution to the Ulster crisis more difficult to attain. For most of the period between 1912 and 1914 loyalist militancy had been closely regulated by the political leadership of the movement, and it had been interwoven with its constitutional strategies. Indeed, though paramilitarism was the most conspicuous aspect of unionist endeavour in these years, and the aspect which was most celebrated by the unionists themselves, it is arguable that for some of the key leaders – notably Carson – militancy was subservient to the process of negotiation. More prosaic, but possibly more significant than coups such as Larne, was the steady process of debate within Westminster, and between leading unionists and Liberal ministers. The Irish Unionist Parliamentary Party had unquestionably been relegated as a result of local initiatives such as the Ulster Unionist Council or the Ulster Provisional Government (planned between 1911 and 1913, and constituted in September 1913), but the party fought the Home Rule Bill with tenacity through each parliamentary circuit, and it remained the chief point of contact between unionism and the ideologues of home rule. Carson negotiated in private with Asquith in December 1913 and January 1914 and it is arguable that the rumours of this diplomacy, combined with its ultimate failure, nudged Carson towards his decision to sanction the gun-running.[36]

The Liberal government subsequently moved a little further than Asquith had been prepared to do in January 1914: in March Lloyd George pursued the possibility that those Ulster counties with unionist majorities might vote themselves out of the home rule polity for a six-year respite. But Carson, famously, did not want 'a sentence of death with a stay of execution for six years'; and in any case the Curragh incident intervened to redirect loyalist energies away from parliamentary negotiation and back to military preparations.[37] The decision of fifty-eight cavalry officers at the Curragh camp, Kildare, to refuse to participate in any offensive (as opposed to policing) action against the Ulster unionists was interpreted by nationalists as broader evidence of the British Army's partisanship; it was seen by unionists, on the other hand, as the culmination of a plot to suppress the movement against home rule. It is unlikely whether – given Carson's attitude – anything further could have come of the Lloyd George initiative, but the Curragh affair, which apparently exposed the bad faith of Liberal ministers, ensured the final dissipation of unionist patience: only a significant gesture of appeasement from Asquith could have diverted popular unionism from the descent into violence. A final effort to hammer home an agreement – the Buckingham Palace Conference of 21–4 July 1914–brought simply a restatement of positions, with the Ulster unionists reiterating without enthusiasm their demand for the permanent exclusion of the six north-eastern counties and the nationalists and Liberals reluctantly offering a combination of county plebiscites and temporary exclusion.

The Larne gun-running had made it more difficult for the unionist leadership to accept anything less than a six-county and permanent partition scheme, even assuming that they would otherwise have been willing to retreat. If – as is arguable – the Ulster unionist command had sought to condition the parliamentary process with the implied threat of force, then this strategy was, by July 1914, demonstrably a failure: the Home Rule Bill was still being nudged towards the statute-books, while the concessions offered by the Liberal government were deemed to be too feeble to be worth the effort of debate. Indeed, the constitutional dimension to Ulster unionist endeavour had already been discredited by (from the perspective of popular loyalism) the years of fruitless diplomacy culminating in the failure of the Asquith talks and the further revelations of ministerial perfidy elicited during the aftermath of the Curragh incident. Thus, if Carson had raised loyalist militancy with a view to strengthening his advocacy, then by the spring of 1914 it was he who was the servant of the militants: in April 1914 he privately admitted to Plunkett his inability to control his own forces; in May 1914 his tentative interest in federalist solutions to the challenge of Irish government was briskly rejected by the Ulster unionist press.[38] Militancy had been created as a means to an end, but it was now threatening to become (in every sense) the end of unionism itself.

Nevertheless, these years of resistance to home rule have been judged within the unionist tradition to be a period of unsullied success; indeed, it is possible to go further and argue that the character of Ulster unionist political behaviour at this time has left an indelible and damaging impression, not just on the historical sensitivities of contemporary unionists, but on their strategic thinking. At one level it is not hard to understand this reverence for the men and women of the 1912–16 era: the story has acquired the trappings of a Norse saga, with heroes who faced down monstrous, superior forces, and who ultimately sacrificed themselves in the cause of honour on the battlefields of France and Flanders. Equally, it is hard to escape the contribution of these men and women to the formulation of a long-term strategy for Ulster unionism, a strategy which was maintained through the negotiations of 1916, the Irish Convention of 1917–18 and during the evolution of the Government of Ireland Bill in 1919–20. Like their counterparts within the republican tradition, these northerners have assumed a mythic stature for contemporary unionists, as the selfless patriots who created Northern Ireland.[39]

And yet – though it might seem superfluous to say so – the problems in their achievement should not be overlooked. This is not just a matter of pointing to the contested nature of the Northern Ireland state, and ascribing blame. Judged even within the terms of the broader Irish unionist tradition, the northern unionists of 1912–14 took decisions which not only had a lasting influence within their community, but wrought lasting damage. The decision to fight home rule on the basis of exclusion seems originally to have been taken as a means of separating Liberal pragmatists from nationalist fundamentalists, and thereby wrecking the bill; but it seems clear that the self-interest of the Belfast commercial elite propelled the choice from a merely strategic gambit into a more active campaign goal. Perhaps this was a necessary compromise between unionism and broader democratic principles; perhaps it was merely an acceleration of deeply rooted trends within Irish society and politics. But it also necessarily involved the reduction of a diverse and complex community down to its north-eastern core, and the amputation of some of the most culturally sophisticated and politically interesting members of the wider Irish unionist family.

Exclusion may have seemed like practical politics, but it inflicted wounds on northern nationalists, and also less obviously and perhaps more insidiously on Irish unionism itself. A combination of exclusion and militancy, though still celebrated within contemporary Ulster unionism, separated northerners from their southern allies, and educated the movement into a highly dangerous form of brinkmanship to which it still occasionally clings. In reality the militant strategy was highly flawed, and brought with it the probability of defeat – glorious, perhaps, but certainly bloody and comprehensive. Moreover, the tactic of brinkmanship, while it was arguably forced on to the Ulster unionists by the Liberal government, involved the gradual eradication of constitutional diplomacy, and a resort to armed threat. This in turn led Ulster unionism to the edge of the abyss. In July 1914 unionist strategic thinking combined with Liberal prevarication meant that loyalism was faced with the choice of a humiliating climb-down or political and military self-destruction at the hands of the Liberal government and the British Army. Since 1969 unionist strategies, influenced by the apparent successes of the home rule era, often produced the same political choices: defeat or annihilation.

The definition of the Ulster unionist case which was being offered at the Buckingham Palace Conference in July 1914 remained fixed until the establishment of the Northern Irish state in 1920–1. However, although Carson and Craig had been bargaining for a six-county exclusion agreement from late 1913, the mandate to conclude a deal on these terms was given by the UUC only in June 1916. The occasion for this decision was the Lloyd George initiative of May–July 1916, designed to address the crisis in Irish government created by the insurgents of the Easter Rising. Lloyd George's preferred strategy was an immediate enactment of home rule, with the exclusion of the six north-eastern counties on what looked like a permanent basis to the Ulster unionists, but at the same time looked like a merely temporary arrangement to nationalists. The debate on this initiative was effectively the first time that the UUC in Belfast had a chance to address the implications of the strategy which its leaders had been pursuing for almost three years. The results were, predictably, far from harmonious, with much distress in evidence concerning the impending desertion of the unionists of Cavan, Donegal and Monaghan, and indeed the broader southern unionist community.

The Lloyd George negotiations supplied the first indisputable evidence that the historic unionist alliance was fragmenting, and that the price of Belfast leadership during the third home rule crisis was the salvation of eastern Ulster alone. The chasm between Ulster unionism and southern unionism was already evident in 1913–14, if not before; but because the home rule crisis was not brought to any definable resolution in 1914 the implications of these divisions were never fully worked out, and the forms of unity – if not the substance – remained in place. To the extent that the Lloyd George initiative also ended inconclusively, then a superficial unity between Ulster and southern unionism continued to be possible, and was still claimed; but in reality the attitude of Carson, combined with the unanimous (if doubt-ridden) vote of the UUC, meant that exclusion was no longer a matter of gamesmanship, but was a democratically endorsed tenet of the Ulster movement. The actions of southern unionists within the cabinet in scuppering the initiative underlined the divergence between the two unionisms, and this was confirmed (if confirmation were needed) by the proceedings of the Irish Convention in the following year.

The Convention was designed to divert the energies of the Irish parties, and to clothe Lloyd George's constitutional nakedness before the USA, and in particular before Irish America. In the context of unionism it helped to supply an institutional and ideological cementing of regional divisions within the movement. The Convention, which met from July 1917 until April 1918, had ninety delegates, and included representatives not from Irish unionism as a whole but rather from both the northern and southern movements. Indeed, the very distinctive styles of the two delegations exemplified at a micropolitical level broader divisions within the Irish unionist movement: the southern unionists acted, in the famous verdict of R.B. McDowell, with 'the self-confidence bred by generations of governing', combining a free-booting lack of responsibility to the broader movement with the sober paternalism of the self-righteous but well-intentioned Midleton.[40] The Ulster unionists, by way of contrast, were led by a sober Scots businessman, H.T. Barrie, and were much less flamboyant, both personally and intellectually: they were well regimented, and reported back to an advisory committee of the UUC. The northerners were working within a limited brief – opposition to home rule and, if appropriate, exclusion of the six counties. But even had this not been the case, they lacked the freedom of manoeuvre of the southern unionists, who weaved and dodged unhindered by the watchful eye of any external authority. Nor were these distinctions purely organisational or cultural: a combination of the freedom enjoyed by the southerners with the arrogance of Midleton allowed them to move towards striking a deal with the representatives of the Irish Parliamentary Party at the Convention. While the Ulster unionists looked on aghast, the southerners accepted a moderate home rule proposal as being the mildest of the unpalatable choices available to them. This not only helped to formalise the ideological split within Irish unionism, but helped to divide and overturn southern unionism itself, for the Midletonites, with characteristic courage and tactlessness, had moved out ahead of mainstream opinion within the body of the Irish Unionist Alliance. The Convention, which seemed at one point to be so close to squaring the circle of Irish politics, instead helped to divert and destroy the Irish Party, and to divide and truncate Irish unionism; its proceedings, no less than its failure, helped to elevate extremism at the expense of the centre ground in Irish political life.

If the Convention formalised the divide between southern and Ulster unionism, then the Government of Ireland Bill helped to formalise a divide within Ulster unionism itself. With the failure of the Convention in April 1918, and the end of the war in November, the government returned to the issue of Irish self-government, forming a cabinet committee in October 1919 under the chairmanship of the southern unionist sympathiser Walter Long. Long, who had helped to scupper the Lloyd George détente of 1916, had been battered by the war and in particular by the loss of his son, a youthful and highly decorated brigadier general, who was killed in action in 1917. Like many other Tories, the bitter experience of military conflict had helped to soften the rigidities of Long's politics, and this former apostle of an all-Ireland unionism was by 1919–20 prepared to countenance a nine-county partition scheme.[41] The debates within Long's committee between the advocates of six-county partition and the advocates of a nine-county proposal were eventually resolved in favour of the former; they prefigured similar, if more emotive, discussions within the ranks of the UUC. The fruits of Long's deliberations were published in February 1920 as the Government of Ireland Bill, an ingenious combination of home rule and unionist principles, which proposed a six-county Northern Ireland, complete with a home rule executive and parliament, and a twenty-six county Southern Ireland, endowed with similar constitutional trappings.

If the Lloyd George debacle of 1916 had foreshadowed the split between Ulster and southern unionism which occurred in 1917–18, then the same fraught process of negotiation looked forward to the fracturing of Ulster unionism which occurred between March and May 1920. Both aspects of the disintegration of Irish unionism involved considerable internal acrimony. The Government of Ireland Bill was debated by the Ulster Unionist Council on 10 March 1920, and again on 27 May, with a majority favouring acceptance of the measure: but there was a considerable dissenting minority (comprising 80 delegates out of 390 in May), whom the Belfast-based leadership of the movement made minimal efforts to appease. These unionists of Cavan, Donegal and Monaghan had been willing to acquiesce in the six-county scheme touted in 1916, but a combination of the mounting tension and defensiveness created by the Anglo-Irish War, as well as somewhat brusque handling by the unionists of eastern Ulster, meant that the debates which occurred in the spring of 1920 were considerably more bitter. The unionists of southern and western Ulster were consigned to the purported darkness of Rome Rule in May 1920 with as little compunction as was applied to the southern unionists in 1913–14, when six-county exclusion was first seriously advocated in the north.

The enactment of the Government of Ireland Bill in December 1920 looked forward to the creation of the Northern Ireland parliament in May–June 1921, and it represented the final triumph of an exclusivist unionism over the more generous and diverse alternatives which had been current since the mid-1880s, but which had been killed off as straggling liabilities during the great retreat of the movement after 1912. A once widely (if often thinly) spread movement had effectively withdrawn to the north-east of the island; a socially and culturally diversified movement had been simplified, stripped of the advocacy of Trinity intellectuals and the more tangible support of southern land and Dublin commerce. Perhaps (as its opponents argued) the advocates of an all-Ireland unionism were fighting history, seeking to dilute a relentlessly self-confident nationalism, and to sustain a gentry class which had been inching a retreat since the eighteenth century. Or perhaps these advocates were seeking to reverse the fundamental development of Ulster unionism towards particularism and prominence.

The problem with Ulster unionism may have been, as its most acerbic nationalist critics alleged, that its supremacist impulse meant that it could not function outside of a unionist state. Maybe – modifying this point – the fate of an all-Ireland unionism was sealed by the proverbial unwillingness of Ulster unionists to accept compromise. But in reality the most striking feature of Ulster unionism in the years after 1912 was not its rigidity but rather the nature of its flexibility: the leaders of the movement, based in Belfast and eastern Ulster, wanted no part of a self-governing Ireland, and they were willing to sacrifice territory, partners and principles in order to protect their own loyalist arcadia. The death of Irish unionism came about not because of Ulster unionist inflexibility but because they were too willing to flex in certain directions.[42]

NOTES

1 Quoted in Paul Bew, *Ideology and the Irish Question: Ulster Unionism and Irish Nationalism, 1912–1916* (Oxford, 1994), p. 35.

2 K.Theodore Hoppen, *Elections, Politics and Society in Ireland, 1832–1885* (Oxford, 1984), p. 284.

3 For these themes see Henry Patterson, *Class Conflict and Sectarianism: The Protestant Working Class and the Belfast Labour Movement, 1868–1920* (Belfast, 1980); Aiken McClelland, *William Johnston of Ballykilbeg* (Lurgan, 1990).

4 Hoppen, *Elections, Politics and Society in Ireland*, p. 189; Brian Walker, *Ulster Politics: The Formative Years, 1868–1886* (Belfast, 1989), pp. 156–7.

5 Walker, *Ulster Politics*, pp. 129–53, 192–201.

6 Saunderson's career is examined in Reginald Lucas, *Colonel Saunderson MP: A Memoir* (London, 1908) and Alvin Jackson, *Colonel Edward Saunderson: Land and Loyalty in Victorian Ireland* (Oxford, 1995).

7 R.V. Comerford, 'Gladstone's first Irish enterprise', in W.E. Vaughan (ed.), *A New History of Ireland*, V, *Ireland Under the Union*, I, *1801–70* (Oxford, 1989), p. 441.

8 Ibid.

9 Jackson, *Saunderson*, pp. 186–8.

10 See, for example, R.W. Kirkpatrick, 'Origins and development of the Land War in Mid-Ulster, 1879–1885', in F.S.L. Lyons and R.A.J. Hawkins (eds), *Ireland under the Union: Varieties of Tension: Essays in Honour of T.W. Moody* (Oxford, 1980), pp. 201–35.

11 Peter Gibbon, *The Origins of Ulster Unionism: The Foundations of Popular Protestant Politics and Ideology in Nineteenth Century Ireland* (Manchester, 1975). See also Jackson, *Saunderson*, pp. 113–14 and Philip Ollerenshaw, 'No home rule, no federalism, no dominion: businessmen and the development of Ulster unionism, 1886–1921' (unpublished typescript), fols 12–16.

12 For the Saunderson–Salisbury correspondence see: Hatfield House, Third Marquess of Salisbury Papers, E/Saunderson/1–27. Numerous letters from Salisbury to Saunderson were used by Lucas in his *Colonel Saunderson MP* and were rediscovered during my research for *Saunderson*: these remain with the Saunderson family at Newbury, Berkshire. Copies of most of the Saunderson papers are available in the Public Record Office of Northern Ireland (PRONI), classified under T.2996.

13 Patrick Buckland, *Irish Unionism*, I, *The Anglo-Irish and the New Ireland, 1885–1922* (Dublin, 1972), pp. xvi–xvii.

14 Alvin Jackson, *The Ulster Party: Irish Unionists in the House of Commons, 1884–1911* (Oxford, 1989), pp. 235–40.

15 A useful account may be found in D.C. Savage, 'The origins of the Ulster Unionist Party, 1885–6', *Irish Historical Studies*, 12 (March 1961), pp. 185–208.

16 Martin Maguire, 'The organisation and activism of Dublin's Protestant working class, 1883–1935', *Irish Historical Studies*, 29 (May 1994).

17 Garry O'Connor, *Sean O'Casey*, paperback edn (London, 1989), ch. 1, discusses the precarious world of the Protestant clerk in late Victorian Dublin. For the records of the Dublin Orange Order, see PRONI, Minute Book of District LOL III, D.2947/5/41.

18 Dockrell and Jameson remain fairly elusive. For Cooper and Plunkett see Lennox Robinson, *Bryan Ricco Cooper* (London, 1931) and Trevor West, *Horace Plunkett: Cooperation and Politics: An Irish Biography* (Gerrard's Cross, 1986).

19 Hoppen, *Elections, Politics and Society*, p. 312.

20 The world of Howth Toryism and the political set around Gerald Fitzgibbon are memorably evoked in R.F. Foster, *Lord Randolph Churchill: A Political Life* (Oxford, 1981), esp. pp. 56–7.

21 See the study by Peter Hart, *The IRA and its Enemies: Violence and Community in County Cork, 1916–23* (Oxford, 1998), esp. pp. 272–92.

22 See, for example, British Library, Arthur Balfour Papers, Add. Ms. 49830, fol. 428: Balfour to Goschen (copy), 12 December 1891.

23 Buckland, *Irish Unionism*, I, pp. 129–85; Alvin Jackson, 'The failure of unionism in Dublin, 1900', *Irish Historical Studies*, 26 (November 1989).

24 Jackson, *Ulster Party*, pp. 227–9.

25 Ibid., pp. 253–60.

26 PRONI, Kingstown Unionist Club Records, D.950/1/144.

27 House of Lords Record Office, Bonar Law Papers, 34/1/23: Carson to Lansdowne, 9 October 1913.

28 Buckland, *Irish Unionism*, I, pp. 258–71.

29 W.E. Vaughan, *Landlords and Tenants in Mid-Victorian Ireland* (Oxford, 1994), p. 227.

30 Maria Luddy, 'Isabella M.S. Tod, 1836–1896', in Mary Cullen and Maria Luddy (eds), *Women, Power and Consciousness in Nineteenth Century Ireland: Eight Biographical Studies* (Dublin, 1995); Noel Armour, 'Isabella Tod and Liberal unionism in Ulster, 1886–96', in Alan Hayes and Diane Urquhart (eds), *New Perspectives on Irish Women's History* (Dublin, n.d.).

31 Nancy Kinghan, *United We Stood: The Story of the Ulster Women's Unionist Council, 1911–1974* (Belfast, 1975); Diane Urquhart, 'The female of the species is more deadly than the male?: The Ulster Women's Unionist Council, 1911–1940', in Janice Holmes and Diane Urquhart (eds), *Coming into the Light: The Work, Politics and Religion of Women in Ulster, 1890–1940* (Belfast, 1994), pp. 93–125.

32 Cliona Murphy, *The Women's Suffrage Movement and Irish Society in the Early Twentieth Century* (Hemel Hempstead, 1989), p. 19.

33 Jackson, *Ulster Party*, pp. 307–19.

34 Charles Townshend, *Political Violence in Ireland: Government and Resistance since 1848* (Oxford, 1983), p. 249.

35 Alvin Jackson, *Sir Edward Carson* (Dublin, 1993), pp. 36–8.

36 Ibid., pp. 37–8.

37 Ibid., p. 33. There is a considerable literature on the Curragh incident. As a starting point see, for example, Ian Beckett (ed.), *The Army and the Curragh Incident* (London, 1986).

38 Plunkett Foundation, Oxfordshire, Horace Plunkett Diaries, 1 April 1914: *Belfast News Letter*, 1, 7 May 1914.

39 Alvin Jackson, 'Unionist Myths, 1912–1985', *Past & Present*, 136 (August 1992), pp. 164–85.

40 R.B. McDowell, *The Irish Convention, 1917–18* (London, 1970), p. 127. McDowell revisited this theme in *Crisis & Decline: The Fate of Southern Unionism* (Dublin, 1997), esp. pp. 44–66.

41 Richard Murphy, 'Walter Long and the making of the Government of Ireland Act', *Irish Historical Studies*, 25 (May 1986), pp. 82–98.

42 This essay is a substantially revised version of chapter 5.4, pp. 215–44 of my *Ireland 1798–1998: Politics and War* (Oxford, 1999).

7 Defenders of the Union

Sir Horace Plunkett

Carla King

Introduction

Horace Curzon Plunkett (1854–1932) is generally cited as the leading Irish proponent of constructive unionism, indeed, one of its formulators. Founder of the
co-operative movement, committee member of the Congested Districts Board,
promoter and first president of the Department of Agriculture and Technical
Instruction and one of the formative influences on the United Irishwomen, he
was undoubtedly a force for change in late nineteenth- and early twentieth-
century Irish society. But to what extent did he have, as his nationalist opponents
averred, an underlying political agenda; that is, to win the Irish people for the
Union? This chapter will examine the evolution of Plunkett's political thought in
relation to the Union, focusing mainly on the years 1889 to 1914.

Plunkett's political formation

Plunkett's background was staunchly Conservative. His father, Admiral Lord
Dunsany, was a Conservative peer, the family, substantial landowners in Meath,
Kildare and Louth, having provided Conservative MPs and peers throughout the
nineteenth century. Born in 1854, he was raised in both England and Ireland, and
given a traditional upper-class education at Eton and Oxford, graduating with a
Second in Modern History in 1877. Sharing an interest in Irish history with his
cousin, the novelist and historian Emily Lawless, he was, arguably, more aware of
the force of Irish historical grievances than many of his unionist contemporaries,
frequently referring to them in his speeches and writings.

It was at Oxford, too, that Plunkett began to develop a social awareness, influenced by figures including Ruskin, Goldwin Smith and Toynbee, and he became
acquainted with the ideas of the co-operative movement. On coming down, he
settled in Ireland, acting as agent for his father on the family estate at Dunsany,
and established a co-operative store in the village that was to survive for over
twenty years.

As a third son, Plunkett did not stand to inherit the family estates or title – by
this stage the family assets were in a combination of land, coal mines and ship-
yards. He sought a career in business and in 1879, when threatened with the

family disease of tuberculosis that had already carried off his mother, younger brother and sister (and was some years later to kill his eldest brother Randal), he embarked on a cattle-ranching enterprise in the American West. This was the height of the cattle boom, before the spread of westward settlement came into conflict with the extensive methods of cattle ranching. Plunkett was able to tap large amounts of investment capital among his Irish landlord acquaintances and made a sizeable fortune.

His decision to return to Ireland early in 1889 was brought about by the death of his father. His eldest brother had died in 1883, the next in line, his second brother, John, was an alcoholic and drug addict, incapable of safeguarding the family interests (he died in 1899) and Horace, who had been left a larger inheritance than he expected, was financially free to return home. Nevertheless, he maintained his business interests in America and for many more years made an annual journey to Wyoming. He was later to inspire the establishment of President Theodore Roosevelt's Country Life Commission[1] and to serve as an unofficial negotiator between the governments of the United States and Great Britain during the First World War.[2] Although, as he put it, 'Ireland had the first claim' on him,[3] he was never a strong nationalist in an era of strong nationalisms. Indeed, the title 'an Anglo-American Irishman' used in Margaret Digby's biography of him was Plunkett's self-designation.[4]

It had been Plunkett's practice to break his years in Wyoming with annual trips home so he was well aware of Irish political developments. In January 1881 he noted the change 'for the worse' in the tenants brought about by the Land League,[5] and in April on receiving a threatening letter at Trim, he commented, 'these epistles are now too common to take notice of'.[6] He closely followed the debate around Gladstone's 1881 Land Act, disapproving of it, and he was conscious of the fears of his class during the Land War.

While he evidently enjoyed the life of the 'big house', particularly hunting and visiting, on his return to Ireland in 1889 at the age of thirty-three Plunkett was searching for a role. He was recognised as having a good business head and was called upon frequently to draw up the accounts for his extended family and friends. His proven business acumen was to lend greater credibility to his reform proposals in later years. He soon found a cause in introducing the co-operative movement to Ireland, fostering initially retail co-operation before, within months, his attention shifted to establishing creamery co-operatives. Despite the fact that he embarked on this work while the Plan of Campaign was at its height, and notwithstanding his clear identification with the landlord class, the creamery movement succeeded because it provided farmers with a means of averting a crisis in the butter industry.[7] By the end of 1891 there were fifteen co-operative creameries in the country, while by 1916 there were 446.[8]

On one of Plunkett's trips home he had been involved in the formation of the Irish Cattle Association in 1885. This was an attempt to help Irish farmers to cope with the effects of the depression on cattle prices. With his experience of large-scale cattle ranching in America, he appreciated the competition Irish farmers faced in terms of the scale of their operations. However, this and subsequent efforts ran up against vested interests in the cattle trade and had very limited success. Nevertheless, with the co-operative creamery movement, the Cattle Association and his membership of the Agriculture Committee of the Royal Dublin Society, by the early 1890s Plunkett was beginning to be seen as something of an authority on rural matters.

Constructive unionism

The start of Plunkett's co-operative campaign coincided with Arthur Balfour's term as Chief Secretary for Ireland. While Balfour was initially occupied with coercive measures to combat the Plan of Campaign, he understood the need for ameliorative reforms in Ireland, particularly in the west, where in 1888 he undertook drainage schemes and light-railway development.[9]

Plunkett first approached Balfour for support in 1891 in an unsuccessful attempt to persuade the RDS to assist the co-operative movement. Balfour welcomed Plunkett's initiative in providing practical assistance to Irish farmers, and sought his advice in formulating his proposals for the establishment of a development board for the west, the Congested Districts Board. Indeed Plunkett and another member of the board, the philanthropist James Hack Tuke, participated in drafting the legislation setting it up.[10] Although at times critical of elements of its policy, Plunkett was to serve for twenty-seven years on the CDB.

Despite the introduction of some significant reform measures, there is little evidence that Balfour had any overall vision of Irish future development. His preoccupations were more with British than with Irish politics, although he felt the need for measures of economic development to reduce an Irish sense of grievance. As Catherine Shannon has pointed out, he shared Salisbury's anxiety about the threat posed in the rise of socialism in Britain and tended to see the Fenian element in the home rule movement as linked with British socialists. To allow a home rule victory in Westminster would not only threaten the integrity of the Empire but might encourage English radicals and socialists to imitate Irish tactics and methods.[11] Balfour also shared with his uncle the view that Irish landlords, as a prop to the Union, had to be protected.[12] His predecessor, Sir Michael Hicks Beach, had started with the aspiration to be even-handed in his dealings with all sides in Ireland.[13] During the Plan of Campaign the Under-Secretary, Sir Redvers Buller, had attempted to put pressure on the more intransigent landlords to meet their tenants some of the way. On his appointment as Irish Chief Secretary in spring 1887, Balfour had taken a more confrontational approach towards the Plan, immediately bolstered the police and judicial powers of the Irish administration, beefed up the landlord response and introduced a policy of coercion that earned him the sobriquet 'Bloody Balfour'. The reform legislation had been introduced only when he was convinced that the Plan of Campaign had been broken.

The first public suggestion that there was a government policy of 'killing home rule with kindness' was enunciated in a speech by Arthur Balfour's brother Gerald to his Leeds constituents during the general election of 1895. Like his uncle, Lord

Salisbury, famous for his political gaffes, Gerald Balfour later denied that there was such an intention but by that stage the damage had been done and the claim soon became part of Conservative rhetoric. The nationalist side, racked by the Parnellite split, did very badly in the 1895 election and the anti-Parnellites, in particular, were ready to spot a government conspiracy to take advantage of their weakness to try to wean the electorate away from support for home rule. John Dillon, especially, tended to see in every reform effort an attempt to 'draw a red herring across the path of Irish nationalism'.

Andrew Gailey has cast considerable doubt on the claim that there was a programme of reform aimed at undermining the nationalist demand on the part of successive Conservative chief secretaries, notably Arthur and Gerald Balfour and George Wyndham and some of their Dublin Castle advisers.[14] He has demonstrated that the Balfours were more concerned with their British electorate and with achieving continued Liberal unionist support than with a concerted aim to undermine Irish nationalism. In relation to one important piece of what has been seen as constructive unionist legislation – the Local Government Act of 1898 that replaced the old grand jury system with elected councils – Gailey has shown that this was an inevitable follow-on to legislation already on the statute-books in Britain.[15] Moreover, the ending of the Plan of Campaign meant that the country was more peaceful, allowing an opportunity for long-overdue reform measures to be undertaken.

Plunkett and rural reform

If it is at least questionable whether reform measures were indeed aimed at undermining the demand for home rule in the case of the Balfours, what about Plunkett's own motivations? It is important to look at the sequence of events here. Plunkett founded the co-operative movement in 1889 in an attempt to move away from the polarisation of Irish politics prior to the Parnell split, in fact when Parnell was at the height of his popularity. In 1890 Plunkett tried to enlist Parnell's support for his new efforts, and it is quite likely, given the latter's economic ideas,[16] that he might have responded favourably, had the meeting arranged by T.P. Gill in the House of Commons taken place. Unfortunately, Parnell did not turn up. Instead, Plunkett engaged the help of Mulhallen Marum, home rule party MP for Kilkenny, who addressed several meetings on behalf of the co-operative movement before he died suddenly of a heart attack in September 1890. A year later Plunkett tried unsuccessfully to persuade Dillon to support his efforts.[17] The point is that had Plunkett's aim been to undermine the home rule argument, he is unlikely to have tried so hard from the beginning to work with nationalist leaders.

From its inception the co-operative movement aimed at being non-party-political and cross-class. This may have seemed naïve, and in the Irish context it was certainly unusual, but the alternatives were to have made it a unionist body, in which case it would have remained very small, or a nationalist body, in which case it could not have been led by Plunkett, and at the time there was no one else with the drive and dedication to make it succeed. From its inception, there were accusations that the movement was landlord led, even a landlord plot. Yet, whatever the likelihood of Irish farmers joining the co-operative movement from purely economic motives, for principled nationalists such as Fr Tom Finlay,[18] T.P. Gill and George Russell to have worked with him, and for the Parnellite side to have given him their support in the early years, they must have believed in his intentions sufficiently to risk their credibility with their own side. Nor did Plunkett believe that the home rule demand had died with Parnell. In October 1896 he and Lady Fingall witnessed the Parnell Anniversary demonstration in Dublin. He commented in his diary: 'Nothing could be more complete [in its] proof of the survival of the national sentiment than this great function in spite of the disintegrating factionalism in nationalist politics'.[19]

Although Plunkett had never made a secret of his unionism, his decision to stand for Parliament in 1892 challenged the non-party image he was trying to maintain for the co-operative movement. Arthur Balfour, while he admired Plunkett's work, told him that he would never have made him a member of the CDB had he been a unionist MP.[20] Plunkett had been expressing an interest in entering politics since early 1890.[21] His family had a tradition of political service and his charming but ineffectual brother John was already MP for South Gloucestershire. He seems to have believed that there was a new spirit emerging in the party and that he might work with it in the interest of reform. His selection for what was one of only three safe southern unionist seats was itself a recognition of his achievement. Yet he was initially quite diffident in cautioning his election agent, Dunbar Barton: 'I ought to warn supporters (if I ran for Irish constituency) that my opinions are too new to be surely permanent'.[22] In his first election speech at Rathmines he claimed that he had hoped it would not be necessary to touch politics at all, 'for my Irish work is in itself totally apart and distinct from politics', and while referring to 'the great danger of home rule', he also expressed an interest in schemes of imperial federation.[23] It was quite a complex address with none of the reassuring unionist certainties for which many of his listeners may have hoped. If his advisers had expected to mould him, they were soon to be disappointed. In unionist terms Plunkett could be something of a loose cannon. He was however elected for South Dublin on 8 July 1892, with a large majority.[24] It was characteristic of him that his first major speech after his election was to an Orange gathering at which he urged toleration of Catholics. He wrote in his diary:

> At night I spoke to a large Orange demonstration in Leinster Hall. I was told the R.C.s would never vote for me again if I did so. But I had more fear of the Orangemen as I was determined to plead for tolerance towards tolerant R.C.s. This I did I think successfully.[25]

Even before Plunkett's entry into political life he had shown signs that he was not likely to make a conventional unionist politician. On founding the Irish co-operative movement he had sought and was given assistance from the British movement, which was a largely working class and socialist body. For many years, often accompanied by Lord Monteagle, he attended the annual Co-operative Congresses, to his amusement travelling third class on the train. He commented in his diary on the Ipswich congress of 1889:

> I was greatly impressed with the tone of the arguments used by the represen-
> tatives of the working men. Most dignified speaking – always to the point. No
> one can realise what the working man has done for himself until they have
> heard them speaking of their aims and ambitions. Those are indeed high.
> I never before realised how much the working man is doing for himself
> compared with what is being done for him.[26]

It was through the co-operative congresses that Plunkett began lifelong friend-ships with Sidney Webb and Beatrix Potter. At the Manchester Congress in 1892 he met the socialist Tom Mann, remarking, 'I liked the man. He is the best kind of labour leader. Honest and strong, even violent where he scents injustice. Very able in argument and withal fair.'[27] Plunkett's willingness to work with these socialist co-operators is worth contrasting with the views of his Conservative Party col-leagues. The early months of 1893 saw the rise of organised labour in the new unionism and socialism of the Social Democratic Federation and Socialist League, developments that Lord Salisbury, the Balfours and other Tory leaders viewed with unmitigated horror.[28] Indeed, Arthur Balfour believed the Irish land movement and the British socialists to be part of the same force.[29] Plunkett was never a socialist, although later in life he was close to Fabianism. Yet from early in his career he showed a willingness to work with people from different social and political backgrounds.

Plunkett and unionism

Plunkett's unionism was more than a family tradition and it was firmly held. Nevertheless, in 1888, he commented in his diary: 'I am a pessimist about Union-ism. But I don't think home rule means such a collapse as some people think.'[30] Four years later to the privacy of his diary Plunkett was willing to concede that the home rule side had an argument:

> Christopher Redington and old Tuke dined with Dunning and me at Royal
> Hotel. I was very seedy. But I had a long talk on Irish affairs & politics with
> C.R. who is a very able exponent of Morley's home rule theories. When
> confined to abstract discussion the home rulers certainly have the best of it.[31]

His point was that, whatever the theory, he did not believe at this time that in practice, given the politicians on the nationalist side, home rule would be bene-ficial to Ireland. Part of this may have been prejudice. A common unionist argu-ment against home rule was that the Irish were too irresponsible and hopeless to be capable of ruling themselves. On the other hand, the 1890s was not a good time for nationalist politics, with the party shattered by the Parnell split and consumed by its own factionalism. By 1894 the combined membership of all sides of the party had dropped by about 70 per cent of its 1890 level. Michael Davitt and Dillon, at the head of the anti-Parnellite section, were at times dismayed by the conduct of several of their parliamentary colleagues and struggled hard to impose some discipline in the party.[32]

One of Plunkett's favourite axioms was that there should be more business in politics and less politics in business. His support for the Union was based on the argument that however detrimental to Irish interests it had been in the past, by the close of the nineteenth century for the country to be linked to the most successful economy in the world and part of a multinational empire would benefit it significantly. Three days after Plunkett's maiden speech to the House of Commons in February 1893 William Gladstone introduced his second Home Rule Bill. Plunkett took an active part in the unionist opposition to the bill and his speeches and writings afford an insight into his beliefs at this time.

As part of the debate, the *Pall Mall Gazette* ran a series of leading articles through July 1893 on 'The Case against Home Rule' from various perspectives. Plunkett's Catholic cousin, the Earl of Fingall, was asked to contribute an article on 'The Case against Home Rule from a Catholic Point of View'. As the earl was far more interested in the Meath hunt than in politics, Plunkett, a non-practising member of the Church of Ireland, wrote it for him. It began with an assertion that Irish Catholics, 'enjoying a liberty and freedom of action unequalled in any country in Europe and unthought of in the days of the Irish Parliament, our legitimate demands from the State are reduced to comparative insignificance'. The only official disqualification of Irish Catholics was now confined to 'one high officer in Ireland' and their only remaining grievance was the question of higher education, which, he maintained, was likely to be settled in the near future. This was aimed to counter the case against the Union. In its defence Plunkett argued that it was necessary to curb the influence of the Catholic clergy, who, he claimed, had exercised their influence in a class sense, on the side of the tenants and against the landlords. Thus the Union would serve to counteract and control such involvement.

Plunkett assumed that the Irish party, if accorded its own parliament, would exercise its authority in a partisan way. Therefore, much of his effort in the debate on the Home Rule Bill was aimed at defending the jobs and interests of existing office-holders, then disproportionately Protestant and unionist.[33] He argued that:

He had never accepted the views that Irishmen need be afraid of persecution on account of their religious belief;[34] but he thought that they were likely to suffer on account of their political opinions. He knew Ireland just as well as any other Member, and he was of opinion that the danger through politics was greater than that through religion. Many Catholics had been subject to persecution owing to their political views, and he was satisfied that political conditions would predominate over the religious.[35]

Like Arthur Balfour, Plunkett sought to decouple the link achieved by Davitt, Parnell, Devoy and others in 1879 between the demand for home rule and the land question. That connexion had, of course, been severed partly by Parnell himself in 1882 but Plunkett argued in 1893 that in having tackled the land question the government had removed it as a force behind the home rule demand:

> There never was a time when the demand for home rule could find any strong or effective expression unless it was tacked on to . . . the remedy of some particular grievance, or the attainment of some immediate, definite, and substantial gain. The entire force of the demand in its latest phase had been due to certain desires, some legitimate and others illegitimate, in connection with the land. Now, there was absolutely no nucleus to the home rule comet. The land question was so well advanced towards settlement that that, as a political engine for home rule agitation, had exploded.[36]

Nevertheless, he showed signs of independence from the unionist line in voting against a Conservative amendment to exclude Irish representation from Westminster in the event of home rule being granted,[37] resulting in Edward Carson threatening to denounce him in the constituency through the Irish press.[38]

A major consideration for Plunkett in his political career was his hope of winning unionist support for reforms in Ireland. There was a feeling among a forward-looking minority of unionists that a new approach was necessary and in his thinking Plunkett was, as Gailey points out, in a line of succession of the so-called 'Howth set'. However, while this group had advocated educational reform and the concession of denominational education in the 1870s and 1880s, Plunkett emphasised broader economic and social reform.[39] Unionism was strongest in the north of the country, where the social base was much wider. In the south it was wedded to a now almost moribund landlord class. What the reformers within unionism were hoping for was a series of initiatives that would give the party a positive content, rather than confining itself to opposition to home rule. The problem was going to be in gaining wider unionist acceptance for such an approach. Already in early 1893 Plunkett was having misgivings:

> Had meeting of Irish Unionist members at IIA rooms on Bridge Street, Westminster. I like not my colleagues. They are altogether too narrow and it is only a question of time how long they will exist as an active party. I must try & keep quiet & watch.[40]

Later he was more scathing: 'Meeting of Irish Unionist Party. Farce. Parliament met for new session. No freshness or interest — virtually continuation of old session'.[41] In the meantime the co-operative movement continued to grow. In 1894 the Irish Agricultural Organisation Society (IAOS) was formed with Plunkett as President and Fr Finlay SJ as Vice-President. It was the central organising body of the co-operative movement, with a Dublin office; a weekly newspaper, the *Irish Homestead*, followed a year later.

By the end of 1894, Plunkett was trying to win over the unionist party to his new policy of rural transformation. On 17 December 1894, he reported in his diary:

> At 10 AM a little conference which I got together which may exercise some influence in Irish history. T.W. Russell, John Atkinson, Dunbar Barton, Col. Dease & a few others let me urge them to press the Unionist Alliance to preach the Economic arguments against home rule in the nationalist parts of Ireland. They approved principle, details to be brought before I.U.A. Executive.[42]

Here we have what does look like an attempt to foster a 'constructive unionist' policy within the southern unionist grouping. It came not from the government but from Plunkett and a small group of associates. When he put the idea to Arthur Balfour the latter's response was lukewarm: 'He approved. But he evidently feels scared about the Ulster farmers' land views & can attach little importance to the nationalist parts of Ireland'.[43] To his chagrin, the Alliance turned down his proposal and he had to face defeat.[44] He was so disappointed that he considered resigning his seat and sent letters of resignation to Arthur Balfour, now leader of the Conservative Party in the House of Commons, on 27 May and to his constituency boss, Ian Hamilton, on 11 June.[45] It is not clear whether this was a genuine attempt to withdraw or an effort to put pressure on the party to introduce reform, because his diary entry on writing to Balfour was: 'Cannot serve party & country. Won't give up Irish industrial work. Will he have me for the sake of having a combined worker & talker from Ireland on such terms? Doubtful'.[46] If he did hope to induce the party to action over Ireland he was unsuccessful, for two weeks later Balfour informed him that the Conservative leadership was not contemplating Irish legislation in the next Parliament, 'at least not much', Plunkett observing that 'they will make a great blunder if they don't take the great, perhaps the last, opportunity they will have of making a unionist settlement of the Irish Qu[estio]n'.[47] There is a hint in Plunkett's diary that he intended setting up a political grouping with Robert Yerburgh, MP for Chester, who was active in the co-operative movement in Britain.[48] However, as it happened, the government resigned suddenly, and, faced with an imminent election, Plunkett was persuaded to stand again, probably owing to the difficulty of finding a replacement candidate in time. He was returned with an increased majority.[49]

Having failed to win the unionists over to reform, Plunkett decided to bring his policy to the country in the form of an *ad hoc*, cross-party committee to address social and economic measures. His proposal for the establishment of the Recess Committee came in two letters to the press, dated 27 August and 18 October 1895.[50] In the first he suggested that there were areas of non-contentious reform which could be agreed upon by both nationalists and unionists and suggested agriculture and technical instruction as examples of these. In the second he proposed the setting up of a committee and stressed its informal nature, which would ensure that no members would be committed to anything by agreeing to participate on it. Plunkett felt himself in a position to launch this initiative since he believed that while the nationalist politicians differed from him on the issue of home rule, they accepted his good faith in desiring reform for its own sake. In August he had acted as mediator between the incoming Chief Secretary, Gerald Balfour, and John Redmond in discussions on proposed legislation for that session[51] and at the end of 1894 he had written in his diary: 'I have been on good terms with the Nationalist members for they know that while I disagree in toto with their Irish policy I am always anxious to co-operate with them for the good of our common country'.[52] Whatever his intentions, in his first letter he was tactless enough to state that as a unionist he believed that if the condition of the Irish population improved it would cease to desire home rule. He urged that while nationalists would not agree with him, their opposite goals should not prevent their working together for more limited aims.[53] The problem was, however, that while some nationalists, such as Redmond, held that increased prosperity of the people would not threaten the demand for home rule, others, pre-eminent among them Dillon, were suspicious of any attempts at reform before home rule had been achieved.[54] Justin McCarthy shared Dillon's mistrust. In his reply to Plunkett's invitation, while denying that a material improvement would weaken support for home rule, he stated that he felt unable to participate in what he saw as an attempt to thwart that demand.[55]

Plunkett's invitation, in fact, faced both wings of the Irish Parliamentary Party with a dilemma, one that was to dog them in the years that followed. This was the question of their response to Plunkett's brand of 'constructive unionism'. Some nationalists believed that to show weakness towards unionism would further shake what support remained to them, particularly among their American sympathisers. On the other hand, as F.S.L. Lyons pointed out, the Parliamentary Party 'had always placed social reforms very much in the forefront of their programme and much of their popularity in the country depended on the success they achieved in wringing concessions from the land question, taxation, education and a host of other issues, from successive English governments'.[56] But to gain concessions in these areas would necessarily involve co-operating with their political opponents, rather than concentrating their energies exclusively on the issues of home rule.

Some nationalists believed, with Fr Finlay, that the co-operative movement, in bringing Irishmen of all sides together, represented a step on the way to making home rule possible. Russell replied to charges that the movement was anti-national with the assertion that the only movements showing signs of life which could be identified as signs of nationality – namely, 'the power of growth within, the power of evolving special ideas of culture, industry and society – are movements which the politicians denounce or ignore, and which are non-political'.[57] Among such movements he placed the co-operative movement, the Gaelic League and the Industrial Development Association. To charges that they were trying to solve the agrarian problem before the 'more fundamental' one of the home rule question had been solved, Plunkett replied:

> I hold that the value of any constitutional change must be increased with any improvement in the life of a community which enables it to turn the

improvement, when obtained, to the best advantage. Those who resist progress on the ground that it may make you cease to desire home rule, are only preparing a feast of dust and ashes should they attain their object.[58]

In the event, a committee was formed which included Parnellite nationalists but not the larger, anti-Parnellite group. At the same time, Colonel Edward Saunderson, the leader of the Irish Unionist Party, a County Cavan landlord of the old school, condemned Plunkett's proposal, claiming that the underlying motive was nationalist. He was deeply suspicious of the involvement of Redmond and Gill, who served as Plunkett's close collaborator in formulating the committee's policy. This response, as Saunderson's biographer Alvin Jackson has written, 'permanently soured his political relationship with Plunkett'.[59] On the other hand, the Liberal Unionists Thomas Sinclair and Thomas Andrews provided important assistance, setting up an Ulster Consultative Committee and galvanising support from among Belfast industrialists who had already made demands for improved provisions for technical education. Thus Plunkett was able to gather a middle ground of moderates, ready to move away from the now dormant politics of the national question in pursuit of reforms. He had already drawn on such individuals in setting up the committee of the IAOS and it was a pattern to be repeated in coming years in the A!l Ireland Committee of 1897, the Dunraven Land Committee of 1903 and the Irish Convention in 1917.

Plunkett's letters to the press had not committed the Recess Committee to dealing specifically with agriculture and technical instruction, though he had suggested them as examples of the sort of issue it might consider and he was clearly anxious for some reform in this area. They seem to have been accepted without argument as the first questions to be tackled and in the event no further measures were broached. The committee's report was published in mid-August 1896 and recommended the establishment of a Department of Agriculture and Industries for Ireland. It carried an introductory letter from Plunkett as Chairman to the Chief Secretary, Gerald Balfour, explaining the aims of the committee and requesting legislation to carry out its recommendations.[60] The first section of the report put much of the blame for the contemporary state of Ireland on past misrule and held that it was now up to the government to redress the situation. From this point of view it was published at an opportune time. In September the Royal Commission on Financial Relations between Great Britain and Ireland, set up by the Liberal government in May 1894 to investigate fiscal relations between the two islands, issued its report in which its members agreed almost unanimously that Ireland was being seriously overtaxed. It concluded: 'That whilst the actual tax revenue of Ireland is about one-eleventh of that of Great Britain, the relative taxable capacity of Ireland is very much smaller, and is not estimated by any of us as exceeding one-twentieth'.[61] The Recess Committee's report, issued only weeks before that of the Financial Relations Committee, while it avoided putting a figure on the grant needed for the proposed department, stated: 'The scale on which these requirements would be provided for might depend somewhat upon the claim which may be established for Ireland by the Royal Commission on

Financial Relations'.[62] Since the content of the majority report had been leaked to the *Freeman's Journal* in June and, moreover, there was some overlap in membership between the Financial Relations Commission and the Recess Committee, Plunkett had a good idea what the findings of the commission would be.

If the government was seriously committed to a policy of constructive unionism, here was its opportunity. So great was the sense of outrage in Ireland that, for once, most sides of Irish opinion, including unionists such as Saunderson, A.W. Samuels of the Irish High Court, W.E.H. Lecky of Trinity College and Plunkett, joined the nationalists in establishing the All-Ireland Committee. Meeting between February and May, they pressed the government for fiscal reforms to redress the imbalance. There was concern in Dublin Castle that the reaction to the Financial Relations Report would lead to an Irish demand for repayment of all the excess taxation since the Union, or at the least for sizeable recompense.[63] As Pauric Travers has argued in a detailed analysis of the financial relations question, government alarm at the extent to which Irish popular opinion united around the demand for redress pushed it further towards reform measures: 'While the constructive unionist policy was not new, it received a major boost from the growing consensus that special concessions to Ireland were justified because of overtaxation'.[64] Nevertheless, although the *Financial Relations Report* proved very significant in eventually pushing the reform argument, Gailey has shown that initially the government's response was one of hostility on the part of the Prime Minister, Salisbury, and the Chancellor of the Exchequer, Sir Michael Hicks Beach,[65] confusion in the case of Arthur Balfour,[66] and an attempt by the administration to shelve the issue.[67]

Far from Gerald Balfour having a carefully worked-out policy of 'killing home rule with kindness', of which a Department of Agriculture and Technical Instruction would form a part, in fact Plunkett had to push him hard to achieve the kind of reform he wanted. It is unlikely that the report would have been carried into legislation as faithfully as it was had Plunkett not been on such close terms with Balfour. In September 1895 he had taken the new Chief Secretary and his wife on a week-long tour of the west of Ireland, during which he talked about his co-operative work and 'gave him some broad views on the Irish Question', remarking that he found Balfour 'very receptive'.[68] At the same time he struck up a close friendship with Lady Betty Balfour and subsequently carried on a correspondence with her on political issues for many years. She became Plunkett's ally in converting her husband to the aims of the Recess Committee. However, whereas his wife read and criticised the draft of the report, Balfour could not at first be induced to look at even the published edition. In 1897 he introduced a much more limited measure but, after coming under opposition, it was dropped. As Gailey points out, Balfour was constrained on the one hand by restrictions imposed by the Treasury[69] and on the other he was opposed by the anti-Parnellites. Eventually, following the successful passage of the Local Government Act in 1898,[70] another bill, now more closely reflecting the Recess Committee's proposals, was passed as the Agriculture and Technical Instruction [Ireland] Act, 1899,[71] Plunkett being appointed Vice-President, or working head, of the new department.

By the end of 1895 Plunkett had become an influential figure. He was summoned regularly to the Viceregal Lodge for consultation by Lord Cadogan, commenting: 'I seem to have risen to a dangerous eminence as an unofficial adviser to the Irish Gov[ernmen]t. If they don't take my advice I am despised. If they do – well, "the Castle" will see I am destroyed. One cannot do good without hurting vested interests in Ireland.'[72] Nevertheless, by 1896 Plunkett's own political ideas were shifting. In February he spoke in favour of amnesty for political prisoners,[73] earning him a reprimand from his party convocation. Saunderson was instructed to write to him:

> The opinion of the Committee was this, that though each member of the Party had perfect freedom of action in political matters, it was expected that before taking a grave step on public policy the Committee should be informed beforehand, and thus be enabled to take counsel together. It was felt that without this mutual confidence it would serve no useful purpose to continue the existence of a separate Irish Unionist Party.[74]

Undaunted, the same month he supported a bill introduced by the Parnellites providing for evicted tenants.[75] On 31 March 1897 he was one of only two Irish unionists to vote against the government on the financial relations issue. The previous January Arthur Balfour had brought forward the idea of a Catholic university and Plunkett intended to speak on the issue in the Commons on 22 January, 'But Lecky made such a splendid speech that I could not in my state of health face the contrast'.[76] However, in the years to follow he was firmly and openly committed to the concession of a university.

Given Plunkett's independent line, it was inevitable that he would run into opposition in his constituency. He was well aware of the political complexion of South Dublin before he stood for the seat, writing on 15 February 1892: 'Went to Dublin (K[ildare] St[reet] Club) & spent the evening with Sharman, my agent in South Dublin looking over the registry. If I liked to be a rabid Orangeman I could get in. As I won't it is problematical'.[77] At the end of 1893 he commented 'in the constituency I am not popular, but am respected'.[78] By 1895 relations were beginning to deteriorate: 'Train to Kingstown & some of the ghastly constituency. 6 PM dinner with the Tandys & Primrose League meeting in Town Hall. What an audience! Chill no word for it'.[79] Yet matters improved somewhat when he was returned in the 1895 election with an increased majority. They deteriorated again in early 1896, following his vote against the government on the Evicted Tenants Bill.[80] By February 1897 he wrote:

> I am beginning to get savage letters from [illegible] and Protestant bigots in the constituency about the Govt's liberality on educational questions in Ireland. The landlords are also bitter & altogether I think an election w[oul]d be rather dangerous to me. Abstention rather than opposit[io]n is what I fear.[81]

As hostility mounted in the constituency Plunkett continued to hope that his record on reform at a national level would win him sufficient votes to be re-elected.

However, the southern unionist electorate was somewhat on the defensive. They were beginning to realise their own weakness in the face of measures such as the Land Acts, in which they felt betrayed even by Conservative governments. The electoral reforms of 1884 and 1885 had virtually ended Conservative and Protestant influences in southern Ireland outside the two constituencies of Trinity College and South Dublin. The Local Government Act of 1898, replacing the Grand Jury system with elected councils, effectively removed their power at local level. Lord Ardilaun, one of the leaders of anti-Plunkett faction in the constituency, was so enraged over the Land Act of 1897 that he refused to meet Gerald Balfour, referring to him as a 'common thief'.[82] The fact was that it was virtually impossible even for a Conservative government to carry out reform measures without encroaching on vested, often unionist, interests. In addition to his apparent flouting of unionist policy, Plunkett's work had been directed overwhelmingly to improving rural life but his was an urban constituency and his electorate may not have seen it as relevant to their interests. The last straw for his unionist constituents was his insistence that Gill be appointed Secretary to the new Department of Agriculture and Technical Instruction of which Plunkett had been made Vice-President and working head. Gill was not only a Catholic – and up to then Catholics had only rarely held so senior a post in the Irish administration – but had been an organiser of the Plan of Campaign and an Irish party MP. Nevertheless, as Plunkett's closest collaborator in the work of the Recess Committee, he was the best placed to follow through with the policy it had laid down. He had, moreover, become a close confidant of Plunkett, who thought highly of him. In addition, Plunkett wanted to make a point of employing Catholics at high levels in the new department[83] and proposed Gill as Secretary and another Catholic, W.P. Coyne, to head the Statistics Bureau of the department, threatening to resign his own post if their appointments were refused.[84] After a battle, he had his way over his choices but it probably cost him his South Dublin seat.[85] He was denounced by the Irish Unionist Alliance in May and the hard-line wing of the southern unionist party led by Lord Ardilaun and Professor Dowden campaigned against his re-election. Optimistic to the last, Plunkett was defeated when a second unionist candidate ran against him, splitting the unionist vote, so that the seat was won by a candidate for the now reunited Irish Parliamentary Party, John Joseph Mooney.

The defeat left Plunkett in a difficult situation. As Vice-President of the department, he was an ex officio minister. Strictly speaking, having lost his seat, he might have been expected to resign his post or a new constituency should have been found for him. In fact, neither of these things happened for another seven years.

Two major changes affected the Irish political scene in 1900. In February the two wings of the Irish Parliamentary Party reunited. This brought the Parnellite side, which had initially been well disposed toward Plunkett's work, such as the co-operative movement and the Recess Committee, more closely under the influence of leaders such as Dillon of the anti-Parnellite faction, who were profoundly opposed to Plunkett's approach. The other alteration following the general election of 1900 was the replacement of Gerald Balfour as Chief Secretary with Wyndham, who had been Arthur Balfour's secretary when he was Irish Chief

Secretary and seemed anxious to continue a policy of reforms. Nevertheless, the two men did not get on, Plunkett soon believing that Wyndham was simply an opportunist while coming to the conclusion that the Chief Secretary was trying to block his being found an alternative constituency.[86] They also differed at the level of policy, Wyndham and his under-secretary, Sir Anthony MacDonnell, seeking greater centralisation,[87] which Plunkett interpreted as a 'plot to castleise the Department'.[88] Both his relations with the Chief Secretary and his lack of a parliamentary seat served to complicate Plunkett's position as head of the new Department of Agriculture and Technical Instruction. However, it was an impressive administrative innovation and achieved a good deal in its early years.[89]

Plunkett tried to find another constituency. He considered the possibility of a seat in Belfast and another in East Down, but his support for a Catholic university was likely to alienate potential unionist voters. He was mentioned in connexion with Manchester and had a disastrous campaign in Galway, after which he gave up looking for a seat. It is a little surprising that the government did so little to find him a safe seat. However, he came to prefer what he saw as a non-party position.

Plunkett then handed a hostage to fortune in 1904 with publication of *Ireland in the New Century*. Here he argued, among other things, that the Irish character was in need of strengthening;[90] that Irish nationalist politicians, with their single-minded emphasis on home rule, had failed the Irish public in the area of social reform;[91] and – what aroused most public hostility – that the influence of the Catholic clergy on Irish life had tended to be out of step with economic development.[92] A lengthy controversy ensued. Redmond, who had been gradually distancing himself from Plunkett's movement, took the opportunity to attack him in a speech in the United States:

> Sir Horace Plunkett and all of those associated with him are anti-home rulers. I say to you, a man is a sham and a humbug who pretends that industries can ever be resuscitated effectively in Ireland except under the fostering care of an Irish government.[93]

Plunkett's problem was that he fell between two political stools (he sometimes likened himself to a dog in a tennis court!). Increasingly disillusioned by his own party (in 1903 he complained 'the Tories are stupid and at sea'[94]), he yet felt no kinship with the Irish Parliamentary party, several of whose leaders had been engaged in repeated attacks on him. Furthermore, Plunkett's differences with the Irish party were more than political. As the Irish party had developed, its leadership had been dominated by the larger farmers, graziers and rural bourgeoisie, drawn from occupations such as traders, publicans, auctioneers, solicitors and the clergy. In some of its work the co-operative movement had emphasised a class cleavage between farmers and traders that the nationalists had sought to deny.[95]

Plunkett, rather uncharacteristically, did not take part in the Dunraven Land Conference, although he knew about John Shawe-Taylor's letter before it was published and approved of the Wyndham Land Act that resulted.[96] When Wyndham was forced to resign as a result of the devolution crisis, Plunkett tried hard to have Gerald Balfour reappointed Chief Secretary.[97] Instead Walter Long, a bluff, uncomplicated, English Tory squire, was sent to assuage Irish unionist fears. His appointment spelled the end of experiments with constructive unionism.[98] Nevertheless, Plunkett quite liked him, while finding him limited[99] and tried to interest him in undertaking a reorganisation of rural reform in Ireland. On 7 October he submitted a memorandum entitled *The Need for a Policy* to Long and MacDonnell.[100] Although his suggestions were favourably received, the Conservative Party's resignation in December left little opportunity for its implementation.

The return of a Liberal government raised questions once more about Plunkett's continued occupancy of the Vice-Presidency of the DATI. Initially, somewhat to his surprise, the new Chief Secretary, James Bryce, asked him to stay on pending an inquiry into the working of the department.[101] However, in the face of mounting nationalist opposition, Bryce's successor, Augustine Birrell, requested his resignation in May 1907.[102]

Plunkett's political evolution towards support of home rule

Paradoxically, while the nationalist leaders were still attacking Plunkett and his movement for being 'anti-national', he was gradually coming to the conclusion that home rule was both inevitable and desirable. At the end of 1907 he had concluded in his diary: 'home rule is theoretically right but they are not fit for it'.[103] In November 1908 he had to quell a rumour among his northern unionist supporters that he had become a supporter of imperial home rule, which he denied.[104] However, by the end of 1910 he felt its introduction was inevitable and does not appear to have opposed it, writing: 'home rule looks inevitable – or rather imminent. This will I think help my work, at any rate my work will help home rule'.[105] In August 1911 he told Arthur D. Steele-Maitland, the Conservative Party manager, in private, that he 'was now a home ruler'.[106] In coming to support home rule Plunkett had been greatly influenced by Erskine Childers, whose book *The Framework of Home Rule* was written during 1911.[107] Plunkett discussed its contents in detail with Childers and commented on an early draft of the book, being moved by its arguments in favour of dominion home rule.[108] In April 1912 the Liberal government introduced a Home Rule Bill. Plunkett did not like it but supported it on the basis that he felt a solution of the question to be pressing. Nevertheless, he was reluctant to come out in public in support of home rule because he felt that it would rupture the co-operative movement. At the end of May he wrote to Childers explaining his position:

> I do not take exception to your estimate of the relative importance of the political and what you regard as the subsidiary questions so long as the matter is treated academically. I cannot expect you to understand my obligations to Sinclair, Andrews and the other influential Ulster Unionists who, by breaking away from Saunderson and joining the Recess Committee, enabled me to take the second step in the policy I set before me three and twenty years ago;

nor would it be possible for you to realise the immense injury it would do to the working out of home rule, and conceivably also to the working for home rule, if the remarkable record of harmonious co-operation between thousands of Irishmen, mostly nationalist, were suddenly broken by the formation of an Ulster Unionist section of the IAOS. I still doubt whether this would take place but the weight of authority among those who are intimately acquainted with the movement in Ulster is against me. There is, unhappily, an extremely able leader already in the field and anxious for such a split. I have put the whole case before a large number of strong home rulers in the movement and every one of them begs me to keep silent for a while.[109]

Early in his political career Plunkett had opposed home rule because of the danger of partition. In 1893 he asserted that 'one of his leading objections to the measure [home rule] was that if it were possible to force it on Ulster . . . it would perpetuate and intensify a state of things in which the Boyne seemed to be broader, deeper, stormier than the Irish Sea'.[110] After 1906 a sense of isolation had grown among the northern unionists, who felt that government was no longer prepared to listen to them. By 1910–11 they were moving from a parliamentary approach towards open militancy.[111] It soon became evident that they were preparing to resist home rule, by force if necessary, a position Plunkett saw as 'selfish' and 'unreasoning'.[112] Towards the end of 1913, while recuperating from illness in the United States, he worked out a proposal for a compromise solution to the impasse, whereby the north would be included in a home rule settlement for a period of, he suggested, ten years, with the option of dissociating thereafter. However, it proved unacceptable to the unionists and his plea to the northern unionists published in July 1914, entitled *A Better Way. An Appeal to Ulster not to Desert Ireland,*[113] similarly fell on deaf ears, the outbreak of the Great War putting the question into temporary eclipse. With a growing sense of disillusionment, he struggled on for a dominion home rule settlement that would avoid partition, chairing the Irish Convention of 1917[114] and establishing the Irish Reconstruction Association in 1918, superseded by the Irish Dominion League in 1919, with its weekly paper, the *Irish Statesman* (echoing the title of the British Fabian paper, the *New Statesman*).[115] The league was aimed at achieving self-governing dominion status for Ireland within the British Empire, but by this stage the scope for Plunkett's style of consensus politics was rapidly disappearing. While the league's message of conciliation was attacked by all sides, Plunkett was dismayed at Balfour's submission to the demands of the northern unionists, led by Carson. Although appalled by the violence of the War of Independence (there were at least forty-two attacks on co-operative creameries between 1919 and 1921[116]), he admired the idealism of the Sinn Féin leaders, some of whom he knew personally, and he was increasingly outspoken in his criticism of British government policy in Ireland.

With the establishment of the Free State, Plunkett accepted President W.T. Cosgrave's nomination to the Senate but in January 1923 his home at Kilteragh was destroyed by anti-treaty forces and nine months later he resigned his seat and moved to Weybridge, in Surrey, where he died in 1932.

Conclusion

Two main points emerge from an examination of Plunkett's political thought over time. In the first place, in so far as there was a *policy*, as opposed to a *rhetoric*, of constructive unionism, it emanated not from the Conservative government but from Plunkett and a group of like-minded individuals. At the same time, in the years after 1895 Conservative governments were more open than heretofore to such initiatives. Perhaps this was as much as they could do. Governments rarely have the freedom of action to adopt elaborate programmes and see them through; they are far more likely to respond to the complex interaction of events and interests. Moreover, any resolute policy of reform would almost inescapably have hurt the interests of their unionist supporters in Ireland. While the aim of 'killing home rule by kindness' may have been used as a useful means of smoothing ruffled feathers among unionist supporters in Britain and Ireland, Plunkett at least, and most probably the Balfours, too, did not believe that this was a real possibility. Plunkett reiterated the non-political nature of his campaign very frequently and it is likely that his efforts for rural reform were *sui generis*, and not intended to have a political, so much as a social and economic, purpose.

The second aspect of Plunkett's political development relates to his attitude to the question of the Union. Unlike most of his class, he did not see unionism as a defence against the majority. Rather, he was attracted to the economic and social benefits the Union could confer and his emotional commitment was to a wider British Empire or Anglo-Saxon dominion community. Thus he was flexible on precise political structures and was willing to support quasi-nationalist positions in some areas.

Many of Plunkett's Protestant friends and acquaintances were to move from unionism to nationalism in this period, including Douglas Hyde, Mary Spring-Rice, Roger Casement, Alice Stopford Green, Robert Barton, Erskine Childers, and others. Most of these were to end up as radical nationalists, closer to Sinn Féin than to the Irish Parliamentary Party.[117] What is striking about Plunkett is that rather than any dramatic reorientation in policy, his approach was quite consistent. He started off as a moderate independent-minded unionist and ended as a moderate, non-party home ruler. But in the meantime unionism itself had changed: southern unionists had become defensive and the northern unionists moved towards militancy and isolation. There was no room left within unionism for the kinds of constructive policies that he had worked so hard to have adopted and quite gradually and somewhat reluctantly he sought a solution in dominion home rule.

NOTES

1 See Carla Keating [King], 'Sir Horace Plunkett and rural reform, 1889–1914', Ph.D., National University of Ireland, ch. 6.
2 See Trevor West, *Horace Plunkett, Co-operation and Politics. An Irish Biography* (Garrards Cross, Bucks, 1986), ch. 7.

3   Horace Plunkett diaries [hereafter D], conclusion, 1904. Permission granted by the Plunkett Foundation to quote from Plunkett's diaries and correspondence is gratefully acknowledged. The diaries are in the Plunkett Foundation, Oxford; microfilm copies are in the National Library of Ireland.

4   Margaret Digby, *Horace Plunkett: An Anglo-American Irishman* (Oxford, 1949).

5   D, 3 January 1881.

6   D, 21 April 1881.

7   Patrick Bolger, *The Irish Co-operative Movement: Its History and Development* (Dublin, 1977).

8   For an interesting analysis of the early spread of the co-operative creamery system see Cormac Ó Gráda, 'The beginnings of the Irish creamery system, 1880–1914', *Economic History Review*, 30 (1977), pp. 284–305.

9   Catherine B. Shannon, *Arthur J. Balfour and Ireland, 1874–1922* (Washington, DC, 1988), pp. 50–1.

10   D, 26 and 30 May 1891.

11   Shannon, *Arthur J. Balfour and Ireland*, pp. 72–3.

12   Salisbury's biographer, Gwendoline Cecil, indicated his priorities in Ireland: 'The original and determining personal factor in Lord Salisbury's opposition to home rule was his overmastering sense of an honourable national obligation towards the minorities in Ireland – landholding, Protestant and loyalist – who depended on English protection. Considerations of imperial security or of Ireland's economic solvency came later' (Gwendoline Cecil, *Life of Robert, Marquess of Salisbury*, 4 vols (London, 1921–32), III, pp. 150–1; quoted in Alvin Jackson, *The Ulster Party. Irish Unionists in the House of Commons, 1884–1911* (Oxford, 1989), p. 22).

13   See, for example, his speech in the House of Commons at the beginning of his first term of office as Chief Secretary in 1874, *Hansard* [PD], 3rd series 218 (1874), cc. 110–18; quoted in Alan O'Day, *Irish Home Rule, 1867–1921* (Manchester, 1998), p. 41.

14   Andrew Gailey, 'Unionist rhetoric and Irish local government reform, 1895–99', *Irish Historical Studies*, vol. 24, 93 (1994), pp. 52–68; and *Ireland and the Death of Kindness, The Experience of Constructive Unionism, 1890–1905* (Cork, 1987).

15   Gailey, 'Unionist rhetoric', p. 60.

16   Paul Bew, *C.S. Parnell* (Dublin, 1980); Liam Kennedy, 'The economic thought of the nation's lost leader: Charles Stewart Parnell', in D. George Boyce and Alan O'Day (eds), *Parnell in Perspective* (London, 1991), pp. 171–200.

17   D, 18 August 1891. TCD, Dillon Papers, Ms. 6836. Letter from Plunkett to Dillon asking to meet him, 16 August 1891. Letter of introduction from Gill, dated 14 August 1891. The two men seem to have remained on good terms at this stage, however, see D, 3 June 1892.

18   'Had a long talk with Fr. Finlay. He is a home ruler because he says English never will be able to govern according to Irish ideas and that some day the Irish will face the situation. He admitted that at present it is not a possibility but thinks the IAOS is bringing people together in a way to make H.R. possible' (D, 13 March 1896).

19   D, 11 October 1896.

20   'B also refused to advise me about South Dublin. He would not have appointed me if I had been an MP or candidate & so would have 'lost the best member of the Board'! But things were diff[eren]t now & he must leave it to my judgement' (D, 31 October 1891).

21   D, 20 March 1890.

22   D, 16 June 1890.

23   Address to unionist meeting, Rathmines, reported in *Freeman's Journal*, 4 March 1892.

24   Plunkett (Conservative) won 4,371 votes (54%); Dr ffrench-Mullen (Parnellite) 2,261 (28%) and Sir T.H. Grattan Esmonde (Nationalist) 1,452 (18%).

25   D, 13 July 1892.

26   D, 10 June 1889.

27   D, 7 June 1892.

28 Shannon, *Arthur Balfour and Ireland*, p. 5.

29 Ibid., pp. 72–4.

30 D, 23 March 1888.

31 D, 12 May 1892.

32 F.S.L. Lyons, *The Irish Parliamentary Party, 1890–1910* (London, 1951), pp. 231–2.

33 *PD*, 4th series, 12, 19 July, cc. 4, 24; 13, 16 June 1893, cc. 1226–7.

34 Here he may have been distancing himself from the views of Lord Salisbury, who, he noted in May 1892, 'made a rabid speech to the Primrose League . . . saying H. Rule means religious civil war. My moderate position will I fear be more & more difficult as the time of the election draws near' (D, 7 May 1892).

35 *PD*, 13, 3 June 1993, c. 954.

36 *Ibid.*,11, 19 April 1893, c. 706.

37 D, 10 July 1893.

38 D, 9 August 1893.

39 Gailey, *Ireland and the Death of Kindness*, pp. 14–17. See also, R.F. Foster, 'To the northern counties station: Lord Randolph Churchill and the prelude to the Orange Card', in F.S.L. Lyons and R.A.J. Hawkins (eds), *Ireland under the Union: Varieties of Tension* (Oxford, 1980), pp. 237–87.

40 D, 30 January 1893.

41 D, 12 March 1894.

42 D, 17 December 1894.

43 D, 2 May 1894.

44 D, 13 May 1894.

45 D, 27 May 1895; 12 June 1895.

46 D, 27 May 1895.

47 D, 19 June 1895.

48 'Dinner with Yerburgh to talk over formation of an Anglo(?) Irish Political Alliance, ie a small party of English MPs who agree with my Irish views' (D, 28 May 1895).

49 In 1892 he had 4,371 votes and 54% of the votes cast; in 1895 he had 4,901 votes and 62% of the votes cast.

50 These are reprinted in the *Report of the Recess Committee* (Dublin, 1896), Appendix A.

51 D, 16 August 1895.

52 D, 31 December 1894. However, Margaret O'Callaghan, in *British High Politics and a Nationalist Ireland* (Cork, 1994), p. 148, claims that Irish nationalists 'saw him as a well-intentioned, if effective, paternalist bore'. Perhaps the two views were not incompatible.

53 *Report of the Recess Committee*, Appendix A; H. Plunkett, *Ireland in the New Century* (Dublin, 1904), pp. 213–15.

54 F.S.L. Lyons, *John Dillon. A Biography* (London, 1968), pp. 175–6.

55 *Report of the Recess Committee*, Appendix A; H. Plunkett, *Ireland in the New Century*, pp. 215–16.

56 Lyons, *The Irish Parliamentary Party*, p. 261.

57 George Russell (Æ), *Co-operation and Nationality. A Guide for Rural Reformers from This to the Next Generation* (Dublin, 1912; reprinted 1982), p. 53.

58 H. Plunkett, *The New Movement in Ireland*, (Dublin, 1899), p. 1.

59 Alvin Jackson, *Colonel Edward Saunderson. Land and Loyalty in Victorian Ireland* (Oxford, 1995), p. 125.

60 *Report of the Recess Committee*, Letter from Plunkett to Balfour, 1 August 1896, pp. v–viii.

61 *Report of the Royal Commissioners Appointed to Inquire into the Financial Relations of Great Britain and Ireland*. Final Report with Evidence and Appendices [Cd. 8008], H.C. (1896), xxxiii, 59.

62 *Report of the Recess Committee*, p. 110.

63 D, 31 January 1896: 'Dined with Cadogan [Lord Lieutenant]. They are all much worried over prospect of Irish uniting on Financial Relations Com[missio]n & consequent exorbitant demand.'

64 Pauric Travers, 'The financial relations question, 1800–1914', in F.B. Smith (ed.), *Ireland, England and Australia. Essays in Honour of Oliver MacDonagh* (Canberra, 1990), pp. 41–69.

65 Gailey, *Ireland and the Death of Kindness*, pp. 104–6.

66 Ibid., pp. 106, 112.

67 Ibid., p. 114.

68 D, 15 September 1895.

69 Plunkett seems to have understood this. In a letter of 29 July 1898 he refers to the difficulty of 'screw[ing] money out of Hicks Beach' (Plunkett papers, Plunkett Foundation Oxford, BAL/21, Plunkett to Betty Balfour).

70 Local Government (Ireland) Act, 1898 (61 and 62 Vict., c. 37).

71 Agriculture and Technical Instruction (Ireland) Act, 1899 (62 and 63 Vict., c. 50), passed on 9 August 1899.

72 D, 28 December 1895.

73 *PD*, 37, 17 Feb 1896, cc. 478–81. Arthur Balfour also ticked him off in the House, c. 487.

74 Edward Saunderson Papers, T 2996/2/D1, Saunderson to Plunkett, 21 February 1896; quoted Alvin Jackson, *The Ulster Party. Irish Unionists in the House of Commons, 1884–1911* (Oxford, 1989), p. 107.

75 *PD*, 37, 26 February 1896, Evicted Tenants (Ireland) Bill.

76 D, 19 January 1897.

77 D, 15 February 1892.

78 D, conclusion 1893.

79 D, 7 May 1895.

80 D, 17 March 1896.

81 D, 25 February 1897.

82 West, *Horace Plunkett, Co-operation and Politics*, p. 56.

83 D, 26 October 1899.

84 D, 14 January 1900; 1 February 1900; 21 February 1900. Coyne did pioneering work in the new department but to Plunkett's great sorrow he died in January 1904.

85 Plunkett knew that he was taking this risk. Gill Papers, NLI, Ms. 13495(7), Letter Plunkett to Gill, 18 January 1900; Ms. 13495(2), Letter Plunkett to Gill, 17 March 1900; Ms. 13495(3), Letter Plunkett to Gill, 19 March 1900.

86 D, 29 August 1902.

87 Gailey, *Ireland and the Death of Kindness*, pp. 186–8.

88 Gill Papers, NLI, Ms. 13496(4), Plunkett to Gill, 20 October 1903.

89 D. Hoctor: *The Department's Story, A History of the Department of Agriculture* (Dublin, 1971), ch. 3.

90 Plunkett, *Ireland in the New Century*, p. 58.

91 Ibid., pp. 80–5.

92 Ibid., ch. 4.

93 *Freeman's Journal*, 18 October 1904.

94 D, 22 October 1903.

95 Liam Kennedy, 'Agricultural co-operation and Irish rural society, 1880–1914', D.Phil. Thesis, University of York, 1978; Kennedy, 'Farmers, traders, and agricultural politics in pre-independence Ireland', in S. Clark and J.S. Donnelly (eds), *Irish Peasants: Violence and Political Unrest, 1780–1914* (Manchester, 1983), pp. 339–73.

96 For an interesting discussion of Plunkett's attitude to Dunraven and the conference see West, *Horace Plunkett, Co-operation and Politics*, pp. 111–13.

97 D, 6, 7, 8, 9, 11,12 March 1905.

98 On Walter Long's chief secretaryship and subsequent role in Irish politics, see John Kendle, *Walter Long, Ireland and the Union, 1905–1920* (Montreal and Kingston, 1992).

99 D, 4 May 1905; 5 June 1905; 23 August 1905; 30 August 1905; 6 October 1905.

100 See Andrew Gailey, 'Plunkett and a policy for a New Ireland', in Carla Keating

[King] (ed.), *Plunkett and Co-operatives: Past, Present and Future* (Cork, 1983), pp. 70–91, which contains the text of the memorandum.

101 Copies of Bryce's letter to this effect and Plunkett's reply are in the Gill Papers, NLI, Ms. 13496(6), both dated 20 December 1905.

102 On this see Eunan O'Halpin, *The Decline of the Union, British Government in Ireland 1892–1920* (Dublin, 1987), pp. 81–3.

103 D, conclusion 1907.

104 D, 19 November 1908.

105 D, conclusion 1910.

106 D, 19 August 1911.

107 Erskine Childers, *The Framework of Home Rule* (London, 1911).

108 D,12 March 1911; 24 April 1912. Childers Papers, TCD, Ms. 7850/972, Plunkett to Childers, 27 April 1911. See also, West, *Horace Plunkett, Co-operation and Politics*, pp. 118–24.

109 Childers Papers, TCD, Ms. 7850/979, Plunkett to Childers, 31 May 1912.

110 *PD*, 11, 19 April 1893, c. 702.

111 Jackson, *The Ulster Party*, pp. 307–19.

112 D, 26, 28 September, 1 October 1912.

113 Horace Plunkett, *A Better Way. An Appeal to Ulster not to Desert Ireland* (Dublin, 1914).

114 R.B. McDowell, *The Irish Convention, 1917–18* (London, 1970).

115 West, *Horace Plunkett. Co-operation and Politics*, pp. 177–88.

116 George Russell (Æ), *A Plea for Justice: Being a Demand for a Public Enquiry into the Attacks on Co-operative Societies in Ireland* (Irish Homestead, n.d. [1921?]).

117 This is explored further in an interesting book by León Ó Broin, *Protestant Nationalists in Revolutionary Ireland: The Stopford Connection* (Dublin, 1985).

8 'God will defend the right'

The Protestant Churches and opposition to home rule[1]

Alan Megahey

'Protestantism lay at the core of British national identity', and it was the Protestant religion which, as Linda Colley has shown, helped to forge the nation in the century before Victoria's accession to the throne.[2] Irish Protestants felt themselves to be an integral part of the nation so forged. The anti-Catholicism which helped to define and fuel that Protestantism had even older roots, of course, in the Marian persecutions, the Spanish Armada, the Glorious Revolution. For Irish Protestants, the siege of Derry and the Battle of the Boyne were outstandingly important chapters in their heritage. While constitutionally Catholics had been admitted to the political nation in 1829, anti-Catholicism lived on. In 1900 the Revd C.H. Kelly proclaimed: 'With all the experience of long ages Popery has not improved; with all the religious and civil liberty granted to its Church in this Empire, it is still the foe of true liberty, of free speech, of private judgement'.[3] Kelly was not an Irish Protestant; he was an ex-President of the English Wesleyan Conference, and newly appointed Chairman of the National Council of Evangelical Free Churches in Britain. Irish evangelicals (that is, most Irish Protestants), like English ones, continued to mistrust the Church of Rome. As Edward Norman has pointed out, 'through the seventeenth and eighteenth centuries, and then from the Gordon Riots of 1780 until well into the present century, there were anti-Catholic disturbances in Britain'.[4] The cry of 'No Popery' was not confined to Irish Protestants, though they continued to raise it for much longer than Protestants in the rest of the British Isles. In Ireland a potent mix of religion and politics – particularly in Ulster – ensured that their anti-Catholicism was part of a living and developing tradition. Throughout the nineteenth and twentieth centuries, further names have been added to their roll-call of martyrs, and further episodes have kept alive their very real and widely held feelings of anti-Catholicism.

On 6 May 1882, Gladstone's nephew Lord Frederick Cavendish, newly appointed Chief Secretary of Ireland, and his under-secretary, T.H. Burke, were murdered in Phoenix Park. F.E. Harte, later a Methodist minister, remembered sitting as a boy in Charleston Road Methodist Church in Dublin, where his father was minister, when the news was announced to a shocked congregation.[5] It underlined the different worlds inhabited by Protestants on either side of the Irish Sea. There might be occasional outbursts of 'Anti-Popery' feeling, and even more occasional outbursts of violence in Liverpool or Glasgow, but most Britons were unused to sectarian violence. Not so the Protestants of Ireland. It did not take a long memory for some people in that Methodist church in 1882 to remember the Anketell affair, when a Protestant station master of that name had been 'denounced from the altar' in Mullingar, and subsequently fatally shot outside his house in 1868.[6] They could remember the sectarian riots in Belfast in 1872 which had resulted in 5 dead and 243 injured; in 1880 riots there after a Catholic Lady Day procession had left 2 dead and 10 injured.[7] More pathos, though no deaths, accompanied an attack on a Protestant Sunday school procession in the mainly Catholic town of Coalisland in 1873.[8] Of course, a parallel litany of the victims of violence could be – and often was – recited by Catholics as well. But the point is that they all – Roman Catholics and Protestants alike – lived in a land where 'violence would appear to be endemic'.[9] While Irish Protestants were almost invariably devoted subjects of a Protestant queen and proud inhabitants of a Protestant United Kingdom, their religious heritage had its own unique flavour. Their *Foxes's Book of Martyrs* was not a dead sixteenth-century volume but a continuing saga.

The Protestant Churches in Ireland maintained close relations with their equivalents in Britain. But just as their Reformation heritage had grown on very different ground, so too they differed in other ways. Ireland was the only part of the United Kingdom in which there was no established Church. And crucially it was the only part of the kingdom where Roman Catholics were in a majority – of some three to one in a population of around 4 million. In Ireland Protestants were divided almost equally between members of the Church of Ireland and those who could, until disestablishment in 1871, be called nonconformists or Dissenters. The religious statistics for Ireland (where, unlike the rest of the United Kingdom, a religious question was a part of the decennial census) were as follows:[10]

	1871	1881	1891	1901	1911
Church of Ireland	667,998	639,562	600,103	581,085	576,571
	12.34%	12.3%	12.75%	13%	13.13%
Presbyterian	497,648	470,734	444,974	443,276	439,846
	9.19%	9.09%	9.46%	9.94%	10.02%
Methodist	43,441	48,866	55,500	61,979	62,427
	0.8%	0.88%	1.18%	1.39%	1.42%
Other	52,405	54,798	56,866	62,427	68,031
	0.97%	1.05%	1.21%	1.37%	1.55%
Catholic	4,150,867	3,960,891	3,547,307	3,308,661	3,242,170
	76.69%	76.56%	75.4%	74.2%	73.84%
Total	5,412,359	5,174,851	4,704,750	4,457,428	4,389,045

Thus an overview of the census figures would indicate a marginal strengthening of the Protestant position, and indeed in the nine counties of Ulster this was even more evident. The Catholic population there fell from 48.9% of the total in 1871 to 43.6% in 1911. Despite this marginal advance, however, Protestants in the last quarter of the century were not confident. David Hempton and Myrtle Hill summed it up well:

> Disestablishment of the Irish Church, educational competition, the 'invasion of Ulster' by the Irish National League after 1883, agrarian violence, Cullen's anti-Protestant leadership of the Catholic Church, sectarianism in Belfast and the perceived economic superiority of the Lagan valley over the rest of Ireland, all coalesced to persuade Ulster Protestants that they were facing a Catholic-inspired nationalist threat to their entire way of life.[11]

The mid-century 'Protestant Crusade' to gain converts and to win victory for the reformed faith in Ireland had palpably failed.[12] Then in 1886 came the greatest threat thus far. Gladstone's home rule scheme threatened – in the eyes of all the Protestant Churches – to cut them adrift from Protestant Britain, render them an oppressed minority within Ireland, and undermine their traditions, liberty and way of life.

The Church of Ireland, the largest and most geographically spread of the Protestant denominations, had faced unpalatable legislation from Westminster within the recent past – when it was disestablished. But unlike the Presbyterian tradition, it had no history of opposition to government, and indeed until 1870 had been an integral part of the state. Unlike the other Protestant bodies, its strength was not concentrated in the counties of the north-east. It relied heavily on the landed interest for its income and support. It now faced a dilemma. Lord Plunket, Archbishop of Dublin, addressed the problem early in 1886. He emphasised the Church's 'attitude of neutrality as regards political questions which it had wisely observed in the past'. But the question before them was now of quite a different order. The loyal Anglicans of Ireland could, he maintained, legitimately protest against anything 'severing the sympathies of those people from their attachment to the Crown', or that would 'lead to the disintegration of the great Empire to which they belonged'.[13] That set the tone for the Church of Ireland's official stance against home rule. They took their stand not so much on anti-Popery, though that sentiment was not absent, but more on the grounds of patriotism and indeed conservatism. When the General Synod met in special session in March, Plunket went further and asserted that 'behind the claim for home rule . . . there lurks the demand for entire separation, and for a very advanced form of socialism'.[14] For a property-owning Church with strong links with the propertied classes, that was a fearful spectre. A month later, Bishop Alexander of Derry (later, in 1896, to become Primate) hurried over to London to share Irish Anglican concerns at a great anti-home rule meeting in the Albert Hall.[15] 'Although his speech was characteristic of a man of peace', Shane Leslie's aunt reported somewhat ambivalently, 'he managed to work in a great deal that was most stirring'.[16] It was not an entirely comfortable message for an Anglican bishop to propound, in an atmosphere which was increasingly tinged with hints of threats of violent resistance. Colonel Edward Saunderson, prominent churchman and leader of the Irish unionists, may have 'clung to his ambiguities, rejecting a rising "in arms" against any home rule executive – while pledging Ulster's refusal to acknowledge such a regime'.[17] His parliamentary colleague and Orange leader, William Johnston of Ballykilbeg, was less ambivalent. Even before Gladstone's conversion to home rule, he was making clear the consequences of the passing of a Home Rule Bill: 'on that day the Orange Volunteers would be mustered to Ulster, under able and efficient officers, and the Royal Assent to such a Bill would be a declaration of civil war in Ulster'.[18] In February 1886 Lord Randolph Churchill made his celebrated visit to Ulster, which certainly appeared to give support from the highest levels of the Tory Party to those who contemplated a resort to arms.[19] In late May, while in a London 'thick and hot with political passion' the final stages of the second reading of the Home Rule Bill were taking place,[20] the *Irish Ecclesiastical Gazette* Anglican newspaper was tackling the question of what to do if it passed. What if the Bible itself, the bedrock of Irish Protestantism, forbade any resort to arms? What of St Paul's strict injunction: 'Let every soul be subject unto the higher powers. For there is no power but of God: the powers that be are ordained of God. Whosoever therefore resisteth the power, resisteth the ordinance of God: and they that resist shall receive to themselves damnation'.[21] In an article headed 'Romans XIII' there was an admission that 'Obedience to the powers that be is an abstract duty imposed on all Christian persons'. The word 'abstract' was important; it may be that there comes a time when 'public events have created an exception', that 'throughout the passage the apostle speaks of *good* government', and that this 'feature of the apostle's words should be borne in mind by those who think they see in them only the law of unconditional obedience'.[22]

For Presbyterians this dilemma was somewhat less unsettling. For over two centuries they had, along with Catholics, been dissenters in Ireland. When an Irish Presbyterian minister wanted to voice his support for Gladstone, he wrote to tell him that Ireland's troubles were attributable to the 'late Established Church' and to 'an oppressive and heartless landlordism'.[23] Without agreeing with his conclusion that home rule was therefore acceptable, most Presbyterians would have agreed with this analysis. The trouble now was that, as the Presbyterian newspaper put it, 'Mr Gladstone has mixed up the land question with the home rule question'.[24] That was unacceptable, to such an extent that armed resistance could be contemplated, and 'if ever it should come to civil war . . . we do not doubt for a moment but that the Protestants and loyalists could hold the country against all odds, and sweep it of disaffection from the Causeway to Cape Clear'.[25] Presbyterian militancy had been exacerbated by centuries of ascendancy domination; they now faced the threat of a new ascendancy 'of one class and creed in matters pertaining to religion, education and civil administration'.[26] That threat was spelled out in the anti-home rule motion of the Presbyterian General Assembly in March. And the seconder was Thomas Sinclair, leading Presbyterian businessman and ex-Gladstonian Liberal.[27]

Gladstonian Liberalism relied heavily on the nonconformist vote, and so it was particularly galling to Irish Methodists, who were constitutionally as well as theologically linked to the English Wesleyan Methodists, that their English brethren failed to appreciate that 'home rule for Ireland means the ruin of the country. Its inspiration is religious antipathy, its methods plunder, and its object Protestant annihilation'.[28] The Methodists of Ireland were few in number, relatively apolitical when compared with the Presbyterians, and generally lacking those links with landlordism and the political establishment that characterised the Church of Ireland. Now they, even more enthusiastically than the larger Protestant Churches, proclaimed their solidarity with their 'brother Protestants of Ireland', and voted in conference overwhelmingly for maintenance of the Union.[29]

The aftermath of the defeat of the Home Rule Bill at its second reading on 8 June led to the most protracted and violent spell of rioting Belfast had seen. Thirty-two people were killed and 371 injured in four months. Clergymen like Dr Kane and Dr Hanna were accused of fomenting the trouble. Even before the riots, Kane, Anglican and prominent Orangeman, had used the language of the Old Testament to 'commit their cause to the God of Battles', averring that they would 'by their swords defy the combined efforts of false friends and ancient enemies'.[30] 'Roaring' Hugh Hanna, who had created the enormously successful St Enoch's Presbyterian Church in Belfast, had similarly warned that a resort to arms was being 'discussed in pulpits and platforms by grave and reverend gentlemen, who have never before been heard talking of an appeal to the arbitrament of the sword'.[31] Now the danger had passed, though the propaganda continued, especially against those within the Protestant ranks who had come out as home rulers, thus identifying themselves with that 'congeries of men of all creeds, any creed, and no creed, secularists, socialists, et hoc genus omne' who were in favour of 'separation'.[32] The Irish Loyal and Patriotic Union continued to bombard people in Britain with leaflets showing that the Irish Churches, as well as other bodies, stood four-square for the Union.[33] In 1888 an anti-home rule letter was addressed by 864 of the 990 non-Anglican Protestant clergy in Ireland to Salisbury and Hartington, and there seems little doubt that many English nonconformists were beginning to have doubts about the wisdom of Gladstone's Irish policy.[34]

The Union was again threatened in 1892, when the Liberals were back in power, and Gladstone determined to make another attempt at bringing in home rule, despite the disarray among Irish nationalists and English nonconformists in the wake of the Parnell divorce case scandal. Even before the election a huge unionist convention met in Belfast, with clergy prominent on the platform.[35] A prime mover in this was the same Thomas Sinclair who had seconded the Presbyterian General Assembly's anti-home rule declaration in 1886, and who seemed anxious to avoid inflammatory language. The convention, as one Presbyterian minister turned judge later remembered it, 'never even hinted at armed resistance',[36] and Dr Kane appeared on the platform in the company of Catholic priests and spoke in a conciliatory fashion.[37] While the second Home Rule Bill was under consideration at Westminster in the spring of 1893, the regular annual meetings of each of the Protestant Churches were taking place, and their opposition to home rule was reiterated. On this occasion, even the Northern Executive of the previously strictly non-political Congregational Union passed an anti-home rule resolution.[38] As in 1886, the defeat of the home rule measure – this time in the House of Lords – was not the end of the matter as far as the Churches were concerned. Considerable activity resulted (more than after 1886) and co-operation with political organisations continued to bring home to the voters of Britain the solid opposition of the Irish Churches to any form of home rule. The Irish Unionist Alliance, for instance, at the request of the Dean of St Patrick's, voted a grant of £50 towards the printing and distribution of a booklet containing a report of the Church of Ireland's resolutions against home rule.[39] It was the Anglican Dr Kane who proposed an Irish unionist vote of appreciation to the English Nonconformist Unionist Association for the success of its work among those who as a result 'ranked patriotism and duty higher than the claims of party politics' – that is, they voted against the Liberals in the 1895 election.[40] Again in 1900 it was 'the influential advocacy of our cause by the Presbyterian and Methodist ministers' which was held to have swung the contest against the Liberals in a number of constituencies in England and Scotland.[41]

'I am riding a long patient race in Ireland', wrote the Conservative Chief Secretary of Ireland in 1902; 'I shall pass a Land Bill, reconstruct the Agricultural Department and Congested Districts Board, stimulate Fishing and Horse-breeding; and revolutionise education. Then I shall "nunc dimittis" and let someone else have a turn'.[42] Thus George Wyndham summarised his continuation of that policy which under his predecessor had been saddled with the phrase 'killing home rule with kindness'. He commented that 'the "parochialism" of the Ulster right wing is beyond belief', but was perhaps unaware of just how much his policies contributed to a growing sense of insecurity among Protestants, particularly – though not exclusively – among those in Ulster.

Surveying the recent past, T.W. Rolleston, the Dublin Protestant home ruler, stated his belief that 'the expectations that were raised by the pettifogging and impracticable Bills of Mr Gladstone . . . were never at all so near realisation as they once seemed to be'. Then, looking forward, he predicted: 'The two Irish nations must first be made one before another frontal attack can have any chance of success'.[43] But that is precisely what did not happen. The 'struggle between two nations, the Protestant and the Roman Catholic' if anything intensified in these years.[44] While the sectarian Belfast riots which followed the first Home Rule Bill were not repeated after the second, the 1890s did see disorder on other fronts. Street preaching by Protestants came under particular attack: at Arklow in 1890, Cork in 1894, Dublin and Arklow in 1895, Trim in 1899. The Methodists found the 1894 riots in Cork particularly galling, and they were joined by the Cork Unionist Clubs Committee which issued a 'strong protest against the violent action of the mob', calling for 'equal civil and religious liberty for all classes' and demanding that Morley 'administer the law impartially'.[45] But Morley was a Gladstonian Liberal; what could you expect? That Protestants should feel equally, indeed increasingly, threatened during the subsequent Conservative administrations was more surprising. When R.L. Crawford launched his anti-ritualist and anti-Romanist journal, the *Irish Protestant*, in 1901, he did so because it was a 'crucial period in the history of our country' as a result of the 'Romanisation of Ireland by the Balfour brothers'.[46]

The fires were stoked by M.J.F. McCarthy, a Cork Catholic, graduate of Trinity, Dublin, and barrister. His first book, *Five Years in Ireland*, was published in March 1901 and had reached its tenth edition by November 1903. His *Priests and People in Ireland*, published in 1902, was in its fifth edition by 1905. Other books followed, all on the same theme, 'that Priestcraft is omnipresent, all-pervading, all-dominating' and that 'sacerdotal interference and domination in Catholic Ireland . . . will be found to be the true and universal cause of that universal degeneracy upon which we so commiserate ourselves'.[47] They furnished Protestants with ammunition to attack the influence of the Catholic Church. His books found their way onto thousands of Protestant bookshelves. His lectures were widely reported and hugely attended. He attacked the United Irish League, founded in 1898, supported by the clergy and strong in Ulster. Like the Ancient Order of Hibernians – which saw phenomenal growth in Ulster in the years 1905–9 – it was virtually a Catholic secret society, a counter-poise to the Orange Order. He attacked the sectarian Catholic Association which was founded in 1902. Its handbook was so shockingly extreme that the Church of Ireland General Assembly formally deplored it in 1903, and later that year Archbishop Walsh censured it, though McCarthy managed to see in the Catholic Archbishop's words a further threat to Protestants.[48] 'The Irish split' of 1890, as one historian has claimed, 'put an end to "Tudorism" in Manning's phrase and made the Catholic Church for twenty five years the dominant political power outside north-east Ulster'.[49] That was certainly how it looked to many Irish Protestants.

In 1896 the Papal Bull *Apostolicae Curae* had declared Anglican orders invalid, causing distress to members of the Church of Ireland, if not to other Irish Protestants. All Protestants, however, could feel aggrieved by other examples of 'Papal aggression'. In February 1901 Catholics – even of privy counsellor rank – were forbidden to attend memorial services for the late Queen, thus reinforcing Protestant fears that Catholicism was disloyal and undermining of the Empire.[50] In June a curial directive ruled that Protestants ('heretics') could not be godparents to a Catholic child.[51] In that same month the Catholics held a Corpus Christi service in Belfast, preceded by an open-air procession of 15,000 people, who marched 'silently, without bands, and with furled banners'. It seemed to many an ordinary Protestant that 'the Catholic priest had taken over his streets'.[52] There was, on a different level, concern about priestly influence in education. The question of providing a Catholic university for Ireland revealed divisions within Irish Protestantism, and also the 'bonds between English and Irish anti-Catholicism'.[53] In addition, English anti-Catholicism had its own causes in the early years of the century. There was the controversy about 'Rome on the rates' and the Education Act of 1902.[54] Liverpool experienced sectarian riots in 1901–2.[55] Even London had its own furore over a proposed Catholic procession to mark the Eucharistic Congress of 1908.[56] But despite the efforts by George Wise in Liverpool, or John Kensit in London, none of these raised the temperature or caused the fear and panic that arose in Ireland over the Papal *Ne temere* decree.

Issued in 1908, the decree dealt with marriages in which one of the partners was a non-Catholic, and laid down regulations regarding the bringing up of children of any such marriage in the Catholic faith. It was condemned in the Church of Ireland General Synod of 1908, and by all the other Protestant Churches thereafter, but it took the McCann case of 1910 to create a *cause célèbre*. The Revd William Corkey, minister of Townsend Street Presbyterian Church in Belfast, brought to light in November 1910 the case of Mrs Agnes McCann, who had contracted a Presbyterian marriage; her husband, Alexander, was a Catholic. Their marriage was happy, and as agreed they each attended their own church. There were two children. Then (it was claimed) Mr McCann's priest visited the house to tell the couple that their marriage was invalid in the light of the *Ne temere* decree. Agnes McCann refused to remarry in a Catholic ceremony, her husband began to ill-treat her, and in the end vanished, along with their two children and their furniture, leaving his wife destitute. She had turned to her own minister, Mr Corkey. This was the scandal he now publicised, particularly in a lecture – subsequently published – to the Knox Club in Edinburgh. In it he spelled out the dire consequences of *Ne temere*. It was 'a danger to the Commonwealth, because it strikes at the home'; it challenged 'the supremacy of British Law'; it meant 'that the Church of Rome can absolve a man from the solemn marriage vow'; it showed 'that Rome is still prepared to inflict cruel punishment on any members of the Protestant Church over whom she gets any power'; it was 'a proselytising instrument to help in the reconquest of Britain for Rome'.[57] The Revd J.B. Armour, the Presbyterian home ruler, was not impressed: 'The general opinion among those who know the woman is that she is no great shakes and to use her case for purely political purposes shows the straits to which the Ulster Tories are reduced'.[58] Even the unionist cleric the Revd F.E. Harte – he who as a boy had learned in church of the Phoenix Park murders – felt uncomfortable while speaking against the decree at the Grosvenor Hall that 'there was rather too much of a political atmosphere'.[59] Certainly, while the details of the case are shady there can be no doubt at all of its effectiveness as a rallying-cry for Irish Protestants. It saw the Protestant Churches acting together in a way that foreshadows their political unanimity a year later. And in January 1912 the Ulster Women's Unionist Council launched a petition against the decree which within a month had collected the signatures of 104,301 women,[60] foreshadowing the signatures on Ulster's Solemn League and Covenant nine months later.

The McCann case gave a focus to all the frustrations and fears which had been building up among Irish Protestants since the rejection of the second Home Rule Bill. The timing was perfect: William Corkey delivered his lecture in Edinburgh on 21 February 1911 – the day on which Asquith introduced the Parliament Bill into the House of Commons. The general elections of 1910 had left the Liberal government dependent upon the Irish nationalists' votes, and the Parliament Act would remove from the constitution the Lords' veto, upon which Irish Protestants had been able to rely in 1893. Irish Protestants felt they had played their part in ensuring a significant dent in Liberal support. The election in January 1910 was preceded by a manifesto 'To the Electors of Great Britain' by eleven ex-

Moderators of the General Assembly, declaring their conviction that the interests of all the people of Ireland were best safeguarded by maintenance of the Union: 'no more important manifesto' appeared during the election campaign, the Presbyterian *Witness* declared.[61] From an Anglican point of view, it was significant that 'the Protestants of Ireland have stood together in the present political crisis'.[62] Surveying the results of the December election, R. Dawson Bates, secretary of the Unionist Associations of Ireland, reported that many of the favourable results in Britain were 'mainly due to the distribution of leaflets dealing with the attitude of the Church of Rome towards the Protestant religion in Ireland, and to the influential advocacy of our Cause by the Presbyterian and Methodist Ministers who represented us'.[63] On the home front, for at least one candidate, it was sufficient as an election poster to declare 'home rule means Rome rule', and to append beneath that the long petition by Mrs McCann to the Lord Lieutenant seeking justice for herself and her children.[64]

The passing of the Parliament Act in August 1911 was the signal for renewed unionist activity in Ulster, directed by Edward Carson, the Dubliner who since February 1910 had been leader of the Irish unionists. Carson wanted to be sure that 'the people over there really mean to resist', as he wrote to James Craig.[65] A great demonstration at Craig's family home, Craigavon, with 50,000 men on parade, gave Carson himself, and the public at large, proof that Ulstermen meant business. It was this demonstration which, as A.T.Q. Stewart puts it, 'determined both the policy and the methods to be followed during the next three years'.[66] For the churches, the determination to resist home rule was only deepened by a further papal intervention, in October, when the *motu proprio* 'Quantavis diligentia' seemed to suggest that the Church was now claiming that its clergy should be immune from 'process of civil or criminal law of every sort in any lay court'.[67] Coincidentally, just over a week after its publication – though before there had been any reaction in the press – the Church of Ireland and the Presbyterian Church held the first meeting of representatives appointed by the respective Churches to discuss matters of mutual interest. High on the agenda were matters relating to the *Ne temere* decree. Such ecumenical contacts and co-operation would increase greatly over the subsequent two years of political ferment.

The Presbyterians were the first to mobilise against the new home rule threat, with a Convention on 1 February 1912. It was chaired by Thomas Sinclair, the former Liberal and leading Presbyterian layman, and attended by 'almost half the adult male Presbyterian population in Ulster'.[68] The emphasis in the resolutions passed was a religious one: that 'our civil and religious liberties would be greatly imperilled'; that 'the philanthropic and missionary enterprise of our Church at home and abroad would be greatly curtailed'; that 'Presbyterian minorities in all parts of Ireland (many of them consisting of settlers from Scotland)' would be in danger; that children would be at risk from the 'denominationalising' of education by the Catholic hierarchy; and that 'industrial and agricultural interests would be seriously crippled'.[69] The reference to Scottish settlers was significant. During the 1893 home rule crisis, the Irish Moderator had attended the Church of Scotland's annual meeting, chiding his Scots brethren for their 'hollow expressions of sympathy', and emphasising Irish fears at the 'prospect of being handed over to the tender mercies of a Parliament dominated by Romish priests'. For his trouble he had been put in his place by Lord Balfour of Burleigh who said he had heard too much about 'the Roman Catholic Church'.[70] This time, the efforts to elicit support from Scotland paid off much more significantly.[71] It was noteworthy too that the Presbyterians made the point that they were appealing to a government 'with whose policy, apart from the question of home rule, so many of us are in general sympathy'.[72] But for most Presbyterians, this home rule issue was 'not a political question'. As the Revd Robert Barron put it, 'in ordinary political questions, I took no part and expressed no opinion'.[73] This issue was different. 'In those days', he remembered afterwards, 'I often spoke and preached on the subject, and I urged the people to resist even to death'.[74] The Presbyterian newspaper felt the same, and believed that 'history will justify Protestant resistance to the present attempt – humiliating on the part of England, hypocritical on the part of Rome – to establish Roman ascendancy in Ireland'.[75] And yet another affair seemed to underline the risks Protestants faced. In July the same Robert Barron organised a Sunday school outing which was attacked in what became known as the 'Castledawson outrage', when some fifty pupils and teachers were 'attacked and battered' by a party of some two hundred and fifty men 'wearing green hats'.[76] The Belfast Presbytery were not slow to appoint a commission on the matter, and to 'present a statement of their case to their Brethren in England and Scotland'.[77] The Methodists followed the Presbyterians with their anti-home rule convention in March at the Ulster Hall. They were anxious to 'disavow, as utterly alien to the spirit which we have inherited from the fathers and founders of the Methodist Church, all feelings of enmity or ill-will to any class in the community'.[78] They reiterated their conference's anti-home rule statements of 1886 and 1893, adding their anxiety caused by *Ne temere*. And in a flourish characteristic of this small, evangelical and puritan Church, they emphasised their fear of 'very wide and far-reaching evil consequences, especially imperilling the best interests of education, temperance and Sabbath observance'.

All the Protestant Churches were officially represented at an Easter Tuesday parade and service at Balmoral (outside Belfast), attended by the recently appointed leader of the Conservative Party Andrew Bonar Law, who himself boasted Presbyterian Scots and Ulster forebears. In an ecumenical united front, the service was conducted by the Presbyterian Moderator and the Church of Ireland Primate. The numbers were double those who had paraded before Carson at Craigavon, and in addition the proceedings were attended by seventy MPs from Britain. The demonstration had its effect. When Bonar Law got back to London he revealed to a friend just how much the experience had meant to him: 'The demonstration last week was a great surprise to me. It may seem strange to you and me, but it is a religious question. These people are in serious earnest. They are prepared to die for their convictions'.[79] Three months later, Bonar Law attended another demonstration, this time at Blenheim, and it was he who caused some surprise by his bold statement: 'I can imagine no length of resistance to which Ulster can go in which I should not be prepared to support them, and in which, in my belief, they would not be supported by the overwhelming majority of the British people'.[80]

In the months after the Balmoral demonstration further church pronouncements were forthcoming. In April the General Synod of the Church of Ireland met in Dublin in a special session which opened with the singing of the hymn which was rapidly becoming the national anthem of the Irish Protestants, 'O God our help in ages past'. The Primate, J.B. Crozier (who had been Bishop of Down until Archbishop Alexander's resignation in the previous year), opened his address with words similar to those of Plunket in 1886: 'Our Church knows no politics, and our Church is tied to no political party'. As to the question of home rule, however, he noted that 'the vast majority of the members of all the Protestant religious bodies in Ireland are absolutely united'. And again, like his predecessor, he dwelt upon the threat to the unity of the Empire and the likelihood of 'anarchy and civil strife' should home rule be enacted. Although there was no specific mention of 'Rome Rule', Crozier did tackle the 'action of Ulstermen at this crisis', noting their resolve 'to resist extra-constitutional measures by extra-constitutional means'. The body of 402 synodsmen then voted for a resolution reaffirming 'constant allegiance to the Throne, and our unswerving attachment to the Legislative Union'. It was passed with only five dissentients. Further resolutions of a similar nature were passed, and the proceedings ended with the singing of the national anthem.[81] One of the few dissentients was the Revd J.O. Hannay, whose claims then and later that 'The resolutions of the Synod are not "The Voice of the Church"' were dismissed by the 'sturdy Northerner' Archdeacon Pooler as a 'rhodomontade of nonsense'.[82]

In June 1912 even the Reformed Presbyterian Church, which was strictly non-political to the extent of advising its members to abstain from voting at elections, passed a resolution condemning home rule, 'because the measure transcends ordinary politics'.[83] The statements and utterances from pulpit and platform throughout that summer of 1912 were certainly hardly the stuff of normal political discourse. 'Their cause was just. The unchanging God was on their side', declared the Methodist minister L.W. Crooks.[84] 'They were prepared to lay down their lives in defence of their principles', said the Rector of Newtownards, the Revd W.L.T. Whatham.[85] 'It is not sufficiently realised', said Bishop D'Arcy of Down, 'that behind Ulster's opposition to home rule there is an immensely strong conviction which is essentially religious. We contend for life, for civil liberty, for progress, for our rightful heritage of British citizenship. We also contend for faith and for the freedom of our souls'.[86] But the greatest and most publicised proclamation of such views came on Ulster Day, 28 September 1912. A clergy subcommittee helped with the planning: the Dean of Belfast, the Presbyterian Moderator and the Methodist President.[87] When the day came, its religious overtones were evident to all.

Looking back on it, St John Ervine caught that religious mood.

On the day itself, a magnificent morning of fine and durable weather that made the hills around the city look blue in the sunlight, Belfast suspended all its labours and became like a place of prayer. Very solemnly, the people went to church to prepare their minds for their responsibilities, as postulants prepare themselves for consecration.

It was to be a day of dedication, when men and women sang 'O God our help in ages past' 'like a hymn of battle'.[88] A.F. Moody, later to become Presbyterian Moderator, recalled 'the signing of a covenant with a fervour equal to that of the old Scottish Covenanters at Greyfrairs'.[89] Looking forward to the day, an Ulster newspaper noted that it would be 'solemnised by prayer and hallowed by the sanctities of religion'.[90] Looking back on it *The Times* was even more struck by the Covenant as 'a mystical affirmation. Ulster seemed to enter into an offensive and defensive alliance with Deity'.[91] Certainly the language of the Covenant, signed by almost half a million men, was redolent of the Old Testament, and deliberately so.

A year later, preaching in Belfast Cathedral on the anniversary of 'Ulster Day', the Bishop of Down and Connor surveyed the events of past and present: 'The steps which have been taken of late are of the most awful import. They have been taken, we believe, in the path of plain duty – in defence of things for which a man must be prepared, if need be, to make the utmost sacrifice'.[92] The signing of the Covenant had been followed by the establishment of the Ulster Volunteer Force, soon to be armed by guns brought in from Germany. The pulpit rhetoric of 1886 ('the God of Battles') had been translated by 1914 into active preparations for armed resistance. And clergymen were as involved in those preparations as they had been in the rhetoric. Archdeacon Atkinson blessed the UVF colours at Lenaderg.[93] To the Presbyterian Moderator, the Revd James Bingham, the members of the UVF were 'a great and noble army'. And placing himself alongside them he declared that they 'had a right to resist' and he was 'ready to share with them in their resistance'.[94] William Corkey, of McCann case fame, 'enrolled as a member of the UVF', and felt that subsequent events 'proved how right Ulster was to remain under the British flag'.[95] The Revd O.W. Clarke, Rector of Connor, supplied his car for and took delivery of five bundles of rifles landed at Larne.[96] For Quakers, the possible resort to arms conflicted with their belief 'that war and the taking of human life are irreconcilable with the spirit and teaching of our Lord Jesus Christ', yet they too had a 'desire to defend our rights as citizens of the United Kingdom'.[97] James Richardson, a leading northern Quaker, explained in a letter how he was coping with the dilemma: 'we seem to be stolidly preparing for civil war in our different ways. Some by working, some by praying, and some by drilling and arming; some, like me, by getting up Ambulance Work'.[98]

Had Irish Protestantism 'quite simply lost its nerve'?[99] It is certainly true, as we have seen, that for two decades before the Covenant was signed it had watched with increasing unease what it regarded as the 'appeasement' of the Catholic Church and of Irish nationalists by governments both Liberal and Conservative. But the events of 1912–14 were not some sudden sea-change in the nature of Irish Protestantism. They did not denote a new 'Ulsterism' on the ground that, as one writer has put it, 'the entire Ulster population had, on fundamental matters, come to accept the conceptual framework of the Ulster-Scots'.[100] The stand which the Irish Protestant Churches took, and which Ulster Protestants in particular rallied to, was rooted deep in the history of Irish Protestantism. Protestants stood together because they were not Catholics, and since the early nineteenth century had felt excluded from the concept of Irish nationalism which had been formulated by Daniel O'Connell, who 'never could decide whether his Protestant fellow-countrymen were indeed his fellow-countrymen'.[101] For the majority of Irish Protestants, the Archbishop of Armagh was right when he declared in 1912: 'There is a popular clap-trap cry which means so little, or may mean so much – the cry of "Ireland a nation once again". But when we come to examine it in practice, how utterly absurd it is.'[102] When that nation gained self-government, it did so with Ulster (or six of its counties) excluded. That was the result of the Protestant crusade against home rule. Well could Lord Oranmore lament in his diary early in 1914: 'It seems as if the Government would yield on the exclusion of Ulster and then what will become of us all in the South'.[103] But, as Lieutenant Colonel Frederick Crawford admitted in 1920, with reference to the Covenant's claim that home rule would be disastrous to Ulster, and 'the whole of Ireland': 'We had to recede from "whole of Ireland" and stick to Ulster only or we should have lost all'.[104]

Shan Bullock, writing of a Protestant boyhood in County Fermanagh, quotes from Isaiah, Ecclesiastes and the Gospel of John, and asks: 'Is it a small thing that a boy shall grow to manhood, his life resonant with such sentences, hundreds and hundreds of them?'[105] The lives of hundreds of thousands of Irish Protestants were filled with such resonances, visually represented on many of the banners carried by the Orange Order on each 12 July. The things that united the Protestants were far more important than those which divided them, and generally they, like James Craig, had 'no difficulty in moving from one Protestant church to another, sitting, perhaps, under a Presbyterian minister in the morning, and under an Episcopalian or Methodist at night'. Huge numbers of them met together in Orange lodges and at temperance meetings. Their children were members of the many 'uniformed organisations' like Scouts and Boys' Brigade, organised by the Churches and giving a focus to the social life of the young. It is not surprising that in Armagh members of the Boys' Brigade on Ulster Day 1912 'joined with members of the Anglican Church Lads' Brigade in publicly demonstrating their unionism through parades'.[106] Their loyalty to King and Empire was soon to be tested more severely. 'The Orange and Protestant Friendly Societies had over 10,000 members in uniform by late 1914; while veterans of the Boys' Brigade accounted for nearly half of all Protestant recruits in Dublin'.[107] No doubt many of the members of the UVF had learned their marching skills in B.B. or the Church Lads' Brigade. 'How little did we think', wrote Archdeacon Atkinson who blessed the UVF colours at Lenaderg in May 1913, 'that in the next year those battalions would be marching in Flanders as part of the Ulster Division in the Great War, and numbers of those gallant young men within the next few years sleeping their last sleep on the banks of the Somme'.[108]

The Great War submerged the home rule issue. No doubt some few clergymen might believe that 'at every crisis God had miraculously intervened to save Ulster unionists', and point to the fact that 'when the whole world believed home rule to be inevitable Germany marched her forces across the Belgian border'.[109] Whether or not such Divine intervention was a factor, the situation was changed after that war, and Ireland was politically – though not ecclesiastically – divided. The strength of the Protestant Churches was concentrated increasingly in Ulster where '[T]he war, and the battle of the Somme specially, were presented as a Unionist blood sacrifice: the Union permanently sealed in blood.'[110] Those who had put their trust in the 'God of Battles' had got rather more than they bargained for on the battlefields of Europe, and rather less than they had fought for in the partitioned island of Ireland.

NOTES

1 'In sure confidence that God will defend the right we hereto subscribe our names': Ulster Covenant, 28 September 1912.
2 Linda Colley, *Britons: Forging the Nation 1707–1837* (London, 1992), p. 369.
3 *Free Church Year Book and Official Report of the Fifth National Council of the Evangelical Free Churches held in Sheffield, March 13 to 15, 1900* (London, 1900), p. 17.
4 E.R. Norman, *Anti-Catholicism in Victorian England* (London, 1968), p. 19.
5 F.E. Harte, *The Road I Have Travelled* (Belfast, n.d.), p. 15.
6 See H.E. Patton, *Fifty Years of Disestablishment* (Dublin, 1922), p. 139.
7 See I. Budge and C. O'Leary, *Belfast: Approach to Crisis* (London, 1973), p. 89.
8 See Frank T. Wright, *Two Lands on One Soil* (Dublin, 1996), p. 428.
9 A.T.Q. Stewart, *The Narrow Ground* (London, 1977), p. 113.
10 See W.E. Vaughan and A.J. Fitzpatrick, *Irish Historical Statistics: Population 1821–1971* (Dublin, 1978), p. 49. The totals for years 1871, 1881, 1901 and 1911 have been corrected from the original.
11 D. Hempton and M. Hill, *Evangelical Protestantism in Ulster Society 1740–1890* (London, 1992), p. 167.
12 Desmond Bowen, *The Protestant Crusade in Ireland 1800–70* (Dublin, 1978).
13 *Irish Ecclesiastical Gazette*, 23 January 1886.
14 *Journal of the General Synod of the Church of Ireland* (Dublin, 1886), p. liv.
15 J. Biggs-Davidson and G. Chowdharay-Best, *The Cross of St Patrick* (Bourne End, 1984), p. 261.
16 Shane Leslie, *Long Shadows* (London, 1966), p. 128.
17 Alvin Jackson, *Colonel Edward Saunderson: Land and Loyalty in Victorian England* (Oxford, 1995), p. 89.
18 *Fermanagh Times*, 2 December 1885.
19 See R.F. Foster, *Paddy and Mr Punch* (London, 1993), ch. 12 ('To the Northern Counties Station: Lord Randolph Churchill and the Orange card'); R.R. James, *Lord Randolph Churchill* (London, 1959), ch. 8 ('Home rule').
20 John Morley, *The Life of William Ewart Gladstone* (London, 1903), III, p. 321.
21 Romans 13, verses 1 and 2.
22 *Irish Ecclesiastical Gazette*, 29 May 1886.
23 The Revd C.H. Irwin to W.E. Gladstone, 12 May 1886, British Library Add. Ms. 44497, 205.
24 *Witness*, 19 March 1886.
25 Ibid., 16 January 1886.
26 *Minutes of the General Assembly* (Special Meeting, March 1886), p. 13.
27 For Sinclair, who bulks large in the Presbyterian story, see Graham Walker, 'Thomas

Sinclair: Presbyterian Liberal unionist', in Richard English and Graham Walker (eds), *Unionism in Modern Ireland* (Dublin, 1996).

28 *Christian Advocate*, 8 January 1886.

29 Ibid., 25 June 1886; 2 July 1886.

30 *Belfast News-Letter*, 3 May 1886.

31 Ibid., 9 January 1886.

32 *Christian Advocate*, 21 April 1887.

33 See, for example, ILPU leaflet no. 65, 2nd series (1887), 'Irish public opinion on home rule'.

34 See David W. Bebbington, 'Nonconformity and electoral sociology, 1867–1918', *Historical Journal*, 27, 3 (1984), pp. 633–56.

35 Appropriately enough, the huge pavilion erected for the convention was later used by Dwight L. Moody when he visited Belfast in 1893 for another of his evangelistic campaigns.

36 J. A. Rentoul, *Stray Thoughts and Memories* (London, 1921), p. 224.

37 Biggs-Davidson and Chowdharay-Best, *Cross of St Patrick*, p. 249.

38 The Congregationalists had not spoken out officially in 1886, and reverted again to silence on the issue in 1912; M. Coles, *I Will Build my Church: The Story of the Congregational Union of Ireland 1829–1979* (Belfast, 1979), p. 27.

39 Irish Unionist Alliance Executive Committee Minute Book (1893–4): Public Record Office of Northern Ireland (PRONI), D 989/2.

40 Minutes of the Council of Unionist Clubs of Ireland (19 May 1896): PRONI D 1327/1–1.

41 Unionist Associations of Ireland, Minute Book of Joint Committee (3 December 1900): PRONI D 1327/2/1.

42 J.A. Mackail and G. Wyndham, *Life and Letters of George Wyndham* (London, 1924), II, p. 436.

43 In a pamphlet privately published in 1900 and quoted in T.W. Rolleston, *Portrait of an Irishman* (London, 1939), p. 60.

44 W.F. Monypenny, *The Two Irish Nations* (London, 1913), p. 17.

45 *Christian Advocate*, 27 April 1894; subsequently, in a bizarre twist to this tale, when a Jew was mistaken for one of the preachers, he and other Jews were assaulted, and a Jewish shop was gutted. See Louis Hyman, *The Jews of Ireland* (Shannon, 1972), p. 221.

46 See Henry Patterson, 'Independent Orangeism and class conflict in Edwardian Belfast: a reinterpretation', *Proceedings of the Royal Irish Academy*, 80c (1980), p. 8.

47 M.J.F. McCarthy, *Priests and People in Ireland* (Dublin, 1902), p. 7.

48 M.J.F. McCarthy, *Rome in Ireland* (London, 1904), p. 314, and generally ch. 11.

49 Erich Strauss, *Irish Nationalism and British Democracy* (London, 1961), p. 209.

50 *Irish Ecclesiastical Record*, IX (January–June 1901), p. 262.

51 Ibid., p. 374.

52 See Sybil Baker, 'Orange and Green: Belfast 1832–1912', in H.J. Dyos and M. Wolff (eds), *The Victorian City: Images and Realities* (London, 1973), II, p. 800.

53 Alvin Jackson, *The Ulster Party: Irish Unionists in the House of Commons 1884–1911* (Oxford, 1989), p. 180.

54 See G.I.T. Machin, 'The last Victorian anti-ritualist campaign, 1895–1906', *Victorian Studies*, 25 (Spring 1982), pp. 277–302.

55 See P.J. Waller, *Democracy and Sectarianism: A Political and Social History of Liverpool* (Liverpool, 1981), pp. 189–208.

56 C. A. Devlin, 'The Eucharistic procession of 1908: the dilemma of the Liberal government', *Church History*, 63 (September 1994), pp. 407–25.

57 W. Corkey, *The McCann Mixed Marriage Case* (Edinburgh, 1911), pp. 14–15; see also his autobiography, *Glad Did I Live* (Belfast, 1963); also R.M. Lee, 'Intermarriage, conflict and social control in Ireland: the decree *"Ne temere"*', *Economic and Social Review*, 17 (October 1985), pp. 11–17.

58 J.B. Armour to his son, 9 February 1911: PRONI D 1792/A3/2/6 – reproduced in J.R.B. McMinn, *Against the Tide* (Belfast, 1985), p. 87.

59 F.E. Harte, *The Road I Have Travelled* (Belfast, n.d. [1945]), p. 92.

60 J. Holmes and D. Urquart, *Coming into the Light: The Work, Politics and Religion of Women in Ulster 1840–1940* (Belfast, 1994), p. 98.

61 *Witness*, 14 January 1910 (editorial).

62 *Warden*, 21 January 1910 (the *Warden* became the *Irish Churchman* later in 1910).

63 Report dated 4 January 1911: PRONI D 1327/2/1; see Patrick Buckland, *Irish Unionism 1885–1923* (Belfast, 1973), p. 303.

64 Smiley election poster: PRONI D 1900/24.

65 Letter of 29 July 1911, quoted in St John Ervine, *Craigavon: Ulsterman* (London, 1949), p. 185.

66 A.T.Q. Stewart, *The Ulster Crisis* (London, 1967), p. 48.

67 *Ulster Echo*, 21 December 1911; the papal directive or motu proprio was usually referred to in Ulster as *motu proprio* (the name of the type of directive) rather than by its actual title 'Quantavis diligentia'.

68 Graham Walker, 'The Irish Presbyterian anti-home rule convention of 1912', *Studies*, 86 (1997), p. 74.

69 Buckland, *Irish Unionism 1885–1923*, pp. 78–9.

70 *Evening Dispatch*, 23 May 1893.

71 Walker, 'Irish Presbyterian anti-home rule convention', pp. 75–6.

72 Buckland, *Irish Unionism 1885–1923*, p. 79

73 R. Barron, *The God of My Life* (Belfast, n.d. [1928]), p. 105.

74 Ibid., p 209.

75 *Witness*, 16 August 1912.

76 Barron, *The God of My Life*, pp. 212–16.

77 Presbyterian Church House, Belfast, *Belfast Presbytery Minutes*, 18 July 1912.

78 Buckland, *Irish Unionism 1885–1923*, p. 80; see also full report in *Christian Advocate*, 15 March 1912.

79 Diary entry by George Riddell, 14 April 1912; in *The Riddell Diaries*, J.M. McEwen (ed.) (London, 1986), p. 40.

80 Robert Blake, *The Unknown Prime Minister* (London, 1955), p. 130.

81 *Journal of the General Synod, Special Meeting* (Dublin 1912), pp. xlvi–lii.

82 *Irish Churchman*, 26 April 1912; *Church of Ireland Gazette*, 12 July 1912.

83 *Witness*, 28 June 1912.

84 *Belfast News-Letter*, 8 July 1912.

85 Ibid., 13 July 1912.

86 *Irish Churchman*, 30 August 1912.

87 They were aged, respectively, 55, 65 and 69, and were born, respectively, in Dublin, Belfast and Burslem; see Minutes of Ulster Day Committee, 27 August 1912: PRONI D 1327/3/1.

88 Ervine, *Craigavon*, p. 235.

89 A.F. Moody, *Memories and Musings of a Moderator* (London, n.d. [1938]), p. 12.

90 *Fermanagh Times*, 22 August 1912.

91 *The Times*, 6 May 1913.

92 *Irish Churchman*, 10 October 1913.

93 See S.H. King and S. McMahon, *Hope and History* (Belfast, 1996), p. 35.

94 *Witness*, 2 June 1914.

95 W. Corkey, *Glad Did I Live*, p. 116.

96 Buckland, *Irish Unionism 1885–1923*, p. 250.

97 *The Friend*, 10 October 1913.

98 Letter dated 18 December 1913; quoted in C.F. Smith, *James Nicholson Richardson of Bessbrook* (London, 1925), p. 162.

99 T.P. McCaughey, *Memory and Redemption: Church, Politics and Prophetic Theology in Ireland* (Dublin, 1993), p. 133; see also p. 90.

100 D.H. Akenson, *God's Peoples: Covenant and Land in South Africa, Israel and Ulster* (Ithaca, 1992), p. 149.

101 D. George Boyce, *Nationalism in Ireland* (London, 1982), p. 144.

102 *Journal of the General Synod, Special Meeting* (Dublin, 1912), p. xlvii.

103 Entry for 15 February 1914; see J. Butler, 'Lord Oranmore's journal', *Irish Historical Studies*, 29 (November 1995), p. 560.

104 Buckland, *Irish Unionism 1885–1923*, p. 410.

105 S.F. Bullock, *After Sixty Years* (London, n.d. [1931]), p. 69.

106 Alvin Jackson, 'Unionist politics and Protestant society in Edwardian Ireland', *Historical Journal*, 33, 4 (1990), p. 860.

107 David Fitzpatrick, 'The logic of collective sacrifice', *Historical Journal*, 38, 4 (1995), p. 1029.

108 S.H. King and S. McMahon, *Hope and History*, p. 35.

109 J.W. Good, *Ulster and Ireland* (Dublin, 1919), p. 145.

110 Keith Jeffery, 'The Great War in modern Irish memory', in T.G. Fraser and K. Jeffery (eds), *Men, Women and War* (Dublin, 1993), p. 150.

9 The problems of unionist literature

Macaulay, Froude and Lawless

Norman Vance

Is there such a thing as unionist literature? Thanks to the genius of Yeats, and the remarkable talent of many of his friends and contemporaries around the time of the home rule debates, the literary aspects of Irish nationalism have been frequently acknowledged and exhaustively studied.[1] But unionist literature is a less promising prospect. One problem is that there are too many different unionisms, ranging from the Liberal unionism of the historian W.E.H. Lecky, MP for Dublin University (1895–1902), or the aristocratic Anglo-Irish conservatism of Lord Ernest Hamilton, MP for North Tyrone (1885–92), son of the Duke of Abercorn and author of *The Soul of Ulster* (1917), to the militant truculence parodied in the Belfast industrialist Cahoon or the machine-gun-toting McConkey, foreman of the Green Loaney Scutching Mill, in George Birmingham's satirical novel *The Red Hand of Ulster* (1912).

McConkey at least was not a literary man. Unionist pamphlets and political essays such as those in *Against Home Rule. The Case for Union* (1912), introduced by Edward Carson, tend to be incurably factual, statistical and ephemeral. There is indeed a substantial body of popular Orange ballads, dating from the later eighteenth century,[2] and some of these introduced the young Yeats to 'the pleasure of rhyme'.[3] But they really merit separate study, and are not necessarily explicitly unionist. They tend to be politically anti-Catholic rather than pro-Union, and because Catholics hoped for emancipation under the Union many Orangemen actually opposed the Act of Union of 1800.[4]

There is also a considerable body of Ulster regional writing which is gradually becoming better known, but that too is not the same thing as 'unionist literature'.[5] Unionism was not originally confined to Ulster, and Ulster writers, even Ulster Protestant writers, are not necessarily unionists. St John Ervine's ill-judged articles in the *Belfast Telegraph*, *Ulster the Real Centre of Culture in Ireland* (reprinted as a pamphlet in 1944), were motivated by Ulster unionist defensiveness against partisan onslaughts from southern nationalists, especially Sean O'Casey in *Time and Tide*. But Ervine's canon of Ulster writers was a more or less meaningless list which included nationalists as well as unionists and argued not so much for unionist literature as for a richly pluralist literary culture which, he claimed, was no longer possible in the separated southern counties.[6]

Literary culture, at least in Britain, tended to be wary of industrial society even when it worked. Matthew Arnold's *Culture and Anarchy* aligned the worship of material success with narrow views and cultural philistinism.[7] Insofar as formal unionism originally derived in part from a sense of economic and social community and interdependence between industrial Belfast and the great industrial centres of England and Scotland, it could stimulate qualified literary praise of engineering and economic prowess from the northern writers Samuel Ferguson and St John Ervine and interesting minor verse such as Thomas Carnduff's *Songs from the Shipyard* (1924).[8] But this kind of unionism provided little scope for romantic ruralism or superfine aestheticism if that was what true culture was all about. Its most effective supporters and exponents were not poets and dreamers but industrialists, lawyers and soldiers. Perhaps the most academically distinguished unionist writer was Cyril Falls of Fermanagh (1888–1971), Chichele Professor of the History of War at Oxford, son of an army officer turned Conservative MP and himself an army officer turned historian of European, British and Irish wars. Even after discounting obvious aesthetic and political prejudices, derived from Matthew Arnold and nationalist polemic, which foster the crude stereotypes of unionist mercantile philistinism, dourly practical unimaginative northerners and killjoy Calvinists suspicious of literature as of life itself, it has to be said that there are few obviously unionist literary figures of obvious genius.

Algernon Swinburne, though English, is a possible exception: at best he was a subversive poet of disturbing originality, at times near genius. Eccentric and enthusiastic, he was a good hater. In middle life, horrified by the Phoenix Park murders and unhappy about the Land League, he came to dislike Parnell and Gladstone so violently that in 1886 he wrote indignantly to *The Times* about the 'Disunionists' – 'Parnell, Gladstone and Company (unlimited in liability)'. Two months later he followed this with a poem, 'The Commonweal. A Song for Unionists', which included some good lines. Gladstone's glittering career was summed up as 'the road of splendid shame'.[9] But Swinburne was more concerned to denounce Gladstone and political murder than to enter imaginatively into what positive value, if any, unionism or the Union might have.

On the whole, the sense of sudden dire emergency which brought organised unionism into being in the late nineteenth century seemed to discourage the merely literary, particularly if the literary tended to approximate to the trivial. It certainly did not help that the unionist *bête noire* Augustine Birrell, Liberal Chief Secretary for Ireland during the crucial years 1907–16, was also well known as a rather lightweight essayist and man of letters, author of three volumes of *Obiter Dicta* (1884, 1887, 1924). An attempt to promote literary support for the unionist cause prompted the unionist-minded Rudyard Kipling to growl that the unionists needed drilling rather than doggerel,[10] though he did eventually publish the sombre poem 'Ulster 1912' in the *Morning Post* on 9 April 1912:

> The dark eleventh hour
> Draws on and see us sold
> To every evil power
> We fought against of old.[11]

Kipling was another good hater. This threnody is strong on disparagement, like Swinburne's 'The Commonweal', and invokes Isaiah's condemnation of violence and iniquity in a manner that catches something of the deadly seriousness of God-fearing Ulster unionists. There were Methodist preachers who had preached in Ireland among Kipling's forebears. But it is hardly Kipling at his best. Swinburne and Kipling grumpily expressed a few militant unionist sentiments after making literary reputations for other reasons, and Kipling attracted a very sympathetic political and literary study by Cyril Falls, but even they can hardly be described as essentially unionist writers.[12] That is not to say that there is no such thing as 'unionist literature', but it has received little attention as such.[13]

I

This is partly because it is so difficult to get it in focus. 'Unionist literature' could be ancient or modern, purely fictitious or sternly historical, British or Irish, active or passive, northern or southern, Orange ballads and ephemeral broadsheets or serious imaginative writing. While what could be termed nationalist literature and the Irish literary revival which nurtured it from the late nineteenth century are in the nature of protest movements against the Union and the dominant culture of England and can be at least retrospectively constructed as limited and coherent, the product of the Yeatsian moment, as it were, 'unionist literature', associated at some level with the dominant culture, has no clear beginning, need not be confined to the modern literary categories of fiction, poetry and drama and can mean almost anything.

Since a union has by definition two or more partners the writers of 'unionist literature' do not have to be Irish. There were English, Scottish and Irish vested interests in maintaining political and other connexions between Ireland and the British mainland for centuries before the formal Act of Union of 1800, so unionist writing can be much older than the nineteenth century. To concentrate only on Irish examples, it could be argued that the category includes works such as the Irish historical compilations (in Latin) of Sir James Ware (1594–1666), Auditor-General of Ireland under Charles I, who created on paper a literary community of the Irish and the English-in-Ireland in his list of Irish writers, or Thomas Leland's would-be 'philosophical' but rather Protestant *History of Ireland from the Invasion of Henry II* (1773) which was intended to invite comparison with the work of the contemporary Scottish historians William Robertson and David Hume.

There is indeed a (rather unhelpful) sense in which almost all enduring post-medieval literature in English, constantly circulating in and helping to reinforce a degree of cultural unity among different English-speaking communities in Britain and beyond, could be regarded as at least passively or unconsciously 'unionist literature' unless it is explicitly anti-English (like some famous passages in Swift), unless it specifically declares some kind of separatist or anti-unionist programme. Those writings not specifically annexed to the cause of literary nationalism by tradition-builders such as the Young Ireland propagandists or Yeats himself can be regarded as (culturally speaking) unionist by default. So, particularly for the non-English, the study, let alone the writing, of English literature might itself be an implicitly unionist activity.

It has been observed that the Scots and the Scottish universities led the way in the formal academic study of 'English' literature from the early eighteenth century, following the Act of Union with Scotland of 1707.[14] A crucial role was played by Hugh Blair (1718–1800), Professor of Rhetoric and Belles Lettres at the University of Edinburgh, editor of Shakespeare (1753) and of a major collection of British (not 'English') poets (1773), itself a kind of cultural Act of Union. Ambitious Scots, reinventing themselves as 'North Britons', might still sound strange of speech to English ears, but it was now very much to their advantage to write pure and polished English and to participate in English literary culture, annexing themselves to and enriching an essentially English, now 'British', cultural tradition partly invented for the purpose.

Inevitably, the cult of English literature and polite letters extended to Ireland and Irishmen. After North Britons there were West Britons. This was originally a positive term, provisionally accepted even by the great repealer Daniel O'Connell in 1836, considered as possibly complementing rather than contradicting Irishness by the Irish poet Samuel Ferguson, though it subsequently became a dismissive label for those suspected of anti-nationalist attitudes.[15] Literary West Britonism antedated the Act of Union. Edmund Burke's early work of cosmopolitan literary theory *A Philosophical Enquiry into the Origin of our Ideas of the Sublime and the Beautiful* appeared in London in 1757. Irish Presbyterian ministers were often educated at Scottish universities, particularly Glasgow, and read Hugh Blair's *Lectures on Rhetoric and Belles Lettres* (1783) as a matter of course. Scottish universities provided a better and more modern model for higher education in Ireland than clerical and classical Oxbridge. Dr Johnson's circle in England included not only the literary Scot James Boswell but the literary Irishman Edmond Malone (1741–1812), a graduate of Trinity College Dublin, and, like Burke, an important Shakespeare scholar and editor of Dryden's prose (1800). While the University of Oxford's professors of poetry were still lecturing in Latin, mainly about non-English literature, English Literature was taught, in English, both at Trinity College Dublin and (from 1845) at the new Queen's Colleges in Galway, Cork and Belfast. One of the leading Edwardian scholars of Shakespeare and Renaissance drama was F.S. Boas, Professor of History and English in Belfast from the turn of the century, a northern unionist and imperialist who praised Shakespeare's version of Henry V as 'the supreme embodiment of the imperial spirit of the Elizabethan age'.[16] Boas was able to build on the work of the Trinity professor, poet and scholar-critic Edward Dowden (1843–1913), another unionist and one of the great pioneers of academic English studies. Dowden is an unduly neglected figure:[17] his major work on Shakespeare, Shelley and Walt Whitman and his intelligent respect for the achievement of his contemporary George Eliot have been overshadowed by savage Yeatsian disparagement and his notorious lack of interest in contemporary Irish writing in English. The threat of home rule legislation drove Dowden into self-conscious political as well as literary unionism. He tried to get Kipling to write for the unionists and coaxed minor lyrics from

Swinburne and Alfred Austin for the cause.[18] It was hardly Dowden's fault that his particular brand of unionism, southern, literary and ecumenical in that he insisted on changing an anti-Catholic reference in Swinburne ('priest' became the vaguer 'beast') to avoid offending Catholic unionists, has not survived.

But Dowden was a man of (mainly English) letters before he was a unionist. Self-advertising unionism never used to be necessary. Until or unless the connexion with Britain came under extreme duress or became manifestly dysfunctional, most Irish writers could tacitly accept it as a fact of life and concentrate on other things: they were usually under no particular pressure even to articulate the status quo of a more or less informally united kingdom, let alone strenuously defend it. Later seventeenth-century Irish-born writers such as Nahum Tate or William Congreve are passive literary unionists in the sense that they are seemingly apolitical or conservative, at least on Irish issues, are happy to write for a British, mainly English, audience and pay no particular attention to distinctively Irish subject-matter, idiom or literary form. Closer to our own time, something similar could be said of the Belfast-born scholar-critic and romantic fantasist C.S. Lewis. Tacit literary unionism tends not to be noticed as such, while literary nationalism seeks to draw attention to itself.

But, even though the trumpet-notes of nationalist rebellion will always sound more grandly than the woodwind of ostensible pastoral content or the gentle percussion of unexcited ordinariness, there is an active as well as a merely passive unionist tradition in English letters. Over the centuries the pressure-points which gave rise to Irish national excitement or outrage, or which could be retrospectively assimilated to nationalist narrative, were always likely to produce pro-English apologia and a quasi-unionist counter-narrative. From the Danes to the Paratroop Regiment, the Armed Invader has inflamed Irish nationalist passions and nationalist rhetoric. But the Armed Invader may be a hero, even a deliverer, in someone else's rhetoric. Catholic Ireland still execrates Oliver Cromwell for the massacres of Drogheda and Wexford but in 'Oliver's Advice' the Armagh Orangeman Colonel William Blacker (1777–1855) reclaimed him as a type of loyal Protestant fortitude, reincarnate in the Williamite wars and 1798 and afterwards:

> He comes, the open rebel fierce – he comes, the Jesuit sly;
> But put your trust in God, my boys, and keep your powder dry.[19]

Cyril Falls wrote dispassionately as a modern critical historian in his *Elizabeth's Irish Wars* (1950) and *The Birth of Ulster* (1936) but earlier literary unionists saw no reason to be fair-minded with this material. Through literary alchemy the iron heel of oppression can be transmuted into iron justice and stern but splendid discipline, necessary to promote ultimate union and peace beyond conquest, and it was in this spirit that Edmund Spenser described the ineffectual brutalities of Lord Grey de Wilton in Ireland in 1580 under the grim figure of Artegall, champion of Justice, in Book V of *The Faerie Queene*. In his *View of the Present State of Ireland* (1596) Spenser sets out a unionist cultural agenda which was never fully achieved: 'I think it best by an union of manners and conformity of minds to bring them [conqueror and conquered] to be one people, and to put away the dislikeful concept both of the one and the other'.[20]

Elizabeth's Irish wars coincided with the earlier part of Shakespeare's career, and Shakespeare, as well as non-English Shakespeare scholars, can easily be claimed for literary unionism. The patriotic *Henry V*, easily annexed for the British war effort by Laurence Olivier's film in 1944, was originally associated with a much earlier war effort, Essex's expedition to Ireland in 1599 to put down Tyrone's rebellion. The unhistorical incorporation of the Irishman Captain Macmorris among Henry's soldiers at Agincourt is an early unionist statement to the effect that rebellion is unnecessary, that English and Irish interests can be the same. Macmorris's famous outburst, 'What ish my nation? Ish a villain, and a bastard, and a knave, and a rascal. What ish my nation? Who talks of my nation?' (III.ii.123–4), is an attempt to dislodge separatist thinking, to resist the view that divided and war-torn Ireland should stand apart, and to claim a larger and less problematic identity in the service of an increasingly united kingdom.[21] For Shakespeare's present-minded audience this was the kingdom in which Camden's *Britannia* (1586), the Welsh-descended Tudor dynasty and the Scottish heir to the throne (James VI of Scotland) had already encouraged the idea of 'Britishness' rather than Englishness.

'Britain', rather than just England, began to acquire an empire in the eighteenth century. The Union Jack acquired additional significance when it was planted on previously foreign soil, and a notional union of peoples and interests acquired substance overseas in the face of new experiences of difference and strangeness which could make more domestic difference seem of little account. The connexion between unionism and imperialism which is particularly apparent in writers such as Rudyard Kipling is of long standing. While the Act of Union of 1707 was with Scotland rather than Ireland, the latter was soon an honorary member of the Union for purposes of imperial sentiment, not least because Scots and Irish officers and troops did much of the fighting, and Scots and Irish emigrants did much of the settling. When Canadian confederation was achieved in 1867 by its own Act of Union between different provinces (the signatories included the Glasgow-born John Alexander MacDonald of Ontario and the Ulster-born Thomas D'Arcy McGee of Quebec) the Scots-born Alexander Muir celebrated this as a supremely British occasion by writing the words and music of 'The Maple Leaf for Ever', harking back to General Wolfe and eighteenth-century British conquest ('In days of yore/From Britain's shore/Wolfe the conquering hero came') to the enduring irritation of French Canada. The Irish shamrock is securely placed between the Scottish thistle and the English rose:

> The Thistle, Shamrock, Rose entwine
> The Maple leaf for ever!

> On Merry England's far-famed land
> May kind Heaven sweetly smile;
> God bless Old Scotland evermore,
> And Ireland's Emerald Isle!

Then swell the song, both loud and long,
Till rocks and forest quiver,
God save our King, and Heaven bless
The Maple leaf for ever!

Similar unionist sentiments were possible in relation to the land just a little
further south. In March 1774, just thirteen months before the outbreak of the
American Revolutionary War, the Dublin-born painter John Dixon published in
London an allegorical mezzotint, *The Oracle. Representing Britannia, Hibernia, Scotia
and America*. The first three appear as allegorical maidens, obviously sisters, closely
grouped together, while America sits a little apart, as is geographically appropriate, and all four gaze at a magic-lantern image, projected by Father Time, of a
triumphant and unified future.[22]

II

It is perhaps hardly surprising, therefore, that the triumph of empire is a concern
of the first important actively unionist writer worthy of the name, Thomas Bab-
ington Macaulay, sometime legal member of the Council of India and Whig
historian of the siege of Derry and the Battle of the Boyne as well as of much else.
After Gladstone disestablished the Irish Church Macaulay's sharp criticisms of
Gladstone's earlier views on Church and state were particularly attractive to
disgruntled Irish Protestants, belligerent unionists in the making.[23] Macaulay
robustly attacked O'Connell and repeal in Parliament, on 6 February 1833, and
wrote vividly and well about the sacred things of Orange tradition, attracting
correspondence from the Ulster Orange leader and anti-Catholic novelist William
Johnston of Ballykilbeg.[24] But he was no Orangeman himself, observing with
ponderous detachment: 'it is impossible for the moralist or the statesman to look
with unmixed complacency on the solemnities with which Londonderry com-
memorates her deliverance, and on the honours which she pays to those who
saved her'.[25] Scots-descended, Macaulay's real unionist significance lies in his
brash progressive materialism, sturdily protestant Britishness and imperial sentiment, admired and invoked by unionists as epitomising the Britain they wished to
stay united to. The sentiment was savagely deplored by Irish nationalists such as
John Mitchel in his famous *Jail Journal*,[26] while the style was fastidiously regretted
by Matthew Arnold, always more disposed to praise what he took to be Celtic
literature than the celebration of crassly philistine achievement. Macaulay's famous defence of industrial society ('steam engines and independence') against the
romantic regrets of Robert Southey in his *Sir Thomas More, or, Colloquies on the
Progress and Prospects Society* (*Edinburgh Review*, January 1830) was followed by a
celebration of the scientific materialism and essential Britishness of Francis Bacon
(*Edinburgh Review*, July 1837). As MP for the new constituency of Leeds he
belonged with the new commercial and industrial Britain which would naturally
incorporate Belfast but not Westport or West Cork. He wrote about Roman
heroism when he was in India, but he was also thinking about Britons. Macaulay's

Horatius holding the bridge against impossible odds, so that 'even the ranks of Tuscany/Could scarce forbear to cheer',[27] is a type of heroic fortitude in the service of the Empire, which had been defended by Irish soldiers such as Sir Robert Rollo Gillespie of Comber, County Down, who died in 1814 storming a fort in the Himalayas, calling for 'one charge more for the honour of Down'.[28] In the same Romano-British imperial tradition, not long after the Indian Mutiny of 1857, Kipling's uncle, the painter Edward Poynter, represented a Pompeian senti- nel standing 'Faithful unto Death' even as the volcanic ash rained down upon him.

If Macaulay is one of the major literary unionists, another historian, James Anthony Froude, author of *The English in Ireland in the Eighteenth Century* (1872), needs to be considered in the same light. He was an admirer of Julius Caesar as military dictator and imperial statesman and an advocate of firm government and the Protestant interest in Ireland, both of which he felt had been neglected or betrayed by successive administrations up to and including Gladstone's, so his history and his politics annoyed Irish nationalists and English Liberals intensely. In 1872, long before the heyday of James Craig (born in 1871) and Edward Carson (born in 1854), he told an American audience: 'if I know anything of the high-spirited, determined men in the north of Ireland, they would no more sub- mit to be governed by a Catholic majority in a Dublin Parliament, than New England would have submitted to a convention of slave-owners sitting at Richmond'.[29]

Froude has been accused of persistently libelling the Irish people, and he cer- tainly regarded the Catholic Irish as a race apart, inferior in intelligence and energy to Irish Protestants. But he felt this was hardly their fault. He insisted his main concern was for the Irish peasantry, 'by far the most deserving class in the country', and his opposition to home rule was because he felt that for them and for the country as a whole Catholic ascendancy, a new politics dominated by priests and Catholic landlords, would be no improvement on Protestant ascend- ancy. Rackrenting Protestant landlords might well have been a problem in the past, but the Catholic middlemen who had benefited from Gladstone's first Land Act (1870) had shown no particular desire to pass on any of the benefit to Catholic under-tenants.[30]

Like many subsequent unionists, Froude was anti-Catholic on political grounds rather than anti-Irish. He knew more than most about past political intrigue; his pioneering research on the sixteenth century had painstakingly explored Jesuit plots and conspiracies against Protestant England. A famous religious doubter in early manhood, a more or less secular Protestant after singeing his wings in the flame of Newman's intense and magnetic Catholic spirituality in Tractarian Oxford, a convert to Thomas Carlyle's secular Calvinist ethic of work and duty, he first visited Ireland in the turbulent 1840s and found he loved the country and its people. He was deeply impressed not just by the hospitality but by the general intellectual culture of at least one Irish evangelical family whom he got to know when he briefly acted as tutor to the sons of Revd William Cleaver, Rector of Delgany in County Wicklow and the eldest son of a former Archbishop of

Dublin.[31] He also found he had considerable sympathy for the often beleaguered position of impoverished Protestant gentry in Catholic areas. It was clear to him that systematic and extensive Protestant settlement in Ulster had secured a degree of loyalty to the British crown. Would the whole of Ireland have been more stable and peaceful if this had been successfully extended to the south?

He explores this possibility in his vividly readable historical novel *The Two Chiefs of Dunboy* (1889), which begins in the mid-eighteenth century. Colonel Goring, a Cornish Calvinist, attempts to establish a model colony on his estate of Dunboy on the borders of Cork and Kerry, importing colonists from Cornwall and Presbyterian artisans from Ulster to develop coastal fisheries and copper mining. Froude's mentor Carlyle had sympathetically edited Cromwell's *Letters and Speeches* and Froude makes Goring a latter-day Cromwell:

> He carried his habits as a soldier into his relations with his Commander above. Under Cromwell he would have been the most devoted of the Ironsides. In default of an appointed leader to give him orders, he looked out for direct instructions to himself in Providential circumstances.[32]

Colonel Blacker's Orange ballad 'Oliver's Advice' had already assimilated the piously militant Cromwellian spirit to Irish loyalist tradition and Froude tries to work out some of the implications. Goring, loyally British, is responsible to government for putting down smuggling along the coast, a continuing source of tension which helps to keep colonists and natives apart, though unwise English legislation governing and hampering Irish trade set up the conditions for smuggling in the first instance. Spenser had dreamed of English and Irish eventually becoming one people, but, through Goring, Froude accepts racial difference and apartness as necessary, even desirable. This implicitly endorses – and exaggerates – the sectarian division between Catholic Irish and unassimilated Protestant settlers in Ulster: 'Too close a Union with the Irish had produced degeneracy both of character and creed in all the settlements of English which had been made in previous centuries. It was on this rock more than any other that they had split'.[33]

Needless to say, it all ended in tears. Goring was murdered by Morty Sullivan, the displaced Chief of Dunboy turned smuggler and outlaw, and Morty's own death soon followed.[34] Goring's enterprising colonial experiment was too little, too late: 'the spirit of the Cromwellians had died out of the land and was not to be revived by a single enthusiast'.[35] Froude's sternest criticism is not for Morty or desperate Irish patriots but for the 'English statesmen whose reckless negligence was the true cause of their crimes'. A pessimist where Macaulay was incurably optimistic, Froude brings his novel to an end with an Irish lament not for Goring but for Morty Sullivan: 'Mine was the best of masters that Ireland could produce. May our souls be floating tomorrow in the rays of endless glory'.[36]

Froude had taken his epigraph for the novel from Shakespeare: 'Under which King, Bezonian? Speak, or die' (*Henry IV*, Part II, V.iii.116). Would the Pope or the British monarch hold sway? Ireland and the Irish were dying because too little had been done to make British rule work. The Irish novelist Emily Lawless (1845–1913), daughter of Lord Cloncurry, was similarly alert to the tragic possibilities for both coloniser and colonised under a dysfunctional union. Her grandfather had voted against the Act of Union, and although her own politics were unionist she was imaginatively aware of the problems. Mr Gladstone himself felt he could learn about the peculiar difficulties of the country from reading her work. Her historical novel *With Essex in Ireland* (1890) revisits the excitements of 1599 which had produced Shakepeare's *Henry V*, but my Lord Essex, seen through the eyes of a devoted follower, gradually shrinks from glittering Renaissance hero coming to take charge of 'our Kingdom' to beleaguered and ineffective adventurer, let down, rather like Froude's English in Ireland, by intrigue at home and the inadequacy and indifference of English statesmen.

Lawless's earlier novel *Hurrish* (1886), set in Clare during the Land War, is a kind of answer to nationalist novels of landlord and tenant such as Charles Kickham's enormously popular *Knocknagow, or the Homes of Tipperary* (1879). *Hurrish* is melodramatic, but sympathetic to rural distress. Good and evil are not distributed along class lines. Landlord and tenant both suffer from the poverty of the land, and Hurrish is an O'Brien as well as his landlord. Lawless uses the strange bare rock of the Burren as background and metaphor for the desolation and bizarre inequality of contemporary Irish life. As the opening paragraph reveals, 'in valleys and hollows, where the washings of the rocks have accumulated, a grass grows, famous all over cattle-feeding Ireland for its powers of fattening'. But the general impression is of bleak, inhospitable rock, 'skeletons – rain-worn, time-worn, wind-worn – starvation made visible, and embodied in a landscape'.[37] The wearily repetitive violence of the sea suggests a land as embattled as its people: 'the spray rose in the air like the dust of a submarine explosion, and fell again with a thud that was like the fall of many fortresses, draining away through their twenty thousand mouths, and streaming back to sea, to be promptly caught and sent back upon the same errand again and again, and over and over again'.[38]

But the culture of endemic violence, which repels the pale, idealised Alley Sheehan, a nun by the end of the novel, is a consequence of misgovernment and despair. Hurrish, strong, gentle and noble, is a Fenian, as Kickham had been in the previous generation, but Lawless makes the man better than his inherited and largely decorative and rhetorical politics. He shrinks from the violence and intimidation shown to 'landgrabbing' tenants who take land from which others had been evicted, but accidentally kills one such, the brutal Mat Brady. He is arrested but acquitted of murder, only to be murdered by Mat's ambitious and vengeful brother Maury. He lives in local memory as a folk-hero, not only because he was a strong man who triumphed over the law and the 'polis' but because he had a reputation as a 'dacent man'.[39]

Heroism and villainy are moralised rather than politicised. While the novel invokes the atmosphere of lawlessness and structural violence in rural Irish society the actual violence it describes is occasioned by private enmity, obsession and revenge rather than the quarrels of landlord and tenant. Poor Irishmen kill each other, tragically, and if Mat Brady is represented as a bestial indigenous 'Caliban' that is a matter of nature, not politics: there is no obvious Prospero figure, no grandee colonist who opposes or degrades him, and in fact the landlord gives him a tenancy, unwisely, when he asks for it.[40] Maury Brady escapes to America, abandons involvement in politics and makes good as a merchant in San Francisco. Irrespective of 'politics', which seems to mean the politics of subversion and insurrection, there is still hope for an uncertain future from the indigenous virtue described in the novel: 'Kindliness, faith, purity, are good spirits which may steer a boat through even as rough waters as any that it has travelled through, and bring it into safe anchorage at last'.[41]

The different modes of unionist writing, like the different modes of unionism, did not solve the problems of Ireland which nationalists and unionists confronted. If anything, moral imagination, compassion and a sense of tragedy complicated the issues. But writers such as Macaulay, Froude and Lawless did something to supply a sympathetic and more human dimension by giving different kinds of imaginative access to the prospects, possibilities and problems of Irish life in continuing connexion with England.

NOTES

1 See W.I. Thompson, *The Imagination of an Insurrection* (New York, 1967); Malcolm Brown, *The Politics of Irish Literature: From Thomas Davis to W.B. Yeats* (London, 1972); P. Costello, *The Heart Grown Brutal: The Irish Revolution in Literature from Parnell to the Death of Yeats, 1891–1939* (Dublin, 1977).
2 Some of this material is used for illustrative purposes in Geoffrey Bell, *The Protestants of Ulster* (London, 1976). For a useful bibliography see Georges-Denis Zimmerman, *Irish Political Street Ballads and Rebel Songs 1780–1900* (Geneva, 1966).
3 W.B. Yeats, *Autobiographies* (London, 1955), pp. 14, 472.
4 See R.F. Foster, *Modern Ireland 1600–1972* (London, 1989), pp. 283–4.
5 The best introductions are probably still John Wilson Foster, *Forces and Themes in Ulster Fiction* (Dublin, 1974) and Terence Brown, *Northern Voices: Poets from the North of Ireland* (Dublin, 1975).
6 See Norman Vance, *Irish Literature, a Social History* (Oxford, 1990), p. 192.
7 See Martin J. Wiener, *English Culture and the Decline of the Industrial Spirit 1850–1980* (Cambridge, 1981).
8 Samuel Ferguson, 'The forging of the anchor', *Blackwood's Edinburgh Magazine* (1832), and 'Dialogue between the heart and the head of an Irish Protestant', *Dublin University Magazine* (1833); St John Ervine, *Changing Winds* (1917) and *The Ship* (1922), discussed in Vance, *Irish Literature*, pp. 183–7.
9 A.C. Swinburne, letter to *The Times*, 6 May 1887; 'The Commonweal. A Song for Unionists', ibid., 1 July 1886, and in *Collected Poetical Works* (London, 1927), II, p. 1194.
10 See Edward Dowden to Edmund Gosse, 20 October 1912, in Edward Dowden, *Letters of Edward Dowden* (London, 1914), p. 383.
11 Rudyard Kipling, 'Ulster 1912', in Rudyard Kipling, *The Years Between* (London, 1919), p. 9.
12 Cyril Falls, *Rudyard Kipling, a Critical Study* (London, 1915).
13 The only recent published discussion know to me is Patrick Maume, 'Ulstermen of letters: the unionism of Frankfort Moore, Shan Bullock and St John Ervine', in Richard England and Graham Walker (eds), *Unionism in Modern Ireland: New Perspectives on Politics and Culture* (Dublin, 1996).

14 Robert Crawford, 'The Scottish invention of English literature', in Robert Crawford, *Devolving English Literature* (Oxford, 1992), pp. 16–44.

15 Discussed in Vance, *Irish Literature*, pp. 122–3.

16 Quoted in Edna Longley, '"A foreign oasis?" English literature, Irish studies and Queen's University Belfast', *Irish Review*, 17–18 (1995), p. 31.

17 But see Terence Brown, 'Edward Dowden: Irish Victorian', in Terence Brown, *Ireland's Literature: Selected Essays* (Dublin, 1988).

18 Dowden to Gosse, 20 October 1912, in Dowden, *Letters*, p. 383.

19 William Blacker, 'Oliver's Advice', in John Cooke (ed.), *The Dublin Book of Irish Verse 1728–1909* (Dublin, 1909), p. 30.

20 Edmund Spenser, *A View of the Present State of Ireland*, W.L. Renwick (ed.) (Oxford, 1970), p. 153.

21 Discussed in Philip Edwards, *Threshold of a Nation: A Study in English and Irish Drama* (Cambridge, 1979), pp. 74–7.

22 Discussed by Linda Colley, *Britons: Forging the Nation 1707–1837* (London, 1994), pp. 132–3.

23 See Robert Staples, *Irish Loyalty and English Gratitude; or Repeal of the Union the Certain Result of the Destruction of the Irish Church* (Dublin, 1869), p. 4, referring to Macaulay's essay, 'Gladstone on Church and State', *Edinburgh Review* (April 1839).

24 William Johnston diary, 17 and 23 January 1856, William Johnston Ms., Public Record Office of Northern Ireland, D880/2/1.

25 T.B. Macaulay, *History of England*, ch. 12, Everyman edition (London, 1906), II, p. 397.

26 John Mitchel, *Jail Journal* (1854) (Dublin, 1982), pp. 20–8.

27 T.B. Macaulay, 'Horatius', stanza lx, in T.B. Macaulay, *Essays and Lays of Ancient Rome*, popular edition (London, 1988), p. 857.

28 For Gillespie see *Dictionary of National Biography* and Richard Hayward, *In Praise of Ulster* (London, 1938), pp. 150–1.

29 J.A. Froude, 'Ireland since the Union' (1872), in J.A. Froude, *Short Studies on Great Subjects* (London, 1891), II, pp. 554–7.

30 Ibid.

31 See W.H. Dunn, *James Anthony Froude: A Biography* (Oxford, 1961), I, pp. 62–6.

32 J.A. Froude, *The Two Chiefs of Dunboy, or, An Irish Romance of the Last Century* (London, 1889), p. 59.

33 Ibid., p. 99

34 Ibid., p. 455.

35 Ibid.

36 Ibid., p. 456.

37 Emily Lawless, *Hurrish: A Study* (Belfast, 1992), p. 3.

38 Ibid., p. 58.

39 Ibid., p. 195.

40 Ibid., pp. 9, 80.

41 Ibid., p. 196.

10 Scientists against home rule

Greta Jones

In 1887, in the middle of the crisis provoked by Gladstone's home rule proposal of 1886, John Tyndall (1820–93), professor of natural philosophy and super-intendent of the Royal Institution, London, wrote to Thomas Henry Huxley to organise a memorandum criticising Gladstone to be signed by the members of the Royal Society.[1] He solicited 'a brief expression of opinion on the part of our leading scientists to strengthen the hand and increase the courage of the Gov-ernment'. Although Tyndall and Huxley believed the majority of the Royal Soci-ety were anti-home rule, the proposed memorandum never materialised. Huxley agreed with Tyndall's sentiments but, as ever the politician, he warned him about the reluctance of scientists to be drawn into political controversy and the dangers a memorandum might pose to the unity of the Royal Society.[2] There was, there-fore, no public expression of unionist sentiment on the part of the most pres-tigious institution of science in the United Kingdom in 1887. However, these were merely the opening shots in what was to be a long campaign against home rule among a significant section of scientific opinion in Britain and Ireland lasting through the introduction of the first Home Rule Bill in 1886, the second in 1893, the third in 1912 and the electoral victory of Sinn Féin in 1918.

This chapter will concentrate upon teasing out the specifically scientific concerns of anti-home rulers, although the complexities of the issue in any individual case need stressing. There were scientists for whom the case against home rule was based predominantly upon their fears for science, scientists who opposed home rule for much the same political and religious reasons as the non-scientific com-munity and the majority, for whom political views and apprehensions about sci-ence were inextricably mixed up and difficult to disentangle. However, as Irish nationalism became more overtly Catholic and Gaelic in character at the end of the nineteenth century, fears about the implications of home rule for science grew, encouraged by the belief that the project of scientific modernisation would be put in jeopardy by the creation of an Irish parliament.

What was meant by the nineteenth-century concept of scientific modernisa-tion? By the second half of the century prominent scientists were involved in systematic public exposition of the value of science and scientific research as a means to aid economic development and increase national strength. This meant convincing government, industry and public opinion of the need to invest in science. A major target of these scientists was the reform of the curriculum in schools and universities to increase the amount of science education, including the provision of experimental laboratories for basic training in research. From being an important but often private vocation, science was to be put at the centre of national life, expanded in the education system, the means to pursue a career in science put in place and the importance of research recognised by the provision of research facilities.

This agenda appears unproblematic to twentieth-century eyes as a description of how science is conducted but it was an ideal far from being realised in the mid-nineteenth century. Scientific education in the schools was either non-existent or minimal, as were school laboratories. There were few posts for scientists in universities and facilities for research there were poor. Science was seen, primarily, as an adjunct to the professional training of doctors and engineers. While scientific research was done at universities, it was not seen as an integral part of their function. Professors were usually paid by student fees and the temptation was to pack courses and devote most of their time to teaching. Laboratories were rare and the money needed to fund them hard to obtain.

The leading propagandist for scientific modernisation in the nineteenth century was Thomas Henry Huxley (1825–95).[3] Huxley's other claim to fame was as the defender of Darwinian evolution. In a series of brilliant and often polemical articles and lectures, he defended Darwinism as a particular exemplification of the philosophical basis of all scientific investigation. The term coined to describe this philosophy was 'scientific naturalism'; that is, the possibility of establishing laws of development in man and nature without reference to Divine intervention or to theological considerations. His own position on religious questions he referred to as 'agnostic', a term he coined himself. Science could not prove or disprove the existence of God, but nor could theology invalidate scientific laws.

Huxley's involvement in the debate over evolution considerably enhanced his public profile. He became the exemplification of the 'modern' scientist and helped make Darwinism an icon of scientific modernity. However, there was a real sense in which for Huxley and the colleagues and supporters he drew around him – Hooker, Tyndall and Lubbock – the cause of scientific modernisation and Darwinism were truly interconnected. Reforming scientific education required that the older universities move away from their original character as religious foundations for the training of clergymen and that the curriculum in 'sensitive subjects', in particular those which touched on Creation and on human origins, be rid of the influence of theology. The right to teach scientific naturalism was regarded by Huxley and his supporters as a test of the freedom of science from clerical interference.

Although the foundations for Huxley's fame were laid earlier, it was the Darwinian controversies of the 1860s which made him a household name. However, there were scientists belonging to an earlier generation who resisted the lure of Huxley and his followers and among them were prominent anti-home rulers. William Thomson, Lord Kelvin,[4] was described 'up to 1885 as a broad Liberal but, as was natural in an Ulsterman, [he] became an ardent unionist on the introduction of the home rule bill'.[5] Kelvin, though very much taken up with the application of science to industrial and economic development, was 'conventionally religious and hostile to Darwinism'.[6] George Gabriel Stokes, Lucasian Professor of Mathematics at Cambridge, elected as MP for Cambridge University 1887–91 and 'the first scientific man who represented either University in Parliament since Sir Isaac Newton', was, according to his biographer, 'like all Irishmen of his way of thinking, a very loyal subject',[7] but he too was deeply pious. Stokes was regarded as a scientific conservative and an obstacle to Huxley's influence over the Royal Society.[8]

The exception in this generation of Irish scientists was John Tyndall.[9] He was four years older than Kelvin and a year younger than Stokes but distinguished from them by his association with the circle of scientific reformers who gathered around Huxley and lent their public support to the Darwinian cause. He shared their belief in the need to proselytise the cause of science aggressively and their agnosticism in regard to conventional religious belief. Tyndall's public lecturing, popular science books and position at the Royal Institution gave him a prominent national profile rivalling Huxley's, a source of some pride to Irish patriots. W.E.H. Lecky referred to him in 1868 as intellectually Ireland's 'best representative'.[10]

Tyndall was, however, not universally approved of in Ireland. In 1874 his address to the meeting of the British Association for the Advancement of Science in Belfast on the subject of scientific naturalism and evolution, conceived in close liaison with Huxley, earned him immediate notoriety.[11] Yet he also had his supporters. The *Northern Whig*, published in Belfast, believed that not only was Tyndall 'justified in letting his convictions be fully known but it is on scientific principles and not through sectarian prejudices and passions that his exposition must be considered'.[12] The *Dublin Daily Express* concurred: Darwinian theory would probably startle some of its readers, but 'such hypotheses should receive a free and fair discussion and nothing has done more injury to religion than the attempt to down new scientific theories as atheistic without inquiry into their bearings on their evidence'.[13] Much to the consternation of the Catholic Church, Tyndall's supporters could even be found among their ranks.[14]

Huxleyism, whether identified as a gospel of scientific progress, the defence of evolutionary ideas or religious scepticism evoked sympathy among a section of the Irish public. It also had a following among scientists in Ireland who wanted to realise the objective of scientific modernisation as defined by Huxley. They included John Joly (1857–1933), Professor of Geology at Trinity College Dublin, George Johnstone Stoney (1826–1911), born in Kingstown, County Dublin and Professor of Natural Philosophy at Galway 1857–82, and his nephew George Francis Fitzgerald (1851–1901), Erasmus Smith Professor of Natural Philosophy at Trinity College.[15] All three were actively engaged in promoting science education. Stoney was Secretary to the Queen's Colleges in Ireland 1852–83, and Superintendent of the civil service examinations, becoming a noted authority on Irish educational matters.[16] Fitzgerald was appointed a Commissioner of National Education in 1898 and a member of the Board of Intermediate Education in 1900 as well as actively campaigning to set up Trinity's first large-scale experimental physical laboratory. John Joly was a member of the Dublin Educational Association and the author, in association with the Trinity anatomist D.J. Cunningham, of a memorandum sent in 1899 to the Irish Intermediate Education Commission in which they set out proposals for a programme of science education for secondary schools.[17] After Fitzgerald's death in 1901 Joly took up the cause which had been dear to Fitzgerald's heart of expanding the laboratories in Trinity. He set up the 'science fund', lobbying government and industry for money to expand facilities for research. In 1903 Joly finally persuaded Lord Iveagh, owner of the Guinness Breweries, to part with £35,000 for the construction of a modern laboratory.

Writing in 1886, Fitzgerald believed that 'experimental science in Ireland was nearly the same as snakes in Ireland',[18] a situation he actively sought to remedy and in which he believed government should be persuaded to take a role. Underlying this was a much more ambitious vision – the belief that science could alleviate Ireland's economic problems. This could be done partly by the application of science and technology to her economic problems but also by the spread of scientific attitudes through education to her population at large. In a lecture to the Irish Industrial League in 1896 Fitzgerald argued that there should be a single system of schools and colleges ending the separation of science and classical education. All students should be taught at least one biological or physical science because science inculcated 'accuracy in observing, in experimenting, in classifying, in judging and consequently in doing'.[19] The product of a science education was a critical and evaluative attitude, a search for constant improvement, and this was one key to curing Ireland's problems of depopulation and low productivity.

Fitzgerald, along with Sir Horace Plunkett, the founder of the Irish Agricultural Association, was among those who assiduously lobbied in the 1890s for a government department committed to addressing the agricultural problems of Ireland through education and scientific research.[20] In 1899 they were successful in obtaining an Act of Parliament setting up the Department of Agriculture and Technical Instruction (DATI), and Plunkett, who shared Fitzgerald's views on the relationship between economic and social progress and science, became its head.[21] DATI inaugurated a golden age for science in Ireland. Scientific education expanded at secondary level. The Royal College of Science in Dublin received additional funding and the numbers of students increased.[22] DATI earmarked money for agricultural research. The first experiments in Mendelian genetics in Ireland took place under DATI's auspices.[23]

Potentially all the various political factions in Ireland from constructive unionists to nationalists could unite under this agenda. Catholic priests, for example, were prominent in the movement for agricultural improvement which led to the creation of DATI. In reality, however, controversy dogged DATI as it did other aspects of the Huxleyite project. Central to the problem was the question of education and the aspirations of the Catholic Church, particularly with regard to third-level or university education.

In 1845 the Queen's Colleges at Belfast, Cork and Galway were founded – they opened over the subsequent four years – to provide non-denominational education and therefore meet the objections of Catholics and Presbyterians that Trinity College, a Church of Ireland foundation, was unsuitable for the education of their young. By the 1870s the Fawcett reforms had opened up Trinity College fellowships – studentships were already available – to non-Anglicans. The Queen's Colleges and the gradual detachment of Trinity from its predominantly Anglican origins were not, however, acceptable compromises in the view of the Catholic bishops. In 1854 they founded the Catholic University of Ireland, a private foundation under their control, for the education of Catholics in a denominational atmosphere. In 1883 it was transferred to the Jesuits. With the exception of its flourishing medical school, this proved a weak institution short of student fees and charitable income. Securing government funding without sacrificing their control over appointments, the curriculum and administration became a prime objective of the Catholic bishops.[24] The result was conflict between the scientific modernisers and the Catholic Church.

The ethos of scientific modernisation in Ireland, as in England, was wrapped around the pill of scientific naturalism, scepticism and Darwinism, a fact which made it all the more difficult for the bishops to swallow. Darwinian evolutionism had considerable influence over Irish scientists.[25] The anatomy department at Trinity was by the 1880s a redoubt of evolutionary biology and the influence of Darwin also spread among physical scientists.[26] Robert Ball (1840–1913), Astronomer Royal of Ireland 1874–92, who entered Trinity in 1857, described himself as 'an instantaneous convert to the new doctrines'.[27] In one of his popular books on astronomy published in 1892, Ball added chapters on the Darwinian theory, which he treated as the equivalent in organic nature of an evolutionary process taking place in the physical universe. Joly incorporated Darwinian evolution into his geological teaching. Fitzgerald was also involved in the controversy over scientific naturalism, arguing in a series of letters to *Nature* in 1898 against the idea that the probable origin of life in crystalline forms implied an intelligent designer.[28] Catholic clergy complained that just as Tyndall's speech was 'carried by the periodical press into every town and village where there is a reading room or railway stall so Sir Robert Ball's Darwinism will now profit by popularity of his astronomy and get publicity it never had a chance of before'.[29] James Joyce's capacity in *Ulysses* for putting his finger upon the tender spots in Irish intellectual life is illustrated by his having Leopold Bloom musing as he goes about Dublin. 'Fascinating book that is of Ball's. Parallex I never exactly understood. There's a priest. Could ask him'.[30] Bloom also plans a visit to the eminent Professor Joly.

In 1874 the Catholic Church was disappointed at the failure of the Devonshire Commission on the reform of education to recommend government funding for the science faculties of the Catholic University. They attributed this to Huxley's influence over the commission. *The Tablet* complained that 'denied endowment and legal recognition, the Catholic University should, in the opinion of the Royal Commission found and endow chairs open to Messrs Carpenter, Tyndall, Huxley, and Herbert Spencer and all the scientific rationalists of the day'.[31] The nationalist newspaper *The Nation* agreed: 'the Catholic bishops were said to be exorbitant in their demands when in the matter of university education they sought for some effective control over professorial teaching. Ought they to give sanction to a university system in which Professor Tyndall might day after day deliver lectures containing the doctrines of his address?'[32] Subsequent government inquiries into the universities in Ireland were dogged by the question of whether the Catholic bishops would allow the teaching of Darwinism and the generally hostile or evasive answers they gave to this question. In a memorandum he drew up on university education in 1905, Joly listed some of them: the Bishop of Limerick: 'I would let him [Huxley] go on as long as his Science did not come in contact with Revelation'; the Revd Fr Delaney said the Church should decide how far evolution should be taught; Bishop O'Dwyer believed it was likely that laity on a governing body of a university would follow the bishops in faith or morals.[33]

There were other considerations besides the right to teach Darwinism which made many scientists uneasy about home rule. They feared Irish nationalism would disrupt scientific relationships within the British Isles to the detriment of Ireland. Irish science was sustained by a community of feeling and myriad relationships between the British and Irish scientific communities. The *Dublin Daily Express*, commenting on Tyndall's address to the British Association at Belfast in 1874, editorialised that more Irishmen had been elected fellows at Cambridge than in the University of Dublin over the preceding twelve years, a proof, they claimed, that Irish civilisation was conducive to scientific eminence.[34] Ireland supplied two Lucasian professors of mathematics to Cambridge in succession. Joseph Larmor (1857–1942) was Professor of Natural Philosophy, Queen's College Galway 1880–5 and then moved to Cambridge in 1885, eventually succeeding Stokes in 1903. Alexander Macalister moved from Trinity's department of anatomy to become Professor of Anatomy at Cambridge in 1893. Robert Ball was appointed Lowndean Professor of Astronomy in Cambridge in 1892. William Ridgeway (1853–1926), a leading figure in the development of British anthropology and Professor of Greek at Queen's College Cork 1883–94, became Professor of Archaeology at Cambridge in 1892 and Reader in Classics from 1907. Irish scientists like Fitzgerald, Joly and Stoney were the equals of and could claim respectful attention from their colleagues in major British universities.[35] Letters flew across the Irish Sea and the Irish trooped off to scientific jubilees and presentations for their fellow Irish scientists in Britain.[36] As the Irish migrated to scientific posts in England, so the English, Welsh and Scots took up places in Ireland. Huxley was particularly assiduous in placing scientific men he regarded as allies in positions of influence to help spread the gospel of scientific reform and evolution. His protégés at the Royal College of Science Dublin included W. Thistleton–Dyer (1843–1928) who was Professor of Botany there from 1870–2 and Alfred Cort Haddon, who moved to Dublin from Foster's Physiological Laboratory in Cambridge to take up a post in zoology, 1880–1900, on Huxley's recommendation.[37]

There was alarm that the agenda of Irish nationalism would diminish these connexions. Fitzgerald already felt he was struggling against the tendency, familiar to scientists in the twentieth century, for scientific excellence to concentrate in certain geographical areas, rendering the work of those on the periphery more difficult. As his obituary commented, his research was 'rendered more arduous by limited funds and distance from other scientific centres'.[38] Although scientific migration favoured the dominant area of science – giving its young scions their first jobs in the periphery and drawing off the most eminent from the outlying regions – it none the less, given other favourable factors, also helped limit the inequalities which could arise. Glasgow, after all, held on to Kelvin, and it was only Larmor's assiduous wooing of Ernest Rutherford which finally brought him from Manchester to Cambridge.

Now, however, all professional appointments, including scientific posts, were coming under the scrutiny of Irish nationalists.[39] The nationalist newspaper *The Leader* argued that DATI had failed to meet its 'national responsibilities' by employing 'foreigners':

> The Department rightly insists on the qualifications of teachers who are to undertake this responsible work; but this insistence *must not* mean the employment of other than Irishmen. Already Scotland and England have supplied officers to the Board. It would be fatal, at any time, but more particularly in the present transitory condition of the Irish mind to make this transfer of fiscal and administrative powers an opportunity for a further influx of foreigners; for they can never appreciate or rightly understand the Irish temperament.[40]

The problem was further compounded by the increasing tendency to define Irishness in terms of Catholicism and nationalism. This Joly felt was leading to the increasing marginalisation of Trinity. In 1899, Joly argued that the chances of employment in the public sphere in Ireland of graduates of Trinity were severely impaired by what he called this politico-religious barrier: 'Where are our young men to get any public employment in Ireland? except in a limited part of Ulster'.[41]

The problem in science was illustrated by comments over appointments in dental surgery, mechanics and a professorship in mathematical physics in the National University Cork (formerly Queen's College Cork) in 1913. The editorial in *The Leader* complained

> two Protestants and a Jew were candidates as against three Catholics. Two of the Catholics are natives of the city, but this did not prevent the majority of the Academic Council giving them a curt go-by. The history of the appointments has been sufficiently told and it only remains to point out the moral. This was that these three appointments put further away than ever the possibility of a Catholic and nationalist atmosphere in this worthy successor of the old Queen's College and means three votes added for Protestants in all future elections for appointments.[42]

Many home rulers were embarrassed by the increasing sectarianism accompanying appointments but the pressures on them were considerable. Alex Anderson, Professor of Natural Philosophy at Galway, complained bitterly to Joseph Larmor about lobbying which had gone on in 1912 in Galway over the chair of mathematics and the effect this had upon the quality of the appointment. Anderson claimed:

> the representatives of the Academic Council dealing with the qualifications of the candidates were entirely ignorant, and it was evident the RC professors had to do what they were told. They looked like a flock of sheep . . . it will be impossible in the future to get good men for the chairs when they become vacant unless a good Catholic happens to turn up.[43]

All these factors contributed to anxiety in the scientific community. Ball's son recalled an encounter in 1893 between his father and a priest in Dublin which summed up, in a humorous fashion, the fears entertained by many.

> When the second home rule bill was under discussion he chanced to be at an entertainment in Dublin where many eminent men were gathered together. A cleric who had attained high preferment in the Catholic Church was at pains to assure the Astronomer Royal that whatever changes might be made in Ireland when home rule was achieved, men of his standing would not be interfered with. I am glad to hear it was the reply. As the name of Sackville Street has recently changed to O'Connell Street, I had grave apprehensions lest a nationalist government would begin to tamper with the constellations. I feared I should live to see the day when I should look on the great O'Brien sloping slowly to the West.[44]

Scientific opponents of home rule in Britain were not so closely acquainted with developments in Ireland and they tended to frame their objections in more general political terms – the integrity of the Empire, the rights of Protestants and of Ulster in particular, and, among Huxleyites, an abiding contempt for Gladstone. Or, like the anthropologist and naturalist John Lubbock, a Liberal MP, they were alarmed about the implications of Irish nationalism for the unity of the United Kingdom as a whole. Lubbock attacked Irish home rulers for the idea that Celtic racial and cultural distinctiveness demanded expression in a separate political identity. He did not believe a community composed exclusively of the Celt could, in any case, be found anywhere in the British Isles and he urged Huxley to use his authority to denounce the idea:[45] 'No expression of my opinion would be accepted because it would be supposed that I spoke more as a Liberal Unionist than as an Ethnologist but I wish you could give in something which . . . I might quote on your authority'.[46]

There was, also, a hard-edged anti-Catholicism to the Huxley circle which contributed to their anti-home rule position. Tyndall made constant deprecating references in private and public to 'enslavement by the Romish priesthood'.[47] This hostility to the Catholic Church was exacerbated by Huxley's controversies with prominent Catholic apologists over the Darwin question.[48] Huxley thought the Catholic Church one of the most unregenerate foes of the 'spirit of the age' represented by modern science and Darwinian evolution. Like many English liberals of the time, he saw Catholicism as the historic enemy of British political independence and constitutional liberty.

Those with closer connexions to Ireland, however, saw how divisive the language of militant political Protestantism could be. Irish liberals were gravely alarmed by Gladstone's pamphlets in 1875 attacking ultramontanism, which, while strongly appealing to his British non-conformist constituency, they thought wrong and intemperate. Gladstone's subsequent conversion to home rule was all the more galling to them in the light of his rhetoric during this controversy.[49] Tyndall, writing to an Irish correspondent over a proposed Dublin anti-home rule convention, warned against anti-Catholicism *per se* as the basis for opposition to home rule. He wrote that those whom Gladstone would 'hand over to their hereditary foes' were not confined to Ulster and he would use the word Protestant with reluctance 'for are not Roman Catholics to be met with here and there whose loyalty to the Union is as uncompromising as that of any Protestant?'[50] To many Irish scientists Protestant sectarianism as well as Catholic denominationalism would destroy the space in which common intellectual activity embracing all denominations could take place.

In England fears about denominationalism in higher education were eventually put to rest largely through the integration of Catholics into third-level education.[51] Nevertheless, tensions between Catholics and scientific modernisers arose in England, too. For example, by the 1850s London University was a stronghold of the scientific naturalists. W.B. Carpenter, the evolutionary physiologist, became Second Registrar in 1856. In 1858 Alexander Bain, a philosopher of the mental sciences, was appointed to the Examining Board and in 1860 Huxley became its Science Examiner and the man who launched its first science degree.[52] English and Irish Catholics often made use of the external examination system set up by London University and the revised courses in philosophy and mental science occasioned by Bain's appointment led to bitter attacks from English Catholic circles on the university.

> Up to 1858, the textbooks [of the London University] were Whately, *Elements of Logic*, Paley's *Principles of Morals*, and Butler, *Three Sermons on Human Nature*, a sorry selection certainly. However, in the year 1858 they discarded the textbooks in favour of subjects and instead of logic and moral philosophy proposed an examination in logic, morals and moral philosophy. Now things began to look serious. The then prefect of studies at Stonyhurst instantly took alarm and communicated his suspicions to the heads of all our English Catholic Colleges. They unanimously agreed with him in the fact that the change would tend to the exclusion of Catholics from the modern University Degree. They felt that Catholics would be at a disadvantage as being debarred by their faith from that freedom or, as they would call it, licence of philosophical speculation which is allowed and approved in non-Catholic schools.[53]

The gospel of scientific naturalism, however, had put down roots in English higher education which Catholic objections could not dislodge. The case was different in Ireland. In 1883 the Royal University of Ireland was created, bringing together the Queen's Colleges and the Catholic University in a loose federation with a common examination board.[54] When, in 1884, the examining board of the Royal University of Ireland set the first joint examination in philosophy, it was roundly denounced in the *Irish Ecclesiastical Record*, the chief organ of the Catholic Church in Ireland.

> Considering how largely Catholics predominate in Ireland, as also the fact that the Royal University was established with the special object of relieving their educational grievances it cannot be held unreasonable to demand (1) that as many questions should be based especially on standard works of Catholic philosophy as are based upon the corresponding works of non-Catholic philosophy; (2) that the terminology familiar to the Catholic student should be employed as freely as that which is familiar to his rival and (3) that any alternatives which are offered should be as favourable to one side as to the other.[55]

The Revd Thomas McGrath DD singled out cosmology, psychology and ethics for special condemnation.[56] Catholics, in his view, could not accept basing the discipline of mental philosophy upon mind and matter and instead he asked for the Aristotelian categories of bodies, essences, constituents and properties to be included in the syllabus. McGrath claimed the Church was also disturbed by the nature of the exam questions which eschewed the formula of 'stating, proving and solving' in favour of 'commenting and discussing'. In ethics he objected to the concept of pleasure, pain and aversion being introduced into the discussion of the origin of moral nature. In response to these demands a separate paper in philosophy was provided in the following year's examination and the government began the process of endowing chairs of scholastic philosophy at the Queen's Colleges at Cork and Belfast, effectively providing separate departments of Catholic philosophy.

In 1901 the appointment of the Robertson Commission on Irish Universities, which reported in 1903, signalled further change in higher education. Trinity was excluded from its remit but between June 1906 and January 1907 another commission headed by Sir Edward Fry and concentrating exclusively on Dublin University (Trinity) reported. Hard on the heels of the Fry Commission, an Irish Universities Bill was announced by the Chief Secretary for Ireland, James Bryce, to a deputation of the Irish Presbyterian Church on 25 January 1907. This proposed the creation of a National University of Ireland (the title 'Royal' being dropped to appease nationalism) which would incorporate Trinity, the Queen's Colleges and University College Dublin – the successor to the Catholic University. This would go further in integrating administratively the constituent colleges than the Royal University, whose function had been primarily that of an examining body.

This brought all the potential conflicts to a head. The prospect of being submerged into a university in which the Catholic Church, through its representation in University College Dublin, would have a predominant influence provoked the most serious alarm in Joly:

> I have enjoyed in Trinity College over 24 years of teaching work conducted under conditions of perfect freedom from interference. My work of research, my writings have never been hampered by the fear that I was under the supervision of those who viewed Biology, Geology or Science generally as curbed by boundaries fixed in theological grounds and immovable for all time.
>
> But now collegiate relations are to arise within a college of a kind which must subject us to just such limited ideals of education. I do not desire to criticise those ideals or to decry the sincerety [sic] and high principles of those who hold them. I am far from saying that such a College would not be beneficial to the Roman Catholic community . . . but what I do say is that the ideals which find favour with Roman Catholic theologians are not ours.[57]

In his statement of 1907 Bryce put a positive interpretation on the changes. The new university would enable students from different denominations to 'form friendships and grow up and mingle with one another in the classroom and the playfield'. The new university would be free from any theological test and public money would not be used for any religious instruction. There was, he went on in his address to the Irish Presbyterians, no such thing 'as Protestant mathematics and Catholic mathematics (laughter). There is no such thing as Catholic philology and Protestant philology'.[58] Nevertheless, Bryce proposed 'alternative graduation and courses in controversial subjects such as history and philosophy', alternative papers for examinees and that separate professorships in history and philosophy should be established.[59] Bryce failed, however, to take into account the potential conflicts in science and suggested a formula to cover other subject areas which aggravated the fears of the anti-home rule scientists. He proposed, 'no question should be put in an exam paper offensive to any student',[60] and in lectures 'no Professor or teacher must misuse his position by teaching or writing anything as professor which could be reasonably offensive to the faith of any student attending his course'.[61] Joly rightly believed the list of 'offensive' subjects included evolution and he complained, 'I cannot teach palaeontology without evolution'.[62] He commented bitterly on Bryce's exegesis: 'What a vista of educational freedom and thoroughness is here opened up. What an idea for a great University!'[63]

Joly's preferred solution was non-denominational and mixed university education. Catholics attended Trinity and were among its fellows, though they incurred the hostility of their Church for doing so. However, if this process was accelerated he believed something might be saved. Joly proposed, therefore, that Trinity reserve places on its governing body for Catholics as of right, augment the teaching staff by ten fellowships reserved exclusively for Roman Catholics for a period of ten years and make special arrangements for Catholic worship to take place within Trinity.[64] Joly's plan, however, failed to win acceptance even within Trinity and the chance of its success outside in the world of Irish politics was nil. The real battle was taking place elsewhere, between the Catholic Church's aim thoroughly to denominationalise any new institution and the government's reluctance to fund an institution directly under the control of the Catholic bishops.

The fight of anti-home rule scientists turned, therefore, to the more modest objective of keeping Trinity outside the proposed new institution. In February 1907 the Dublin University Defence Committee was formed and a manifesto issued which warned that sectarian divisions in the proposed university 'would be felt in all questions of policy, in the making of appointments, in the arrangement of studies and in the control of teaching'. It believed 'it is contrary to our best traditions that the boundaries of science should be fixed directly or indirectly by ecclesiastical authority or the impulse of speculation arrested by clerical intervention'. This sterling statement of Huxleyism was supported by, among others, J. Kells Ingram, Mrs Lecky, the Earl of Rosse, Whitley Stokes, Samuel Prenter in Ireland and G. Stoney Johnstone.[65]

The Cambridge–Trinity politico-scientific networks sprang into life to assist the Dublin University Defence Committee. William Ridgeway's political and academic connexions proved crucial in this respect. For over a generation Ridgeway had been at the hub of university politics in both Trinity and Cambridge, particularly in the elections for the university seats. He helped secure Carson's election for Trinity in 1892, Larmor's for Cambridge University in 1911 and tried to persuade Joly to stand in 1918 for Trinity when Carson took up a parliamentary seat in Belfast. It was Ridgeway who helped Joly arrange a series of public meetings in England in support of Trinity. Joly left Dublin in February 1907 to attend these and to meet Augustine Birrell, who, meanwhile, had replaced Bryce as Secretary for Ireland. Robert Ball chaired the meeting at Cambridge on 2 March and Carson attended. A memorial was drawn up by Ball and Ridgeway and issued on 11 March 1907, which protested against arrangements which 'must subject teaching and research to limitations injurious to liberal education and free inquiry'. It was signed by, among others, George Darwin, R.J. Strutt, J. Peile, the Master of Christ's and J.B. Bury, another Irish exile in Cambridge and strong Darwinian. Further public meetings were held at Oxford on 15 March and at Bristol where Professor Purser the Trinity classicist threatened 'we will make a good show in Birrell's own fortress'.[66] The physicist Oliver Lodge wrote from Birmingham that the university 'has already memorialised the Irish secretary on behalf of TCD's independent university status'.[67] Only the Ulsterman Larmor could not be persuaded. Ulster Presbyterians were, on the whole, unenthusiastic in the cause of Trinity, and Larmor, a graduate of Queen's College Belfast and former fellow of Queen's College Galway, was more worried about their fate than Trinity's:[68] Joly wrote to Purser, 'he hopes we may escape but he will not aid us so long as the Queen's Colleges are in danger. He thinks the absorption of the Queen's Colleges in the new Catholic College would be fatal for the former'.[69]

Both Trinity and Queen's College Belfast (the latter became a university in its own right under the 1908 Irish Universities Act) were eventually excluded from the new National University. This outcome had as much to do with the unwillingness of the Catholic Church to operate in a mixed religious institution as it did to the pleas for intellectual freedom made by Joly and his allies. A National University which excluded Trinity and Queen's College Belfast would be predominantly Catholic and nationalist and, as events proved, this resulted in the increasing denominationalism of third-level education for Irish Catholics. Exclusion was not the most desirable option in the view of the anti-home rule scientists, but it was the best that could be achieved in the circumstances. Ridgeway wrote to Larmor that the new National University of Ireland should be 'left to work out their own salvation in a Catholic University erected on the ruins of the Royal. They can go at their own gait and be as obscurantist as they please whilst the other University will be able to work with freedom'.[70] Not everyone in Ireland was as sanguine about the outcome. While Trinity was saved, it was at the price of conceding ground to the opponents of scientific modernisation and thus changing, perhaps irrevocably, Irish intellectual life.

Larmor's election address of 24 January 1911 for the Cambridge University seat encapsulated the two objectives of anti-home rule scientists – the advancement of science and the preservation of the Union of Ireland with Britain.[71] However, politics often took second place to science.[72] Carson was one of Ridgeway's 'oldest and closest friends' but, nevertheless, Ridgeway believed it desirable that the university MPs represented academic interests as well as being strong anti-home rulers. This he considered he had achieved 'in Larmor's case here, when I burst the caucus' but he recalled, 'I had difficulty in the case of Ned [Carson] . . . when he stood and I told him that I could not support him if a true academic candidate came forward such as Lecky'. He summed up this double strategy when trying to persuade Joly to stand for the Trinity seat in the 1918 election: 'Woods is being run by Kelleher who is, I believe, a strong home ruler and from Woods' address I infer that he is a disguised home ruler. This further justifies my support of Samuels but I could not support Samuels against you, who are an ideal scientific researcher and reformer'.[73]

Were the anti-home rule scientists correct in seeing the interests of science and the maintenance of the Union as bound together? To a large extent Catholic denominationalism and political and intellectual separation were taking place even prior to the actual legislative Act of Separation in 1922 and the scientists proved relatively powerless to stop it. The Catholic Bishops did not gain full legislative control over the new National University but they did achieve *de facto* influence and any residual non-denominational atmosphere in the Queen's Colleges was weakened in the decade after the Irish Universities Act of 1908. Bitter sectarian feuding over appointments went on and nationalist feeling within the student body pressurised the staff and made the Queen's Colleges at Cork and Galway, now transformed into the constituent colleges of the National University of Ireland, uncomfortable places even for moderate Catholic home rulers. The senate of the National University made proficiency in the Irish language obligatory for those matriculating from the university, a measure which, if it did not prevent, certainly further discouraged Protestant and unionist participation.[74]

The position for scientist anti-home rulers deteriorated further at the end of the First World War. Sinn Féin emerged in the election of 1918 as the largest party in

Ireland destroying the more moderate Redmondite wing of Irish nationalism.[75] Joly was in despair. He told Larmor in 1919 that 'the result of the election leaves one with the feeling that a life's work for scientific reform and non-denominational education is swept away. I am too old to renew the struggle'.[76] Larmor meanwhile spent the early 1920s obsessing about the outcome of the British–Irish negotiations for his beloved Ulster. In the process a man described as 'difficult to know' and who 'hid his thoughts' became unusually voluble on the subject in his correspondence to largely uncomprehending English scientists.[77]

The Huxleyite project was in danger in the years leading up to 1922 but it required the breaking of the Union for its final nemesis. All the apprehensions of the anti-home rule scientists were vindicated by the events that followed independence. In the newly created twenty-six-county state, the next decades saw the denominationalisation of education increase even further. The proportion of clerics and the clerical orders in the population grew and this was reflected in secondary-level education.[78] Legislation made the Irish language compulsory for most professional positions in the public service and in education. Links with the scientific community in the rest of the British Isles diminished. Trinity became more isolated and the atmosphere of vituperative sectarianism directed against it increased, encouraged by the project of building a new national, Catholic and anti-British consciousness.[79] Resources for science shrank – Trinity College in particular felt the effect of this – and the new state lost the financial support of both the newly created Department of Scientific and Industrial Research created in 1916 and the Medical Research Council founded in 1919.[80]

Most important of all, the achievement of the Huxleyite project in creating a 'neutral space' in which scientific education and research operated free from denominational influence disappeared. By 1926 the Royal College of Science, non-denominational and directly funded by the government, had been absorbed, against the wishes of staff and students, into University College Dublin, the descendant of the Catholic University. DATI also ceased to exist. In 1923 its technical education department was taken under the wing of the Department of Education and its agricultural section absorbed by the Department of Agriculture. The College of Agriculture it ran was incorporated in University College Dublin as a Faculty of Agricultural Science. In 1922 the Royal Irish Academy, under attack for being insufficiently 'national', wrote a memorandum in its own defence for the new government, the bulk of which was devoted to its services to the Irish language and only a few final paragraphs to the glories of the physical science tradition in Ireland.[81] In this ideological climate a whole history of involvement with Darwinism and Huxleyism, an interesting and potent part of Irish history, faded from memory.

Historians have recently deconstructed the Huxley phenomenon, leading to a better understanding of its rootedness in the social and economic fabric of the late nineteenth century. It has been described by Adrian Desmond as militant non-conformity stripped of the theology. Huxley 'bore witness', enthused his followers, to spread the gospel of the new church of science, and encouraged them to remake society in a better image by practical missionary work animated by all the passion characteristic of the evangelical revival. However, in spite of Huxley's implacable conviction that he was working for truth and the public good, they have pointed out how much his rhetoric served as a tool to advance the professional interests of scientists. Many of the classic encounters between science and religion, seen at the time as iconic images of the battle between freedom of thought and religious obscurantism, have been shown to have grown in the telling. The opponents of Darwin, cast by Huxley into outer darkness, have been demonstrated to have been, in some instances, excellent scientists whose contribution to understanding the history of life was indispensable. The doubts they expressed about the validity of natural selection are now known to have been shared by many of those who defended Darwin. The story of the triumph of reason and progress, led by the scientists, over darkness and superstition has been shown to have 'mythic' qualities.

We now have a Huxley mediated through the lens of historical reconstruction. However, the general social influence of Huxley can only be appreciated by tracing its manifestations in society at large. Ireland shows how the ideology of Huxleyism, conveyed by classic public confrontations at national level, nevertheless percolated from the metropolitan elite into society at large. Stripped of its bombast, it provided a generation of scientists in the late nineteenth century with an organising ideology, a sense of mission and a practical programme of reform. Working through the movement for educational reform, economic development and state involvement in social improvement, Huxleyism helped to change things. The victories in Britain are now commonplace and unremarkable. Huxley won and, therefore, what perhaps has disappeared is a sense of the vulnerability of the Huxleyite project: that the battles, even though often stage-managed by a brilliant propagandist, were real, not concocted, and that Huxleyism might have lost out, at least in the short term, to an alternative vision of science. In Ireland, after some notable successes on the way, Huxleyism lost the battle, and that fact allows us to see better the real intellectual and social impact of the scientific modernisers of the late nineteenth century.

NOTES

1 In 1867 Tyndall succeeded Michael Faraday, whose assistant he had been since 1852, at the Royal Institution. The Royal Institution was a combination of research laboratory and school. One of its functions was to give public lectures. By the 1860s Tyndall was well established both scientifically and socially in London's intellectual elite, and a confidant of Huxley and Hooker. Tyndall married in 1876, Louisa, daughter of Lord Claud Hamilton.

2 Tyndall to Huxley, 27 December 1887, Huxley Papers, Imperial College, London, 8.260.

3 For the best and most up-to-date evaluation of Huxley see Adrian Desmond's recent two-volume biography, *Huxley: The Devil's Disciple* (London, 1994) and *Huxley: Evolution's High Priest* (London, 1997).

4 Sir William Thomson, Lord Kelvin (1824–1907) came from a family of Protestant farmers in Down, of modest though respectable means. He was born in Belfast where

his father was Professor of Engineering. He left while a child when his father took up a post in Glasgow.

5 Silvanus Thompson, *Life and Work of Lord Kelvin* (London, 1908), p. 22. Kelvin denounced home rule 'as a mere political adventure that would, in the long run, bring serious trouble to Ireland'. See Herbert N. Casson, *Kelvin*, (London, 1930), p. 228.

6 Kelvin in particular became a thorn in the flesh of Darwinians because of his calculation, from the rate at which the earth cooled, that insufficient time existed for evolution by natural selection to have taken place, a view later disproved by another Irishman, John Joly.

7 Joseph Larmor (ed.), *Memoir and Scientific Correspondence of G.G. Stokes* (Cambridge, 1907), p. 35.

8 Desmond, *Huxley: Evolution's High Priest*, pp. 41 and 149. George Gabriel Stokes (1819–1903) was born in Skreen, County Sligo. He was Lucasian Professor of Mathematics at Cambridge 1849–1903, president of the Royal Society 1885–90 and MP for the University of Cambridge 1887–91.

9 Like them, Tyndall left Ireland early in his career in 1842, but he maintained contact with his father, an Orangeman and anti-repealer (of the Act of Union) and the correspondence between them in the 1840s recounts the stormy political events in Carlow Town. However, Tyndall's political beliefs were formed by his encounter with radicalism and Chartism in the politically disturbed conditions of Preston and Huddersfield in the 1840s. Politically, he was highly literate, writing on Adam Smith and currency reform for the local Preston paper, in addition to articles in the *Carlow Sentinel*. He became an advanced radical, a believer in industrial progress and in the democratisation of society.

10 Quoted in Donal McCartney, *W.E.H. Lecky, Historian and Politician, 1838–1903* (Dublin, 1994), p. 196.

11 See David Livingstone, 'Darwin in Belfast. The Evolution debate', in John Wilson Foster (ed.), *Nature in Ireland: A Scientific and Cultural History* (Dublin, 1997), pp. 387–408.

12 *Northern Whig*, 20 August 1874, p. 4.

13 *Dublin Daily Express*, 20 August 1874.

14 See the account of John Dillon's intervention in the debate in Greta Jones, 'Catholicism, nationalism and science in Ireland', *Irish Review*, 20 (1997), pp. 47–61. At that time Dillon, the future deputy leader of the Irish Parliamentary Party, was a student at the Catholic University.

15 For a discussion of some of these scientists see Nicolas Whyte, 'Lords of ether and of light: the Irish astronomical tradition of the nineteenth century', *Irish Review*, 17/18 (1995), pp. 127–41.

16 See the entry for Stoney in *Dictionary of National Biography Second Suppplement*, January 1901–December 1911, pp. 429–31.

17 Memorandum of 22 February 1899, Joly Papers, Trinity College Dublin 2313/4/19.

18 G.F. Fitzgerald, 'Experimental science in schools and universities', *Nature*, 35 (1886–7), p. 194. Lecture given 23 November 1886 in Trinity College Dublin at the Dublin Experimental Science Association.

19 See G.F. Fitzgerald, 'Science and industry, lecture to the Irish Industrial League', 7 May 1896, in Joseph Larmor (ed.), *The Scientific Writings of the Late George Francis Fitzgerald* (Dublin, 1902), p. 398.

20 The origins of DATI were in 1893 when an Irish Technical Education Association was founded in order to encourage local councils to implement the Technical Education Act of 1890 which allowed them to raise a rate for the purposes of building a local technical college. This group, together with the *Irish Textile Journal*, Sir Horace Plunkett's Irish Agricultural Association and prominent men of science in Ireland pressed for greater state expenditure on science. In 1895 they succeeded in setting up an informal committee of the House of Commons known as the Recess Committee which reported in 1896. In 1899 the bill which created a new Department of Agriculture and

Technical Instruction for Ireland (DATI) passed and in 1900 DATI was set up. It received an initial grant of £200,000 from the government and subsequently annual support to the tune of £166,000, of which half was from the Imperial Exchequer and half from taxation within Ireland.

21 Horace Plunkett, *Ireland in the New Century* (reprint Port Washington, NY/London, 1970). Plunkett's critical references to the Catholic Church's attitude to economic development and science, especially the comment that it had been 'unprogressive' in these areas, created a political furore which contributed to Plunkett's removal from DATI in 1907.

22 DATI had the power to award capital grants to schools based on the numbers of students taking science. In schools which accepted these grants it had powers over the science curriculum and the right of inspection. In addition DATI could meet some of the costs of equipping school laboratories – a third of the cost of fitting them out and half for the purchase of apparatus. DATI would also pay the costs of training science teachers on secondment from their schools. DATI made two years' instruction in science at secondary level compulsory for receipt of capitation grants. Thereafter, three to four years of optional science instruction was made available. In the case of the secondary school students, one estimate put the increase at sevenfold between 1900 and 1907.

23 See James Wilson, 'Past and present theories in stockbreeding', *Journal of the Department of Agricultural and Technical Instruction*, 10 (1909–10). This is, as far as I know, the first discussion of Mendelism in an Irish journal. See also Wilson, 'The breeding of egg laying poultry', ibid., 14 (1913–14); Herbert Hunter, 'A summary of experiments in barley growing conducted during the eleven years 1901–11', ibid., 13 (1912–13). Hunter's discussion of the Mendelian interpretation of his results can be found in Hunter, 'The improvement of the barley crop', ibid., 19 (1918–19).

24 The increasing prosperity of the Irish Catholic middle classes at the end of the nineteenth century meant a rise in the numbers seeking a university education. Third-level education was also relatively more important in Ireland than England, partly due to the low level of industrial development in many parts of the country. R.B. Lyons, vice-president of the Royal College of Physicians in Ireland and a professor at the Catholic University, estimated in a pamphlet on *The Intellectual Resources of Ireland* that there was one graduate to every 3,095 people in Ireland compared with one to every 6,486 in England. He pointed to the success of the Irish in the newly established civil service exams and predicted a continuing rise in the demand for university training, particularly among the Catholic Irish (*The Intellectual Resources of Ireland, Supply and Demand for an Enlarged Irish University Education* (London, 1873), p. 27).

25 In history, political economy and classical studies Ireland produced some of the most important proponents of the theory of progressive, intellectual evolution in the nineteenth century, for example, the historians W.E.H. Lecky and J.B. Bury and the positivist political economist John Kells Ingram. Frederick D'Arcy, a future Church of Ireland Primate, recounted the influence of Darwinism in Trinity in the 1870s. He believed that, in some cases, this had led to religious scepticism: 'at a somewhat later date I grasped the fact that there was a set containing some of the most brilliant of the younger men in the University who regarded the doctrines of our religion and indeed other things that I had been taught to hold in reverence as subjects for derision' (*Adventures of a Bishop* (London, 1934), p. 66).

26 See A. Macalister, 'The bearing of anomalous anatomy on the evolution theory of the origin of man', *Dublin Journal of Medical Science*, 53 (March 1872) and D.J. Cunningham, 'The lumbar curve in man and the apes with an account of the topographical anatomy of the chimpanzee, orang-utan and gibbon', Cunningham Memoirs, 2, *Proceedings of Royal Irish Academy* (1886), pp. 1–116. See also 'The anatomy of the anthropoid ape', ibid., pp. 117–48.

27 The Ball family were luminaries of Trinity College Dublin. Robert Ball's father taught

botany there and his brother Valentine medicine. See Valentine Ball, *Letters and Reminiscences of Sir Robert Ball* (London, 1915).

28 This was against Professor Japp's address to Section B (Chemistry) of the British Association of the Advancement of Science when Japp argued the origin of life in crystalline forms revealed an asymmetry which implied a designer. Karl Pearson and Herbert Spencer also attacked his address. For Fitzgerald's intervention see his letters 'Chance or vitalism', *Nature*, 58 (6 October 1898) and 'Asymmetry and vitalism', *Nature*, 59 (24 November 1898), p. 76.

29 E. Gaynor, 'Sir Robert Ball on evolution', *Irish Ecclesiastical Record*, 4th Series, 1 (1897), p. 248. Ball earned considerable sums of money as a popular lecturer. The offending book was *In Starry Realms* (London, 1892). Interestingly, in it Ball described the possibility of charting mathematically the proliferation and extinction of species in geographical areas divided into grids for that purpose.

30 *Ulysses, A Reader's Edition*, Danis Rose (ed.) (London, 1997; first published 1922), p. 147. Bloom's library contained at least one book by Ball, *The Story of the Heavens* (London, 1885). This went into six editions. The other astronomy book mentioned in *Ulysses*, *In the Track of the Sun*, is probably, in fact, Ball's *The Story of the Sun* (1893).

31 *The Tablet*, 12 September 1874.

32 *The Nation*, 29 August 1874.

33 Joly Papers, Ms. 2304 (4), November 1905. For the exchanges during the Robertson Commission see Jones, 'Catholicism, nationalism and science in Ireland', p. 50.

34 *Dublin Daily Express*, 20 August 1874.

35 When Joly put himself up for the provostship of Trinity in 1919 the memorial signed in his support reads like a *Who's Who* of nineteenth and twentieth century physics. It included Sir Henry Bragg, Rutherford, Oliver Lodge, Arthur Schuster, Lord Rayleigh and J.W. Strutt. See 'Three Memorials addressed to the Right Hon Lloyd George praying for the appointment of John Joly to the Provostship of TCD', Joly Papers, 2313/IV (28).

36 At the jubilee celebrations for G.G. Stokes in Cambridge in 1899 Joly stayed with Ball; Professor Purser of Trinity stayed at St John's with Larmor and the Earl of Rosse. In 1912 at the 250th anniversary of the Royal Society, the delegates from Ireland included Joly, the physicist, J.A. McClelland from University College Dublin, Sir Howard Grubb of the Royal Dublin Society (the maker of astronomical and other precision scientific instruments), J. Symington, Professor of Anatomy at Queen's College Belfast and Dr Alexander Anderson, Professor of Natural Philosophy in Queen's College Galway.

37 Thistleton-Dyer then went to the Botanical Gardens at Kew, marrying into the Hooker dynasty and eventually becoming curator of Kew Gardens. For Haddon's time in Ireland see Greta Jones, 'Contested territories, Alfred Cort Haddon, progressive evolutionism and Ireland', *History of European Ideas*, 24, 3 (1998), pp. 195–211. E. Perceval Wright and Wyville Thomson were also discussed by Huxley as possible candidates for Irish chairs. See letter to Hooker of 19 October 1868, Huxley Papers, 3. 122. Wyville Thomson, a distinguished naturalist who later took the chair at Aberdeen, was recommended for jobs at Queen's and Trinity by Huxley and spent a year in Ireland. Undated letter to Hooker, ibid., 2. 147.

38 Obit, *Nature*, 63 (7 March 1901), pp. 445–7, at p. 446 (reprinted from *The Electrician*, March 1901).

39 This cast of mind has not altogether disappeared from the discourse of contemporary Irish nationalism. See R. McVeigh, 'The last conquest of Ireland? British academics in Irish universities', *Race and Class*, 37 (1995), pp. 109–21.

40 'Science and art tutelage', *The Leader*, 2, 9 (27 April 1901), p. 138.

41 Joly to Mahaffy, 6 June 1899, Joly Papers, Ms. 4007.

42 *The Leader*, 26, 22 (12 July 1913), p. 523.

43 Anderson to Larmor, 8 May 1912, Larmor Papers, Royal Society of London, Ms. 603 letter 9.

44 Ball, *Sir Robert Ball*, p. 380. Robert Ball is referring to the line in Tennyson's *Locksley Hall* which refers to the 'great Orien sloping slowly to the west'. Thanks to Patrick Maume for identifying this.

45 Huxley in fact had already pointed out the admixture of races in the British Isles and the impossibility of using the term Celtic or Saxon to denote a political or cultural nationality occupying a distinct geographical area. See 'On some fixed points in British ethnology', *Contemporary Review* (1871), reprinted in *Critiques and Addresses* (London, 1883), p. 178.

46 Lubbock to Huxley, 24 January 1887, Huxley Papers, 96.

47 Professor Tyndall on Home Rule, *Irish Times*, 13 May 1893.

48 For Huxley's controversies with John Henry Newman and his disciples see Desmond, *Huxley*, I, pp. 84–5 and 170. The Catholic convert St George Mivart had been an enthusiastic proponent of evolution and friend of Huxley. His subsequent apostasy on the issue of human evolution in a critical treatment of natural selection in *Genesis of Species* (1871) was therefore particularly resented. Added to this, he stood accused by the Darwin circle of an undeserved personal insult directed at Darwin's son (Desmond, *Huxley*, I, pp. 25–8). Mivart, through his influence on Bertram Windle, a future president of Queen's College Cork, did however bring a form of Catholic evolutionism to Ireland.

49 Thomas MacKnight, *Ulster as it is or Twenty-Eight Years' Experience as an Irish Editor* (London, 1896), I, pp. 303–7.

50 Letter of 28 January, 1890, Royal Institution, Tyndall Papers. (The name of the correspondent is difficult to decipher but may be Sir Thomas Dixon, the father of Sir Daniel Dixon (1844–1907), Unionist MP for North Belfast. The Dixons were an important commercial and business family in Ulster.)

51 In Cambridge the solution was increasing the integration of Catholic students within the university. For the role of John Peile, Master of Christ's 1887–1910, also prominent in the Trinity Defence Campaign, see Christopher N.L. Brooke, *A History of the University of Cambridge 1870–1990* (Cambridge, 1993), IV, pp. 60 and 390–1.

52 The Royal Belfast Academical Institution had sought recognition of its degrees from the University of London in 1841. Individual students at the Royal College of Science, Dublin and University of Dublin appear in the graduation lists of London University. In 1853 the colleges in Ireland recognised by London included St Patrick's Carlow, St Patrick's Thurles and St Kyran's Kilkenny. See Negley Harte, *The University of London 1836–1986* (London, 1986).

53 'The Catholic colleges and London University', *The Month*, 1 (1864), p. 395.

54 This allowed the Catholic University to receive covert funding from the government in the form of sponsorship of fellowships for the Royal University of which half fell to their lot.

55 Anon., 'The recent Royal University examination in Metaphysics', *Irish Ecclesiastical Record*, 5 (1884), p. 707.

56 Thomas McGrath, 'Catholic philosophy and the Royal University', ibid., 6 (1885), p. 171.

57 November 1905, Joly Papers, 2304(4). The date may be incorrect. While Joly might have correctly anticipated the direction of the new University Bill in 1905, it is more likely these comments was made following Bryce's statement in 1907.

58 *Irish Times*, 26 January 1907.

59 Bryce's statement of 25 January 1907, Joly Papers, 2304(13).

60 Ibid., 2304(4).

61 Ibid.

62 Ibid., 2304(40).

63 Ibid., 2303(13) 1907.

64 Ibid., 2304(8). Dowden and Prenter supported Joly but at a time when the income and prospects of junior fellows were difficult it did not command sufficient support within

Trinity. Joly also campaigned for reform of the structures of Trinity to make life better for the junior fellows.

65 Ibid., 2304(19). Samuel Prenter was Moderator of the Presbyterian Church in Ireland. Whitley Stokes was Professor of Physics in the University of Dublin. William Parsons, third Earl of Rosse, was an astronomer, patron of science and had constructed the largest telescope then available at his family home, Birr Castle.

66 L.C. Purser to Joly, 5 March 1907, ibid., 2304(22). Purser (1854–1932), born County Longford, was Professor of Latin at Trinity 1898–1904 and thereafter held various administrative positions in the college.

67 Lodge to Joly, undated [February 1907?], ibid., 2304(22), letter 15.

68 Joly found it difficult to gather money for the Science Fund in Belfast: 'the rich men of Belfast are mostly Presbyterian – their ideas you may gather from the fact that one of their orators . . . spoke of TCD as "Nebuchadnezzar's furnace" and was applauded' (letter from R. Kyle Knox to Joly, 24 June 1903, ibid., 4007(69)).

69 Joly to L.C. Purser, 7 March 1907, ibid., 2304(22), letter 18. This letter also contains an account of his meeting with Birrell.

70 Ridgeway to Larmor, undated [1908], Larmor Papers 407, letter 1707.

71 Representation of the University of Cambridge in Parliament: To the Members of the Senate of the University of Cambridge, 24 January 1911, University of Cambridge, Stokes Papers, PA1600 D.

72 It did not always mean that there was agreement on university reform. Fitzgerald welcomed government expenditure on science in the universities, arguing it did not affect individual freedom. Ridgeway was deeply suspicious that it might lead to a reduction in the intellectual independence of Cambridge. He could point to his experience in the government-funded Queen's College as exemplifying what he feared most about state-run institutions of higher education. See Jones, 'Catholicism, nationalism and science in Ireland', fn. 31.

73 Ridgeway to Joly, 2 January 1917, Joly Papers, 2312, letter 328.

74 While the National University of Ireland (NUI) was formally non-denominational, Alfred O'Rahilly (1884–1969), who was a vice-chancellor of the NUI from 1948–51, listed in his half-centenary address to the NUI the means by which its denominational character was preserved. These included the right to make its own appointments, the requirement on its professors not to offend the religious susceptibilities of any among his or her classes, and the right of the institution to have its own philosophy chairs (meaning, presumably, the chairs in scholastic philosophy) (J. Anthony Gaughan, *Alfred O'Rahilly. 1: Academic* (Dublin, n.d.), pp. 245–6). The general Catholic atmosphere also increased substantially over the decades, with religious holidays becoming university holidays and special celebrations attending events in the calendar of the Roman Catholic Church. On the Catholicisation of Cork see John A. Murphy, *The College. A History of Queen's/University College, Cork 1845–1995* (Cork, 1995), p. 233. By 1908 enthusiasm for the Irish language and nationalist politics were irrevocably intertwined in spite of a history of Protestant interest in the language in the nineteenth century.

75 Representatives of Sinn Féin assumed significant administrative positions in Irish education. Alfred O'Rahilly, who had been a protégé of Windle, and was appointed to a chair of mathematical physics at Cork in 1916, was instrumental in easing him out of Cork, leaving Windle very embittered. O'Rahilly was elected in 1920 at the age of thirty-five to Registrar at Cork, eventually becoming President. The Jesuit T. Corcoran, Professor of Education in the National University of Ireland, and a strong influence over the Minister of Education in the new state, was also regarded as representing Sinn Féin in University College Dublin, serving as a member of its governing council 1916–43.

76 Joly to Larmor, 1 June 1919, Larmor Papers, 406, letter 1061. For his role in defending Trinity in 1916 see J. Joly, *Reminiscences and Anticipations* (London, 1920), pp. 218–64.

77 'Larmor', *Obituary Notices of Fellows of the Royal Society*, 5, 3. See Larmor to Lodge, 12

August 1922, written from Portrush, Northern Ireland, Lodge Papers, University College, London, Ms. Add. 89.

78 See Brian Titley, *Church and State and Control of Schooling in Ireland* (Montreal and Kingston, 1983), pp. 135, 146.

79 For the impact of this on the medical profession see Greta Jones, 'The Rockefeller Foundation and medical education in Ireland in the 1920s', *Irish Historical Studies*, 30 (November 1997), pp. 564–80.

80 In 1916 the Department of Scientific and Industrial Research (DSIR) was formed and in 1919 the Medical Research Council (MRC). The Royal College of Science benefited from DSIR studentships in the first few years of the DSIR's existence and some MRC money found its way to Ireland. The ambiguous situation of the newly independent Irish state in relation to research money from these sources is illustrated in the Medical Research Council file on Ireland (FD.1/965) at the Public Record Office, Kew. Because they retained dominion status – *Saorstat Éireann* did not abandon this formally until 1948 – they were in theory eligible. In fact, few applications were made and scientists in *Saorstat Éireann* were thrown on their own resources. An Irish MRC was created in 1937 but with very limited funds.

81 See Royal Irish Academy, Minutes of the RIA, Statement by the Council, 16 March 1922.

Part III

After-effects and entrenchment of the Union

11 A Protestant state

Unionists in government, 1921–39

Patrick Buckland

The first general election in Northern Ireland, in May 1921, returned a large majority of forty unionists opposed by twelve nationalists who refused to take their seats. In the following month King George V opened the new parliament amid general rejoicing, and Sir James Craig, the first Prime Minister, pledged himself to work on behalf of the whole community. Yet, within a matter of months, Ulster unionists had stamped their exclusive mark on Northern Ireland.

The way Ulster unionists behaved in government in Northern Ireland should have surprised nobody with an understanding of the history of Ireland. Their behaviour provided a cautionary tale of the dangers of precipitate constitution-mongering after prolonged periods of political conflict.

Preoccupied with maintaining the Union over the previous forty years, Ulster unionists had developed no political philosophy to take responsibility for a government they had not sought nor expected. They were determined to use the new government and parliament not as stepping stones towards but as bulwarks against Irish unity. To them, members of the Catholic minority were at least a potential fifth column. They had to be kept in their place, allowed little influence on government, and their frequent complaints of discrimination and oppression dismissed.

Many of the charges made against the unionist regime are grossly exaggerated. Nevertheless, in the last analysis, the unionist government did consistently use its powers in the interests of its followers, particularly in such sensitive areas as representation, education and, to a lesser extent, law and order. Northern Ireland thus became a 'majority dictatorship', 'a Protestant State and a Protestant People'.[1]

Often the responsibility for this outcome is laid at the door of bigoted Ulster unionists and Protestants, particularly the people of property exploiting religion and playing on the baser instincts of the Protestant working classes to maintain their own position or to carry out the dirty work of British imperialism. It is a view held by nationalists and given added spice by socialist and Marxist commentators. It is also a very facile view, because it takes too little account of the particular historical circumstances in which Ulster unionists operated and the uneasy position they occupied in the conflict between British imperialism and Irish nationalism.

Achievements

The many criticisms levelled against unionists in Northern Ireland should not obscure their achievement in setting up the government and parliament that had been thrust upon them by the 1920 Better Government of Ireland Act. They had little time to prepare for government, but, under the firm leadership of Sir James Craig, the government and parliament were operating within a matter of months, despite the most unfavourable circumstances in 1921–2.

The whole process of state formation was being undermined as the position of Northern Ireland became a bargaining counter in the negotiations leading up to the Anglo-Irish Treaty. The British government wanted to avoid a breakdown of talks over partition, which, one cabinet minister explained to his wife, would 'be the worst ground to fight on that one can imagine; for the six counties was a compromise, and like all compromises, is illogical and indefensible, and you could not raise an army in England to fight for *that* as we could for Crown and empire'.[2] Thus the government tried to cajole Ulster unionists into accepting the jurisdiction of the parliament of the proposed Free State. The attempt caused great resentment and apprehension among unionists in Northern Ireland, for, as Andrew Bonar Law warned David Lloyd George, what was being demanded of Ulster unionists was not compromise but the surrender of all that they had been fighting for since the 1880s.

Moreover, violence threatened to overwhelm Northern Ireland as a result of the activities of the IRA and other paramilitary or local defence groups. In Belfast alone, between December 1921 and May 1922, 346 people were injured and 236 killed, including 16 members of the crown forces, 73 Protestants and 147 Catholics.

This initial trauma did much to affect the character of government in Northern Ireland. In this confused situation only the Protestant community had a clear sense of direction and the capacity to act decisively. The establishment of law and order was vital to the existence and reputation of the new state, but the way in which it was achieved helped to determine the character of government, giving partisan answers to crucial questions of how and by whom violence should be combated, the forces and powers to be used, and the relative priorities given to security and political considerations.

Discrimination in law and order?

Standing reproaches against the government of Northern Ireland were its reliance upon special powers and the sectarian nature of its police force. The Civil Authorities (Special Powers) Act was a draconian piece of legislation, transferring many of the powers for preserving peace and maintaining order from the judiciary to the executive. According to one unionist MP, it virtually empowered the Minister of Home Affairs 'to do what he likes, or else let somebody else do what he likes for him'.[3] Originally passed on an annual basis, it was eventually made permanent.

The law was enforced by the Royal Ulster Constabulary and the Ulster Special Constabulary, both overwhelmingly Protestant. The Act establishing the Royal Ulster Constabulary provided that one-third of it should be Catholic, but Catholics formed at most some 17 per cent of the force. In July 1936 they comprised 17.12 per cent of the entire force, there being 488 Catholics and 2,361 Protestants. Among the higher ranks, however, the proportion was slightly lower, 16.36 per cent, for there were only 9 Catholics among the 55 officers who held the rank of district inspector and above. This represented a decline in Catholic participation, for 535 Catholics had been serving in the force in January 1924.

There is some justice in the complaints about discrimination. Law enforcement in Northern Ireland was dominated by narrow policing considerations and by hardliners in the Northern Ireland government. The latter believed that law should be enforced promptly and vigorously against Catholic and nationalist transgressors, but with discretion against Protestants and unionists. This was especially true in relation to special powers, and senior officials at Home Affairs doubted whether

> it was ever contemplated that these extraordinary powers should be used against those who are loyal to the Crown. If any of the latter class should be arrested it is a matter for consideration whether the ordinary Law should not be put into force rather than emergency legislation which was passed to deal with disloyal and disaffected persons.[4]

This attitude plus fear of alienating Protestant opinion ensured, for example, that in 1922 the security forces took less than vigorous action against a Protestant murder gang dedicated to the assassination of Catholics. Instead of being interned, some of the gang were enrolled in the Ulster Special Constabulary and their aid enlisted in a newly established Secret Service.

The government realised that the Special Powers Act was provocative and admitted, in private, that the powers of internment and arrest on suspicion both of having committed an act prejudicial to law and order and of being about to do so were very drastic as part of a permanent enactment. Nevertheless, there was never any serious suggestion of abandoning the Special Powers Act. The police and the Ministry of Home Affairs felt more comfortable with exceptional powers behind them and maintained that the very existence of the Act served as a deterrent to potential rebels and evidence of the government's determination to stamp out outrage and sedition. The Act continued to be applied against Catholics and nationalists rather than Protestants and unionists, although not as frequently and promiscuously as is sometimes alleged. It was, however, used too much for Catholics and too little for some Protestants, who in the early years would have liked to have used it even to ban the playing of Gaelic games on the Sabbath.

The reasons for the relatively small number of Catholics in the police force were many, including lower educational qualifications and a reluctance of Catholics to join as a result of pressures from within their own communities. Nevertheless, it was not easy for Catholics to prosper in the force, owing to the attitude of leading members of the government and the agitation by Protestant groups who thought that there were too many Catholics in the force.

There were good reasons for the recruitment and deployment of the Ulster Special Constabulary as the main peace-keeping force in the early violent months of the state. There were no alternatives at the time in view of the gap between the disbandment of the Royal Irish Constabulary and the formation of the Royal Ulster Constabulary, and in view of Westminster's reluctance to use the army as a police force. In addition, members of the Ulster Special Constabulary did perform a useful peace-keeping function within their own communities. Nevertheless, its value as a police force was severely limited not only by its identification with Orangeism but by its hasty recruitment, inadequate training and very loose chain of command. As a result, most Specials had no broad conception of their role or duties and local units often acted as private local armies.

Discrimination in government?

Generally, the institutions of government were narrowly based and intended to serve Protestant and unionist interests, often with scant regard to the feelings of the minority. The civil service, especially in the higher ranks, was overwhelmingly Protestant. By the Second World War, for instance, the already small number of Catholics had dwindled so that the lower ranks were some 90 per cent Protestant and the senior ranks almost entirely so. Certainly in the 1920s and 1930s it was difficult for Catholics to prosper in government service, owing to the susceptibilities of certain ministers and the activities of Protestant pressure groups. The tendency of ministers to take the complaints of these groups seriously eventually led the permanent head of the civil service to expostulate:

> If the Prime Minister is dissatisfied with our present system [of recruitment], I think that the only course would be for the Government to come out in the open and to say that only Protestants are admitted to our Service. I should greatly regret such a course, and am quite convinced . . . that we are getting loyal service from all those who have entered our Service.[5]

The fact that proportional representation in parliamentary elections was regarded by Catholics as a symbolic safeguard did not deter the government from abolishing it in 1929 to maintain the solidarity of Official Unionism. It is doubtful whether abolition made much difference to Catholic and nationalist representation in parliament, since it was directed against Labour and Independent Unionists, who were threatening to take votes from the Official Unionists, and the government wanted to make elections a straight fight between unionists and nationalists, between 'men who are for the Union on the one hand or who are against it and want to go into a Dublin parliament'.[6]

Nevertheless, the abolition of proportional representation in parliamentary elections underlined the narrowness of the government's preoccupations, considering the size of its majorities. At successive general elections in 1921, 1925,

1929, 1933 and 1938, the number of Official Unionists returned to the House of Commons was 40, 32, 37, 36 and 39, respectively, giving overall majorities of 28, 12, 22, 20 and 26.

It was in local government that deliberate discrimination was most evident. In 1922 the government abolished the recently introduced system of proportional representation in local elections. Having lost control of key councils, unionists demanded that their new government should redress the balance by abolishing proportional representation and redrawing electoral boundaries so as to restore control to the 'natural rulers' and the largest ratepayers. The government obliged and thus began a process of gerrymandering which facilitated unionist control of local authorities in areas where Catholics and nationalists formed a majority of the population. Unionists were given control of all but two major councils and a disproportionate share of the benefits, particularly in respect of employment and housing.

The *cause célèbre* was Londonderry Corporation, where the government did all it could to ensure that its supporters remained in control of the Maiden City, despite its two-thirds Catholic majority. Protestants comprised 70 per cent of the administrative, clerical and technical staff, and nine of the ten best-paid employees of the corporation. The unionists were able to maintain control as a result of a restricted local government franchise (denying one man, one vote), controversial ward boundaries, and a rehousing policy which confined Catholics to the ward with an already large nationalist majority.

Discrimination in education?

Changes in the electoral system were designed to make public bodies safe for unionism. Changes in education were intended to make public schools safe for Protestantism. When Northern Ireland's education system had been overhauled in 1923, the intention had been to establish a non-denominational system of public primary education. The trouble was that such non-sectarianism was unacceptable to Protestants and Catholics. The latter would under no circumstances submit to public control of their schools, whereas Protestants claimed that they would under certain conditions; namely, denominational control of teaching appointments and compulsory Bible teaching. Such conditions amounted to the virtual endowment of Protestantism by the state and thus contravened the 1920 Government of Ireland Act, which forbade religious endowment and discrimination. Nevertheless, the government eventually gave way to agitation powerfully engineered by the Protestant clergy and the Orange Order and amended the system in 1925 and 1930.

Henceforth, two schools systems operated, the clientele of one being Protestant, that of the other being either Protestant or Catholic. In schools controlled by local authorities, attended almost exclusively by Protestant children, all costs were paid out of central and local government funds. The voluntary schools, Catholic and Protestant alike, received most of their funds from public sources and made up the difference themselves. Had the opportunity of operating publicly maintained schools been open equally to both religious faiths, there would have been nothing inequitable about such an arrangement. However, the option was not so open, since simple Bible teaching, which had to be provided in state schools, was anathema to Catholics. Simple Bible teaching was 'based upon the fundamental principle of Protestantism, the interpretation of sacred Scriptures by private judgement'.[7] For Catholics, however, the Bible was only one source of their faith. According on one nationalist MP, 'it is but a dead letter, calling for a divine interpreter. There are the traditions of the [early] Church . . . There is also the tradition of the Church which is not human opinion but the divine teaching of an infallible apostolate established by Christ Himself'.[8] Education policy drew from Catholic and nationalist leaders some of their most extravagant denunciations of the government of Northern Ireland, but the outlandishness of such outbursts should not obscure the fact that the 1930 Education Act constituted a genuine Catholic grievance. As the Catholic Bishop of Down and Connor argued, this

> unjust and partisan [Act, passed at the] dictation of the Orange Lodges [was] against all principles of justice and equity . . . We form a large portion of the population, and have more children attending primary elementary schools than any other religious denomination. We ask for no privilege, but we claim equality of treatment with our fellow citizens, and we demand our rights.[9]

Obstacles to good government

In many respects it was inevitable that Northern Ireland should become an imbalanced state. It was, and remains, one of the tragedies of Northern Ireland to have been a victim of the conflict between Irish nationalism and British imperialism. From the very beginning Britain's overriding concern was not to secure good government and civic contentment in Northern Ireland but to ensure that events there did not hamper the British withdrawal from Ireland by jeopardising negotiations or agreements with republicans.

Nor was the good government of Northern Ireland a prime concern of republicans. At the same time as Michael Collins was signing peace agreements with James Craig, one of which proclaimed in March 1922 'PEACE IS TODAY DECLARED',[10] he was also sending arms to the IRA in the north intent on bringing Northern Ireland down. Consequently, the settlements of 1921–2 took too little account of the obstacles to good government and civic contentment in the six counties. These obstacles included the nature of the sectarian divide, an ailing economy, and a narrow political culture.

The sectarian divide in Northern Ireland was fundamental and self-perpetuating. The spiritual incompatibility between ultramontane Irish Catholic and Evangelical Fundamentalism was matched by temporal separation, as Protestants and Catholics cut themselves off from one another in three vital areas of life – marriage, residence and education.

Marriages between Protestants and Catholics were infrequent and discouraged. Those mixed marriages which did occur did little to bridge the sectarian divide, for they were subject to considerable isolation and stress. In fact, endogamy, marriage within one's own group, was later identified as the most powerful mechanism dividing people, especially in rural areas.

In urban areas, especially working-class areas, residential segregation was an even more potent divisive force than endogamy. The largest towns, which contained the majority of the urban population, were highly segregated. There were not only clearly defined Catholic and Protestant areas, but clearly differentiated patterns of behaviour.

Segregated education, the education of Protestant and Catholic children in separate schools, reflected and reinforced the effects of endogamy and residential segregation. Nearly all Protestant children attended exclusively Protestant schools; nearly all Catholic children attended exclusively Catholic schools. There is much dispute about the precise effects of segregated education, but its critics are probably right in claiming that it perpetuates and reinforces the division between Protestants and Catholics by physically separating children and by propagating different and mutually hostile cultural heritages – the result of the attitude of teachers just as much as differences in the formal curriculum.

In many respects Protestants and Catholics existed in mutual isolation and mutual ignorance. Unflattering stereotypes took the place of social intercourse and understanding, although the Catholic view of Protestants seems to have been less harsh and entrenched than that of Protestants towards Catholics.

It is possible to apply retrospectively to the interwar years recent analyses of sectarian relationships in Northern Ireland. For Catholics the problem was largely political; for Protestants largely religious. Catholics looked to a united Ireland and objected to Protestant attitudes towards politics. Their attitude to Protestants was not supported by an 'underlying labyrinth of psychological fears'.[11] By contrast, Protestant attitudes towards Catholics were more permanent and psychologically deep-rooted. According to one social psychologist, their objections to a number of aspects of Catholicism are 'underpinned by a complicated psychological network of fears and apprehensions about the political power and dexterity of the Catholic Church'.[12] Despite their divisions, Protestants and Catholics did manage to live together, and had done for centuries. After partition at least, peaceful coexistence was ensured partly by relative isolation and partly by a host of habits and social mechanisms.

The problems of governing Northern Ireland were increased by the collapse of its staple industries, owing to the changing world economy after the First World War. Under the Union Ulstermen had boasted of their prosperity and it was ironic that the decline of the old staples – agriculture, linen and shipbuilding – should coincide with partition, which may have aggravated the problem by cutting up market areas and depriving the Northern manufacturers and traders of their traditional markets in the twenty-six counties. As a result, Northern Ireland came to have, for example, in the interwar years, the highest rate of unemployment in the United Kingdom and the lowest level of income.

The question of unemployment was made the more intractable by the fact that it affected some areas and communities more than others. It was more severe in agricultural than industrial areas; that is, it was worse in the largely Catholic south and west, where there were fewer alternative occupations to compensate for contracting agricultural unemployment. Catholics complained of discrimination against them in jobs, while Protestants were concerned that too many Catholics were being employed at their expense. In fact, the problem of a decaying economy was not one of economics alone but had repercussions throughout an already divided society.

Unionist political culture

The fundamental error of partition was to hand power to Ulster unionists instead of continuing direct Westminster rule over the six counties. Ulster unionists were not politically mature enough to accept the responsibility that had been thrust on them. The whole structure and ethos of Ulster unionism had been based upon a single objective – determined opposition to home rule – and no constructive philosophy had been developed to equip Ulster unionists to govern a state they had neither expected nor wanted. Members of the new regional government were themselves drawn from the Ulster Protestant community, and had been intimately associated with Ulster unionist resistance to home rule. They thus shared all the fears and prejudices of the Protestant and unionist community. It is true that the experience of governing did develop in some ministers a broader perspective and a new sense of responsibility, but these were insufficient to help them initiate policies in the interests of the community as a whole.

Moreover, two other aspects of Northern Ireland's political culture encouraged the government to act in the interests of its supporters. First, there were the divisions within unionism. It is often forgotten that Ulster unionism was an alliance of disparate social, economic and religious groups who found coherence only in opposition to nationalism and Catholicism. Landowners and tenant farmers, businessmen and artisans and labourers, town and country, all had different and competing interests. The term 'Protestant' included the three major denominations – Church of Ireland, Methodist and Presbyterian – separated by considerable theological and historical differences, and also numerous small, fiercely independent sects. Thus, the conflict in Northern Ireland was the more intense not just because Protestant distrusted Catholic but because Protestant distrusted Protestant. The unity of Ulster unionism had constantly to be managed. It was by no means a foregone conclusion that the single-minded alliance would hold together after partition when real problems of government had to be faced.

This problem of government was compounded by the fact that Northern Ireland was, and remains, a small and highly localised society, with a population of some 1.24 million in an area the size of Yorkshire. Everybody knew everybody else's business. There was little mystique in government, and ministers could scarcely distance themselves from supporters and events. As the first Minister for Home Affairs explained in 1923, Northern Ireland 'was in a different position from Great Britain, inasmuch as in a comparatively small community such as

Northern Ireland every action of the Government was scrutinised by the whole population'.[13] Ministers were far too accessible. They could always be sharply reminded of the claims and narrow horizons of their supporters whether they were attending church twice on Sundays or whether they were attending Orange Day demonstrations. Thus in June 1925, during one of the recurrent and successful clerical–Orange educational campaigns, the then Minister of Labour and future Prime Minister, John Miller Andrews, reported to James Craig:

> Already the Protestant pulpits are being used for defending what is called 'Protestant rights'. I had myself to listen to two lengthy harangues on the subject on Sunday last in Little's church at Castlereagh. The Orange Order are working in co-operation with the churches, and I am afraid that the position will be difficult on the 12th July unless something is done.[14]

Something was done and the 1925 Education Act began the process of making state schools safe for Protestantism.

Provisions of the 1920 Better Government of Ireland Act

These obstacles to good government were accentuated by ill-considered provisions of the 1920 Better Government of Ireland Act. The detailed provisions accentuated the difficulty of securing civic contentment in Northern Ireland. The six-county border increased unionist apprehensions and the new government was given real power only in the most sensitive area of community relations. The problems facing Northern Ireland were further heightened by developments in the twenty-six counties, which often seemed designed to aggravate unionist apprehensions in Northern Ireland.

The six-county border was intended to provide a safe haven for Ulster unionists. Yet it did not guarantee security. It was not simply that the political and other aspirations of the 33 per cent Catholic minority were different from those of the majority, but that the minority was large enough to be threatening. There was always the fear elsewhere that in the long run the Catholics' higher birth-rate would enable them to outbreed and outvote Protestants, thus bringing about a union with the south. In some areas, particularly along the border, Catholics already constituted a majority, and it was unionists from Fermanagh, Tyrone and Derry City who desperately sought gerrymandering to maintain control of local government in areas where they were in a minority. Moreover, unionists from these areas were always alert for signs of betrayal by Belfast. After all, the unionists of the three counties of Cavan, Donegal and Monaghan had been sacrificed for the security of the remaining six counties. What was to stop Belfast and the eastern counties giving up other areas where unionists could not defend themselves?

Its limited powers encouraged the Northern Ireland government to pander to the baser desire of its supporters. The constitutional arrangements of the 1920

Act were ill thought-out, sandwiching the new regional government uncomfortably between congeries of parsimonious and partisan local authorities in Northern Ireland and an exacting Treasury in London. Although the government bore formal responsibility for large areas of social, economic and political life, its real power was limited by constitutional restrictions and economic realities. For instance, it was responsible for trade and industry in a severely depressed region, yet could do little to alleviate the resultant distress. On the one hand, its powers of economic and financial manipulation were limited by the terms of the 1920 Act, which reserved major fiscal powers to Westminster. On the other hand, Northern Ireland's potential for economic growth was limited by severe natural disadvantages, particularly its shortage of raw materials and its distance from mass markets.

This impotence caused considerable unrest among government supporters, especially when it could be contrasted with the apparent energy with which the southern government was trying to encourage trade and industry. According to the Lord Mayor of Derry in 1926, the government's inability to safeguard the city's trade against the consequences of Free State protectionist policies was 'making loyalists feel "what is the use of staying under a Government that either don't care a d—n for our interests, or at any rate can't protect them"'.[15] In these circumstances it is scarcely surprising that the unionist government in Northern Ireland took advantage of the powers it did possess and used them in the interests of its supporters. It might not be able to cut the rate of unemployment, but at least it could cater for the claims of Protestant educational theories. It might not be able to safeguard the trade of Derry, but it could at least ensure that unionists remained in control of the city council.

Development of the Irish Free State

The way in which the Irish Free State developed in the interwar years gave Ulster unionists no incentive to broaden their horizons and offer the hand of friendship to their old enemies. The south still maintained the claim to the six counties and yet seemed intent on confirming Ulster unionist fears and thus also hardening the partition of Ireland. Many politicians, especially the long-lived de Valera, frequently stomped around the world condemning partition, to which they attributed any woes Northern Ireland suffered. At the same time, there was no consistent policy to win over the northern majority by offering inducements to unity. On the contrary, southern policies and attitudes seemed to confirm Ulster unionists' worst fears of Dublin rule, for on a wide range of issues little account was taken of their susceptibilities. Indeed, there was a feeling that Northern Ireland, having caused partition and mutilated the motherland, deserved no concessions from southern nationalists. Southern policies were determined by southern economic, political and ideological needs with scant regard for their ultimate consequences for the cause of Irish unity.

After 1922 the Free State proved a very restless dominion. The crown was by degrees taken out of the south, which gradually moved out of the Commonwealth, a process confirmed by the 1937 constitution which made Éire a republic in all but name.

The increasing pursuit of economic nationalism after 1924 had by the 1930s turned the south into one of the most highly protected countries in the world. This affected both northern businessmen and farmers, especially along the borders, and emphasised the different interests of north and south. The distinctiveness of the south was further reinforced by the emphasis given to Gaelic culture and language in an attempt to realise Patrick Pearse's dictum 'Ireland . . . not free merely, but Gaelic as well'.[16]

Although the south did not become a theocratic state after independence, it was some 95 per cent Catholic and the influence of the Catholic Church was all pervasive, even before the liberal and secular Free State constitution was replaced by the strongly Catholic Éire one. Whereas the 1922 constitution declared that all the powers of government were derived from the people of Ireland, the 1937 constitution began 'In the name of the Most Holy Trinity from Whom is all authority and to whom, at our final end, all actions of both men and state must be referred'.[17] Additionally, article 44 of the new constitution recognised 'the special position of the Holy Apostolic and Roman Catholic Church as the guardian of the Faith professed by the great majority of the citizens' and used Catholic social and moral teaching as the basis of law in crucial areas of personal and family life – outlawing birth control and divorce.

The same constitution also reasserted the claim to Northern Ireland. Article 2 laid down that the 'national territory consists of the whole island of Ireland, its islands and the territorial seas', including, that is, Northern Ireland. Article 3 referred to 'the right of the parliament and government established by this constitution to exercise jurisdiction over the whole of that territory'.

Ulster unionists were outraged by the irredentism of the constitution and regarded the rest of it as infringing personal liberty at the behest of the Catholic Church; the more so since the Protestant population of the south declined rapidly after independence, and the Catholic Church, consolidating the position gained under the Union, carved out for itself more extensive control over education than in any other country in the world.

It has to be said that Ulster unionists were not alone in rejecting this combination of Catholicism and nationalism. Others found it stifling, particularly in regard to the censorship of literature, so brilliantly satirised by Mervyn Wall in his Fursey novels set in medieval Ireland, the island of saints and scholars, where he describes the descent of the censor upon the monastery library at Clonmacnoise.

Economic policy did begin to show some sensitivity by the 1960s, but not until the 1970s was there serious discussion in the south as to how far its constitution and laws were repugnant to Ulster unionists and Protestants, and what amendments were needed to make them more palatable.

A stable state

It is one thing to explain how Northern Ireland became a Protestant state for a Protestant people. It is another to explain how, despite its demonstrable defects, it survived undisturbed for so long. Part of the explanation was the way in which the government used what few powers it possessed not simply to limit the political opportunities of opponents but to reward its supporters. In doing so, it underlined common links and smothered potential divisions.

The government also used social welfare policy to good effect. From 1921 it sought to take the edge off working-class discontent in face of rising unemployment and to remove a powerful motive for co-operation between Protestant and Catholic workers. It did so through the so-called 'step-by-step'[18] policy of keeping pace with Britain in relation to the major cash social services. There was no need for the emergence of a democratic Labour movement in Northern Ireland, since all these battles were carried out in Britain and the benefits automatically transferred across the Irish Sea.

The other part of the explanation of the stability of the unionist regime was the absence of effective opposition or control within Northern Ireland and from Britain and the rest of Ireland. The Protestant state was sustained because in Northern Ireland there was nobody to mount an effective challenge to the regime. The Northern Ireland Labour Party was weak and divided. The Catholic minority almost connived at the compromising of its civil rights by refusing to play a full role in public life.

The weakness of the Northern Ireland Labour Party is often a source of surprise to those who think that class is the prime determinant of political action. In this view there should have been an active Labour Party in Northern Ireland, considering its industrial economy, a high degree of unionisation among skilled workers and the demonstrable need for social reform in the depressed interwar years. Yet the party never had a safe seat, even in Belfast. The one or two seats it did gain were achieved not by the straightforward advocacy of social and economic reforms, but by the manipulation of the sectarian balance in a few constituencies and by being different things to different people or by coming forward on a compromise platform.

The government's 'step-by-step' policy in relation to the major welfare benefits had cut the ground from under the party, but the party also contributed to its own weakness. There was a failure of leadership, as the few leaders either left Northern Ireland or quarrelled among themselves. Then there was the question of partition. Until 1949 the party tried to avoid taking a stand on partition, leaving members free to advocate what views they liked on the issue. This tactic only succeeded in exposing the Labour Party to attack from both sides, while its socialism and the Protestantism of many of its members rendered it particularly suspect in Catholic eyes. Catholic voters in the Falls division of Belfast preferred to vote for a Catholic publican and slum landlord rather than a Protestant socialist, for, it was said, 'Catholic representation was required to defend Catholic interests especially on the education question'.[19]

With the high unemployment and mounting distress of the 1930s there was much talk of working-class solidarity and repeated threats by Labour orators to make Craig's knees 'knock like the bones in a jazz band'[20] and to dissolve the Belfast parliament the way Cromwell had dissolved the English one. No such revolution materialised. The most that did occur was the remarkable phenomenon of a non-sectarian riot in Belfast in October 1932, caused by the refusal of the niggardly Belfast Board of Guardians to give relief to the unemployed on the same basis as in Britain.

Under the auspices of the Belfast Outdoor Relief Workers' Committee and the Marxist Revolutionary Workers' Group, a protest movement crossed existing lines of political and religious division. Matters came to a head on 11 October 1932, when, defying a ban under the Special Powers Act on a march on parliament, crowds of unemployed workers gathered on both the Falls and the Shankill. The much reinforced police baton-charged and fired over the heads of the crowds in the Falls, and for the first time in history the Shankill crowd rioted in their support. Rioting lasted for two days and resulted in two deaths.

The 1932 riot represented the fleeting peak of Orange–Green collaboration. Sectarian rioting in various towns was more common than ephemeral demonstrations of working-class Protestants, as the violent rhetoric of Labour orators was matched by the inflammatory and provocative slogans and rallies organised by the Ulster Protestant League, formed in 1931 to safeguard the employment of Protestants. Tension came to a head in July 1935. Three weeks of rioting, sniping and arson resulted in 11 dead, 574 injured, 300 families, mainly Catholic, driven from their homes, and a damning but overstated report of the unionist regime by the National Council of Civil Liberties.

It is a moot question as to how far employers and political and religious leaders deliberately and consistently exploited the sectarian question to keep workers docile and malleable. Nevertheless, such events as the 1935 riot underlined the extent to which political and religious sectarianism inhibited the development of an exclusive working-class consciousness impelling Catholics and Protestants to unite in bold political and industrial action. As one Belfast street orator complained in the 1930s:

> If you took all the Orange sashes and all the Green sashes in Belfast and tied them round a bucket of loaves and threw them in the [River] Lagan, the gull, the common, ordinary sea-gulls, they'd go for the bread, but the other gulls – you's one – you's go for the sashes every time.[21]

Catholics and nationalists were also unable to offer effective opposition. Politically Catholics remained divided between republicans and nationalists (the old home rulers). At first they refused to enter parliament and, despite being the largest opposition party after their eventual entry in the mid-1920s, nationalists refused to act as the official opposition and were prepared to revert to the policy of abstention. In May 1932, for example, all nationalist MPs walked out of parliament, partly out of frustration at the unionist refusal to share power and the limited powers of parliament, which prevented proper discussion of public finance.

There was never a coherent nationalist party complete with headquarters and party organisers on the lines of the Ulster Unionist Council. There were merely loose alliances between local notables – the clergy and the small-town middle class – which produced only ephemeral organisations. Moreover, their prime focus was not the development of Northern Ireland as a whole but the achievement of Irish unity. Thus the 1932 withdrawal was also influenced by de Valera's assumption of power in the Free State. At least one border MP preferred electioneering in the south, looking 'for guidance to the great leader of the Irish people',[22] to sitting in Stormont.

Pending Irish unity, the immediate priority was the defence of Catholic interests. Joseph Devlin, the leader, constantly denied that he led a Catholic party, but there was never a sustained effort to reach beyond the Catholic community and challenge for power on the basis of an economic and social programme. As Devlin declared in 1930, 'it is our duty in Parliament . . . to look after the interests of the faith to which I am proud to belong'.[23] The order of priorities reflected the flourishing position of the Catholic Church in Northern Ireland after partition, especially in the diocese of Down and Connor. Three of the best-known and most effective organisations in modern Ireland had their origins there: the Catholic Truth Society, the Pioneer Association of the Sacred Heart and the Apostolic Work Society. Indeed, the Catholic Church became a focus of much of life as Catholic men and women found outlets for their abilities in the service of their neighbours in the fellowship of the Church.

This retreat and refusal to play a full role in public life rebounded on the Catholic minority. It confirmed the identification of Catholicism with hostility both to the state and the Protestant majority, especially when in 1931 Cardinal Archbishop Joseph MacRory of Armagh declared that the Protestant Church of Ireland 'is not even part of the Church of Christ'.[24] It detracted from the effectiveness of even valid criticisms of the unionist regime, because they could plausibly be dismissed as purely destructive attempts to discredit Northern Ireland in the interests of Irish unity. Furthermore, it tended to develop a spirit of mutual admiration and complacency that made difficult any rapprochement with unionists and the government. By refusing to participate and challenge for positions in official life, Catholics helped unionists to put them in the position of second-class citizens. For instance, the Catholic hierarchy was virtually invited by the British government to challenge the 1930 Education Act before the Judicial Committee of the Privy Council. Instead, Catholics accepted an offer of increased government funding for voluntary schools, which gave them a further incentive to stay outside the state system.

External indifference

The stability of the unionist regime was further ensured by the unwillingness of the British and Irish governments to take a stand against the regime. The Free State and Éire both declared their commitment to Irish unity, but rhetoric apart they did little to achieve it. Once a settlement between Britain and the Free State was achieved, most people in the twenty-six counties quickly abandoned the idea of the coercion of Ulster. This was partly because of the determination of Ulster unionists to maintain partition, and partly because the happy vision of a united Ireland was somewhat marred by the reflection that an influx of a large number of northern Protestants, impatient with the south's Gaelic and Catholic traditions, would overnight turn an overwhelmingly Catholic state into a mixed religious society with a strong, compact and scarcely amenable Protestant minority.

Britain was largely indifferent to Northern Ireland, except during the developing European crisis in the 1930s and over questions of finance. In theory Westminster could have prevented the adoption of discriminatory policies in Northern Ireland and could have taken steps to ensure that policies on such sensitive issues as education, representation and law and order were developed in the interests of the community as a whole. Ultimate sovereignty was reserved to Westminster and the legitimacy of any legislation could be tested by the Judicial Committee of the Privy Council. Yet successive Westminster governments failed to take advantage of such powers.

The reason for this passivity lay less in the traditional British reverence for the sanctity of the rights of parliaments (for, as regards transferred powers, Northern Ireland was just like a dominion). Rather, the passivity was a recognition of harsh political realities. The fact was that there was a built-in unionist majority in Northern Ireland. Thus there was no alternative government to take office, should the unionist government resign in protest against the exercise of Westminster's sovereignty. Only once did Westminster threaten to veto a controversial measure, the Local Government Bill of 1922 abolishing proportional representation in local elections. The reaction of the government of Northern Ireland had been swift and uncompromising. It would resign and hold a general election on the issue, at which it would be returned with an overwhelming majority, thus leaving Westminster with two equally unpalatable alternatives: to climb down or to assume once more direct responsibility for the government of a part of Ireland – the very thing the 1920 Act had been designed to avoid. It was an instructive episode, which starkly underlined the limits of central control over regional government. Westminster was both unwilling and unable to correct the development of discriminatory policies in Northern Ireland. In the last analysis, Ulster unionists behaved the way they did in government because no one was prepared to stop them in the interwar years.

NOTES

1 *Parliamentary Debates* [*PD*], xvi, 24 April 1934, c. 1095.
2 Austen Chamberlain, quoted in D.G. Boyce, 'British Conservative opinion, the Ulster question, and the partition of Ireland, 1919–21', *Irish Historical Studies*, 17 (1970–1), p. 104.
3 Quoted in F.H. Newark, 'The law and constitution', in T. Wilson (ed.), *Ulster under Home Rule* (London, 1955), p. 48.

4 Memo by S.W. Watts, Permanent Secretary, Home Affairs, to R.D. Bates, Minister of Home Affairs, 5 October 1921, Public Record of Northern Ireland [PRONI], CAB 6/27. For a fuller discussion of devolved government in Northern Ireland, based upon the records of the cabinet, see Patrick Buckland, *'The Factory of Grievances': Devolved Government in Northern Ireland 1921–39* (Dublin, 1979). Examples of very different approaches to the unionists in government include P. Bew, P. Gibbon and H. Patterson, *The State in Northern Ireland 1921–72: Political Forces and Social Classes* (Manchester, 1979), and Michael Farrell, *Northern Ireland: The Orange State* (London, 1976).

5 S. Spender, Permanent Secretary, Ministry of Finance, to C. Blackmore, Cabinet Secretary, 8 November 1934, PRONI, CAB 9A/90/1.

6 James Craig, *PD*, viii, 25 October 1927, c. 2276.

7 Daniel Mageen, Roman Catholic Bishop of Down and Connor, quoted in D.H. Akenson, *Education and Enmity: The Control of Schooling in Northern Ireland, 1920–1950* (Newtown Abbot/New York, 1973), p. 114.

8 James McCarroll, MP for the Foyle Division of Londonderry, *PD*, xii, 9 April 1930, c. 815.

9 *The Tablet*, 19 November 1932.

10 Patrick Buckland, *A History of Northern Ireland* (Dublin, 1981), pp. 44–5.

11 K. Heskin, *Northern Ireland: A Psychological Analysis* (Dublin, 1980), p. 44.

12 Ibid., p. 51.

13 Cabinet Conclusions, 29 January 1923, PRONI, CAB 4/69/19.

14 J.M. Andrews to J. Craig, 17 June 1925, ibid., CAB 9D/1/5.

15 M. Scott Moore to C. Blackmore, 27 March 1926, ibid., CAB 9R/57/1.

16 F.S.L. Lyons, *Ireland since the Famine* (London, 1973), p. 635.

17 Ibid., pp. 547ff.

18 Craig enunciated this policy in March 1922, *PD*, ii, 14 March 1922, cc. 18–19.

19 Farrell, *Orange State*, p. 116.

20 Ibid., p. 122.

21 D. Kennedy, 'Catholics in Northern Ireland 1926–39', in F. MacManus (ed.), *The Years of the Great Test 1926–39'* (Cork, 1967), p. 148.

22 John Henry Collins, nationalist member for South Down, quoted in Buckland, *Factory of Grievances*, p. 73.

23 Farrell, *Orange State*, p. 17.

24 *Irish News*, 18 December 1931.

12 The destructiveness of constructive unionism

Theories and practice, 1890s–1960s

Andrew Gailey

At first glance, to describe Irish unionism as constructive appears almost to be a contradiction in terms. More of a dinner party than a political movement, constructive unionists lack the unionist pedigree that, for instance, is instantly recognisable in Carson's Ulster revolt of 1912, or in the 'Ulster says No' banners that sprang up in the wake of the Anglo-Irish Agreement of 1985. Indeed, to their many critics, theirs was the creed of a redundant elite who, condescendingly claiming to have discerned the inevitable drift of Irish history, had decided to cut their losses.[1] Instead, constructive unionism has come to be seen as essentially a late nineteenth-century phenomenon which, however much it appealed to the imagination of an unrepresentative few among Irish unionists, was primarily an English Tory device designed by Arthur and Gerald Balfour to divide nationalism and rule Ireland.[2]

However, as I have attempted to show elsewhere,[3] the Tories' Irish policy was largely determined by English rather than Irish politics. The driving force for constructive unionism came instead from within Irish unionism and was part of a tradition that was as old as the Union itself. For all its adherence to the myths of Grattan's Parliament and the Protestant radicalism of the 1790s, its roots lay in the political legacy of 1800 in which Westminster reasserted its will only to abdicate its responsibilities. Rejecting that the polarisation of Irish society was irreversible, constructive unionists were unionists for whom Ireland was the first love but who saw Ireland's social and economic development as only feasible within the larger sphere of the British Empire. Within Ireland, they sought the reconciliation of all patriots around this goal and attempted to draw out a conservative middle ground within Irish politics.[4] Such ideals enthused Orange Young Ireland, the contributors to the *Dublin University Magazine* and Isaac Butt's Home Government Association.[5] They were also at the core of the acute analysis of Ireland's problems in the 1850s and 1860s by Lord Dufferin, the Ulster Whig peer. But it was the re-emergence in the 1880s of Catholic nationalism and Gladstone's subsequent conversion to home rule that forced the issue and stimulated, in turn, an imaginative response after 1890 from unionists such as Ross of Bladensburg, Sir Horace Plunkett, George Birmingham, Lord Dunraven, Lord Monteagle and Standish O'Grady; of whom some (but not all) were natural Gladstonians in search of a home.[6] Although the tide ran against them after 1905, it returned in the 1960s with the liberal sentiments espoused by Terence O'Neill and given coherence through the journalism of Jack Sayers.[7] These, in their love of country, the pursuit of reconciliation through economic development and prosperity and the desire to broaden unionism into a 'national' creed, were wholly in the tradition of nineteenth-century progressive unionism.

But in arguing for a continuity of tradition one is in danger of minimising the partition of 1921. Are we in fact talking about two separate episodes? It is to shed light on this question that I propose to compare the two periods when constructive unionism was at its height, 1890–1905 and 1963–9. Both were times of major state initiatives, which threatened to transform utterly the very context of Irish politics only for both to end in disarray and controversy. Such comparisons are indeed fraught with danger. Can one usefully compare Wyndham and O'Neill, one mercurial, the other chilly in the extreme? Or Sir Antony MacDonnell with Ken Bloomfield, or Walter Long with Brian Faulkner and so on literally ad absurdum? Equally, what is to be gained by drawing parallels between a nineteenth-century policy directed towards a Catholic, agrarian Ireland and a twentieth-century campaign in an industrial and defiantly Protestant Ulster? Nor can the position of a British administration in Dublin be likened very easily to that of an Ulster unionist government in Belfast.

And yet, although the latter was answerable in the first instance to a local parliament in Stormont, such, in the 1890s, was London's lack of concern for Ireland's internal affairs that the administration in Dublin had often in effect to be responsive to Irish opinion. What with the pressure on parliamentary time and money at the turn of the century, Irish chief secretaries were only allowed to bring forward their legislative programmes if they could be guaranteed all-party support and thus a speedy passage. At the same time, for all the talk at Stormont of self-government, both regimes were ultimately subordinate to and occasionally interfered with by the Westminster government, seeking to defend British perspectives and interests. It was the unpredictable exercise of power and Britain's 'frivolous' preference for the 'vis inertia' that was the daily reality of the Act of Union.[8] And it was this that the constructive unionists exploited for largely the same reasons and in the same ways and with almost the same consequences in the 1890s and the 1960s.

Thus, this chapter will begin by drawing out the similarities between the two periods in terms of the people involved, their ideology and their methods in order to set out the character of a constructive unionist tradition. Naturally, if one is to argue that there was a constructive tradition in unionism, where it 'went' between 1910 and 1963 will need to be tackled. Thereafter, the focus will switch to the achievement of the constructive unionists, highlighting the common factors in both their successes and failures, and attempt to establish why the outcomes in 1905 and 1969 were so different. Finally, some comments will be offered on the significance of this constructive tradition and its continual survival in the face of repeated defeat.

I

At the core of the philosophy of constructive unionism was a profound sense of Irishness. For all their advocacy of unionism, men like Dunraven, Hannay and Plunkett let none forget that they were Irishmen first and dedicated long lives to the improvement of their country.[9] This went beyond an Anglo-Irish love of place and embraced notions of patriotic service and duty, neatly encapsulated by Plunkett's publication in 1908 of *Noblesse Oblige: An Irish Rendering*. In the case of O'Neill and Sayers, such patriotism took the form of both an emotional attachment to an Irish identity and a particular loyalty to the province of Ulster. O'Neill's speeches were unceasing on the virtues of 'our beloved Ulster'. So great was Sayers's pride in the province that he even felt able to argue in 1948, with Europe torn asunder by war and communism, that Stormont could prove the model of a stable, Christian state for the continent![10]

But these sentiments reflected a sense of nationality that stopped well short of nationalism (which constructive unionists saw as socially divisive and republican). While accepting 'the whole range of antipathies', Irish unity (especially if part of the reunification of the British Isles) remained, for Sayers, 'still a civilised ideal, not only for the sake of peace and amity but of national prosperity'.[11] Similar sentiments were crucial parts of O'Neill's Anglo-Irish inheritance, along with the formative experience of fighting with the Irish Guards in the Second World War.[12] What they sought was a definition of Irishness which was inclusive. Hence the attraction of the Gaelic Revival to Protestant clergymen like the Revd J.O. Hannay, for it offered an Ireland which pre-dated the divisions of the Reformation, revitalising 'Irish consciousness and creat[ing] a sense of pure patriotism'.[13] By which, of course, he meant a patriotism that could be genuinely shared; and it was this chance of belonging that explains the gushing adoption of cultural Ireland by the wives of British chief secretaries keen to do their bit in Dublin.[14] But hence also the resentment of Hannay, Plunkett and Æ at the exclusiveness of D.P. Moran's, *Philosophy of Irish Ireland*.[15] Equally the sight in 1963 of southern Ireland fêting John F. Kennedy and emphasising the essentially Catholic nature of Irish–American links offended O'Neill's own sense of Irishness. With Ulster Protestants forming the majority of the Irish in America, O'Neill was determined to establish these historic links by insisting that Ulster was the homeland of the 'Scots-Irish' in America, even building a theme park to prove it.[16]

Nevertheless, for all his Ulster triumphalism, O'Neill never lost sight of the fundamental importance of the British connexion. When a one-time ally, Bill Craig, sought to question this in 1968, O'Neill promptly sacked him. Whether one reads the Ulster liberal Thomas Sinclair in the 1912 summation of the unionist case, *Against Home Rule*, emphasising the guarantees of intellectual liberty, or Plunkett on the economic benefits in his *Ireland in the New Century* (1904), or Dunraven on the marginalisation that threatened from being outside the most powerful empire in the world, the Union with Britain was seen as a crucial modernising and civilising force. Sayers made the same point when in 1948 some in Ulster called for dominion status to escape the 'socialist' onslaught from Westminster. Deriding this attitude as the 'antithesis of unionism', he reasserted

> the need . . . to ally the best of our provincial qualities, integrity, shrewdness and industry, with what we know at bottom to be the broad stream of international progress. By doing that we [will be] less prone to be satisfied with our own efforts and our own standards and the scope of our own backyard.[17]

He was equally strenuous in the defence of what he called 'British standards' in contrast to native Irish corruptibility, particularly in government. But such standards were also to be applied to unionist administrations in Belfast and he was scathing towards those (including the former PM, Lord Brookeborough) who, in defending Harry West over the Fermanagh airfield scandal in 1967, saw 'Northern Ireland in isolation, a law onto itself, who are British when it suits them'.[18]

Admittedly, Sayers was (at least in the eyes of the *Irish Times*) 'a little dazzled by the glories of the Empire; a little overawed by the wonders of the centre of Empire; a little over-conscious of the bonds linking his own region to the Empire'.[19] It is perhaps no coincidence that the main flurries of constructive unionist activity occur at times when the British Empire appeared at its most confident and assertive – for instance, in the apogee of Victorian imperialism or in the aftermath of victory in the Second World War. Many of its leading advocates had seen service abroad in its defence, some at considerable risk to themselves; Hutcheson-Poe lost a leg at Tel-el-Kebir while Sayers almost drowned when his ship was torpedoed in mid-Atlantic in 1939. It took the First World War and his endeavours as a padre in the trenches to bring out the imperialist in Hannay.[20] Conversely, Faulkner's failure to serve in the Second World War contributed to the lack of rapport with O'Neill, who had to endure the ferocity of the Normandy landings in a regiment of Sherman tanks ('so many of which were "brewed up" that they became known by the Germans as "Tommy cookers"'[21]). Like others (e.g. Dunraven, Under-Secretary of the Colonies 1885–7) before him, O'Neill spent part of his early career in imperial administration as ADC to the Governor of South Australia. So influential were Sayers's four years in Churchill's map room – at the very heart of the British war effort against Hitler – that, in his politics, he rarely lost sight of the international perspective, continually urging Ulstermen to contribute on the larger stages of the UK, EEC and the Western world beyond their 'beloved province'.[22]

Nevertheless, the relationship with Britain that many constructive unionists hankered after was a distinctly federal one in which Ireland was less a colony and more a partner in the British Empire.[23] While Westminster never conceded this, her Anglocentric and spasmodic treatment of Irish affairs ensured that constructive unionists were never willing advocates of direct rule. Both Dunraven with his devolution proposals and O'Neill with his defence of Stormont were determined to establish structures which would leave their country free to look after its separate interests; much as Wyndham tried and failed to achieve with his proposed development grant in 1904. The Irish Reform Association's programme aside, it is of note that virtually all constructive initiatives in this period involved the devolution of at least consultative powers to popularly elected national bodies, such as the local government and agriculture assemblies. Equally, in economic matters Dunraven was as much a tariff reformer as any Sinn Féiner; just as O'Neill forever extolled the virtues of Labour's regional policies. Indeed, the Ulster PM spoke for most constructive unionists when he predicted in 1967 that the need for the Union to harness and not stifle such diversity would make it 'inevitable that devolution within the United Kingdom has not run its full course'.[24] T.P. O'Connor's mischievous quip that devolution was merely 'the Latin for home rule' missed the point (as did most unionists) that devolution was essentially unionist in its approach to the government of Ireland.[25]

Devolution served a moral purpose, too, as a bulwark against 'the filthy modern tide' of grubby materialism and class warfare. These concerns led the writer Standish O'Grady to an heroic (and futile) attempt to stir the Anglo-Irish aristocracy out of fatalistic lethargy to re-establish their leadership in the moral vacuum of democratic politics.[26] Equally, it was the need for 'making character ... men ... an educated democracy' that tempted the clerical novelist J.O. Hannay to become Douglas Hyde's 'lieutenant' in the Gaelic League.[27] Less romantically, such concerns were also fundamental to Horace Plunkett's co-operative movement which sought, by fostering the values of self-reliance in a context of communal responsibility, to establish a 'New Social Order' resilient against the temptations of greed and the blandishments of the demagogue.[28] In much the same way Sayers viewed Ulster as the final redoubt of planter values. Here we enter into an imaginary world of the 'Honest Ulsterman', as popularised before the Great War by, among others, the prolific novelist 'G.A. Birmingham' (Hannay's pseudonym).[29] This held that the 'inherent' characteristics of the Ulster race were industry, decency and loyalty. Not given to many words, these were a people whose plain common sense was laced by a fierce independence of mind; indeed, men whose ancestors had defiantly resisted autocratic powers in defence of freedom for three hundred years. For Sayers and O'Neill, the genius of unionism in Ulster lay not simply in its encapsulation of these virtues but in its ability to appear as a political movement that was genuinely classless: 'an almost unique fusion of people and interests' in whose 'wide embrace' were to be found 'men and women of Conservative, Liberal, and even Labour opinions, employers and workers, rich and poor, townsmen and countrymen, Orangemen and non-Orangemen'.[30]

Men and women who, nevertheless, were invariably Protestant. If Catholicism held few attractions for constructive unionists, most acknowledged the need to, at the very least, conciliate Irish Catholics. For the southern unionist minority, not to do so was to risk exile. But this also held true for the unionist majority in Northern Ireland. Sayers, for one, argued passionately for the integration of the minority into the unionist party and the government machine in order to enhance the legitimisation of Stormont and with it the Union. When in 1959 a row broke out within the party over whether Catholics should be admitted as members, he rattled the establishment by putting his paper fully behind the cry to create 'a coalition of all those democratic people of the centre whose belief is in freedom, progress and plenty'. To him, the issue was purely one of tolerance: 'tolerance that will ensure that Northern Ireland becomes the larger unity without which peace and full employment are more difficult to realise'. After all, Ulster could not afford to leave potentially a third of her workforce disaffected. Economic efficiency added to a Methodist commitment to social justice necessitated the mobilisation of Ulster Catholics and thus the transformation of Ulster unionism into an inclusive, supra-class political movement.[31] And it was in this spirit that O'Neill issued his dramatic appeal in 1969 'across the historic divide' to the minority: 'this is your country, too. Help us to make it all it should be'.[32]

Similar ideas perhaps inevitably attracted kindred people. In the main, constructive unionists were men of intellectual independence and experience, tending to look beyond Ireland to larger opportunities, be they in the United Kingdom, the British Empire and later the Commonwealth, or the USA and the rest of the Western world. For all their conservatism, they were always willing to debate and occasionally revise quite radically their beliefs. Above all, they were men keen for decisive action and the exercise of executive power. By way of illustration, one can compare two of constructive unionism's most effective propagandists, Thomas Sinclair (1838–1914) and Jack Sayers (1911–69). Both were proud Ulster-Scots, products of the Belfast bourgeoisie and in different ways Dissenters. Their Christian commitment led both to place high store on the role of the Churches as well as self-help in meeting the moral challenge of the poor without resorting to demoralising state doles. Not that Sayers seriously questioned the validity of the welfare state that emerged after 1945, but he would have had no difficulty accepting Sinclair's assertion that 'Christian charity . . . purifies a plutocracy of its luxury and purges a democracy of its socialism'.[33] Politically both were liberals for whom Gladstone remained the emotional lodestar, his aberration over home rule aside.[34] But such nostalgic allegiance could not outweigh the social and economic advantages of a modernising empire that could confidently combine social unity with individual freedoms. 'The strength of vast empires lies in the skilful blending of various nationalities', opined Sinclair, and through remedial legislation and assured government the Union had protected 'private conscience' from intellectual tyranny, be it autocratic Catholicism in the late nineteenth century or communism and fascism in the twentieth.[35] Neither was naturally a member of the landed aristocracy, which traditionally had lain at the heart of the unionist elite, and (at least in their early days) they were not reluctant to assert their independence, particularly in matters of minority representation in appointments.[36] However, it was as defenders of unionism that they both made their mark. Whether it was in the definition of the creed (through Sayers's nightly leaders in the *Belfast Telegraph* or Sinclair's speech to the Ulster Convention in 1892) or in the mobilisation of supporters (in which Sayers's 'I Back O'Neill' coupons in 1968 performed the same function as Sinclair's Solemn League and Covenant of 1912), these were craftsmen of their trade who profoundly shaped the face of Ulster unionism in their times.

What also characterised constructive unionists was their boundless optimism in the power of the state to reconstruct societies. On taking up the leadership, O'Neill starkly declared to his party, 'our task will be literally to transform Ulster'; indeed, as one senior civil servant reminisced, 'we did feel [in the 1960s] that we were changing the culture' of the north.[37] Moreover, they believed that the opportunity existed in which to do so. 'Ireland is in a plastic state', wrote a euphoric Wyndham to Balfour in the aftermath of his 1903 Land Act. 'We can mould her almost at will'.[38] Both periods saw an abatement in the constitutional conflict and the exhaustion of its main protagonists. In their wake came new, imaginative forces and a widespread expectation of change. They were also times of great prosperity and in London were governments sympathetic to reform and willing prey to the men with the big idea.

Confronted with such openings, constructive unionists tended to adopt the same strategies. Prime among these was the economic assault on what they held to be the roots of nationalism. Thus the Balfour brothers talked of 'killing home rule by kindness' through co-operatives and Land Acts; what Plunkett described as 'the economic and social truth'.[39] Astutely, they insisted that the economic sphere was essentially 'non-political'. Plunkett's invitation to the Recess Committee urged, 'unionists, without abating one jot of our unionism, and nationalists, without abating one jot of their nationalism', to sink their differences for their country's good and leave their politics to 'the justification of time'.[40] In much the same way O'Neill put his faith in economic pragmatism, arguing that nationalism would wither in the face of his modernisation programmes. His was a 'vision of Ulster . . . in which . . . material benefits will create such a spirit that our constitutional position will cease to be an issue in politics'.[41] More graphically, he declared in 1963 his intention 'to write upon this province with the hand of progress', setting in train 'a social and economic revolution as far reaching and overall more beneficent than the industrial revolution' and so 'reveal more and more clearly anti-partition clamour as social and economic lunacy in Ulster'.[42] Nor was there much difference in their efforts to cultivate the Catholic hierarchy, save perhaps in the bribe and then only between a Catholic university and grants for secondary education.

As personalities, Wyndham and O'Neill may have had little in common but they did share a fascination for public relations and the management of opinion. Both recognised how gestures could unite where policies divided and both consequently sought to protect their policies by making speeches richer in vision than in substance. For O'Neill, the image became all-consuming, whether it was photo-opportunities at Catholic schools, orchestrated 'Bobby Kennedy-like' receptions in outlying towns, or regular series of foreign tours to increase the 'appeal' of Ulster to foreign investment.[43] Wyndham preferred to talk loudly at the dinner parties of the establishment but the concern was the same. Given this, it is not surprising that both were assiduous in their courting of the press. In the case of O'Neill, Sayers was only too willing to oblige and in his columns he hounded the Protestant 'lunatic fringe'.

With Sayers's articulate assault leaving antediluvian unionists floundering, he soon became the confidant of the PM and widely regarded as a guru of O'Neillism; in much the same way as Plunkett and Dunraven had been in the 1890s and

1900s. This was especially true of Horace Plunkett, whom the Viceroy, Lord Cadogan, hailed as 'the Irish leader' and with whom cabinet secrets were shared.[44] With their social contacts and their seizure of the ideological initiative through the Recess and Land Conferences and later the editorial and press campaigns of the *Belfast Telegraph* (a paper whose circulation was not only the largest in the province but crucially straddled the sectarian divide), constructive unionists permeated the policy processes. If Dunraven led Wyndham further over devolution than was politic, O'Neill also could become the prisoner of his friends. 'Was he a liberal?' one ally queried. 'I don't think he was ever conscious of what he was – he was more a symbol created by people around him like Bloomfield, who wrote his speeches, Sayers, Malley [his private secretary] and Harold Black, the Cabinet Secretary. They injected him with liberalism'.[45] Thus it was that, while never very numerous or formally organised and restricted in their appeal to some of the more cosmopolitan of the upper and middle classes, constructive unionists came nevertheless to exercise considerable influence; not only through office holding, advisory roles and friendship within the circles of power but because they also offered a perspective in tune with English instincts and a critique all the more devastating from being delivered from within the fold.

II

However, this was not always so. If there was a lasting constructive unionist tradition, then where did it disappear to between 1905 and 1963? Why were its natural exponents so silent? The answer to both these questions lay in the constraints of a society under siege. Ostensibly set up with pluralist intentions, Northern Ireland under threat speedily became effectively a one-party, Protestant state. For all their disquiet over this, constructive unionists found themselves powerless to change matters in the face of periodic IRA assaults and the establishment of an avowedly Catholic state in the south with declared irredentist ambitions towards the north. This, together with the continued reluctance of northern Catholics to accept the new regime, presented an opportunity to unionist hardliners to stifle all debate by highlighting the external threat through a series of 'border scares'. In any case the moderates were themselves unionists first and foremost and, as Carson had after 1912, so they too repressed their liberal instincts to concentrate on the defence of the Union. To do otherwise would seem treasonable. This, together with the acquiescence of British Tory governments that had never shown the political will since 1870 to carry out a radical unionist programme in Ireland, left constructive unionism fading into seeming irrelevance as a near permanent state of civil war or siege was skilfully maintained on both sides of the border.[46]

In the circumstances most constructive unionists accepted these priorities without question. For them too the survival of the state was paramount in the face of regular threat. It is misleading at this stage to view them as a separate faction within the party: on a vast range of issues they saw as one with their fellow unionists and happily identified with the Protestant settler mythology, provincial pride and loyalty to crown, Parliament and Empire. Nor did a British public life reflecting a Protestant majority cause quite the offence that it was to do in a later and very different moral climate. Moreover, as the prime advocates of the imperial civilising mission, constructive unionists provided a sufficient veneer of Britishness to deflect any casual metropolitan concern. Indeed, this role grew enormously in importance with the Second World War and its aftermath and in particular the need for close relations with Westminster in the wake of the Irish declaration of a republic in 1948. That, along with an administrative capacity in a party not noted for the same, ensured their preponderance in the senior offices.[47]

Nevertheless, there were a small number of often highly placed unionists who continued to criticise discrimination and argued instead for the greater integration of the minority. Before 1939, such activities were limited to a few senior cabinet ministers (Lords Londonderry and Charlemont, Hugh Pollock, James Milne Barbour), civil servants (Sir Wilfred Spender), students at Queen's University, and the occasional pronouncements of prominent establishment figures (Major General Hugh Montgomery, the Marquess of Dufferin and Ava) and groups like the Irish Association, keen, with war imminent, to foster better relations with the south.[48] Post-war, there was Morris May and Brian Maginess. The latter, together with the Party Chairman, Sir Clarence Graham, flew a kite at the 1959 Young Unionist Conference calling for party membership to be open to Catholics. This suggestion caused a furore and much closing of ranks (for which read closing of minds). But in the main, where there were signs of an Ulster-British versus Ulster-Loyalist divergence in the 1950s, they were more often than not expressed in private 'non-political' forms such as differing lifestyles, social networks and cultural activities. Public criticism was left to lone voices such as Maginess and Sayers – insiders who in the case of the latter restricted his disquiet to the anonymous columns of the Commonwealth journal, *The Round Table*, whose readership in Ulster would, in all probability, have known each other intimately.[49]

But what was more remarkable about the 1959 controversy was that it became public. In one-party states, forever preoccupied by the enemy without, public unity was almost sacrosanct. This does not mean that the debate between progressive and traditional unionism went into abeyance. Rather through force of circumstances it had become internal, involving no dialogue with Catholic nationalism but no less vigorous for this. The repressive demands of outward conformity also encouraged this debate into the world of poetry and literature, including in 1947 John Hewitt's impassioned plea for the recognition of the communality of the landscape, in which Ulster was seen 'as a region and not as the symbol of any particular creed'. In advocating a strong dose of regionalism within the context of 'a federated British Isles', he was treading a well-trodden path.[50] Writing in defence of the *Telegraph*'s stand in the 1964 election, Sayers asserted 'it's wrong to say that no one backed us. Lots did, but Ulster doesn't have anything like a public opinion'.[51] The task he set the *Telegraph* was to create one. However, it would take the prosperity and security of the 1960s before constructive unionism could begin to wrest the initiative away from populist politicians, whose careers had for so long been based on pandering to the anxieties and prejudices of the Protestant majority. Thus the seeming extraordinary outpourings of progressive politics in the 1890s and 1960s were but public phases in long-standing and fluctuating debate within Ulster unionism over the means to achieve a shared goal.[52]

III

That said, it was in these two decades that constructive unionists made their greatest impact, both in terms of influence and their considerable achievement. The 1890s saw an all-Ireland alliance protest effectively against imperial overtaxation (out of which also came democratic local government in 1898).[53] At the same time, the 'conference plus business' strategy of dialogue with moderate nationalists produced a new department of agriculture and, with the 1903 Land Act, inaugurated a revolution in landholding, so ensuring that socialism would largely pass rural Ireland by. Add in the rapid spread of Plunkett's co-operative movement (within ten years he had established 800 co-ops with 80,000 members and an annual turnover of £2 million), together with the earlier improvements of the Congested Districts Board, railway legislation and the re-housing of 50,000 rural labourers ('the first major public housing enterprise to get under way in the British Isles'), and one can begin to appreciate Arthur Balfour's angry insistence in his old age that 'the Ireland that the Free State took over [was] the Ireland that we made'.[54]

Under O'Neill Ulster was equally transformed with new housing, motorways, towns, businesses and a university. Moreover, with the help of Sayers and the *Belfast Telegraph*, he established a new, popular, moderate consensus. However fragile this proved to be in the end, it remains a unique achievement in twentieth-century Ulster. While hindsight may mock a decade of civic weeks and inter-church activities, they had a spontaneity and confidence that most community workers today can only envy.[55] Liberal unionism was made acceptable, even fashionable, for the first time since 1903 and, at the very least, his rhetoric encouraged Catholics to seek redress from within the constitution. Nor must it be forgotten that O'Neillism mobilised considerable support. There was the 1967 poll and in 1968 acceptance of O'Neill's five-point plan, his famous 'crossroads' speech and the sacking of William Craig two days later, all raising hopes – with O'Neill receiving 150,000 letters of support – of a moderate victory; a triumph to which the *Telegraph* with its 125,000 coupons (the equivalent of 7 million in the UK) backing O'Neill had made a vital contribution. In February 1969 with the Unionist Party splitting into pro- and anti-O'Neill camps, O'Neill won 44% of the vote for his brand of moderate unionism and more than twice as many seats as his unionist opponents; in terms of seats won for unionism, his achievement was not matched by any of his predecessors.[56]

And yet he 'lost'. Attempts to transport this goodwill permanently into the political sphere proved catastrophic with both Wyndham and O'Neill falling victim to the Ulster militants over devolution and civil rights, respectively. By 1910 Ireland was as polarised as she had been in 1886, if not more so, and as she was to be again in 1972. Why was it when conditions for reconciliation were so propitious that the politics of co-operation failed so completely? Was constructive unionism doomed to fail or did these years represent two opportunities lost through political ineptitude?[57]

Whether or not the political opportunity existed, there can be little doubt that some moderates were incapable of seizing it, displaying an essentially amateurish disdain for organisation. Thus, Dunraven's Irish Reform Association was more a collection of faddists, only fifteen of whom bothered to turn up in Dublin to ratify the devolution manifesto in 1904.[58] Indeed, since it was August, the Treasurer, Colonel Hutchinson-Poe, went shooting in Antrim instead of looking for badly needed funds. O'Neill showed similar aristocratic detachment, content to leave such matters in the hostile hands of Glengall Street.[59] It was Sayers who thought up the 'I back O'Neill' coupons, so providing the instant opinion poll that left Craig's coup in December 1968 stillborn. In the vital 1969 election which was to decide his fate and that of the liberal unionist initiative, the Prime Minister did not, with the party now split, give his formal support to all the 'pro-O'Neill' candidates until days before the vote.

To such ineptitude may be added distractions of personality and petty jealousies. At times in the 1890s constructive unionists seemed more a gathering of individuals with little in common, save in the case of Horace Plunkett and Lord Dunraven a shared interest in Daisy Fingall, a 'Society' beauty and occasional confidante of kings and Irish chief secretaries. Indeed, she so captivated George Wyndham in Phoenix Park that he was only saved by the intrusion of his bodyguard, at taxpayers' expense, arriving (like the 7th Cavalry) on horseback. Her real passion, however, was for Wyndham's predecessor, Gerald Balfour, who like a true academic puritan said no. In so doing for the first and only time in his life he sounded like a proper Ulster unionist.[60] The rivalries between Dunraven, Plunkett and Monteagle could not compare with the sheer destructiveness of the clash between O'Neill and Faulkner. In some ways O'Neill was his own worst enemy. Plainly bored in the company of his backbenchers, his relationship with his cabinet colleagues was hardly warmer after his failure to consult them before inviting Lemass to Belfast. Personalities also contributed to his downfall in another way. Increasingly, the media (including Sayers) came to portray events in Ulster in terms of a gladiatorial contest between O'Neill and Paisley which the Prime Minister had to win. But finding himself on the hustings for the first time in decades, O'Neill learned that Old Etonian hauteur warmed few hearts in Bannside. Yet his meagre majority over Paisley became more than a personal humiliation, for it served to undermine the impact of significant progressive gains elsewhere.[61]

In any case many key constructive unionist policies were barely thought through. Thus, on devolution, Dunraven admitted to MacDonnell that they 'have never thrashed the matter out'.[62] Nor did O'Neill know where he was going. 'Terence actually got ahead of me,' wrote Sayers of the Lemass meeting, 'and he had the grace to tell me that he does not know where it will all lead. I would rather that than a pretence that it is all calculated'.[63] Later commentators have been withering in their assessment of O'Neill, some seeing him as an aristocratic fraud raising expectations of which he was incapable or never intended to fulfil.[64] Those who worked with him closely remain vigorous (and largely convincing) in their repudiation of this slur, but to do so is only to condemn him as a strategist. His rhetoric reverberated with the buzzwords of promise without any appreciation of how to turn economic modernisation into political gain. It was as if the politics were to be left to the invisible hand. Hence even close friends like Sayers were 'never able to satisfy my mind about the Prime Minister's liberalism – it is far more intellectual than emotional and even then much of it emanates from Ken Bloomfield'.[65] Nevertheless, the logic of O'Neillism, involving as it did the broadening of the unionist party through incorporating the Catholic middle class into a coalition of the centre, had to involve a confrontation with traditional Protestantism. Sayers for one saw what was inevitable and necessary. Heralding 'a classic struggle between the forces of progress and reaction', he denounced 'the rise of malignant anti-Catholic forces exploiting the psychology of the mob' and bluntly declared 'it is time indeed for any who are not with [O'Neill] to declare themselves and go'.[66] But O'Neill never prepared himself for this struggle or sought to impose any control over the party, and so consequently failed to escape its shackles, preferring to answer Sayers by pointing out that the *Protestant Telegraph* had done a 'roaring trade' on the Twelfth at Ahoghill and making much of its affluent supporters.[67] Given his reluctance to tackle this, the only alternative was to rely on the threat of British intervention to keep his party in line. However, having never been realised in the history of the state, this was a threat that irritated rather than intimidated – especially as it was known that O'Neill was himself determined to prevent such an outcome at all costs. In strategic terms, therefore, O'Neill was sleepwalking to disaster.

It was a common fault of constructive unionists both to presume too much of Irish unionism and to assume (as unionists themselves) the right to speak for unionism as a whole. Linked to this was an unquestioned belief that controversial issues should be settled by a 'few dozen men of intelligence and good will' (as William O'Brien assured Dunraven in 1903) and that 'numbers don't matter' – a view that became more attractive as the sheer momentum of the land and devolution negotiations detached leaders from their followers.[68] In turn, Sayers crucially misunderstood the nature of post-war unionist leadership. Taken in by the image of the titans, Carson, Craig and Brookeborough, he failed to see how far they survived on populism and the 'distribution of the bones'. As a result, on the 'northern democracy' constructive unionists could be significantly out of touch. Thus it was not until John Shawe-Taylor made a 'reconnaissance' (the phrase is telling) that the Dunravenites recognised that the split in the Orange Order (1903) signalled not a diminution of sectarianism but its revival.[69] Fifty years later it took Burntollet to rid Sayers of his 'in-born romanticism about Ulster'. 'That frightful reaction Protestants have to the sight of any large body of Roman Catholics', he now raged to a friend.

> It is compounded of fear and a bad conscience. Let Catholics keep to themselves and say nothing and they can be at least indifferent to them. Let them join together to make a legitimate protest and they are rebels and even in Paisley's words at St Paul's, 'scum'.[70]

Cocooned within an elite that was in spirit too professional middle class, too suburban, too East of the Bann, above all too British, he was emotionally detached from the fears of ordinary Protestants and the appeal of fundamentalism. Delicately O'Neill had had to remind the editor of 'the fantastic gap which still exists between the establishment and the back streets of Belfast'. After all, as Lord Charlemont had the honesty to admit in the 1930s, he was a moderate because he was 'a senator and [had] no seat to maintain!'[71]

Nor by the late sixties had Sayers the means to fill that gap. A power base that had been constructed around the ideological influence of the written word (both in terms of imagination and distribution) was now being undermined by the advent of independent television with its immediacy and egalitarian spirit. What was so striking was the speed with which the moderate consensus, that he had painstakingly cultivated, succumbed to baser instincts as the television screens provided, in the images of violence in Derry in October 1968, the first sight for many of a traditional enemy. When, ultimately, crowds on the streets began to seize the initiative from the government, constructive unionist ideas became a logistical irrelevance. Even before this, for all the Paisleyite concern over the hostility of the *Belfast Telegraph*, Sayers lacked the charisma or the creed to sway the masses.[72] In any case a political philosophy based on reasonableness provided no answer to Plunkett's question, 'How would you meet the man who honestly thinks that if a "comma in the king's oath were changed, the foundation of our religious and civil liberties are undermined"?'[73] Just as Sayers could not comprehend in 1968 why reform of 'nakedly sectarian' local government should be delayed; and then all 'for the sacredness of Londonderry, the belief that to give away what King James could not capture in war was to give away all that William of Orange had ever stood for'.[74] What the moderates lacked was a common political language with popular unionism. Sure, they shared the same phrases but by them they meant different things. For instance, Sayers was an enthusiastic Orangeman because he took literally this commitment to 'religious and civil liberties'. He resigned in 1960 when, in the furore over Catholic membership of the unionist party, it became impossible to deny that to many unionists this was nothing more than a code for Protestant supremacy.

Nor, for all the need to attract Catholics, was there much understanding of their position. What made the inflammatory treatment of Catholicism in Plunkett's *Ireland in the New Century* so depressing was that it was so unintended.[75] Similarly, O'Neill's clarion call to the minority to share in the spoils of 'Northern Ireland Ltd' made little sense when new towns and universities were primarily placed in the Protestant heartlands. It was 'sublime stupidity' (as a Sayers's leader in October 1967 made public) to talk of building bridges between the two communities when only seven out of the previous seventy-nine government appointments had gone to the minority.[76] Such stands won recognition from within his Catholic readership and regular invitations to join the governing bodies of Catholic schools or to speak at their old-boy gatherings. Yet even Sayers had to confess, talking on Radio 4's *Outlook* programme (26 April 1969) after Bernadette Devlin's remarkable maiden speech at Westminster, that:

> I could not agree with all she had said but I saw clearly what I had imperfectly seen before, the depths of the hurts to the human personalities of so many Catholics, those who today are openly claiming their right to full citizenship, to the highest standards of social justice. With many others I can only ask God's forgiveness for the failure of our imaginations.[77]

'I buy [the *Belfast Telegraph*] every night and just look for your words and think, especially tonight: "Well thank God you [are] one decent man who sees things as they really are"', wrote one Derry Catholic woman to Sayers in the aftermath of Burntollet.[78] But in truth such depth of insight had come to him very late.

In many ways this was the Achilles' heel of the constructive unionists. Believers in dialogue, they could exist quite happily at the level of disembodied debates on liberalism and the concepts of rights, injustice and inclusivity but only at the cost of real engagement with popular politics – a world indeed from which to a very large extent they were physically cut off. As a consequence, to appreciate the politics of 'hurt' – be it Catholic or Protestant – required an act of 'imagination', without which constructive unionists could never get beyond a dialogue of the mind. But then to do so is to choose sides, which arguably is what Sayers did in 1968–9, and he went down with the cause as a result.

Therefore, it is not hard to explain the failure of cross-party dialogue in terms of personal inadequacies. However, there were more fundamental problems, of which the most serious was the constructive unionists' heavy reliance on the British government. There is a clear correlation between the level (both economic and political) of British commitment and the credibility of the politics of dialogue. Equally, it was the friendship of the Balfours, not the co-operative movement, that made Horace Plunkett so influential in the 1890s. Just as it was the widely known fact that Wyndham was ready to write the cheque which ensured that Dunraven's Land Conference would be taken seriously. With this kind of backing numerical support did not indeed matter so much. But it did leave the moderate cause extremely vulnerable to governmental whim; as Dunraven discovered to his dismay when devolution proposals, with which Wyndham had connived, were suddenly ditched in a blunt letter to *The Times*. Sayers's influence lay in his relationship with O'Neill, which appeared to be so close that 'at times indeed it is as if Captain O'Neill has a doppelganger flitting through the offices of the *Telegraph*'.[79] So when O'Neill fell, Sayers became marginal.

On top of this, constructive unionism in Ireland was always open to the imposition of English priorities. This was more than a question of general ignorance and prevailing racial stereotypes; even sympathetic ministers were constrained by party, parliamentary and imperial needs; something Dunraven failed to appreciate when fuming at Wyndham for 'not sticking to his guns'.[80] As a result the British government unintentionally raised expectations or fears which far outstripped their limited intention. Consequently, even beneficent measures such as the 1903 Land Act could become yet another cause of grievance. Parliament's insistence that the 1898 Local Government Act conform with English practice (so strengthening the impression of uniformity within the Union) only ensured that there was no minority protection and that local administration would quickly become the engine for the institutional sectarianisation of the landscape, especially in Ulster.[81] Nor did Wilson's largely rhetorical hints of intervention help O'Neill's cause in the 1960s. More disturbing for Ulster unionists was the 'neutral position' the British unionist administration would invariably adopt when forced to intervene in Ireland, especially in the distribution of grants or jobs, rather than indulge in party government. Peter Brooke's denial in 1990 that Britain had any 'selfish or strategic' interest in Ireland was but the latest expression of a long-established instinct. But treating Ireland as a place apart encouraged an all-Ireland perspective which was often reflected in British openness (at least initially) to home rule solutions from democratic local government and devolution to Sunningdale and the Anglo-Irish and Good Friday agreements.[82] This unionism of the islands had its nostalgic attractions for many constructive unionists but such wider perspectives ran counter to the 'little Ulsterism' that had sprung up in the wake of partition. Even in the 1900s few Ulster unionists were particularly interested in the affairs of empire. Nor post-1945 could Sayers find in Ulster much concern for foreign affairs, be it in the Commonwealth or the Berlin Blockade.[83]

Anyway, would 'Saxon gold' work? The assumption that a primarily economic policy of killing home rule by kindness could fundamentally alter emotional and cultural identities was always on its own going to prove too mechanistic a philosophy. The only time that Plunkett saw loyalty on the increase was on the occasion of the Duke of York's visit to the Dublin Horse Show in 1897. William O'Brien, who desired to reconcile Irishmen rather than promote loyalty, saw clearly that no matter how successful the Wyndham Land Act was in terms of sales, it was not even beginning to dispel the cultural hostility that so divided Irish society. Hence his helpless rage at the ease with which Dillon could arouse these suspicions to wreck conciliatory reform after 1903.[84] O'Neill was just as infuriated by the Protestant 'coasters' who failed to turn out for him in 1969 ('good men sleep and others are playing bridge or golf[85]'), but it was the overwhelming reluctance of even moderate Catholics to vote unionist that was the most telling.[86] By the late 1960s Sayers realised that proselytisation by cash had to give way to the mutual recognition of two cultural traditions:

> Community relations are . . . only a beginning. The PM doesn't or won't see that the movement needs a more inspirational basis, that you can't ask Catholics to forget their nationalism in favour of civics and good works. We should be looking for more of a share of the Irish heritage . . . Terence fled from the mention of Wolfe Tone – and I wouldn't plug it – but the answer is that any rapprochement he is looking for can't be confined to a glorification of Ulster alone. That the Red Hand should only be one of two![87]

Yet such an evolutionary approach would at best take two generations to win over the constituencies and in the short term was simply unrealistic for O'Neill to adopt. After all, he continued to equate the Scots-Irish heritage with the Ulster community and dismissed any attempt to reconcile the differing traditions as 'like trying to solve the colour problem by spraying everyone a pale shade of brown'.[88] Only in the 1990s would such ideas attract significant support.[89] And then run into a political storm over whether the goal was cultural integration or the engendering of mutual respect of two distinct traditions; and if the latter, was it, in effect, copper-fastening the sectarian divide?[90] As Horace Plunkett found out a century before, the pursuit of the non-political in the absence of common ground is to chase illusions.

IV

That the story of constructive unionism proved largely one of failure seems self-evident. However, its impact on Irish politics in both these periods was nevertheless quite considerable, if surprisingly destructive; a consequence of the very nature of unionism itself. This, at its simplest, was an alliance of mutually antagonistic groups bound together by the benefits of the Union and the necessity of unity to sustain it. These divisions, especially within Ulster unionism, were as much a question of cultural allegiance as they were of religion or class; between, crudely, those who saw unionism protecting British values and opportunities in Ulster and those who looked at the Union in a more parochial light as the guardian of Protestant position and power in the province. Both perspectives could coexist quite happily in the struggle against a united Ireland but when the spotlight turned to internal affairs both came to view the approach of the other as not merely misguided but fundamentally dangerous to the Union.[91]

In this regard the setting up in the 1890s of representative committees and conferences outside the party system (but with government support) in effect to decide national issues could only threaten the influence of both official nationalism and unionism. Hence the *Freeman Journal*'s bitter jibe at the 'burlesque substitute for home rule' emanating from the 'disinterested guests at Mr Plunkett's dinner table'; and the hostility of a leading nationalist figure such as John Dillon who genuinely feared that killing home rule by kindness would work.[92] At the same time the possibility of reform, however half-hearted, simply reawakened long-standing divisions within the two main political camps. The supposed inadequacy of Gerald Balfour's land reform only inspired T.W. Russell's campaign in Ulster, threatening an electoral catastrophe in Ulster for the unionists in 1900. Similarly, loose talk by government ministers of a Catholic university led to the breakaway Independent Orange Order, critical of the traditional leadership for going soft on their sectarian enemies. It was only the furore over Dunraven's devolution proposals that offered reactionary unionists the opportunity to reassert unity around the cry of the Union in danger, just as Paisley was to seek to achieve over civil rights. Both in 1895–1905 and 1963–9 the adoption of a liberalising policy (ostensibly sympathetic to Catholics) undercut the basis of loyalty and left the rank and file free to criticise leaders without the risk of being denounced as Lundies and traitors. Undoubtedly class antagonisms fuelled both rebellions and, significantly, both periods resulted in the democratisation of party structures

(UUC, DUP) and the ousting of the old guard in favour of a leadership drawn from the ranks.[93]

Fundamentally the 'conference plus business' strategy raised the very large question of whether it was possible to co-operate with one's traditional enemies without endangering one's essential beliefs and integrity. Was nationalism, for instance, an all-Ireland ideal in which compromise was justified in the pursuit of a united Ireland; or was it essentially a revanche of the Catholic dispossessed? Could unionism ever be anything other than sectarian? Faced with issues of such enormity, it is not surprising that nationalists and unionists in this period chose the comforts of trusted prejudice. Given this, constructive dialogue had little to offer, save the risk of the offer that one could not refuse.

Killing home rule by kindness eventually killed only kindness itself and the middle ground that it had fostered. Significantly, it is after the devolution scandal that the first preparations are made for armed resistance in Ulster. Likewise, by 1969, constructive unionism had come to naught as the unionist government caved in under the Paisleyite backlash (just as Wyndham had in the face of the 'Ulster revolt' in 1904–5). Appalled by the violence, a disillusioned Sayers had come by 1969 reluctantly to recognise direct rule as a humiliating necessity.[94] Ironically, it would be this outcome that would offer a lifeline for constructive unionists who with an active British state renewed their influence in subsequent decades through government patronage and quangos.[95] Yet just as in the 1890s, so in the 1960s the greatest impact of the constructive unionist reformers lay in highlighting so provocatively the fissures within unionism and its subsequent inability to develop as a successful philosophy of government. Ironically for one so constructive, Sayers's achievement in the end was primarily destructive, contributing, however unwillingly, to the splintering of Ulster unionism – though perhaps this may prove to have been an essential precondition of any political reconstruction in the province.

But, if these crises were so similar, why were the results so different? Why did unionism survive intact the progressive challenge in the early twentieth century only to disintegrate in the face of a similar challenge in the 1960s? In some ways it is remarkable how long Paisley took to mobilise Protestants *en masse* against their traditional enemies. Compared to the devolution crisis, there was no rapid rallying to the flag. Instead, in the 1969 election both wings of Ulster unionism pushed their quarrel to the brink and over and lost the parliament they both sought to defend. Undoubtedly, this was in part a consequence of miscalculation but there were more telling reasons.

First, for constructive unionists none of the usual constraints of unity applied in the 1960s. It was Stormont not the Union that was in danger (for all the attempt to portray the civil rights movement as the IRA in mufti). Similarly, the obstacles to progress were not nationalists but unionists. By seeking through civil rights greater inclusion within the state rather than its outright rejection, the nationalist challenge (traditionally a focus of unity) forced the liberal-exclusionist contradiction into the open and unionists into deciding and dividing. This, of course, had also been a characteristic of the 1890s. But in the 1960s constructive unionists were deeply entrenched in the governing structure and far more confident that the future lay with them. By 1966, people like Sayers were talking openly of a show-down and of the need to purge the party of the Paisleyites.[96] Rank-and-file protests, as epitomised by the latter, however, were not new in unionist history but to be effective required leadership. Unquestionably one of the major differences between these two periods was Ian Paisley. T.W. Russell, Lindsay Crawford and Tom Sloan never came near in the 1890s to matching Paisley's unique ability to encapsulate Protestant gut feeling and transform it into a cohesive and disciplined movement.[97]

Nevertheless, the difference lay more than in the intensity of the struggle. Unlike in 1905, Ulster unionists were not dealing with a unionist government at Westminster and one too weak to resist Ulster MPs on the rampage. Instead, they faced a Labour government that was winning elections and confident in its self-appointed mission to civilise Britain. And yet, almost irrespective of whichever party was in power, British involvement in Northern Ireland was bound to be markedly different. Whereas in the 1900s (for all the mutual suspicion between the Balfour government and unionist Ulster) the fundamentals were shared, in the 1960s, when the CRA switched the political agenda from security to social and economic liberties, they not only drove a wedge between the London and Belfast administrations but crucially exposed major cultural differences between Great Britain and Ulster, which had evolved unnoticed amid the quasi-independence afforded Stormont by parliamentary convention at Westminster.[98]

What had once been a bond of diversities, forged together by the shared assumptions of Protestantism, empire and the market and renewed with the sac-rifices on the Somme and in the Second World War (in Ulster's eyes, proofs of their belonging), had become over time little more than a veneer of Britishness disguising significant cultural divergence. Perhaps it was ever thus, but while local diversities were respected this didn't matter, for the metropolitan impact was primarily at the level of high politics. However, after 1945 the raft of welfare and educational reform emanating from Westminster not only increased dramatically the scope for government intervention in people's lives and revived implicitly the appeal of inclusivity. More significantly, it transformed the moral and philo-sophical basis of British society. Without the unifying forces of war and empire, the pursuit of civil liberties and social justice increasingly redefined Britain towards a society that was individualistic, pluralistic and secular. Admittedly, for much of the sixties this reflected aspiration more than reality, but it was a devel-opment that sat uneasily beside a virtual one-party state, sustained in part by gerrymandering and widespread if unsystematic religious discrimination.[99] Ulster unionism (particularly when symbolised by Paisley – as it increasingly was in the media) found itself alienated from the emerging metropolitan culture in which Britishness had moved on from the verities of the nineteenth, let alone the seven-teenth, century.[100] With it to varying degrees had moved many (primarily middle class and of a younger generation) who were to seek a more constructive unionist position; as well as unionists like Sayers and O'Neill who embraced the Ulster-Scots heritage for its liberal, intrepid settler myths and less for its sectarian underbelly. Ironically, in the late sixties it was Catholic nationalism, calling for civil rights, which struck far more British chords than Protestant Ulster's defence of the faith. As a consequence British governments of whatever hue were never likely to go back 'on message' as Balfour had in 1904–5.

Moreover, in what was now a battle of ideas, Ulster unionism found that it could no longer control the debate as once it had through its apologists in the established press and the BBC in Belfast. Herein lies the significance of Sayers's accelerating critique and the remarkable collection of reporters he fostered at the *Belfast Telegraph*, breaking down the conformity and complacency within unionist thinking.[101] Even more important were the emergence of independent television and the increasing intrusions of British investigative journalism. The impact of television dramatically intensified the conflict and the sheer pace of events. At the same time by giving the confrontations on the streets an immediacy in the privacy of every home, it very rapidly polarised the community as in 1912. But unlike 1912, its pictures also mobilised the British conscience and world opinion against the unionist cause, determining the shape of British policy in much the same way as had Gladstone's pamphlets on the Bulgarian atrocities nearly a hundred years before.[102] Against the speed, incisiveness and new-style hostility of this reporting, Ulster unionism found itself incapable – both politically and psychologically – of adapting as one; indeed, it found itself a victim both of a very British revolution and of the fossilisation that comes with monopoly.

V

Speaking a year after Sayers's death, O'Neill displayed rare passion when he declared that

> had Jack been listened to at the time that he was talking to us through his leaders in the *Telegraph*, some of the terrible things that have since happened might not have happened. To start with the obvious things, some people might be alive today who are now dead; some people's houses which have been burned down might still be standing. But perhaps even more important than that, our position within the United Kingdom would have been much stronger had his opinion been listened to than it is today. This is one of the tragedies of this whole situation through which we have lived, that they didn't understand, that the message which Jack was trying to impart was not a message of treachery as they thought, but a message of common sense, a message of good will, a message for improving Northern Ireland and (and I hate to use this word) Northern Ireland's image throughout not only the United Kingdom but throughout the world.[103]

Maybe, but such sentiments also provide an eloquent testimony to the destruction of such a vision. And if they were not listening then, nor are they today. 'Sorry, Roy, it is not picking up on constructive unionism' was the bemused response of the head librarian at the *Guardian* in 1998 after a search of the cuttings.[104] For all that individual constructive unionists continued to thrive under the umbrella of direct rule, their political influence, it has been argued, has evaporated with the switch in strategy by the British government from broadening out a middle ground to in the 1990s directly cultivating the terrorist extremes in a series of peace processes.[105] And given such realism, it is perhaps only to be expected that those who choose the middle of the road will eventually be run down.[106] Yet this could also demonstrate the centrality of the issues they represent, of how much their critique lies at the heart of the matter in this conflict, especially in a war that both sides privately acknowledge cannot be won. Whenever, at the realisation of this, both sides stumble resentfully into no man's land, it is the challenges of inclusivity, social justice and the international dimension that they will inevitably have to confront.[107]

In the meantime there can be no denying the many practical benefits that sprang from the politics of dialogue and middle ground. Nor should such experiments be condemned for failing to achieve a political consensus that was simply unrealistic while society remained fundamentally divided over the question of political sovereignty. It may be hard to avoid the conclusion that the experiment in constructive unionism only showed that Ireland was, to all intents and purposes, always a partitioned society. Nevertheless, such a society, if it is not to be racked by permanent war, can only depend on negotiation and the respect for the legitimacy of other traditions. As was acknowledged by David Trimble when in the aftermath of the Good Friday Agreement he declared that, 'We can now get down to the historic and honourable task of this generation to raise up a new Northern Ireland in which pluralist unionism and constitutional nationalism can speak to each other with the civility that is the foundation of freedom'.[108] All of which should ensure that constructive unionism as a perspective will survive for many years to come and will, 'like a dog on a tennis court' (to use Plunkett's analogy), continue to pester and enrage the majority of unionists until the end of the game.

NOTES

1 R.F. Foster, *W.B. Yeats, a Life: the Apprentice Mage* (Oxford, 1997), pp. 442–3.
2 L.P. Curtis, *Coercion and Conciliation, 1880–1892* (Princeton, 1963); Catherine B. Shannon, *Arthur J. Balfour and Ireland 1874–1922* (Washington, DC, 1988). Much more insightful is Margaret O'Callaghan, *British High Politics and Nationalist Ireland* (Cork, 1994), pp. 104–52.
3 Andrew Gailey, *Ireland and the Death of Kindness: The Experience of Constructive Unionism, 1890–1905* (Cork, 1987); Andrew Gailey, 'Failure and the Making of the new Ireland 1879–1905', in D.G. Boyce (ed.), *The Revolution in Ireland, 1879–1923* (London and Basingstoke, 1988), pp. 47–70; Andrew Gailey, 'King Carson: an Essay on the invention of leadership', *Irish Historical Studies*, 30 (May, 1996), pp. 66–87.
4 For the difference between 'middle' and 'common' ground see Duncan Morrow, 'In search of common ground', in Arthur Aughey and Duncan Morrow (eds), *Northern Ireland Politics* (London, 1996), p. 57.
5 Joseph Spence, 'The philosophy of Irish Toryism, 1833–1852', Ph.D., University of London, 1992; D. George Boyce, 'Trembling solicitude: Irish Conservatism, nationality

and public opinion, 1833–86', in D. George Boyce, R. Eccleshall and V. Geoghegan (eds), *Political Thought in Ireland since the Seventeenth Century* (London, 1993), pp. 124–45.

6 See Alvin Jackson's entry on 'Constructive Unionism', in S.J. Connolly (ed.), *The Oxford Companion to Irish History* (Oxford, 1998), p. 113.

7 'The high-principled editor of the *Belfast Telegraph*, who had done so much to sustain the O'Neill administration' (Ken Bloomfield, *Stormont in Crisis: A Memoir* (Belfast, 1994), p. 118).

8 Oliver MacDonagh, *States of Mind: A Study of Anglo-Irish Conflict, 1780–1980* (London, 1983).

9 Andrew Gailey, 'An Irishman's world', *Irish Review* (Winter 1992/1993), p. 35.

10 Andrew Gailey, *Crying in the Wilderness: Jack Sayers, a Liberal Editor in Ulster 1939–69* (Belfast, 1995), p. 25.

11 Ibid., p. 31.

12 Bloomfield, *Stormont*, p. 76.

13 Gailey, 'An Irishman's world', p. 34.

14 Foster, *Apprentice Mage*, pp. 204, 206. Even here there were limits to belonging. When Betty Balfour attempted to put on a 'living pictures' exhibition drawn from scenes out of *The Countess Kathleen*, the Irish Literary Theatre refused to accept Castle patronage and Daisy Fingall had to take on the lead role made famous by the beautiful Maud Gonne. Lady Fingall was not without allure and Yeats found himself fluctuating between nationalist disdain and agreeing to coach privately this latest Kathleen.

15 D.G. Boyce, ' "One last burial": culture, counter-revolution and revolution in Ireland, 1886–1916', in Boyce, *Revolution*, pp. 127–34; Gailey, 'An Irishman's world', pp. 34–5. On Moran see F.S.L. Lyons, *Culture and Anarchy in Ireland, 1890–1939* (Oxford, 1979), pp. 58–62; Roy Foster, 'Varieties of Irishness: cultures and anarchy in Ireland', in *Paddy and Mr Punch: Connections in English and Irish History* (London, 1993), p. 24.

16 Gailey, *Sayers*, p. 96.

17 Ibid., p. 33; David Fitzpatrick, *The Two Irelands, 1912–39* (Oxford 1998), p. 220.

18 Gailey, *Sayers*, pp. 121, 159.

19 *Irish Times*, 31 October 1946.

20 Gailey, 'An Irishman's world', p. 36.

21 Terence O'Neill, *The Autobiography of Terence O'Neill* (London, 1972), p. 23.

22 Gailey, *Sayers*, pp. 27–30, 37–9; Terence O'Neill, *Ulster at the Crossroads* (London, 1969), pp. 184–91.

23 John Kendle, *Ireland and the Federal Solution: The Debate over the United Kingdom Constitution, 1870–1921* (Montreal and Kingston, 1989), pp. 90–103, 128–36, 155–9, 183–9, 231–2.

24 O'Neill, *Crossroads*, pp. 76–97.

25 As the old humbug Gladstone always insisted – John Vincent, 'Gladstone and Ireland', *Proceedings of the British Academy*, 63 (1977), pp. 193–238. See also Richard Shannon, *Gladstone: Heroic Minister 1865–1898* (London, 1999), pp. 365–405.

26 Lyons, *Culture and Anarchy*, pp. 32–5.

27 Gailey, 'An Irishman's world', p. 36.

28 Gailey, *Kindness*, pp. 18–19; Boyce, 'Culture', pp. 119–23.

29 Gailey, 'An Irishman's world', pp. 35–8.

30 Gailey, *Sayers*, pp. 23–4, 57; O'Neill, *Crossroads*, pp. 41, 44, 59–60.

31 Gailey, *Sayers*, pp. 51–63, 102–4.

32 *N.I. House of Commons Debates*, 71, cols 414–15 (29 January 1969). On Catholic unionists see John Biggs-Davison and George Chowdharay-Best, *The Cross of Saint Patrick: The Catholic Unionist Tradition in Ireland* (Kensal, 1984).

33 Graham Walker, 'Thomas Sinclair: Presbyterian liberal unionist', in Richard English and Graham Walker (eds), *Unionism in Modern Ireland* (Dublin, 1996), pp. 22–3.

34 Gailey, *Sayers*, pp. 115, 154.

35 Walker, 'Sinclair', p. 24. Of course, Sayers in an age of ecumenism viewed the Catholic

Church in an altogether different light; indeed, it was the Paisleyites and the Orange Order who posed the greatest threat to freedom of religious expression and who he denounced as 'Nazis' in 1966 (Gailey, *Sayers*, pp. 104, 119–20).

36 Walker, 'Sinclair', pp. 30–1; Gailey, *Sayers*, pp. 51–63, 82–6, 93, 124–9, 134.

37 Jonathon Bardon, *A History of Ulster* (Belfast, 1992), p. 622; Gailey, *Sayers*, p. 80.

38 Gailey, *Kindness*, p. 198.

39 Ibid., pp. 35, 56–7.

40 Trevor West, *Horace Plunkett, Co-operation and Politics* (Gerrards Cross, 1986), pp. 44–55. Andrew Gailey, 'Horace Plunkett and the politics of the non–political, 1892–1908', in John L. Pratschke (ed.), *Papers and Proceedings of the Society for Co-operative Studies in Ireland*, 1 (April 1985), pp. 41–64.

41 O'Neill, *Crossroads*, p. 56; Gailey, *Sayers*, pp. 46–7.

42 *Belfast Newsletter*, 30 November 1963.

43 Gailey, *Sayers*, pp. 101–2, 162. In the first eighteen months of his premiership O'Neill travelled 40,000 miles.

44 Gailey, *Kindness*, pp. 74–5; West, *Plunkett*, p. 93; O'Callaghan, *British High Politics*, p. 148. Even Yeats flattered Plunkett over dinner with the prospect of being the new Parnell (Foster, *Apprentice Mage*, pp. 179, 189).

45 Ed Moloney and Andy Pollak, *Paisley* (Dublin, 1986), p. 178.

46 Paul Bew, 'A Protestant parliament for a Protestant state: some reflections on government and minority in Ulster, 1921–43', in Art Cosgrove and J.I. McGuire (eds), *Parliament and Community* (Belfast, 1983), pp. 237–48; Dennis Kennedy, *The Widening Gulf: Northern Attitudes to the Independent Irish State* (Belfast, 1988).

47 David Harkness, *Northern Ireland since 1920* (Dublin, 1983), pp. 74–80; Patrick Buckland, *The Factory of Grievances* (Dublin, 1979), pp. 266–81.

48 Charles Townshend, 'Synergy and polarity in Ireland', in Charles Townshend (ed.), *Consensus in Ireland* (Oxford, 1988), p. 23; Paul Bew, Kenneth Darwin and Gordon Gillespie, *Passion and Prejudice: Nationalist–Unionist Conflict in the 1930s and the Origins of the Irish Association* (Belfast, 1993).

49 Gailey, *Sayers*, pp. 47–50. See also Jennifer Todd, 'Unionist political thought, 1920–72', in Boyce, Eccleshall and Geoghegan (eds), *Political Thought in Ireland*, pp. 190–206.

50 Tom Clyde, 'A stirring of the dry bones: John Hewitt's regionalism', in Gerald Dawe and John Wilson Foster (eds), *The Poet's Place* (Belfast, 1991), p. 255.

51 Gailey, *Sayers*, p. 90.

52 Jennifer Todd, 'Two traditions in unionist political culture', *Irish Political Studies*, 2 (1987), pp. 1–26. For a highly suggestive and Marxist interpretation of this dialogue see Paul Bew, Peter Gibbon and Henry Patterson, *The State in Northern Ireland 1921–72* (Manchester, 1979).

53 Andrew Gailey, 'Unionist rhetoric and Irish local government reform, 1895–99', *Irish Historical Studies*, 24, 93 (1994), pp. 52–68. On the financial relations controversy see Gailey, *Kindness*, pp. 100–14.

54 Gailey, 'Failure and the making of Ireland', pp. 67–8. The best resumé of the social impact of these policies is Frederick H. Aalen, 'Constructive unionism and the shaping of rural Ireland, c. 1880–1921', *Rural History*, 4, 2 (1993), pp. 137–64.

55 Maurice Hayes, 'Before the deluge', in Sophia Hillan King and Sean McMahon, *Hope and History: Eyewitness Accounts of Life in Twentieth Century Ulster* (Belfast, 1996), pp. 142–3; Sabine Wichert, *Northern Ireland since 1945* (London, 1991), pp. 86–9.

56 Mark Mulholland, 'Ulster at the crossroads: the 1969 election', paper delivered to the Irish History Seminar at Hertford College, Oxford, on 26 January 1999; Wichert, *Northern Ireland*, pp. 91–2, 100–6.

57 On this debate see Lyons, *Culture and Anarchy*, pp. 54, 57–84; Foster, 'Varieties of Irishness', 'Parnell and his People: the ascendancy and home rule' and 'Thinking from hand to mouth: Anglo-Irish literature, Gaelic nationalism and Irish politics in the 1890s', in *Paddy and Mr Punch*, pp. 21–39, 62–77 and 262–80; Paul Bew, *Conflict and*

Conciliation (Oxford, 1987) and *Ideology and the Irish Question: Ulster Unionism and Irish Nationalism, 1912–16* (Oxford, 1998).

58 Gailey, *Kindness*, p. 300.
59 Gailey, *Sayers*, p. 95.
60 West, *Plunkett*, pp. 112–13; Elizabeth, Countess of Fingall, *Seventy Years Young* (London, 1937).
61 Bew, Gibbon and Patterson, *The State in Northern Ireland*, pp. 194–5. Gailey, *Sayers*, p. 146.
62 Gailey, *Kindness*, p. 299.
63 Gailey, *Sayers*, p. 92.
64 For a summary of this critique see Feargal Cochrane, 'Meddling at the crossroads: the decline and fall of Terence O'Neill within the unionist community', in English and Walker (eds), *Unionism*, pp. 148–68. See also David Gordon, *The O'Neill Years: 1963–9* (Belfast, 1989).
65 Gailey, *Sayers*, pp. 84, 144; Bloomfield, *Stormont*.
66 *Belfast Telegraph*, 16 March 1966.
67 Gailey, *Sayers*, pp. 99–100, 110–11; Cochrane, 'Meddling', p. 156.
68 Gailey, *Kindness*, p. 221; Lyons, *Culture and Anarchy*, p. 73.
69 Gailey, *Kindness*, p. 301.
70 Gailey, *Sayers*, pp. 111, 144–5.
71 Bew, Darwin and Gillespie, *Passion and Prejudice*, p. 50.
72 Gailey, *Sayers*, p. 164. King and McMahon, *Hope and History*, p. 144.
73 Gailey, *Kindness*, p. 301.
74 Gailey, *Sayers*, p. 140.
75 Ibid., pp. 213–15.
76 Ibid., pp. 85–6, 126; see also on O'Neill's insensitivity towards the minority, p. 156.
77 Ibid., pp. 134, 142, 150–1.
78 Ibid., p. 142; Paul Arthur, *Political Realities: Government and Politics of Northern Ireland* (London, 1984 edn), p. 91.
79 *Hibernia*, 3 January 1969.
80 Earl of Dunraven, *Past Times and Pastimes* (London, 1922), II, p. 38.
81 David Burnett, 'The modernisation of unionism, 1892–1914?', in Walker and English (eds), *Unionism*, pp. 41–62. 'As if it had ever been anything else', wrote an irritated Dufferin and Ava after listening to Balfour insisting that Ireland must not be treated as a separate entity within the Union (Gailey, *Kindness*, p. 152).
82 Ibid., pp. 138–53.
83 Gailey, *Sayers*, pp. 29–36.
84 Gailey, *Kindness*, pp. 33, 57, 218–20, 305, 316–17.
85 Mulholland, 'Ulster at the Crossroads'; O'Neill, *Crossroads*, p. 27.
86 Gailey, *Sayers*, pp. 146–8; Eamonn McCann, *New Left Review*, 55 (May/June 1969), p. 6.
87 Gailey, *Sayers*, pp. 129–31.
88 Ibid.
89 But see Alan Finlayson, 'The problem of "culture" in Northern Ireland: a critique of the Cultural Traditions Group', *Irish Review*, 20 (Winter/Spring 1997), pp. 78–81.
90 Aughey and Morrow, *Northern Ireland Politics*, p. 184.
91 Todd, 'Two traditions in Unionist political culture', pp. 1–26; Patrick Buckland, 'The unity of Ulster unionism, 1886–1922', *History*, 60 (1975), pp. 211–23.
92 Gailey, *Kindness*, p. 56.
93 Ibid., chs 4, 6, 9; but see also Alvin Jackson, *The Ulster Party: Irish Unionists in the House of Commons, 1884–1911* (Oxford, 1989).
94 Gailey, *Sayers*, p. 160.
95 Duncan Morrow, 'Filling the gap: policy and pressure under direct rule', in Aughey and Morrow (eds), *Northern Ireland Politics*, p. 154.
96 Gailey, *Sayers*, pp. 99–100.
97 Steve Bruce, *God Save Ulster* (Oxford, 1986), pp. 91–6, 211–13. Aided and abetted by

techniques of political mass mobilisation that were unique to the twentieth century and were first espoused in Ulster by Sir Edward Carson, on whom Paisley consciously modelled himself. See Gailey, 'King Carson', p. 86.

98 Todd, 'Unionist political thought', pp. 190–206. Gailey, *Sayers*, pp. 23–4, 44–6, 75, 108–9, 147.

99 Peter Clarke, *Hope and Glory* (London, 1996); Arthur Marwick, *The Sixties* (Oxford, 1998).

100 Bruce, *God Save Ulster*, pp. 91–2.

101 Men of the calibre of John Cole, W.D. Flackes, Martin Wallace, Roy Lilley, Eric Waugh, Dennis Kennedy and Alf McCreary.

102 Bardon, *Ulster*, pp. 650–1, 655.

103 Gailey, *Sayers*, pp. 161–2.

104 Roy Greenslade to the author, 21 August 1998.

105 'BT9 is dead', *Fortnight*, February 1998, p. 5; Morrow, 'Common ground', pp. 56–64; Colin Coulter, 'Direct rule and the unionist middle classes', in English and Walker (eds), *Unionism*, pp. 169–87.

106 Cochrane, 'Meddling', p. 161.

107 Norman Porter, *Rethinking Unionism: An Alternative Vision for Northern Ireland* (Belfast, 1996), offers in 'civic unionism' one such response and is notable not only for its vigour and imagination but for the enthusiastic reaction it provoked. But see also Edna Longley's wide-ranging review of the issues in 'What do Protestants want?', *Irish Review*, 20 (Winter/Spring, 1997), esp. pp. 116–19: 'a future can only be built upon the "middle" ground so automatically and cynically sneered at'.

108 *Daily Telegraph*, 23 June 1998.

13 Loyalists since 1972

Gordon Gillespie

Introduction

By 1971, after more than two years of the 'Troubles', the Northern Ireland (NI) community was extremely polarised. Catholics continued to seek reforms within NI while the Irish Republican Army (IRA) campaign sought to undermine the province's position within the United Kingdom. The differences between the legitimate objectives pursued by nationalists, reform within Northern Ireland and the aim of a united Ireland by constitutional means, and the illegitimate use of violence and coercion through a republican terrorist campaign were often confused by loyalists hearing similar messages from nationalists and militant republicans alike. The loyalist sense of fear and isolation was further increased by statements from British sources which appeared to echo the nationalist argument that the island of Ireland (rather than Northern Ireland or the British Isles as unionists would see it) was the geographical area to be considered in any political debate.

The lack of confidence in the established authorities which was felt by both unionists and loyalists led to the emergence of new groups in several areas. On the political front the failure of the Ulster Unionist government to defeat the perceived nationalist attempt to undermine NI led first to the appearance of the Revd Ian Paisley's Democratic Unionist Party (DUP) in October 1971 and then to former NI Home Affairs Minister William Craig's Ulster Vanguard in February 1972. While Paisley's new party gained support from Protestant fundamentalists and urban working-class loyalists, Craig's pressure group represented both working-class and middle-class unionists who had become alienated from the Ulster Unionist Party (UUP). Initially Vanguard was perceived as the more radical group as a result of Craig's support for an independent NI, hardline statements and links with the paramilitary Ulster Defence Association (UDA) and Loyalist Association of Workers (LAW).[1] One measure of Vanguard's success was the organisation of a forty-eight hour industrial stoppage (held on 27 and 28 March 1972) in protest at the introduction of direct rule. The strike weapon was one which would continue to be used intermittently by loyalists throughout the Troubles with various degrees of success.

Throughout the rest of 1972 and early 1973 Vanguard remained within the

UUP, though its links with the UDA and LAW were a source of embarrassment to many in the mainstream of the party. Craig's 'conditional loyalty' to Britain was also something which did not sit well with many Ulster Unionists, although his views at this time may well have been more representative of most unionists, let alone loyalists, rather than those prepared to accept the will of Parliament under all circumstances. The problem of how the UUP should deal with Vanguard remained unresolved until March 1973 when Craig and some of his supporters broke with the Ulster Unionists over their refusal to reject the government White Paper (*Northern Ireland Constitutional Proposals*) and formed the Vanguard Unionist Progressive Party (Vanguard).

On the industrial front loyalist workers' groups began to emerge in the early phase of the Troubles with the intention of creating an alternative to the all-island ICTU. The first of these groups, established in September 1969, was the Workers' Committee for the Defence of the Constitution, which later developed into the much larger, UDA-linked, LAW.

The early 1970s also saw the creation of the UDA, which quickly became the largest of many loyalist paramilitary organisations. The abolition of the Ulster Special Constabulary (or B-Specials) in April 1970 had, many loyalists believed, created a gap in the province's defences against republicanism which the Ulster Defence Regiment (UDR), a locally based British Army regiment, had failed to fill. Intimidation and the (at least partial) collapse of law and order had created something of a 'security vacuum' which was filled by local vigilante groups. In September 1971 many of these local groups coalesced to form the Ulster Defence Association. As with any large organisation, the UDA contained many different factions and served a number of functions, from the more beneficial aspects of helping locals with social problems to the illegal acts of extortion, intimidation and sectarian murders – the latter often being claimed under the name of the Ulster Freedom Fighters (UFF). While the UDA arguably served a useful purpose in so far as it provided a sense of security for many working-class Protestants, as well as a medium to channel the frustrations of young working-class loyalists by manning local barricades and taking part in marches and demonstrations, such activities only further increased Catholic fears. Nor should the purely sectarian dimension of the paramilitary organisations be overlooked; for many such organisations provided a veneer of dubious respectability for those interested in 'getting at the Fenians'.[2] The smaller (an estimated 1,500 members in 1972) and more disparate Ulster Volunteer Force (UVF), which had been formed in 1966, continued to coexist with the UDA, at times co-operating with the larger organisation and at others becoming involved in internecine conflict. Somewhat paradoxically, while the UVF has often been perceived as more ruthless than the UDA, it has arguably also been more imaginative in its political thinking.[3]

Some of the paramilitaries' activities inevitably brought them into conflict with the security forces. One incident in July 1972 (later described as 'the UDA's finest hour') demonstrated many of the problems which the security forces have faced when strong loyalist opposition is supported by the wider Protestant community. On 27 June 1972 the IRA began a temporary ceasefire in the hope of drawing the

British government into talks that would lead to its withdrawal from NI. Coming only months after the abolition of Stormont, loyalists were naturally suspicious of the British government's intentions. Barricades began to be set up around loyalist areas as a reaction to Secretary of State Whitelaw's apparent indecisiveness over how to deal with the IRA, the emergence of nationalist 'no-go areas' in Derry and the continuation of sectarian killings on both sides. On 1 July the UDA set about building four permanent no-go areas, three in Belfast and one in Portadown. Two days later a crisis emerged when residents of Ainsworth Avenue, on the borderline between the (Protestant) Shankill and (Catholic) Springfield roads, approached members of the UDA and asked for a permanent barricade to be set up in nearby March Street, effectively creating a no-go area. The local army commander initially agreed that barricades could be put up to seal off the area except at specified junctions; however, when it was discovered that these barricades would also enclose approximately fifty Catholic families in the area the decision was overruled by Army Headquarters. On learning of the army's about face the UDA quickly assembled 8,000 men in battledress, armed with iron bars and clubs. The loyalist paramilitaries were faced by only 250 troops. General Robert Ford telephoned Whitelaw and warned him that if the UDA advanced on his soldiers they were likely to be overrun unless he had authority for the troops to fire. Whitelaw gave permission to open fire, but only as a last resort.[4] Discussions between Ford and the UDA leaders led to an agreement whereby there would be no permanent barricade but the army would carry out patrols and set up a checkpoint at the disputed area. Unarmed UDA men would be allowed to move unhindered behind this checkpoint. On the following day the *Belfast Telegraph* summed up the outcome:

> The trial of strength in the area between the Shankill and Springfield Roads last night is as near as the UDA has come to a pitched battle with the army. It was averted only at the cost of the generals admitting that a private paramilitary group has the right, through might, to mount patrols in a sealed-off enclave of a British city. Both sides may claim a 'victory' of sorts, with some justification, but in fact the losers are all those who value democratic rights.[5]

Whitelaw has subsequently portrayed the Ainsworth Avenue incident as a major success for the authorities but in this he ignores the fact that the security forces had neither the manpower nor the training to control the situation and could only threaten to escalate the conflict in order not to lose control to the loyalists.[6] Equally the government could not afford the political consequences of another Bloody Sunday. As events were to demonstrate over the next twenty-five years, the government was only successful in 'facing down' loyalists when they were prepared to use a massive security force and, crucially, also only in circumstances where unionists were not prepared to support loyalist demands.

In contrast to the March Street stand-off events of February 1973 showed that loyalists could be seriously embarrassed when they did not have at least the tacit support of most of the Protestant community. On 5 February, when it was announced that two men were to be held under the Detention of Terrorists

Order, loyalists called a general strike for 7 February. Although the strike brought much of Belfast industry to a standstill, it was also characterised by widespread violence – throughout the day 5 people were killed, 43 people received gunshot wounds, 35 fires were reported, 8 bombs exploded and 68 people were arrested.[7] The unionist condemnation which followed the February 1973 strike was a significant blow to loyalist prestige and the loss of face caused by subsequent apologies was a factor in speeding the demise of LAW (which was in any event riven with personality clashes and accusations of financial irregularities).

Developments, 1972–4

In the period following the introduction of direct rule the Conservative government sought to establish a new Northern Ireland administration based on a cross-community government allied with an Irish dimension. It was not until late November 1973, however, that a power-sharing executive was agreed by the Ulster Unionists, Alliance and the SDLP. While many unionists and some loyalists, despite deep misgivings, might have been prepared to accept nationalists in a NI administration, provision for an Irish dimension, in the form of a proposed Council of Ireland, was an entirely different matter.

In late October 1973 a group of loyalist workers and politicians met at Vanguard's East Belfast headquarters, ostensibly to discuss the ongoing IRA bombing campaign and the possible formation of a new loyalist workers' organisation. Loyalist shipyard worker Harry Murray was chosen as chairman of the new (as yet unnamed) body and attempted to mediate between the competing political and paramilitary groups which sought to control the nascent organisation. In the following weeks the small group of loyalist workers attempted (largely without success) to expand their membership across Northern Ireland. In the wake of the agreement to form a power-sharing executive and the subsequent Sunningdale Agreement of 9 December the group's objectives changed from security concerns to opposition to Sunningdale.[8] Other loyalist groups also began to coalesce – members of the UUP, DUP, Vanguard and members of the Orange Order launched the United Ulster Unionist Council (UUUC) on 6 December while loyalist paramilitaries formed an umbrella organisation, the Ulster Army Council, four days later.

By February the loyalist workers' group, now known as the Ulster Workers' Council (UWC), was intent on calling a strike but was dissuaded from this by Vanguard leader William Craig on the grounds that a general election would soon be announced and that this would provide the mandate required for any subsequent action against the Sunningdale Agreement. However, although the February 1974 general election returned one pro-Sunningdale and eleven anti-Sunningdale MPs from NI the new Labour government's policy was to persist with the Sunningdale package, despite its unpopularity among unionists. With loyalist politicians failing to make any headway in their protests at Westminster and Stormont, loyalist workers and paramilitaries began to contemplate a date for a strike. In early May, however, differences between the groups still remained, with some UDA members insisting that the rump of LAW, not the UWC, represented loyalist workers. The UWC and the UDA were also in disagreement over who would control the proposed strike. Many loyalist politicians were as yet uncertain as to the value of the strike and it was only with difficulty that Murray and fellow UWC member Billy Kelly were able to persuade them to lend even tacit support to the strike. On 14 May the assembly voted to continue to support the Sunningdale package, leading Harry Murray to announce a 'constitutional stoppage'.

The UWC strike was not a well-organised, precisely planned event; rather it consisted of the daily 'fire-fighting' of problems by strike leaders, the use of roadblocks, intimidation by paramilitaries and control of electricity distribution by loyalist workers in power-stations. It was also characterised by growing support among the unionist community at large, not because the waverers wanted to be on the 'winning side' (as nationalists and supporters of the Sunningdale package have argued), but rather because the strike began to appear to be a tool which could successfully bring about an end to the Sunningdale deal. Even the horrors of the Dublin and Monaghan bombs, through which thirty-three people were killed, appear to have had remarkably little impact on unionist support for the strike and its objectives.

The resignation of the Faulknerite unionists from the executive spelled the effective end of the Sunningdale deal so that the 'threat' of a united Ireland posed by the Council of Ireland receded and the strike was called off on 29 May. Significantly, many of the strike leaders viewed the stoppage as a political defeat since an Irish dimension remained government policy. The strike had, however, given some of the paramilitaries a taste for politics. In October 1973 the UVF had launched the Ulster Loyalist Front, which advocated labourite social policies, although the UVF's magazine welcomed the decision of the National Front to organise in the province, stating: 'We may not always agree with NF policy but we agree that there is room and need for a strong patriotic loyalist party to emerge in Northern Ireland'.[9] In May the UVF were given the opportunity to come in from the cold when they were deproscribed and in June the Volunteer Political Party (VPP) was set up. When VPP Chairman Ken Gibson contested West Belfast in the Westminster general election of October 1974, however, he received only 2,690 votes, compared to the DUP candidate's 16,265. In the wake of this defeat the VPP withdrew from electoral politics and instead became the UVF's 'political consultants'. Although it has been argued that loyalist politicians failed to win electoral support because of a 'dirty tricks' campaign which smeared them as communists, the fact that loyalists failed to make any significant impact (at least before the 1990s) arguably had more to do with a general unionist perception of them as thugs and criminals who might have a role to play in 'defending Ulster' but were not the material from which elected representatives were made.[10] The banning of the UVF in October 1975 following a series of murders merely confirmed the organisation's return to the political wilderness and it was not until 1979 that a new party associated with the UVF, the Progressive Unionist Party (PUP), was launched by Belfast councillor Hugh Smyth.

1976–9

For loyalist paramilitaries the late 1970s were mainly characterised by inter- and intra-paramilitary disputes and a number of high-profile convictions as the result of arrests by security forces.[11] By mid-1977 violence from Protestant sources had virtually disappeared.

Relations between paramilitaries and loyalist politicians were soured in 1975 when a majority of the UUUC rejected William Craig's NI Convention proposal for a temporary voluntary coalition which would include the SDLP, a proposal supported by (among others) the UDA's leading political thinker, Glen Barr, and another senior Vanguard member, law lecturer (and future UUP leader) David Trimble. Having split in two over the issue of voluntary coalition Vanguard ceased to function as a political party in November 1977. The abortive United Unionist Action Council strike of May 1977, led by Ian Paisley and supported by the UDA, but which lacked widespread unionist support, resulted in further recriminations between paramilitaries and politicians.

At the beginning of 1978 the UDA established its own think-tank, the New Ulster Political Research Group, which the following year proposed an independent Ulster but found little public support.

1979–84

The return of the Conservative Party to power under Margaret Thatcher in May 1979 had appeared to offer loyalists the hope of a government more sympathetic to unionist concerns. As events developed, however, such optimism seemed misplaced. In October 1980 republican prisoners launched a hunger strike on the issue of political status for prisoners – two months later this ended in confusion over exactly what had been agreed, thereby sowing the seeds for a future conflict.[12]

In early 1981 the security situation appeared to be deteriorating (the murder of the former Stormont Speaker, eighty-six year-old Norman Strong, and his son at their home being one notable IRA 'success'), bringing UDA leader Andy Tyrie to comment that loyalists might have to cross the border to 'terrorise terrorists'. At the same time Paisley launched a protest against closer British–Irish relations by signing a 'covenant' (based on the Ulster Covenant of 1912) at Belfast City Hall and undertaking a series of rallies on the 'Carson Trail'.[13]

Despite their decline in support, loyalist paramilitaries had not given up hope of gaining a niche in the political market for themselves, and in June 1981 the UDA launched the Ulster Loyalist Democratic Party (later the Ulster Democratic Party – UDP), chaired by John McMichael.

The wider political agenda was, however, to be set by republicans. On 1 March Bobby Sands, IRA leader in the Maze, launched a fresh hunger strike which would eventually lead to the deaths of ten republican prisoners. Sands's victory in the Fermanagh–South Tyrone by-election two months later was viewed by loyalists and unionists alike as demonstrating widespread Catholic support for the

IRA's campaign of terror. In the same month loyalist paramilitaries reactivated the Ulster Army Council. The degree of polarisation generated by the hunger strike was demonstrated in the outcome of the May 1981 district council elections when the DUP finished ahead of the UUP for the first and only time beyond the personalised system of European Parliament elections.[14]

The trend of events apparently continued to run against the loyalist and unionist cause when, in September 1981, the Labour Party Conference voted to campaign actively for a united Ireland 'by consent' – a term which certain Labour spokesmen increasingly sought to define in such a way as to render it meaningless. Although the republican hunger strike was called off in early October, tension remained high. On 14 November UUP MP the Revd Robert Bradford was murdered by the IRA and DUP MPs Paisley, Peter Robinson and John McQuade were subsequently suspended from Westminster after protests about lax security. Paisley also promoted the idea of an unofficial home guard-style 'third force' to protect Protestants and threatened that unionists would make NI ungovernable. On 23 November a loyalist 'Day of Action' in support of tougher security measures was marked by stoppages and rallies in Protestant areas. These events subsequently led to Paisley's US visa being withdrawn in December, partially, at least, at the behest of influential Irish-American politicians.

The improved relations between the British and Irish were temporarily damaged by disputes between the two governments over the Falklands War. This trend was reversed, however, after Sinn Féin, contesting their first NI elections, received almost 65,000 votes (10.1 per cent of the poll), in elections to a new NI assembly. The outcome brought near panic among the British establishment which blamed the promoter of the new assembly, Secretary of State James Prior, for enabling Sinn Féin to demonstrate its electoral support. The growing fear of the British, and even more of the recently elected Irish coalition government under Garret Fitzgerald, that Sinn Féin could replace the SDLP as the largest nationalist party in NI, led increasingly to a policy aimed at propping up the SDLP which culminated in the Anglo-Irish Agreement of 1985.[15]

The Anglo-Irish Agreement and its aftermath

It is difficult to convey the degree of shock, anger and sense of betrayal felt by unionists and loyalists which the Anglo-Irish Agreement prompted. From the loyalist perspective, Thatcher, who spoke of 'making Britain great again' and had fought a war to recapture the Falkland Islands, had sacrificed the Protestant community to make life easier for Little Englanders. The agreement promised peace and prosperity but the secretive manner in which it was negotiated (at least as far as unionists and loyalists were concerned), allied to the formalisation of a consultative role for the Irish Republic in Northern Ireland's affairs, ensured, almost from the outset, that these objectives would not be achieved, because the agreement would never be accepted by most Protestants. Equally importantly, the agreement again highlighted the dangers inherent in a situation where the Republic represented the interests of northern nationalists and republicans while the role of the British government was to be merely a neutral arbiter. It reaffirmed for many loyalists and unionists the belief that they would have to rely on their own efforts to defend themselves. It required only a small step for some of Ulster's 'defenders' to begin a campaign of sectarian murder against Catholics and in 1986 the number of loyalist paramilitary murders increased sharply.[16] On the wider political agenda, however, mainstream paramilitaries were generally prepared to follow the line taken by the UUP and DUP, with Andy Tyrie noting that the UDA would 'support anything the unionist leaders and politicians suggest'.[17]

With unionists unable to bring direct pressure to bear on those involved in the Anglo-Irish Agreement, loyalists instead attacked those elements which symbolised the agreement, including the Maryfield Secretariat outside Belfast in December 1985. Secretary of State Tom King also found himself unceremoniously dumped into a decorative flower pot outside Belfast City Hall by loyalist councillor George Seawright and was more circumspect about his public appearances thereafter. More seriously, there were attacks on the homes of more than 500 RUC members, with 150 families being forced to move.

While unionists and loyalists were united against the agreement they were divided in what action should be taken. Nowhere was this clearer than in the aftermath of a unionist 'Day of Action' held on 3 March 1986. The one-day stoppage brought NI to a halt but also saw rioting in loyalist areas of Belfast, with shots being fired at the RUC. The strike highlighted the differing extent to which unionists and loyalists were prepared to take their opposition. As the DUP's Peter Robinson noted:

> In 1986 with the Day of Action [UUP leader James] Molyneaux immediately came out and said, 'I want nothing more to do with it', because there were a few cars burned and a few windows broken. That showed that that section of the loyalist community wasn't coming with it again, so you have never really had another strike of the 1974 variety.[18]

Thus, while the UUP had second thoughts about the danger to life and property which such direct confrontation entailed, the DUP believed the risk worthwhile. In August 1986 Robinson and 500 loyalists 'invaded' the County Monaghan village of Clontibret, leading to two members of the Gardai being attacked and the area being daubed with anti-agreement slogans. One week later, when Robinson was remanded in Dundalk, Gardai seemed unwilling, or unable, to protect him and his supporters from stone and petrol-bomb attacks by republicans, thus reinforcing the view among unionists that the Irish government was hostile to all but submissive Protestants. In November of the same year, only days before a second near 200,000-strong anti-agreement rally in Belfast, Paisley launched Ulster Resistance, an organisation dedicated to the destruction of the agreement. In practice, however, the organisation probably had more to do with an attempt to constrain loyalists from more extreme action.

Ulster Resistance was not the only new, somewhat shadowy, organisation to oppose the agreement. In the autumn of 1985 the Ulster Clubs had emerged in

Portadown from groups opposing the rerouting of local Orange marches and which had adopted a wider political agenda aimed at attaining unionist unity and opposing the encroachment of Irish nationalism. The organisation highlighted the link between Protestant faith and unionist politics, with the Clubs' leader Alan Wright, a member of the Salvation Army, stating: 'at the end of the day my politics are not divisible from my faith. It's Protestantism versus Rome'.[19]

If the Ulster Clubs were largely content to restrict their activities to civil disobedience and street protests, the same could not be said of Ulster Resistance, which, although retaining links with individual DUP members, became disenchanted with the DUP as the party began to move towards dialogue with the government. By the late 1980s the organisation appeared to be attempting to acquire weapons and in April 1989 one of its founding members was arrested in Paris along with two other men following an attempt to secure weapons from South Africa.

One other enduring legacy of the anti-agreement campaign was the increased alienation of loyalists from the RUC, accelerated by the death of Keith White during rioting in March 1986, the first Protestant to be killed by a plastic baton round.

An attempt to break the political impasse which characterised the post-agreement months emerged from an unusual source. In January 1987 the New Ulster Political Research Group published *Common Sense*, a document calling for a devolved NI government based on consensus and shared responsibility, a written constitution and a bill of rights. The report was generally well received as a well-intentioned attempt to break the political deadlock but was attacked by the DUP on the grounds that it attempted to recreate a power-sharing executive similar to that which the UDA had helped destroy in 1974. In response one of the report's authors, John McMichael, reminded Paisley,

> the principal objection to that treaty [Sunningdale] was because of the Council of Ireland clause which allowed the Government of Éire a formal role in the affairs of Northern Ireland. As to the power-sharing executive, it was undemocratically structured and appointed and did not have the consent of a broad enough section of the community.[20]

Somewhat belatedly in July 1987 a joint UUP/DUP task force issued a report highly critical of the effectiveness of unionist opposition to the agreement and suggested that discussions be opened with the government; however, this was effectively buried by the respective party leaders.

The Anglo-Irish Agreement had a number of consequences: loyalists were again dangerously alienated from the government, unionist political leadership was perceived to have failed and the 'horror' of a united Ireland was believed to have been brought closer. The reaction also followed a similar pattern to earlier political shocks to the system. Loyalist paramilitary murders increased but so too did the realisation that if working-class Protestants wanted something done, whether socially or politically, they would have to do it themselves.

At approximately the same time a major shake-out in the membership of the UDA's Inner Council also left the organisation's future direction unclear.[21] By the early 1990s, however, it was evident that the new generation of loyalist paramilitary leaders was, if anything, even more ruthless than its predecessor. It has been estimated that at least eighteen people with Sinn Féin connections were murdered by loyalist paramilitaries in the five years up to August 1993.[22]

1988–94

In January 1988 John Hume began discussions with Sinn Féin leader Gerry Adams as part of the 'Irish Peace Process'. While Hume's aim was to move Sinn Féin towards full acceptance of constitutional politics and thereby end the IRA's 'long war', joint statements issued with Adams as part of this policy convinced most Protestants, and loyalists in particular, that the SDLP was becoming party to a 'pan-nationalist front'. Attempts by the British government to bring republicans in from the cold, notably Secretary of State Peter Brooke's November 1990 statement that Britain had no 'strategic or economic interest' in NI, also increased loyalists' sense of insecurity.

In the meantime the issue of collusion between loyalist paramilitaries and the security forces re-emerged in August 1989 after the UFF handed leaked security documents to a BBC reporter and claimed the army, UDR and RUC all provided them with information. The subsequent inquiry by senior English police officer John Stevens into the theft and leaking of intelligence documents led to the revelation that UDA 'intelligence officer' Brian Nelson, who had been arrested at the request of the Stevens Inquiry, had been working for army intelligence. During the course of the inquiry fifty-eight people were charged or had their files sent to the Department of Public Prosecutions. The accused included ten UDR members, twenty-six UDA men and six members of the UVF.[23] In May a summary of the Stevens Report concluded that although information had been leaked to loyalists by elements within the security forces the problem was restricted to a small number of individuals and was neither widespread nor institutionalised. Nevertheless, the disruption to the paramilitaries which the inquiry caused helped accelerate the change in UDA leadership.

There were, however, indications that loyalist paramilitaries were becoming more politically astute. In April 1991 a joint statement from the UDA, UVF and Red Hand Commando announced a ceasefire under the name of the Combined Loyalist Military Command (CLMC), aimed at aiding progress in the political talks organised by Peter Brooke. While the CLMC called off its ceasefire after the talks broke down in early July, the paramilitaries stated their willingness to call another ceasefire if talks resumed. The parties linked to the paramilitaries, the PUP and UDP, also began to cultivate the support of the loyalist grass-roots more seriously.

At the same time, however, attacks on the 'pan-nationalist front' continued with a number of indiscriminate attacks on Catholics. By the end of 1991 the UVF had killed nineteen people and UDA and UFF fifteen. The same pattern was repeated in the following year. In February 1992 the UFF murdered five Catholics at a bookmaker's shop on Belfast's Ormeau Road in retaliation for the IRA's murder of seven Protestant workers at Teebane crossroads the previous month. This led to an increase in antagonism between Orange marchers and nationalist demonstrators in the same area in July and helped lead to the creation of local nationalist 'concerned citizens' groups campaigning against Orange marches passing through nationalist areas.

Another result of the upsurge in loyalist killing was the banning of the UDA in August 1992 although the timing of the ban arguably had more to do with appeasing nationalist politicians than addressing security concerns. In practical terms the ban had little immediate impact, with the UDA's headquarters in East and West Belfast becoming the Ulster Information Service and Loyalist Prisoners' Association offices, respectively.

During 1993 loyalist fears were heightened by a continuing IRA campaign (including leaving car bombs in the centre of predominantly Protestant towns) while at the same time Sinn Féin claimed to be promoting 'a meaningful peace process'. In June it emerged that a 1992 Labour Party discussion document had suggested that local parties be given six months to agree a form of devolved administration and that if the parties failed to reach agreement the British and Irish governments would then begin talks aimed at bringing about joint British–Irish authority over the north. On 8 July Irish Foreign Minister Dick Spring told the *Guardian* that if there was not clear evidence that NI inter-party talks would restart soon then the British and Irish governments should negotiate a framework agreement for NI without any input from local parties. The resulting agreement would be put to a referendum in both NI and the Republic.

Convinced that they were facing a united pan-nationalist front, and with no support from the British government, loyalist attacks on Catholics of all shades of opinion escalated. This led to an absurd state of affairs in August when the UVF-linked Red Hand Commando threatened to attack bars or hotels holding Irish folk nights because the music was part of the pan-nationalist front.

For most loyalists the true face of this pan-nationalist front became evident in October when the IRA murdered nine civilians in a bomb attack on the Protestant Shankill Road.[24] Loyalists retaliated by proving they could be just as ruthless as republicans. On 30 October two UFF gunmen entered the Rising Sun bar in Greysteel, County Londonderry and fired randomly at customers celebrating Hallowe'en. The UFF, claiming it had attacked the 'nationalist electorate' in revenge for the Shankill bombing, killed seven people and wounded a further thirteen. With twenty-seven people dead in October alone the prospects for a peaceful political settlement did not seem bright.

Relations between unionists and the government sank even lower in late November when it emerged that the government, despite categorical denials, had been conducting secret negotiations with Sinn Féin for several years. On 22 November the CLMC confirmed that their representatives had also met government officials twice since the summer, stated that they were earnestly seeking peace, but also warned that they were preparing for war if peace was 'bought at any price'.[25]

The Downing Street Declaration of December 1993 created the framework for the political settlement which was to follow five years later. For loyalists, the crucial elements of the declaration were the recognition by the Irish government that a united Ireland could only be achieved 'on the basis of consent, freely and concurrently given, North and South' (Downing Street Declaration, para. 4). The Irish government also accepted 'that the democratic right of self-determination by the people of Ireland as a whole must be achieved and exercised with and subject to the agreement and consent of a majority of the people of Northern Ireland' (para. 5) while the Taoiseach stated that, in the event of an overall settlement, the Irish government would support proposals for change in the Irish constitution which would reflect this principle of consent (para. 7).

Although the document was rejected by the DUP, the UVF stated that it did not feel threatened by the declaration and that it would not support another 'publicity stunt' by Ian Paisley. The UFF was less positive, however, stating that, 'despite its grand claims regarding consent freely given, [it] is part of a wider agenda and once again ignores the reality that the status of Northern Ireland within the United Kingdom was dramatically changed with the imposition of the Anglo-Irish diktat'.[26]

On 15 June, in reply to a series of queries about the declaration posed by UDP leader Gary McMichael (son of John McMichael), Taoiseach Albert Reynolds stated: 'The Irish Government have a strong moral duty towards the Nationalist community in Northern Ireland, because of experience in the past, to ensure that the principles of equal citizenship, equality of treatment and parity of esteem are translated into practice'.[27] In taking this position Reynolds wasted an opportunity to move away from the traditional narrow defence of nationalist interests towards the more balanced approach (one increasingly adopted by the Fine Gael opposition) that it was the moral duty of the Irish government to protect the interests of all of the people of Ireland, irrespective of political outlook.

Political developments did not, however, stop paramilitary activity. Nevertheless, despite atrocities such as the UVF's murder of six men at The Heights bar in Loughinsland in June and ongoing IRA activity, there were continuing rumours that an IRA ceasefire was imminent. This led the CLMC to state, on 14 July, that if the IRA ended its campaign it would respond in order to allow 'magnanimous dialogue'.

In the event the IRA ceasefire announcement of 31 August was greeted with scepticism and caution by loyalists. The CLMC called on UUP leader Molyneaux and Paisley to meet John Major in order to find out 'if the constitution is being tampered with' and 'what deals have been done'. However, although there was no let up in the loyalist campaign, paramilitaries appeared to be slowly edging towards their own ceasefire. Early in September the CLMC set out a list of issues on which it required assurances before it was prepared to call a ceasefire. These included: an assurance that no secret deals had been done between the government and the IRA; that the constitutional position of NI within the UK was assured; and that there would be no 'change' or 'erosion' within NI 'to facilitate the illusion of an IRA victory'. The statement added: 'change, if any, can only be honourable after dialogue and agreement'.

On 10 October loyalist leaders were given permission to enter the Maze prison by the Northern Ireland Office to discuss a ceasefire with loyalist prisoners. Three days later, on 13 October, a statement from the CLMC, read by former UVF leader Gusty Spence, announced that as a result of assurances on the position of NI within the UK that they were declaring a ceasefire. The announcement continued by stating that its permanence would depend on a continued cessation of republican violence. It offered an apology to innocent victims and concluded by stating: 'Let us firmly resolve to respect our differing views of freedom, culture and aspiration and never again permit our political circumstances to degenerate into bloody warfare'. One of the most telling sentences of the CLMC announcement was, however, the statement that 'The Union is safe'.

1994–8: new opportunities – old problems

With the declaration of the CLMC ceasefire the UDP and PUP could at last begin to argue realistically that they were more than people 'with an insight into the thinking' of various paramilitary groups. In this quest for political acceptability they were helped by the ongoing, if slow, decline of the DUP's electoral support. The new breed of loyalist politician also spoke a new language. Where Paisley's fire and brimstone voice of 'Old Testament' loyalism consigned nationalism and republicanism to damnation, the disciples of new-style loyalism spoke of inclusivity and the legitimacy of the pursuit of the nationalist agenda by democratic means.

Emerging from the shadow of the gunman, however, proved more difficult for the loyalist parties than they might have envisaged. They were faced with the problem of maintaining their core support while attempting to win over a wider unionist community sceptical of their 'criminal' connections, while also voicing their support for loyalist prisoners and, in some cases at least, justifying their retention of weapons. While attempting to anchor the paramilitaries to democratic methods, breaches of the CLMC ceasefire meant that, at times, loyalist politicians appeared to apologise for violence.

Improving relations between the British and Irish governments and loyalists received a temporary setback in February 1995 when the Frameworks Documents were published. These were rejected by unionists and loyalists alike because of the documents' nationalist rubric and perceived lack of political balance.

Another old problem, republican opposition to Orange marches, was also re-emerging with a vengeance. The rerouting of an Apprentice Boys march away from Belfast's lower Ormeau Road in April 1995 reinforced loyalist and unionist fears that their interests were being sacrificed in order to appease republicans. The view that the Lower Ormeau Concerned Citizens (LOCC) group which organised the anti-Orange, and supposedly local, protest was anything other than a Sinn Féin front was given little credence by loyalists.[28]

With this attitude prevalent among unionists at large the events of Drumcree in July 1995 were highly predictable. On 9 July the RUC and Orange marchers became involved in a stand-off (later referred to as the 'siege of Drumcree') after police prevented Orangemen from marching along the nationalist Garvaghy Road in Portadown on their return from a church service. Orangemen, who claimed they would have been prevented from marching along the road for the first time in nearly 200 years, refused to accept the decision. As the stand-off continued rioting escalated in loyalist areas across NI. On 11 July, following mediation between the police and Orangemen by Paisley, UUP MP Trimble and others, a compromise was reached between the two sides and 500 Orangemen marched along the road (despite protests from local nationalists) but without any loyalist bands. Rather than providing a resolution to the marching issue, however, Drumcree merely set the stage for future confrontations.

On the wider scene political progress had reached stalemate over the issue of the decommissioning of paramilitary weapons. The CLMC made a significant contribution to this debate on 25 August by stating that, provided the rights of the people of NI were upheld they would, 'not initiate a return to war. There will be no first strike'. A week later Gary McMichael added that loyalists were ready to decommission their arms if the IRA would do the same. Despite this, tensions within loyalism about the direction the peace process was taking remained. Paramilitary punishment attacks and the acquisition of weapons continued, while pressures within the prisons also led to loyalist attacks on the homes of prison officers.

Loyalists had also become disenchanted with the attitude of the Irish government, believing, as a senior loyalist told the *Belfast Telegraph* on 15 August, 'Dublin must stop dancing to Sinn Féin's tune'. The political process did, however, continue to make slow progress with a 'twin-track' policy of talks and an International Body to examine the issue of decommissioning being agreed by the British and Irish governments in late November.

Early in 1996 the peace process once again became bogged down over the issue of decommissioning. The report of the International Body (the Mitchell Report), published on 24 January, set out a list of principles on non-violence for those involved in political talks and proposed decommissioning during talks rather than before or after. Prime Minister Major backed the report's proposals but then created a wave of nationalist antagonism by supporting the (mainly unionist) suggestion of elections to provide a democratic mandate to all-party talks. This new 'precondition', allied to Sinn Féin's refusal to sign up to the report of the Dublin-based Forum for Peace and Reconciliation (because it included a clause stating that the consent of a majority in NI was required for any new political agreement), helped precipitate the breakdown of the IRA ceasefire on 9 February.[29]

In the following months the CLMC ceasefire came under pressure from a resumed IRA campaign but, although fractured, it did not break down completely. This continued to be the case even after the CLMC was declared 'inoperative' in May as a result of internal loyalist disputes. On 30 May the PUP and UDP made their first major foray into electoral politics by contesting the election for all-party negotiations. Though receiving only 3.5 and 2.2 per cent of the vote, respectively, the unique system of election, in which the ten most successful parties were guaranteed representation at the talks, saw the loyalist parties involved in negotiations in June.

The summer months were again dominated by confrontation between Orange marchers and republicans centred primarily on another Drumcree stand-off but further complicated by the boycotting of Protestant businesses by nationalists in certain areas. The extent of government concern that the loyalist ceasefire was on the verge of total collapse was demonstrated on 22 July when Major met PUP and UDP representatives for talks at Downing Street.

Another worrying development was the increasingly independent and sectarian line taken by the Mid-Ulster UVF led by Billy Wright which murdered a Catholic taxi-driver outside Lurgan on 8 July. On 2 August the UVF announced that the Portadown unit of the Mid-Ulster Brigade was to disband, but within days reports suggested that some of its members were joining a new organisation.

On 28 August the CLMC ordered the expulsion of Portadown loyalists Billy Wright and Alex Kerr from NI and warned of 'summary justice' if either man failed to comply with their 'directive'. Wright defied the threat. On 4 September a 2,000-strong Portadown rally in his support was addressed by the Revd William McCrea, DUP MP for Mid-Ulster, who condemned the death threat and said he was there in support of freedom of expression.[30] He added that the only charge levelled against Wright was that he disagreed politically with the PUP.[31]

The growing antagonism between the DUP and Robert McCartney's UK Unionists on one side and loyalists on the other was illustrated by the former's unsuccessful attempt to have the PUP and UDP ejected from the talks for breaching the Mitchell principles on non-violence in light of the CLMC threats against Wright and Kerr.[32] The antagonism between the two sides continued throughout the year and late November saw the appearance in loyalist areas of graffiti attacking Paisley and McCartney.[33]

With community relations already tense, at the end of September UFF and UDA prisoners in the Maze announced they were withdrawing their active support of the peace process because of IRA activity and 'politicians' inactivity'. On 7 October, while PUP representatives met UVF prisoners in the Maze to discuss the peace process, two IRA bombs exploded at Thiepval Army Barracks, Lisburn. Thirty people were injured, one seriously, in the first IRA bombing in NI since August 1994. When loyalist leaders met to assess the situation the following day the ceasefire was again close to collapse. However, the meeting adjourned without a final decision being taken. In the event it was widely believed that only the fact that the soldier badly injured in the attack, James Bradwell, did not die until 11 October prevented the ending of the loyalist ceasefire at that time.

Antagonism over the halting and rerouting of Orange marches continued, however, with a group calling itself the Ballymena Loyalist Residents' Association stating it would continue to blockade a Catholic church at Harryville while Orangemen were prevented from marching in nearby Dunloy by republicans.

Against this background loyalists were again fearful of the efforts of a seem-ingly united pan-nationalist front to bring about another IRA ceasefire, no matter what the cost. The situation was summed up by loyalist prisoner Michael Stone, who claimed that circumstances changed dramatically when the IRA resumed its bombing campaign, combined with republicans organising opposition to Orange parades:

> Sinn Féin was plainly agitating over the parades, trying to erode our political identity. The provocation of bombings and the loss of life, their campaign to destroy our political and cultural identity as Ulster loyalists . . . these were the major factors in our decision to withdraw our active support [for the peace process].[34]

The year ended with the UFF planting a booby-trap bomb under the car of a leading Belfast republican and the CLMC, which had apparently not sanctioned any paramilitary activity, in disarray.

Loyalist fears of the pan-nationalist front were eased somewhat in February 1997 when John Hume warned Sinn Féin that without an IRA ceasefire he would 'look elsewhere' for political progress. In the following month, however, it was clear that not all loyalists were convinced that the peace process was moving in the right direction with the Portadown-centred, and Billy Wright-led, Loyalist Volun-teer Force (LVF) later committing a series of sectarian murders. The UFF also murdered a Catholic man, but refused to admit responsibility. While loyalist par-ties participated in the talks process the list of unclaimed attacks committed by loyalist paramilitaries nominally maintaining a ceasefire grew, leading to a policy widely described as 'no claim: no blame'. The intention of the paramilitaries committing such attacks was undoubtedly to provide the loyalist parties with a degree of plausible deniability, thus allowing them to continue in the talks process. Tensions within loyalism also continued. In June Robert Bates, a former member of the Shankill Butchers gang, was murdered (allegedly in revenge for his involvement in the killing of a UDA man in 1977) while, in August, a Portadown bar said to be frequented by LVF members was smashed up by a gang of men believed to be from the UVF.

The district council elections of May 1997 gave the loyalist parties some cause for optimism: the PUP, with 2.2 per cent of first-preference votes, won six council seats, while the UDP with 1 per cent won four. The political situation had, how-ever, already been transformed by the arrival of a new Labour administration backed by the political authority of a massive majority at Westminster and deter-mined to drive the search for political agreement forward.[35] In July the peace process began to make progress once again when the IRA renewed its ceasefire, opening the way for Sinn Féin to participate in all-party talks in September. The talks quickly demonstrated something of the realignment in unionist politics with the UUP and loyalist parties prepared to test the commitment of republicans to the peace process in negotiations, while the DUP and UK Unionists refused to become involved in discussions with Sinn Féin on the principle that the republicans could not be committed to democratic methods while the IRA retained its weapons.

For the loyalist parties many difficulties remained, however, not least the final collapse of the CLMC as a result of internal loyalist disputes in October. The desire of the British and Irish governments to make progress on the political front also led loyalists to believe that the government was giving undue prominence to republican concerns and on 23 December UDA and UFF prisoners again stated that they believed the government was working to a republican agenda.

The murder of LVF leader Wright (who had been jailed in March) in the Maze prison by INLA prisoners in late December again revolutionised the situation and led to a wave of sectarian murders by loyalists in retaliation. The peace process staggered into 1998 against a background of loyalist and republican murders, leading to the UDP being temporarily expelled from the all-party talks in January and Sinn Féin similarly excluded in February. By April the talks were heading towards their deadline and, although on the brink of collapse on several occasions, an agreement was concluded on Good Friday, 10 April. Even so, confrontations between DUP and PUP supporters at Stormont in the hours leading up to the agreement again highlighted divisions within loyalism over the merits of the peace process.[36]

Loyalists and unionists once more found themselves divided on the merits of the Belfast Agreement with the DUP, UK Unionists, the Orange Order and a significant section of the UUP opposed to the deal. Unlike 1974, however, on this occasion the majority of loyalists linked to paramilitary groups supported the agreement. It was fitting, therefore, that on 14 May, the anniversary of the UWC strike, the UDA leader in the Maze should tell the BBC that as far as he was concerned, 'the war is over'. On the following day the LVF, though opposed to the Belfast Agreement, also announced a ceasefire.

With the endorsement of the agreement in a referendum the process of bringing its terms into effect began. The UVF and UDA quickly appointed contacts between their organisations and the arms-decommissioning body, and prepared to contest elections to the new NI assembly.[37] Despite optimism on the part of the UDP and the PUP,[38] however, only two PUP candidates were elected and it is arguable that this was largely due to personal votes for Billy Hutchinson and David Ervine rather than support for their party. In the event the PUP received 20,634 votes (2.6 per cent) and the UDP 8,651 (1.1 per cent). The result also highlighted the fact that almost as many unionists and loyalists opposed to the Agreement were returned to the assembly as those in favour.

Although a political package had been agreed by most of the parties and validated by a referendum, stability had not yet been established on the ground. In July a wave of arson attacks on Catholic churches was attributed to the LVF and the decision by the NI Parades Commission to ban the Garvaghy Road march led to further recriminations, rioting and the deaths of three young Catholic brothers as the result of an arson attack on their home in Ballymoney. Although loyalist tempers continued to simmer over the ban on the Portadown march and ongoing attacks by republican dissident groups, the LVF announced on 8 August that their 'war' was over. The decision was widely seen as an attempt by the organisation to have their prisoners included in the scheme for early releases which resulted from the agreement. A week later the political scene was again turned upside down when a 'Real IRA' bomb in Omagh left twenty-nine (predominantly women and children) dead and many more seriously injured. The revulsion created by the Omagh atrocity, for a time at least, isolated the remaining 'men of violence' outside the peace process from any public support and swiftly led to further ceasefire declarations.

By the autumn of 1998 the horror of the Omagh bombing had helped enhance a general mood in favour of peace, even if not necessarily in favour of the Belfast Agreement. For loyalists, however, a number of difficulties remained to be addressed. The issue of the acceptance by nationalists of Orange marches as a part of loyalist culture still had, to say the least, some way to go. Loyalists also required reassurance over fears of discrimination against Protestants in job appointments and the marginalisation of British culture.

Where the loyalist parties were concerned, the issues of prisoner releases, continuing punishment attacks and the retention of paramilitary weapons were likely to restrict growth in support from the wider unionist community for some time. The emergence of new loyalist paramilitary groups such as the Red Hand Defenders and Orange Volunteers, their attacks on Catholic homes and businesses and their relationship with groups supposedly on ceasefire also posed questions about the 'modernisation' of loyalism. On the key constitutional issue, however, most loyalists seemed content to believe that the Union was indeed safe. This was not the result of any new statement which had been made by the British government. At the very beginning of the Troubles the (now almost forgotten) Downing Street Declaration of August 1969 had stated that: 'Northern Ireland should not cease to be part of the United Kingdom without the consent of the people of Northern Ireland'. The difference now was that nationalists had also accepted that position and loyalists could, at last, put some faith in their words.

NOTES

1 On 18 March 1972 Craig told a 60,000-strong loyalist rally at Belfast's Ormeau Park: 'if and when the politicians fail us, it may be our job to liquidate the enemy'.
2 See Sarah Nelson's excellent, *Ulster's Uncertain Defenders* (Belfast, 1984) for a detailed account of the development of the UDA in this period.
3 See David Boulton, *The UVF 1966–73: An Anatomy of Loyalist Rebellion* (Dublin, 1973); Roy Garland, *Seeking a Political Accommodation: The Ulster Volunteer Force Negotiating History* (Belfast, 1997); Jim Cusack and Henry McDonald, *UVF* (Dublin, 1997).
4 William Whitelaw, *The Whitelaw Memoirs* (London, 1989), p. 97.
5 *Belfast Telegraph*, 4 July 1974.
6 Whitelaw, *Memoirs*, pp. 97–8.
7 Paul Bew and Gordon Gillespie, *Northern Ireland: A Chronology of the Troubles 1968–1993* (Dublin, 1993), pp. 58–9.
8 Gordon Gillespie, 'Loyalist politics and the Ulster Workers' Council strike of 1974', Ph.D. thesis, the Queen's University of Belfast, 1994.

9 *Combat*, 5 April 1974.

10 Garland, *Political Accommodation*, p. 34.

11 In March 1977 twenty-six members of the UVF were jailed for a total of more than 700 years while, three months later, a further nine UVF members were sentenced to more than 100 years.

12 In December 1980 six UDA prisoners also held a five-day hunger strike demanding segregation from republicans and at the end of the month a prison officer was murdered by the 'Loyalist Prisoners' Action Force'.

13 In February 1981 Paisley led 500 men up a hill at night in County Antrim where they waved firearms certificates. Paisley subsequently was derided by some loyalists as 'the Grand Old Duke of York' for leading his men to the top of the hill and back down again.

14 The election was held just over two weeks after the death of Sands and a week after the death of another republican hunger striker, Francis Hughes. On the eve of the by-election five soldiers were killed by an IRA landmine in County Armagh.

15 The IRA's near 'success' in the attempt to murder the British cabinet by bombing the Grand Hotel, Brighton, in October 1984 also brought a fresh impetus to improve Anglo-Irish relations on security grounds.

16 Loyalist paramilitaries murdered 14 people in 1986, 11 in 1987, 22 in 1988 and 18 and 19 in the following two years (W.D. Flackes and Sydney Elliott *Northern Ireland: A Political Directory, 1968–1988* (Belfast, 1988), p. 469). In 1991 the figure doubled to 40, with 39 and 48 being murdered by loyalists in 1992 and 1993, respectively.

17 Arthur Aughey, *Under Siege: Ulster Unionism and the Anglo-Irish Agreement* (Belfast, 1989), p. 74.

18 Interview with the author, 9 March 1990.

19 Quoted in Steve Bruce, *The Edge of the Union: The Ulster Loyalist Political Vision* (Oxford, 1994), p. 25.

20 *News-Letter*, 25 May 1987.

21 Five of the UDA's eight-man Inner Council were replaced between December 1987, when McMichael was murdered by the IRA, and October 1988 (David McKitterick, *Dispatches from Belfast* (Belfast, 1989), p. 173). In October 1988 leading UDA member Jim Craig was murdered by loyalists because of his alleged involvement in racketeering and collusion in the death of McMichael. Information provided to the police by the informer Brian Nelson or discovered by the Stevens Inquiry was also damaging to the UDA. In 1991 Tommy Lyttle was sentenced to seven years' imprisonment for possession of files which could be used for terrorist purposes.

22 McKitterick, *Dispatches*, p. 261.

23 Bew and Gillespie, *Chronology*, p. 234. In March 1993 six former UDR members were awarded damages as a result of wrongful arrests arising from the Stevens Inquiry.

24 The IRA claimed the bomb was intended to kill members of the UFF who, they said, were meeting in a room in the former UDA office situated above the shop.

25 The fact that the UVF at least was still preparing for war was demonstrated by the unsuccessful attempt to smuggle a major arms shipment from Poland in November 1993.

26 Paul Bew and Gordon Gillespie, *The Northern Ireland Peace Process 1993–1996* (London, 1996), p. 40.

27 *Belfast Telegraph*, 24 June 1994.

28 The view that the LOCC and other such groups were being strongly influenced by Sinn Féin was reinforced on 4 March 1997 when RTE's *Prime Time* programme quoted Adams as telling SF members at Athboy:

ask any activist in the North did Drumcree happen by accident and they will tell you 'no' . . . three years of work on the lower Ormeau Road, Portadown, and parts of

Fermanagh and Newry, Armagh and Belleghy and up in Derry . . . . Three years' work went into creating that situation, and fair play to those people who put the work in

(*Irish Times*, 5 March 1997).

29 Nationalists and republicans seemed convinced that the Conservative government's perilous majority led them to follow an exclusively unionist agenda. Thus, when Major announced an election to all-party talks on 24 January 1995, Hume said the government was attempting 'to buy votes to keep themselves in power'. A similar accusation was made in the IRA statement announcing the end of their ceasefire in February 1996. This statement claimed that 'selfish party political and sectional interests in the London parliament have been placed before the rights of the people of Ireland'.

30 Wright demonstrated the divergent regional opinion of loyalists towards the peace process by telling the rally their turnout would 'show these people in Belfast that they cannot dictate to dear old Portadown'.

31 *Irish Times*, 5 September 1996.

32 The DUP and UK Unionists made another unsuccessful attempt to have the loyalist parties expelled in January 1997.

33 Graffiti on a number of walls carried a message (erroneously referring both to the 1914 UVF gunrunning and Paisley's 'Carson Trail') which noted: 'Carson 1912: Clydevalley. Paisley 1996: "Hand in Guns". Some Carson'.

34 *Belfast Telegraph*, 30 November 1996.

35 The PUP, contesting three constituencies in the general election, received 10,928 votes.

36 At 11 p.m. on the night of 9 April nearly 150 DUP protesters (who had earlier heckled Trimble outside UUP headquarters) entered the grounds of Parliament Buildings at Stormont. At a DUP press conference at Castle Buildings one hour later Paisley and other party leaders were harangued by PUP supporters, one of whom was pulled from the scene by PUP spokesman David Ervine.

37 Ervine believed that the PUP were capable of winning 4 of the 108 seats. Interview with the author, 20 April 1998.

38 The NI Assembly elections returned 18 UUP, 24 SDLP, 20 DUP, 18 SF, 6 Alliance, 5 UKU, 2 Women's Coalition, 2 PUP and 3 anti-agreement unionists. The shredding of the unionist bloc vote led to the UUP's lowest-ever share of the vote (172,225, 21.3%) while the DUP received 145,917 (18%), UK Unionists, 36,541 (4.5%), PUP, 20,634 (2.6%) and UDP, 8,651 (1.1%). Overall thirty pro-agreement unionists and loyalists were returned and twenty-eight anti-agreement.

14 Bigots in bowler hats?

The presentation and reception of the loyalist case in Great Britain

Alan Parkinson

Introduction

Walter Ellis, a Protestant Ulsterman, bared his soul in a mid-1990s *Sunday Times* article. In this, Ellis maintained:

> In Northern Ireland the Protestants proudly proclaim their loyalty to England and the Crown, and are regarded as vulgar aliens. The Catholics, who have, after all, bred the IRA and vote regularly for secession from Britain, are, by contrast, seen as loveable rascals, no less a part of the nation than the Scots or the Welsh – and better company. The Prods are used to being shunned. Nobody likes us. We are regarded for the most part as bloody-minded scum, lost down one of history's blind alleys. The English are not touched by our devotion. Rather, they think we ourselves are 'touched'. Proper Paddies, in fact. Vile is how they see us, just like the Boers, and when we pledge our loyalty, they shy away, embarrassed, as though we had just broken wind.[1]

Ellis's comments ring true for many Ulster Protestants, especially those living outside Northern Ireland. They feel embarrassed and frustrated by the speeches and actions of their political and religious leaders and impotent in their efforts to repair the damage inflicted on their community by their political marginalisation and stereotyping in the national media. This perception of loyalists as 'vulgar aliens' is partly attributable to unionists' failure to present themselves in an appealing manner, via their own literature and propaganda. However, the chief reason for this poor image lies in the nature and content of British media coverage of the conflict in general and loyalism in particular. Why has there been such a dearth of analytical coverage of unionist issues? What images of Ulster loyalism predominate British coverage and what are the effects of these on the British public's attitudes to the Irish conflict? I turn first to the nature of Ulster Unionist Party propaganda.

Spreading the word – the dilemmas of unionist propagandists

Unionists freely admit they lost the propaganda 'war' to their nationalist opponents early in the conflict and have rarely managed to gain the initiative in this vital area. Despite the occasionally effective pamphlet or overseas counter-republican initiative (such as the visit of unionists to America during the 1981 H Block crisis and subsequent trips to the United States to counteract damage inflicted by Sinn Féin visits), there was an absence of a carefully orchestrated propaganda campaign aimed specifically at the Great Britain market until the Ulster Unionist Information Institute (UUII) was established in 1988.[2] This was in stark contrast to the anti-home rule campaign at the start of the century when an energetic crusade was mounted on the British mainland.[3]

One explanation of unionists' propaganda failure was their unshakeable certainty in the moral supremacy of their position. The notion that they were 'so right', that they did not have to 'sell' their case, was held by unionists for many years. With in-built control of the state and an uncritical overseer in London, unionists before 1968 did not feel pressurised into justifying their political policies or philosophies. Another reason for unionist antipathy towards propaganda has been their conviction that the media was so much against them that contesting republican claims was a lost cause. This was particularly so during the early years of the Troubles when, after many decades of virtually ignoring Northern Ireland, external media agencies saturated the province, appearing to sympathise with the Catholic position. Unionists believed that, on account of the complex political background to the Northern Irish situation, and the very essence of the tabloid press, the media's focus was firmly on the more sensational aspects of the Irish story. In recent years unionists have appreciated more fully the need to promote their case and a London-based publicity department was established in 1996, to 'promote the cause of the Union; to argue the benefits, cultural, social, political and economic, of maintaining and strengthening the unity of the Kingdom'.[4] In its defence of the Union, the Unionist Information Office highlighted the contrast between the government's 'pro Union stance in Scotland and Wales' with its 'at best neutrality' position in Northern Ireland. However, even with the belated opening of a public relations department in London, unionists' difficulties in presenting an attractive image in Great Britain were to receive a further jolt with allegations of internecine bickering emerging from within that London organisation.[5]

Much of the early unionist propaganda was directed towards demythologising the claims perpetuated about Northern Ireland by the civil rights movement and, especially, Bernadette Devlin. The concentration on 'hate' propaganda relating to one personality or subject, a classic propaganda technique, was significant. Unionists realised that the intricate nature of the Ulster conflict meant that it would be better understood in terms of stereotypes, and they resorted to aping the tactics of their opponents by their caricaturing of Devlin. The British media had been quick to reassess the Mid-Ulster MP's image as a modern Joan of Arc and unionists capitalised on her fall from grace following her involvement in the Derry riots of 1969. They exploited Devlin's participation in the riots – 'the highlight of her career as a public figure' – claiming that it illustrated she was more interested in street politics than parliamentary debate.[6]

The main targets of Unionist Party 'hate' propaganda since the early 1970s have, of course, been republican terror groups, most notably the IRA. Perhaps unionists' most memorable propaganda triumph occurred when the Stormont government's Information Service concentrated their response on the casualties of the Provisionals' bombing campaign. The result was the 1972 booklet 'The Terror and the Tears', the popularity of which was to take even unionists by surprise.[7] Brian Faulkner, Prime Minister of Northern Ireland at the time, later noted that the demand for it was 'overwhelming as Ulster folk circulated thousands of copies to friends and relatives across the globe'.[8] 'Terror and the Tears' was successful because of its lack of political dogma. The theme of the twelve-page booklet was 'the inhumanity of the IRA', which was illustrated in graphic, pictorial fashion.[9] Innocent victims of the violence – children, women and pensioners – were selected. One section, labelled 'D Day IRA style – suffer little children', concentrated on child victims of the violence. A photograph showed a wounded girl sobbing as the coffin of her UDR father was removed for burial, while another depicted an ambulanceman removing the body of an infant killed in a 1971 IRA attack at a funeral showroom on Belfast's Shankill Road. The caption at the foot of the photograph encapsulated loyalist thinking:

> If there is power in the sobs of children and the tears of husbands and fathers, then the cause espoused by the terrorist is on the point of death. Its followers now are but walking dead animated husks, soulless and mindless, disowned by any creature capable of pity and compassion.[10]

Unionist criticism of IRA violence was a major feature of their propaganda and continued even into the 1990s.[11] While the tone of such literature was usually virulent, its nature was to change from the early 1980s, when unionists turned their wrath on the political 'godfathers' of such violence. Republicans were not the only quarries for regular unionist onslaught. Loyalist venom was also periodically directed at those agencies which threatened to bring Irish unity closer. Such a target was the SDLP, especially following the publication of the Forum Report in 1984. In 'The Way Forward' unionists rejected joint sovereignty and castigated the SDLP for their refusal to consider devolution seriously, claiming that British insistence on the principle of 'widespread consent' had given the party 'an absolute veto on the Assembly's progress'.[12] Other less likely targets for unionist vilification proved to be Conservative administrations in London. Thus a 1995 unionist critique of the Framework Document castigated its Irish dimension and considered the document to be presenting 'a case to take us out of the United Kingdom into an all Ireland'.[13]

The slow expansion in the number of unionist publicity initiatives, including the setting up of the UUII in 1988 and the establishment of the Unionist Information Office in London during 1996, illustrates unionists' growing awareness of their profound shortcomings in the area of propaganda. The purpose of the UUII news-sheets was 'to inform and update people throughout the United Kingdom and the wider world of the views of Ulster unionists' and the UUII publications have featured the research of specific unionist groups (including their legal committee's 'simple guide' to the complex subject of extradition) and acted as a vehicle for leading unionists, including Martin Smyth, James Molyneaux, Enoch Powell, John Taylor and David Trimble, to air their views on a variety of issues, normally coinciding with their own portfolios or areas of expertise.[14] One enlightening article voiced unionist disdain regarding the British public's perennial misunderstanding of the Ulster problem.[15] Ken Maginnis maintained that, burdened by 'a legacy of imperial guilt', British mainlanders exhibited 'self-consciousness' when the whole question of Northern Ireland was raised. At the heart of this 'self-consciousness' lay 'a sense of guilt, well fuelled by republican propaganda about an Irish debt to be paid'. Maginnis argued that the practicalities of this made the repaying of such 'debts' difficult. British authorities eased their consciences and deflected external pressure by 'transferring the guilt to Ulster unionists'. According to Maginnis, such a psychological rationale explained Britain's 'apologetic and dilatory approach to 20 years of violence'.

The widespread acceptance of unionists' inability to project themselves is illustrated by an *Independent on Sunday* article 'selling the unionists'.[16] This 1995 article started with the premise that loyalists were 'the image-maker's nightmare' and asked six advertising agencies how they would counteract the 'negativism' of unionism which 'seems to be losing them a PR battle with the republicans'. It believed that the existing unionist image as 'dour, stubborn, bigoted, articulate (though excessively noisy) and tribal' was a 'caricature' and that the unionists had 'a genuine case which can be powerful, even moving'. The paper justified its claim that unionists had a case:

> They are the majority community in Northern Ireland, an entity that has existed longer than about half the world's sovereign states . . . What if they [unionist leaders] set out, using all the artifices of modern politics, to win the hearts and minds of the British public? Would it – could it – change the character of the debate?[17]

Such a loyalist image problem is, therefore, partly due to miscomprehension of their political position, but it can also be attributed to their initially slow awareness of the power of propaganda and the underdeveloped public relations skills of their representatives. Despite the undoubted validity of their argument and frequent opportunities to capture the moral high ground at the expense of republicans, Ulster unionists have rarely been able to capitalise on anti-IRA sentiment in Great Britain, partly because of the lack of sophistication of their political literature and its failure to reach the uncommitted audience. However, the chief explanation for unionist inability to maximise opportunities for capitalising on

British repudiation of republican terrorism has been the national media's tendency to present loyalists in stereotypical, one-dimensional terms and to adopt a news agenda which has, by and large, promoted news items and subjects for analysis more pertinent to the arguments of unionism's political opponents.

Why don't they like us? Loyalists and the British media

Introduction

As I endeavour to illustrate below, the British media's analytical coverage of the Irish conflict has been generally limited, and this has been even more pronounced in its treatment of the unionist community. With the main protagonists in the conflict being perceived to be republican terrorists (and their political representatives, Sinn Féin), the British Army and government and, to an ever-increasing degree, the government of the Irish Republic, unionists have, for prolonged periods of the Troubles, been restricted to the periphery, and this has been reflected in media coverage. Apart from significantly less media space being afforded to the numerically greater Protestant community, those images which have emerged tend to be negative in their nature. These include the contradictory nature of 'loyalism', unionist bigotry and resistance to political compromise, and the shadowy, criminal essence of loyalist paramilitarism. I turn first to unionism's failure to dominate the media agenda in Northern Ireland.

Following the republican agenda

The complex nature of the Irish problem means that its comprehension can only be aided by detailed coverage of events and political attitudes. However, the vast majority of TV items have been factual accounts of military actions and violence – what has been dubbed by one commentator as 'a shopping list in death and destruction' – and this paucity of analytical coverage has added to the British public's misunderstanding of events in Ireland.[18] What investigative journalism there has been has tended to concentrate on attacking state agencies, an approach more likely to relate to nationalist or republican thinking than that of unionists.[19] My own research has illustrated the dearth of analytical coverage of the grievances and political nature of loyalism. Of the 60 programmes on Northern Ireland transmitted by Thames Television between 1969 and 1989, only 14 looked in significant detail at the unionist community, compared with 23 which had their main focus on the Catholic community.[20] Only 14 editions (out of a total of 71) of BBC1's *Panorama* between December 1968 and February 1995 looked specifically at the unionist community, compared with 26 which focused on the Catholic community. Channel Four coverage was less even-handed. A.A. Gill, writing in the *Sunday Times*, described the station's Irish 'anniversary' season as being 'decidedly pro-republican', adding that this was 'about as big a surprise as Monday morning'.[21] Not only were loyalists the subjects of significantly less coverage than nationalists, but the manner in which their case was presented was far from flattering. Hence, there were several programmes featuring loyalists' internal divisions, their intransigence and intimidatory behaviour and their tendency to be the chief stumbling-blocks on the road to progress.[22]

Although the majority of the national press is supposedly right of centre, this did not manifest itself in many papers expressing open support for political loyalism. Indeed, while many on the political right wearied of events in Ireland, restricting their support and sympathy to the army and government, those papers on the left were more open about espousing the political goals, if not the methods, of Irish republicanism. The *Guardian*, arguably more than any other daily, consistently pursued a pro-nationalist line.[23] Its revered owner and editor C.P. Scott had been an ardent supporter of Irish unity and had backed H.H. Asquith and David Lloyd George during the home rule campaign.[24] More recently, the paper has kept to a broadly nationalist agenda, 'reflecting the ideas which led to the New Ireland Forum and then to the Anglo-Irish Agreement'.[25] During the 1981 hunger strike, the paper's Irish correspondent, Anne McHardy, called for the British government to indicate its intention to quit Northern Ireland:

> The unionist refusal to even consider a future outside the United Kingdom may perhaps be the strongest argument for Britain to at least indicate that it wants to leave. At present the guarantee can be paraphrased as 'we would not object to going if the majority wanted us to'. Perhaps after 12 years of stalemate, it's time to say 'we really would like to get out. How can we help you to survive without us?' If Britain did make such a declaration it would then throw the ball into the Irish court.[26]

Other papers adopted a more pragmatic stance to the issues of troop withdrawal and unity. In calling for the British authorities to 'show courage' in dealing with the Irish question, the *Daily Mirror* exhibited a clear antipathy to the unionist cause in their warm response to the Forum Report:

> It is time to right the wrong and reunite Ireland. It is the only solution which makes sense . . . If the British Government offered serious resettlement grants to Northern Irish who preferred to come to Britain, then the long march to peace could begin. That is the way forward. It is time to take it.[27]

The Economist was another journal which stressed the political advantages afforded by Irish unity.[28] As early as 1970, *The Economist* pointed out that the British government 'does not want to take Northern Ireland over' and a decade later they suggested that Ulster unionists 'should be told . . . that they cannot set their conditions for remaining in the United Kingdom'.[29] It suggested that 'a better hope for Protestants is that, slowly, both north and south will come to see that together they would be cleverer, stronger and richer than they have been while apart'.[30]

It would be wrong to deny that loyalists gained some capital from possessing, to varying degrees, the same opponents and friends as those in Great Britain. Press condemnation of IRA atrocities was hostile and universalistic in its nature, and vilification of Sinn Féin leaders like Gerry Adams and Martin McGuinness intensified following IRA attacks, especially on the British mainland. However, there was a differential in terms of the scale and nature of coverage afforded to such attacks in Great Britain and those occurring in Northern Ireland, with the mainly factual account of the latter campaign tending to camouflage a sectarian dimension related to such outrages. While the media, in the main, sustained their support for the army in the province, and sympathy was also extended to casualties emanating from locally recruited security forces (namely, the RUC and the Ulster Defence Regiment/Royal Irish Rangers), this tended to be muted in comparison with army casualties.[31]

A contradictory and divided movement?

Accusations of hypocrisy and division have been hurled at unionists by politicians and journalists alike, for the apparent contradiction between unionist principles and action. These have been especially vehement when unionist ire has threatened to derail British political initiatives and has been accompanied by paramilitary violence or intimidation. Exasperation and confusion have also been associated with the British response to such instances of 'disloyal' behaviour, such as the 1974 Ulster Workers' Council strike. The venomous television broadcast of Prime Minister Harold Wilson reflected not only the growing impatience of the British public (for whom the broadcast had been primarily targeted), but the schism which existed between British and Ulster unionist perceptions of what was occurring in Northern Ireland. Wilson's speech tweaked at unionism's most sensitive area. His claim that unionist loyalty was inherently selfish in its nature deeply offended many opponents of the strike:

> People who benefit from all this [economic subsidies] now viciously defy Westminster, purporting to act as though they were an elected government; people who spend their lives sponging on Westminster and British democracy and then systematically assault democratic methods. Who do these people think they are?[32]

Ironically, therefore, in his endeavour to win support in Great Britain, Wilson gave sustenance to the strikers in Ulster by delivering a speech which, in uniting disparate strands of unionism, reflected British failure to appreciate strength of feeling within the unionist community. Thus, by underplaying the political opposition to the Sunningdale Agreement which was prevalent in Northern Ireland (and, indeed, which had been expressed in the electorate's anti-Sunningdale verdict at the February 1974 election) and their miscomprehension of both the nature of the strikers' demands and the growing measure of support for them in the province, the British media predictably turned to loyalist 'contradiction' in their quest to explain unfolding events.[33] Hence, not one of Britain's many right-of-centre papers expressed any sympathy for the UWC. Even the *Sun* was not prepared to side with the loyalists during their crisis, interpreting their defiance of parliamentary will as clear contravention of their claims to be 'loyal' British citizens:

> the rest of us cannot and will not go on indefinitely trying to save a people who seem intent on destroying themselves . . . The so-called 'loyalists' have for half a century been an oppressive majority . . . Ulster men and women on both sides have to realise that ordinary British people are losing patience as well as hope for a sane settlement.[34]

Division in the ranks of unionism was a leading theme of media coverage of the early phase of the conflict and great attention was paid to the power struggle involving Terence O'Neill's 'liberal' wing of the Unionist Party and dissident leaders, most notably Brian Faulkner and William Craig. *This Week* interviewed these three unionist leaders and Llew Gardner's report covered 'the activities of the three separate factions of dissident unionists'.[35] Five years later the same programme returned to a similar subject when they interviewed loyalist grassroots supporters on Belfast's Shankill Road. On this occasion the interviewees spoke of Faulkner's 'betrayal' in joining the power-sharing experiment, and Peter Taylor, appreciating the irony in their criticism of Faulkner, posed the question, 'Can Brian Faulkner survive the attacks of the Protestant hardliners, the people from whom he has drawn so much of his support in the past?'[36]

Although unionism was not to experience the same degree of dissension and media exposure thereafter, disagreement both within the Unionist Party and between the DUP and UUP was to continue. The quality of unionist leadership was considered on a number of occasions.[37] In the wake of the Brighton bombing *The Times* suggested that the unionist population 'are owed a political leadership that is capable of distinguishing between conciliatory moves which do and conciliatory moves which do not put the Union at risk'.[38] Nearly a decade on, following loyalist castigation of Peter Brooke's RTE gaffe, the *Independent* bemoaned the dearth of fresh talent in unionism's ranks, suggesting that this was partly a result of the absence of devolved government. The paper argued:

> In Britain, the rigidity of the unionists' veteran leaders is seen as a substantial contributory factor in prolonging Ulster's agony . . . It is regrettable that because there is no devolved government in Northern Ireland promising and moderate young unionists who might have replaced or diluted the old guard have had no political jobs in which to cut their teeth. In the late 1980s, they gave up and moved into other professions. The older generation lives in the past, rarely venturing into the republic, and unaware of the extent to which its citizens have been Europeanised.[39]

Bigots in bowler hats?

The most enduring image of Ulster loyalism and the one which has dominated media coverage over the past thirty years is the perceived bigotry of Ulster loyalists, epitomised collectively by Orangemen and individually by Ian Paisley.[40] Arthur Aughey has noted how loyalism, despite the massive increase of media interest in the Irish conflict, has been presented to the British audience as 'nothing other than a primitive local cult given to rituals of a barbaric nature'.[41] One-dimensional usage of the term 'sectarian' and a tendency to dismiss unionists' cultural and political aspirations as merely ideologically bereft stubbornness have resulted in this all-pervading image of unionist bigotry, which largely explains the existence of loyalist marginalisation. Another result of this one-dimensional coverage is that people in Great Britain are barely more aware of the reasons why Orangemen want to walk in Northern Ireland today than they were when the conflict started thirty years ago.

Mainland interest in Orange parades has rarely been evident except when the likelihood of violence was high. Thus, the BBC provided scant coverage, even at local level, of the tercentenary celebrations of the Boyne victory, yet covered in depth the parades in 1969, 1970, 1986, 1991 and at Drumcree since 1995, when violence was anticipated. Interestingly, Patrick Buckland has shown that such parades are by no means the only cause of sectarian violence and claims that Orange processions were 'a precipitatory factor' in only six out of fifteen major riots between 1813 and 1914.[42] Orange parades have increasingly been interpreted as being 'provocative' or 'triumphalistic' in their nature and, as such, parades passing through nationalist areas have been regarded as constituting a threat to public order and, more recently, the much-vaunted peace process. This was, in the main, the tone of the reporting of the Drumcree stand-offs in County Armagh between 1995 and 1997. Suggesting that the government had made an error of judgement in allowing the 1996 Drumcree parade eventually to proceed, David Dimbleby argued that the peace process might prove to be the 'victim' of such 'triumphalism' and, in an interview with the Prime Minister, he stressed 'the perception that the majority population always gets its own way in Northern Ireland'.[43] Other critics of unionism maintained that the 'boneheadedness' of unionist leaders and their refusal to compromise 'confirmed the political bankruptcy of unionism'. *The Economist* leader went on:

> If the current crop of unionist leaders cannot achieve, or even propose a compromise about a short stretch of road in Portadown, what chance is there that they can bring themselves, or their followers, to accept a broad political compromise that would also be acceptable to moderate nationalists?[44]

In an age when interest in and awareness of the cultural manifestations of political organisations (including Sinn Féin) have provoked considerable media attention, little interest has been shown in Orangeism's cultural aspect. While this feature of loyalism has been consistently understated, that of 'triumphalism' has been spotlighted in many reports and programmes. Although a minority of writers have been increasingly aware of the psychological complexities of Orangeism – how fifth-column fears and a more pronounced awareness of their marginalisation have outstripped any feelings of 'triumphalism' – most still interpret it nearly exclusively in terms of this latter feature. Writing in the *Evening Standard* after Mo Mowlam's decision to allow the Drumcree Orangemen to proceed down Portadown's Garvaghy Road, Kevin Myers observed how 'within the peculiar psyche of Northern Ireland unionists, the right to march close to or even through Catholic or nationalist areas seems to be a key ingredient to the renewal of identity'. Myers concluded: 'The last gnawed old bone of identity, or assertion of Top Dogness, is the Orange right to march at this time of the year. That right can be deflected, rearranged and even bartered. But it cannot be surrendered. The Orange mentality does not allow it'.[45]

The blockers of progress?

Another leading image of contemporary unionism is that of fervent, unbending opposition to political reform and progress. This was normally most apparent in response to government initiatives on Northern Ireland, when unionists frequently appeared to constitute the only barrier to a political solution. For instance, most of the press were in unison over the worthiness of the Anglo-Irish Agreement in 1985 and condemned the 'blinkered outlook' of unionist leaders.[46] One paper went as far, five months after the signing of the Agreement, to suggest that the 'sense of betrayal' which unionists felt was 'not the result of an act of the Westminster Parliament' but was rather 'one of the unionists' own leadership'.[47] Even papers which were not unsympathetic to the unionist plight despaired of its eternally depressing nature and implored their leaders to say 'yes' to the Framework Document in 1995.[48] The *Independent* suggested that it was in unionists' interests to participate in discussions about the province's future, but questioned their right to establish a veto over all political change. It argued: 'If unionist politicians fail to co-operate, they might find that cross-border institutions are developed without them . . . The Protestant community effectively retains a veto over Northern Ireland's constitutional status, but not over all political change'.[49] When political talks were in danger of collapsing, the scapegoats have usually been unionists. This was evident during the media's analysis of the failure of the first round of all-party talks organised by Secretary of State Peter Brooke in 1991.[50] A long-standing opponent of the unionist case and a former adviser to Harold Wilson, Joe Haines berated the 'patience' of British governments in endeavouring to 'talk round' Ulster unionists, who shared similar 'wrecking' motives with the IRA. Haines maintained: 'If you don't like the game, object to the rules. That's what the Ulster unionists are up to in the talks about Ireland's future. The unionists and the IRA are playing a different game from all the others. Talks which succeeded would diminish the role of both'.[51] John Ware's *Panorama* edition during these talks also suggested it was 'the unionists that people mostly blame for the failure of the talks' and forecast that unionism's lack of modernity would relegate Ulster's Protestants even further on the political sidelines. Ware intimated that the longer unionists refused 'to cast themselves in a modern mould, the more likely the future of Northern Ireland will be determined without them'.[52]

Shadowy figures

Images of loyalists as intimidatory, shadowy figures have not been restricted to accounts of Protestant paramilitarism. During the 1974 UWC strike, loyalist 'intimidation' and the erroneous assumption that the strike was successful on account of paramilitary as distinct from populist support received greater media treatment than detailed analysis of the strikers' grievances or demands. In his *Mirror* report, 'The Crippled City', Terence Lancaster argued: 'It has been a revolt because it has been more than a simple withdrawal of labour. Behind the strike has been the barricade, the bludgeon and the boot. And behind all of these has been the gun'.[53] This direct association of the gun and the strike was not a totally accurate one, but it was a predominant feature of media coverage of the strike.[54] Even the Conservative press, perceived to be 'sympathetic' to loyalists, condemned the strikers as 'bully boys' in their consistently pro-law and order editorials. Direct comparisons were made between the IRA's volunteers and UWC strikers. Vincent Mulchrone wrote in the *Mail*: 'What the IRA failed to do in 5 years the Protestants have done in 6 days. The Protestant strikers have brought the Province to the edge of chaos if not civil war'.[55]

This deliberate decision to focus on loyalist-associated violence rather than investigating the reasons behind such community tension was also reflected in the media's coverage of another political initiative, the Anglo-Irish Agreement. Here, journalists concentrated on a new spate of sectarian murders, intimidation of workers and an unprecedented petrol-bomb campaign on the homes of police officers, and one asked: 'Are the politics of the streets taking over?'[56] A few months earlier *TV Eye* had highlighted loyalist attacks on 'over twenty-five' police homes which, Peter Gill argued, were 'part of a campaign to force the British government to abandon the Anglo-Irish Agreement'.[57]

Such reports of intimidation and street disturbances differed little from those of paramilitary violence. In a number of *Panorama* editions loyalists were portrayed as 'villains', either as shadowy figures in the terrorist 'underworld' or as ill-disciplined security force members. One such programme, 'Allies in Arms', presented a fascinating account of the 'remarkable' liaison between a foreign government (South Africa) and 'a shadowy paramilitary organisation in Northern Ireland'.[58] Reporter Robin Denselow compared the 'embattled nature of white South Africans with the siege mentality of Ulster Protestants'.[59] In stressing such a mutual friendship theme, the programme underestimated the common interest factor in such an arms venture. Perhaps *Panorama*'s most vicious and certainly pervasive indictment of the Protestant community was a 1990 edition, 'Ulster's Regiment – A Question of Loyalty', which revealed 'disturbing evidence that leaks from within the locally recruited UDR are the source of sectarian attacks'.[60] Apart from precipitating the government's subsequent decision to create a new Royal Irish Regiment by amalgamating the Ulster Defence Regiment and the Royal Irish Rangers, the programme also intensified loyalists' feelings that the media was pursuing a witch-hunt against them.

Liz Curtis has pointed out that the British media have made a clear distinction in their analysis of the activities of republican and loyalist paramilitaries, tending to understate the deeds of the latter group by labelling their actions as 'criminal'.[61] However, it is inevitable that the media have made a distinction between the groups, considering their very different motivations and theatres of war, but it would be hasty to deduce from this that they 'favour' one group more than the other. Indeed, by castigating loyalist paramilitaries and depicting them as 'criminals', the British media ensured that their political motivation was obscured, unlike that of the IRA, whose political rationale was, on account of skilful Sinn Féin propaganda and reflective comment in the British media, more coherent. Undoubtedly the abiding image of loyalist paramilitaries, as far as the British public is concerned, has been that of a motley band of criminal, psychopathic, amateurish mavericks who, if anything, have inclined to conform more to the 'Irish' stereotype than the more 'professional' volunteers of the IRA.[62] These impressions of loyalist paramilitaries were confirmed by the events which accompanied the burial of three IRA activists at Milltown Cemetery in March 1988.[63] Apart from the melodramatic nature of Michael Stone's attack and the presence of TV cameras at the funeral, it was the assassin's psychopathic tendencies which distinguished this act from other terror attacks and gained it widespread media coverage.[64] It was Stone's foolhardy, almost suicidal, mission which appeared to personify the chaotic, criminal essence of loyalist terrorism. Labels such as 'Rambo', 'psychopathic killer' and 'loner' were bandied about in the press and one report noted how Stone was 'still smiling as he fired into the backs of men, women and children trying to get away'.[65] Press refusal to side with paramilitary groups in Northern Ireland was illustrated in their response to the killing of Loyalist Volunteer Force (LVF) leader Billy Wright in the Maze prison towards the end of 1997. In a lengthy report on his funeral in Portadown, the *Daily Mail* noted how several thousand 'had been drawn to this small town to pay homage to a man whose business was murder and who died by his own methods'.[66] Other papers, while also expressing a lack of regret over the shooting, suggested that the killing was more meaningful in terms of the breaching of security at the Maze. *The Times* urged Mo Mowlam to 'move quickly to rebuild confidence among Northern Ireland's peaceable pro-union majority', and suggested that she 'should ensure that there is no further erosion of security'.[67]

Media sympathy for the unionist case

It is important from the outset to distinguish between the mutual sharing of 'enemies' (and, to a lesser extent, 'friends') by the British media and Ulster loyalists, and the existence of any enthusiastic, deep-rooted empathy or political sympathy for Ulster unionism. Certainly sections of the British press shared with the latter an antipathy towards the IRA and, albeit to a lesser degree, the government of the Irish Republic. Undoubtedly the most frequent subject of tabloid editorial comment has been associated with the activities of the IRA and the 'war' on terrorism, especially when it has spilled over onto the British mainland, and virtually every section of the British press has been sympathetic to the security-force victims of such violence.[68] However, in practice the correlation between Tory tabloid castigation of republican terrorism and overt political support for Ulster unionists was far from evident in their leading articles.

Therefore, British press support for governmental initiatives in Northern Ireland, including the Anglo-Irish Agreement (1985), the Downing Street Declaration (1993) and the Framework Document (1995) was universal. It was at such times, when they appeared most isolated and vulnerable, that unionists depended upon substantial editorial backing. Although substantial and sustained support rarely manifested itself during such stressful periods for unionism, the occasional feature, or report, expressed sympathy with loyalists' political plight. Commenting on the 1986 by-elections in the province, Peregrine Worsthorne suggested that, in ignoring unionists' political will, Westminster was encouraging more extreme elements within loyalism to adopt 'unconstitutional' methods.[69] In an article, 'The threat from threatened Ulster', Worsthorne asserted: 'No wonder Ulstermen feel threatened. They are threatened and the almost total indifference shown to last week's election results . . . will not encourage them one little bit to go on putting their faith in the protection of the ballot box'.[70] Other journalists maintained that Westminster's dismissive treatment of unionist politicians had sustained those most opposed to the Union. In demanding that Ulster should be 'treated like any other province of the United Kingdom', the *Mail*'s Andrew Alexander maintained that the 'contemptuous' treatment of unionists by successive governments had been 'a stimulus to those who wanted to overthrow majority rule'.[71]

The political haemorrhaging which might befall complacent governments who continually ignored the demands of unionists was spelled out by the *Sunday Telegraph*. Commenting on increasing loyalist concern over the content of the Framework Document, the paper warned that unionist MPs 'menaced' the Tory majority at Westminster and that growing loyalist dissent could result in 'a shot across the Government's bows in the final stages of the negotiations'.[72] *The Times*, which warmed to the unionist position in the 1990s, complained that there was still miscomprehension at Westminster about the substance of unionism. Following John Major's Guildhall speech, in which he made tentative gestures to Sinn Féin, *The Times* bemoaned the sidelining of the majority of Ulster's political representatives. Its leading article asserted: 'The inability of the British political class to comprehend the extent to which unionists have been militarised and disenchanted since the Anglo-Irish Agreement in 1985 remains a serious obstacle to discussion of the province'.[73]

The Times differed from the *Daily Telegraph* in its support for devolved government in Northern Ireland. In calling for a 'rethink' of government policy and the establishment of an administrative assembly, *The Times* alleged that 'wooing Sinn Féin has done nothing but raise the party's profile and alarm the Protestant community in Ulster' and proceeded to warn the Prime Minister to 'think again if his desire to be remembered as a peace broker in Ireland is sincere'.[74] The *Daily Telegraph*, on the other hand, pursued an integrationist approach. Although this was out of step both with government policy and grass-roots unionist opinion, the paper was unequivocal in its support for the Union, realising that the secession of Northern Ireland

from the United Kingdom would inevitably have ramifications for the constitutional futures of Wales and Scotland. This pronounced 'national' interpretation
of what unionism entailed, as distinct from the narrow 'provincial' unionism
proclaimed by Ulster Protestants (characterised, as it was, to some English eyes at
least, by unseemly, sectarian traits) was pivotal to the *Telegraph*'s policy on Ulster.
Therefore, any attempts to redefine 'unionism' were warmly applauded by the
newspaper. Praising 'a remarkable conference' organised by the Friends of the
Union at Hatfield House (the home of the Conservative House of Lords leader, Viscount Cranborne), the *Daily Telegraph* welcomed the creation of a unionist 'think-
tank': 'For too long, democrats and unionists have punched beneath their weight;
thanks to this think-tank there is now a real chance that their voices will be given
the same consideration in the counsels of government as those of the terrorists'.[75]

A constant theme of right-wing press coverage was the need to improve security both in the province and in Great Britain. Perhaps more than any other paper,
the *Daily Telegraph* was vociferous both in its condemnation of terrorism and its
criticism of periodic governmental lapses in security. Indeed, the paper placed
greater emphasis on the short-term primacy of winning the security 'war' at the
expense of immediate political progress. After the killing of ten Protestants by the
IRA in 1976, the *Telegraph* argued 'no purely political action will suffice' and
maintained that what was required was 'a firm and consistent security campaign,
visibly, impartially and relevantly directed towards suppressing terrorism from all
quarters'.[76] In another leading article around this time, the *Daily Telegraph* had
criticised those advocating military withdrawal, suggesting that 'if we wash our
hands of Ulster we are in fact washing our hands of responsibility for our own
security and survival', and castigated the failure of the authorities to protect their
fellow citizens in Northern Ireland. The *Telegraph* neatly pinpointed the predicament of Ulster's majority community:

> They have had to live in a society in which the forces of evil, malice, madness
> and violence which are everywhere present, so far from being properly
> repressed by public authorities, have been most improperly and outrageously
> rewarded. We are accustomed to saying that crime does not pay. It has paid
> handsomely in Ulster. Who can wonder now that a minority of Protestants
> learning the evil lesson now deal in the same coinage?[77]

Loyalists have been, for many years, aggrieved at the differing media response to
terror attacks committed in Northern Ireland and those executed in the rest of the
United Kingdom. Unionist disquiet was particularly evident in the wake of the
Warrington bombing.[78] By contrast, the more devastating Shankill Road bombing
later in 1993 failed to gain the headlines acquired by the Warrington blast.[79] An
interesting dimension of the coverage of the Shankill explosion was the focus on
the IRA volunteer killed planting the bomb, rather than the relaying of the
sectarian nature of the attack and its effects on the close-knit Protestant community in West Belfast.[80]

Another theme of the press coverage of the Shankill attack was the perception that the local people's response to the bombing was in marked contrast with that which followed the Enniskillen blast six years before. In his report in *The Times* Nicholas Watt noted that the mood on the Shankill was 'one of revenge with none of the spirit of reconciliation that followed the Enniskillen bomb' and warned that the attack would 'set off a chain of reprisals'.[81] The Enniskillen bomb, contextualised as it was as an attack on the wider community and not as a sectarian outrage, failed to result in unionists reclaiming the moral high ground and meant that they would be unable to capitalise on any lasting sympathy in their anti-Hillsborough campaign of the late 1980s. This contextualisation blended with the existing media interpretation of the conflict and resulted in the outrage being denied a political dimension. Thus, the coverage of the explosion concentrated on the high number of casualties, the unique scale of forgiveness to emerge from the grieving and the sacrilegious nature of the IRA's attack on the 'war dead'. It was these factors which made Enniskillen 'different' in the eyes of the British media, and not the belief that one section of the Ulster community was being specifically targeted by terrorists emanating from another section of that community.[82] The central theme of the press coverage of the attack was the welcoming of the propensity of the bereaved and injured to forgive their attackers, rather than focusing on blatant breaches of security in the province which had led to this and many previous attacks.[83] John Burns's *Express* report is a good illustration of the media's tendency to eulogise this 'newly found' Protestant capacity to forgive their opponents.

> In other homes [apart from Gordon Wilson's] in this backwater town there are tears for the victims. Yet no one talks of bloody vengeance against the killers and all strive to hide from you their tears. Time and again you are rocked by the unfailing niceness of the bereaved. Whenever their self-control slips they quickly apologise for their tears, yet you want to weep with them.[84]

Previously unchallenged, one-dimensional images of loyalism were questioned in this post-Hillsborough period. Features illustrating loyalist triumphalism and bigotry were replaced by references to the sense of betrayal, political marginalisation, isolation and insecurity. Robert McCrum suggested in the *Listener* that the accepted image of loyalists as 'the parochial, aggressive bigots of legend' needed 'some adjustment', maintaining the reality was that 'they, historical bullies, have also become victims and losers'. Witnessing an Orange parade, McCrum observed:

> For all their boot-faced graveness, these are a war-like, clannish people. Unsure of their future identity, anxious for a secure place, punctilious about the obligations of loyalism, they are always ready to go over the top to protect their territory. They believe they are God's Chosen. Their slogan is 'No Surrender!' The more their cause seems lost, the greater their intransigence.[85]

There was also comparatively little coverage of Protestant disillusionment at grass-roots level and there were few indications of the effects of republican violence on their Protestant victims. However, there were several notable exceptions. John Taylor's forthright and searching *This Week* edition, 'No Surrender', probed far beyond the prototypical images of unionist bigotry and intransigence, managing to convey the changing fortunes and predicament of loyalists during the post-Hillsborough period. Hence, the programme provided a timely reassessment of loyalism's triumphalistic image and argued that unionists were increasingly motivated by fear and anxiety. Taylor neatly summarised the unionist predicament: 'There are hard decisions ahead for Ulster's Protestant population, but they say they will never bargain their loyalty to the crown. That can never be surrendered. In the strength of that belief lies both their triumph and their tragedy'.[86]

Another programme which endeavoured to unfathom the esoteric nature of the loyalist psyche was Gavin Hewitt's 1986 *Panorama* report, 'The Loyalists of Ulster'. In emphasising the all-embracing character of unionist resistance, Hewitt noted how the 'high-risk strategy' implicit in the Hillsborough Accord 'touches on the Protestants' rawest nerve – betrayal by the English'. The *Panorama* team covered a wide range of loyalist opinion, including the influential Ballylumford power workers, a Fermanagh security-force widow and Ulster Clubs members. Hewitt stressed 'the contradiction that tears at the souls' of Protestants. In his conclusion he asserted,

> the Protestants are on the march, but their destination is unclear. They face a difficult choice; if they rebel they might well weaken what they desire most. If they accept the Irish having a say in their affairs, they believe the door would have been opened to a united Ireland. Either way they lose.[87]

This 'partial revisionist' media approach to evaluating unionism involved explaining the increased level of loyalist paramilitary operations, as well as accounting for their more clinical methods. It also meant that some journalists accepted for the first time that they had a responsibility to explain the stereotype (for instance, loyalist bull-headed intransigence), if not question the stereotype itself. This meant that when unionists were, on account of changing political and security circumstances, becoming progressively marginalised, media agencies were more likely to express increased levels of sympathy, albeit temporary in their nature. Such an instance was the media's initial response to the IRA's 1994 ceasefire. Although the main reaction was a welcoming one, verging on euphoria, several papers warned against complacency and the need to respect unionist opinion. Reports suggested that, in accepting the agenda of nationalists and republicans, there was a danger of permanently marginalising Protestants and the paradoxical image of unionists as 'underdogs' surfaced.[88] The *Sunday Times* was adamant that, in welcoming the ceasefire, the government should refrain from 'ditching' the unionists. The paper, which had once exposed the inequitable policies of unionist governments, now warned against 'betraying' the unionist community.[89] Its leader, 'Peace – But Not At Any Price', cautioned:

However intoxicating the so-called peace process becomes, we must never become entangled in a betrayal of the unionist community . . . Ulster unionists have stood by us in times of great peril; we must not betray them now. We owe them more than a shabby sell-out. Mr Major should ensure they do not get one.[90]

The *Sun* and *Daily Mail* also admonished the government for 'selling out' the unionists. The *Mail* spelled out a catalogue of increasing pressures on unionists who, they warned their readers, needed 'reassuring', and to be 'convinced they will never be sold down the river'.[91] The *Sun*, which had become increasingly sceptical of the Hillsborough Agreement, did acknowledge that the ceasefire signalled 'peace at last' but advised politicians to approach the future with caution: 'The slaughter must stop but not at any price . . . We must not be fooled by the terrorists' weasel words . . . Until the majority votes otherwise it must remain a part of the United Kingdom. There must be no appeasement, no surrender, no sell-out'.[92]

Probably the most pertinent analysis of loyalist reaction to the 1994 IRA ceasefire came several weeks after the Provisionals' original announcement. Fergal Keane's *Panorama* report, 'The Uneasy Peace', presented a balanced portrait of the problems and concerns of unionists, as well as observing change and friction within the loyalist rank and file. Keane argued that the greatest shifts in the Protestant community had emanated from 'the hidden world of loyalist paramilitaries' and maintained that the ceasefire had laid down 'a daunting challenge' for the unionists to carry out 'a searching investigation of their identity'. In highlighting the confusion which loyalists were experiencing over discerning such an identity, Keane observed how their 'loyalty' was under severe strain, which had been exacerbated by the IRA ceasefire. He concluded: 'Ulster Protestantism is on the move but has yet to define its voice . . . A moment of decision is approaching for the Ulster Protestants. The unfamiliar peace could prove to be the most fundamental test of their British identity'.[93]

Although the British media was not to sustain this 'underdog' theme, papers such as the *Daily Telegraph* and *The Times* were increasingly supportive of unionist demands. When UUP leader David Trimble expressed his unease with elements of Senator Mitchell's document, both papers sided with the Ulster unionist leader. The *Daily Telegraph* criticised Mr Mitchell and both governments for producing a document which 'would mean political suicide for the leader of Ulster's largest party' and suggested that the British Prime Minister 'should start using the muscle of the British state to secure a decent deal for the pro-Union majority in their own country'.[94] *The Times* was equally vociferous in its pre-publication condemnation and castigated Tony Blair's 'failure to defend the interests of those who put their faith in democracy'.[95] *The Times* leader suggested that Mitchell's paper was 'Sunningdale-exhumed and dressed in vivid green' and asked if the British Prime Minister was going 'to allow the most important issue of his premiership so far to be hijacked by the republicans?'[96]

British public opinion and the loyalists

What, then, has been the effect of the transmission of these, mainly negative, media images on public opinion in Great Britain? Opinion polls relating to Northern Ireland have, in the main, focused on a limited number of issues; namely, those of troop withdrawal, Irish unity and, to a lesser degree, relations with Irish administrations. Although public opinion findings have not been entirely damning for unionists, polls on the withdrawal and unity issues have given them little cause for celebration. While the number of those in favour of withdrawal tended to fluctuate, depending on the scale of IRA activity and the proposed timescale of any such withdrawal, it is fair to conclude that there has been a marked contrast between British political responsibility for providing a military presence on the streets of Northern Ireland and the British public's desire to lessen such a military profile.[97] British respondents have tended to be more reflective in their attitudes towards the question of Northern Ireland's long-term political future, and although support for an 'Irish' role in that future grew after the 1985 agreement, a majority backed the constitutional guarantee.[98] While polls pertaining to withdrawal and unity obviously provide insights into attitudes to the unionist predicament, they failed to provide a 'rounded' mainland response to the images and demands of loyalism or test the degree of support for its political objectives.

My own survey in six centres in Great Britain attempted to 'bridge' such a gap. I constructed a ten-question survey which aimed to obtain respondents' views on a number of easily recognisable loyalist images and received nearly 200 responses from people in London, Surrey, Devon, South Wales, Lancashire and Glasgow over a three-month period in 1995.[99] The survey confirmed the existing view that even after a quarter of a century of detailed media coverage there remained widespread ignorance of the Irish conflict in general and the unionist case in particular.[100] While 'indifference' was the most common response to the plight of Northern Ireland's loyalists (36 per cent expressed such sentiments with 26 per cent claiming 'sympathy' and 20 per cent declaring their 'hostility' to the unionist case), nearly four times as many admitted having 'limited support' for unionism than those expressing 'considerable sympathy' (46 per cent and 12 per cent, respectively). Predictably, perhaps, respondents expressed their condemnation of the Orange Order, unionist leadership and loyalist 'intransigence'. Nearly four times as many believed Orangeism to be a 'negative' influence on events in Ulster than those thinking it to be a 'positive' one, while nearly three times as many believed unionists feared compromise more than nationalists. Observing photographs of unionist leaders and the then unelected leader of Sinn Féin, only 11 per cent thought Ian Paisley and Jim Molyneaux (Ulster Unionist Party leader at the time) to be more significant figures than Gerry Adams.[101] A large majority of respondents (76 per cent) backed the move towards increased consultation with the Dublin government and even more (79 per cent) believed that Irish unity would ultimately occur.

These statistics belie a considerable number of expressed statements of sympathy for unionists (especially emanating from Glasgow and Lancashire). However, these expressions of sympathy tended to be overshadowed by respondents' criticisms of loyalists' 'intolerance' and 'intransigence'. For instance, a Lancashire training adviser said he could begin 'to understand their fears for the future of their culture' but confessed to having 'no time for the religious intolerance upon which that culture is based'. Likewise, a London lecturer conceded that loyalists 'probably have become marginalised in recent years', but he wasn't 'especially sympathetic' about their plight because he felt they had not 'presented themselves as forward-looking or willing to negotiate'.

Summary

A number of central themes have been discussed in this chapter. First, since the social, cultural and political manifestations of their loyalism are reported within the long-established mainstream contextualisation of the Northern Irish problem, unionists have rarely been able to enjoy the satisfaction of seeing their case presented in anything other than stereotypical terms. On account of the predominance of investigative programmes into allegations of state transgressions in Northern Ireland and due to the complex nature of their political philosophy (not to mention their own presentational shortcomings), loyalists have been especially susceptible to simplistic, one-dimensional media coverage and have been the subject of significantly fewer programmes or articles than nationalism or republicanism. Despite press condemnation of unionist 'enemies' such as PIRA or successive Irish governments, unionism has rarely received sustained press support when it was urgently required (therefore, the British press provided virtually unanimous support for governmental initiatives in Northern Ireland) and there has been a clear shortfall between media condemnation of republican terrorism and open support for the plight of loyalists. Thus, although there was an improved press awareness of the loyalist predicament in the 1990s, it would be disingenuous to overstate the significance of a marginal shift in the tenor of press coverage.

The consequence of the combined effect of inadequate unionist propaganda and analytical media coverage on the British public's understanding of the conflict was a diminished appreciation of the loyalist case in Great Britain which meant that the British public was less likely to align itself with unionists. Indeed, it was this direct correlation between the low calibre of information available to the British public and the subsequent dearth of support for unionism which has been the kernel of my argument. Due to the dearth of analytical coverage and the media's insistence on presenting the Irish problem in a simplistic fashion, unionists continued to be misunderstood in Great Britain. If one accepts that there is a 'British' as well as an 'Irish' problem, and that British knowledge of their most enduring news story over the last thirty years has barely improved, then one should be disturbed by the continuing intolerance in Great Britain towards both traditions in Northern Ireland, and especially the unionist one. Or perhaps, after all, such a characteristic is not confined to the 'bigots in the bowler hats' . . .

NOTES

1 *Sunday Times*, 26 June 1994.
2 Even then, the appeal of unionist literature tended to be confined to the 'converted', local audience, a theme which I develop later.
3 See Alan Parkinson, 'Ulster will fight and Ulster will be right!', MA, University of Westminster (1989).
4 'The Unionist', Unionist Information Office, Great Britain (Autumn 1996).
5 Rumours that the new manager of the Unionist Information Office, Patricia Campbell, was planning to sue the party for alleged religious discrimination warranted headlines in a number of broadsheets. See *The Times*, 27 July 1996.
6 'Ulster – The Facts', Ulster Unionist Party (n.d. [1970]).
7 'The Terror and the Tears', Ulster Research Department (1972).
8 Brian Faulkner, *Memoirs of a Statesman* (London, 1977), p. 145.
9 'Continuing the Terror and the Tears – More Facts about the Inhumanity of the IRA', Unionist Research Department (n.d. [late 1972]).
10 Ibid. Other sections of the booklet portrayed people carrying out everyday activities, but juxtaposed those with photographs of the aftermath of terrorist attacks in Belfast's Oxford Street and the Abercorn restaurant ('Next time you go into a cafe . . . think of the girls maimed for life!').
11 See I. Reynolds, 'Prov think', *Ulster Review* [Journal of the Ulster Young Unionist Council], Summer (1995).
12 'The Way Forward', Ulster Unionist Council (April 1984).
13 'Framed – A Critical Analysis of the Framework Document', Ulster Unionist Information Institute (1995).
14 *Ulster Unionist Information Newsletter*, 1 (Autumn 1988). Thus, James Molyneaux's 1988 party conference address was quoted in detail, as was David Trimble's maiden speech in the House of Commons. Clearly such a style was more suited to committed, local readers, rather than to the 'external' audience.
15 Ken Maginnis, 'Britain's Failure to Understand the IRA', Ulster Unionist Information Institute (Autumn 1988).
16 *Independent on Sunday*, 19 March 1995.
17 Ibid. One of the advertising agencies, Saatchi and Saatchi, even depicted Ian Paisley as the Ulster equivalent of Nelson Mandela, asking, 'What would it take for us to be recognised as a repressed minority?'
18 This was a theme of Rod Stoneman's 1983 film for Channel Four, 'Ireland – The Silent Voices'.
19 This explains the large number of programmes related to miscarriage of justice cases which, nearly exclusively, affected Catholics. In the one instance where this was not the case (namely, that of the UDR, or Armagh Four) there was significantly less TV coverage than that afforded to the Birmingham Six or Guildford Four.
20 For a more detailed analysis of Thames Television coverage of Northern Ireland issues see Alan Parkinson, *Ulster Loyalism and the British Media* (Dublin, 1998). This trend was apparent also in London Weekend Television coverage. Of 45 programmes transmitted by LWT between October 1972 and May 1988 only 10 dealt with chiefly loyalist issues, compared with 19 which had, as their central focus, nationalist issues.
21 *Sunday Times*, 10 July 1994.
22 This was reflected also in a number of *This Week* editions, including 'Ulster – The Power Game' (6 February 1969); 'Ulster – The Loyalists Say No!' (18 September 1975); and 'Intimidation' (11 September 1986).
23 For a detailed analysis of the *Guardian*'s treatment of the unionist case see Parkinson, *Ulster Loyalism*.

24 C.P. 'Great' Scott was editor of the Manchester *Guardian* from 1872 until 1929 and its proprietor from 1905 to 1929.

25 G. Taylor, *Changing Faces: A History of the Guardian 1956–88* (London, 1993), p. 156.

26 *Guardian*, 6 August 1981.

27 *Daily Mirror*, 15 August 1984. The *Mirror*, founded in 1903 and Britain's second most widely read daily, had a readership of 2,442,078 in September 1997.

28 The *Observer* and *New Statesman* were in this category also. Indeed, even right of centre journals such as the *Spectator* (18 December 1971) argued that British opinion would be for 'a change of mind to take place whereby the majority in Northern Ireland become prepared seriously to consider the conditions under which the unification of Ireland could be made acceptable'.

29 *The Economist*, 16 May 1970 and 23 May 1981.

30 Ibid., 23 May 1981.

31 Indeed, as *Panorama* coverage of the UDR illustrates, this could be quite hostile.

32 Quoted in Robert Fisk, *The Point of No Return: The Strike Which Broke the British in Ulster* (London, 1975), p. 183.

33 See Bill Rolston, *The Media and Northern Ireland: Covering the Troubles* (Basingstoke, 1991).

34 *Sun*, 29 May 1974.

35 'Ulster – The Power Game', *This Week*, 6 February 1969.

36 'The Price of Peace – The Protestants', ibid., 24 January 1974.

37 Ironically, praise for unionist leaders could be most commonly found in the obituary columns of the nation's press (this was true of Harold McCusker and Jim Kilfedder).

38 *The Times*, 19 October 1984.

39 *Independent*, 25 January 1992.

40 A case study analysing the manner in which initial media stereotyping of Ian Paisley mitigated against sympathetic portrayal of the unionist case can be found in my Ph.D. thesis, 'Loyalist case in Great Britain 1968–96', University of Wales, Swansea, 1996.

41 Arthur Aughey, *Under Siege: Ulster Unionism and the Anglo-Irish Agreement* (Belfast, 1989).

42 See Patrick Buckland, *The Factory of Grievances: Devolved Government in Northern Ireland 1921–39* (Dublin, 1979).

43 *Panorama*, 15 July 1996.

44 *The Economist*, 13 July 1996.

45 *Evening Standard*, 7 July 1996.

46 Ibid., 15 November 1985.

47 *Guardian*, 15 April 1986.

48 *Evening Standard*, 22 February 1995, criticised the 'predictability' of the unionist response to the Framework Document, suggesting that unionist anger had been 'expressed in typical fashion – a walkout'.

49 *Independent*, 23 February 1995.

50 I noted twenty-five 'strong' criticisms of unionist tactics in my sample of media coverage of these talks, compared to one 'mild' criticism of suggestions that the SDLP might withdraw from the discussions.

51 *Daily Mirror*, 3 June 1991.

52 *Panorama*, 'No Surrender – No Progress', 21 October 1991.

53 *Daily Mirror*, 24 May 1974.

54 Apart from two UDA bomb attacks in the Irish Republic, two Catholics were killed in pub attacks in County Antrim.

55 *Daily Mail*, 22 May 1974.

56 *This Week*, 'Intimidation', 11 September 1986.

57 *TV Eye*, 'The Thin Green Line', 24 April 1986.

58 *Panorama*, 'Allies in Arms', 11 December 1989.

59 Footage of Orangemen marching in Ulster was intermixed with that of cattle-driving Boers in South Africa's Orange Free State.

60 *Panorama*, 'Ulster's Regiment – A Question of Loyalty', 19 February 1990.

61 Liz Curtis, *Ireland: the Propaganda War* (London, 1983).
62 The criminal activities of loyalist paramilitaries were highlighted in several TV programmes, perhaps most spectacularly by Roger Cook's exposure of loyalist paramilitary racketeering (*The Cook Report*, 21 August 1987).
63 Three were killed and over fifty injured in the attack committed by loyalist Michael Stone.
64 Both the *Daily Mirror* and *Today* devoted over five pages to the story and the latter contained nine photographs of the attack.
65 *Today*, 17 March 1988.
66 *Daily Mail*, 31 December 1977.
67 *The Times*, 29 December 1977.
68 However, this is not to say that the London-based media gave the same coverage or degree of sympathy to locally recruited security-force casualties as they did for members of the British Army.
69 These were caused by the mass resignation of unionist MPs in protest over the Anglo-Irish Agreement.
70 *Sunday Telegraph*, 21 January 1986.
71 *Daily Mail*, 25 October 1982.
72 *Sunday Telegraph*, 15 January 1995.
73 *The Times*, 17 November 1993.
74 Ibid., 20 May 1994.
75 *Daily Telegraph*, 1 December 1997.
76 Ibid., 6 January 1976.
77 Ibid., 24 December 1975.
78 Two children were killed and over fifty people injured in the 1993 blast at a Warrington shopping centre. Newspapers led for days on the story and even a *Panorama* edition, 'An Ordinary Boy', was devoted to the incident.
79 Eleven were killed and nearly sixty injured in the Shankill bombing.
80 The IRA maintained that they were trying to kill a leading loyalist paramilitary who, they alleged, had been in a meeting in a different part of the same building earlier in the day. While such an 'excuse' was condemned, the press tended to accept the rationale behind the attack, labelling it a 'blunder'.
81 *The Times*, 25 October 1993.
82 Interestingly, Robert Rodwell's report in the *Evening Standard* (9 November 1987) dealt with the victims of the blast without mentioning their religion, but ended with a reference to '8 Roman Catholic youths' being shot in North Belfast later that night.
83 The personification of this unique tone of forgiveness was local draper Gordon Wilson who lost his daughter, Marie, in the attack. In her Christmas speech, the Queen commented on Wilson's 'inspiring example of tolerance' and how he had 'impressed the whole world by the depth of his forgiveness'.
84 *Daily Express*, 10 November 1987.
85 *Listener*, 19 November 1987.
86 *This Week*, 'No Surrender', 10 November 1988.
87 *Panorama*, 'The Loyalists of Ulster – A People in Torment', 10 February 1986.
88 See Alan Parkinson, 'Loyalists: the new underdogs?', *Belfast Telegraph*, 6 October 1994.
89 The *Sunday Times'* Insight Team investigated allegations of 'discrimination' and 'misgovernment' against the Stormont authorities and published their critical findings in 1972.
90 *Sunday Times*, 4 September 1994.
91 *Daily Mail*, 2 September 1994.
92 *Sun*, 31 August 1994.
93 *Panorama*, 'The Uneasy Peace', 17 October 1994.
94 *Daily Telegraph*, 8 April 1998.
95 *The Times*, 8 April 1998.

96 Ibid., 11 April 1998. Interestingly, it changed its position inside three days and, following the end of negotiations, the newspaper again threw its considerable weight behind a governmental initiative on Northern Ireland, claiming that 'after the longest of Good Fridays has come the best of news'.

97 The level of loyalist paramilitary activity was also a factor, with nearly double those who had been demanding withdrawal in 1972 doing so three years later. This is developed in greater detail in my Ph.D., 'Loyalist case in Great Britain', pp. 340–1.

98 In 1987 64 per cent were in favour of the constitutional guarantee, with 23 per cent opposing it (MORI/*Daily Express*, 19–24 January 1987), while an overwhelming majority (92 per cent) backed closer negotiations with Dublin, as exemplified by the Framework Document (quoted in the *Daily Telegraph*, 24 February 1995).

99 A detailed account of the survey's findings is provided in my book, *Ulster Loyalism*.

100 Forty-five per cent had 'little knowledge' of Northern Ireland affairs and over 50 per cent had 'limited knowledge' of the unionist case.

101 Only 4 per cent felt Ian Paisley had 'strengthened' the unionist case, while 53 per cent believed he had 'considerably weakened' it.

15 Unionism, Conservatism and the Anglo-Irish Agreement

Arthur Aughey

This chapter explores the nature of Ulster unionism and British Conservatism and examines how unionists and Conservatives perceived the provisions and purpose of the Anglo-Irish Agreement of 1985. It seems appropriate to do this since there has been a general and mutual incomprehension. The generality of the Conservative Party found it difficult to understand the extent of unionist hostility to that agreement. The generality of unionists believed that the signing of the agreement by a Conservative government (especially one led by Margaret Thatcher) was a gross betrayal. The chapter outlines the distinctive characteristics of unionism and Conservatism and the extent to which these characteristics correspond with each other or diverge. Attention is paid to the way in which the Anglo-Irish Agreement evolved amid the priorities of the Thatcher government. These priorities are assessed in the light of assumptions which I have based on readings of Carl Schmitt's *The Concept of the Political* and Francis Fukuyama's *The End of History and the Last Man*.[1] The appropriateness of this reading perhaps requires some initial justification.

It is often said, sometimes accurately, that people in Northern Ireland tend to have an unhealthy obsession with their own problems. When applied to academics it often means that they have a habit of ransacking the work of thinkers who have nothing to say about Ireland at all in order to make a point about the political situation there. Sometimes this ransacking is appropriate in so far as it may shed some new light onto well-studied territory. The Anglo-Irish Agreement is such well-studied territory and, it could be suggested, requires some new angle of approach. I do not suggest an interpretation along the lines of 'Schmitt and Fukuyama on the Irish Question' which would be overegging the pudding. Rather I take a specific reading of aspects of the ideas of Schmitt and Fukuyama to be a way of exploring the official hopes placed in the Anglo-Irish Agreement as well as the difficulties which lay in the way of that agreement delivering on those official hopes. Elements of both works can provide, I suggest, a distinctive perspective on the Northern Ireland situation. They allow us to examine the formal thinking which informed the approach of the Conservative government and upon which an optimistic view of the agreement was based. They also permit us to explore those resistant features of politics in Northern Ireland, in particular unionist politics, which created difficulties for that view and which compelled a subsequent reassessment of it. In the flux of events, manoeuvres and detail, such an approach might provide some fixed point or points for understanding the complexity of issues at the heart of the agreement controversy. The chapter goes on to examine the enduring legacy of the agreement in the relationship between Conservative politics and Ulster unionism and what that legacy means for unionist trust in the good faith of any British government.

Unionism

At the heart of traditional unionist political argument has been the *fact* of the Union, a fact which involves two distinct, though practically interrelated, ideas. The first holds that membership of the United Kingdom represents a clear and unequivocal definition of Northern Ireland's British political status. To live in Northern Ireland, in other words, *ought* to mean that one is accorded equality of citizenship with everyone else who lives in the United Kingdom. As the 1984 Ulster Unionist Party policy statement *The Way Forward* argued, 'only rights can be guaranteed, not aspirations'. To adapt a Burkean phrase, the proposition is that real rights and not pretended rights are founded in the fact of the Union. And that fact is nine points of the law in unionist politics. In practice, this is an idea which has issued in a determination to accept no political initiative which could be judged to attenuate British citizenship in Northern Ireland. It is a position which has been held with a stubborn constancy and which has come to be taken as definitive of the unionist mentality in general – 'not an inch', 'what we have we hold', 'no surrender'. This is a style which requires some explanation in modern British politics, a politics which for most of the post-war period has stressed the prime value of compromise and adaptation. If that has not always been the universal *practice* of British politics, it has been an almost universal *assumption* of British political culture.

A way of understanding this unionist view may be found in the work of the German jurist Carl Schmitt. The most famous of Schmitt's works is his *The Concept of the Political* which was published in 1932. His object was to capture the ultimate distinction to which all action with a specifically political meaning can be traced. If the appropriate distinctions in morality are good and evil, in aesthetics beautiful and ugly, in economics profitable and unprofitable, then for Schmitt the specific 'distinction to which political actions and motives can be reduced is that between friend and enemy'. The 'friend/enemy' distinction is a criterion denoting 'the utmost degree of intensity of a union or separation, of an association or dissociation'.[2] It is irrelevant, according to Schmitt, whether one rejects this criterion, finds it barbaric or atavistic, hopes that it will some day disappear or imagines that enemies no longer exist.

As an ultimate criterion of the political, in the sense of a 'in the final analysis' grounding, this does not mean that communities are actually engaged in war or civil war. The distinction remains, irrespective of reason or idealism, as 'an ever present possibility for every people existing in the political sphere'.[3] In Schmitt's uncompromising and startling view there is little room for equivocation: 'If a part of the population declares that it no longer recognises enemies, then, depending on the circumstance, it joins their side and aids them. Such a declaration does not abolish the reality of the friend-and-enemy distinction'.[4] Those who have been close to political life in Northern Ireland will be familiar with the meaning of that. That is how collectively, as a political people, unionists have understood their struggle with Irish nationalists. It is an understanding which is equally reciprocated and defines the nature of 'extremism' in the political culture of the north.

The difficulty which mainstream British public opinion has with that view, especially as it was expressed at the time of the Anglo-Irish Agreement, is intimated in Schmitt's work as well. Stable political communities, experiencing an orderly and settled administration of public affairs under the rule of law, represent not only an achievement of civilisation but a decisive outcome of previous conflicts and struggles. For instance, Schmitt was fond of quoting Arthur Balfour's introduction to Bagehot's *The English Constitution* to the effect that the 'whole political machinery presupposes a people so fundamentally at one that they can safely afford to bicker; and so sure of their own moderation that they are not dangerously disturbed by the never-ending din of political conflict'.[5] That is a satisfactory condition, one experienced by citizens in Great Britain and assumed to be the norm by the political class. The conventions of Parliament, in other words, ought to regulate the passions of political conflict. But it has not been the condition of Northern Ireland politics and therein lies the gap in understanding which was to become all too evident after the signing of the Anglo-Irish Agreement. Unionists did not believe that the machinery of the agreement allowed for safe bickering on the basis of the common acceptance of the rules of the game. They believed that a significant concession had been made to the objective of their enemy by assumed friends in the Conservative government. And this gap in understanding was to be evident in the differing responses of the generality of Conservative and unionist politicians to the agreement afterwards.

The second and related unionist idea is that Northern Ireland's British status, founded on the democratic consent of the majority, should be durable. This attitude is fixed in terms of the justice of the constitutional arrangements guaranteeing Northern Ireland's place within the United Kingdom. In other words, partition is legitimate and there ought to be no change in the status of Northern Ireland unless and until there is a change in the will of the majority, understood now, at least in (polite) Ulster unionist circles, as the 'greater number'. Historically, these principles of status and durability, founded on the 'fact' of the Union, have provided a clear mandate for unionist politicians to reject any set of arrangements predicated on the idea or assumption of the *natural political* unity of the island of Ireland (which is how unionists generally chose to interpret the provisions of the Anglo-Irish Agreement). For Ulster unionists today, whatever may have been the case in the past, there is no natural political unity in Ireland. There are held to be two states or two nations or two peoples on the island of Ireland. Therefore, unionist hostility to the Anglo-Irish Agreement was not a manufactured political tactic. It reflected a long-standing claim for the mutual recognition of these distinctive entities – Northern Ireland as a part of the United Kingdom and the Republic of Ireland as a separate state – which it appeared that the Agreement had substantially qualified.

Such an understanding may suggest a self-serving disposition to British politicians and officials dealing with a problem of violent instability. Any pragmatic means – even a modification of normal constitutional propriety like the agreement – ought to be tried to address this problem. Yet looked at another way – the way unionists looked at it – it appeared that the British government was behaving in a manner which contradicted its duty to uphold the fact, status and durability of Northern Ireland based on the expressed will of the unionist majority. And in these circumstances it was quite rational for unionists to challenge this change in British policy. To adapt another Burkean phrase, it was logical to qualify the expressive value of the civil state (Conservative constitutionalism) with the assertive value of the uncivil state (to do what is necessary to preserve the Union from the ill-advised actions of government). When the Anglo-Irish Agreement was signed on 15 November 1985 outraged unionists believed that such an uncivil state had been created and that it was their duty to reassert their rights in street protest and political boycott. This met a generally uncomprehending response among most of the population of the rest of the United Kingdom, who failed to acknowledge the fine distinction which unionists made between the action of government and the constitutional legitimacy of that action.[6] This was all the more revealing of the dissociation of history from current practice in British politics. Only a few years later there was official commemoration of the Glorious Revolution of 1688, a revolution the principles of which unionists believed themselves to be upholding, principles which put a premium on legitimacy and not power.

Conservatism and British political culture

Certain of these traits of Ulster unionism find their echo in the history and character of British Conservatism. But there are profound differences: Conservatives have traditionally understood their distinctive political genius to lie in the capacity to fashion institutions which reconcile order with personal liberty (a balance, it could be argued, which is to be found in justifications of the agreement). Since the last century Conservative politics have been bound up with the political institutions of the United Kingdom as the expression of the peculiar genius of the British people. A 'constitutional patriotism' was celebrated as the reflection of those leading traits of the British political character, a vigorous commitment to personal liberty on the one hand and the practical wisdom of slow, piecemeal, gradual constitutional adaptation and change on the other.[7] This is a recognisably Conservative ideology, not because it is the property of that party – it wasn't and isn't – but because it was the Conservative Party which, at the end of the nineteenth century, seized the opportunity to present itself as the constitutional (and patriotic) party. That meant becoming the Unionist (British) Party, a label which it still bears, a label which carries with it a formal responsibility for constitutional tradition and sovereignty.

This is a political disposition which has associated the proper governance of the territory of Britain with the institution of the Conservative Party and with the particular competence of its parliamentary leadership. Conservatives, it is argued, are sensitive to the various traditions within the United Kingdom. It is this claim which has been the prevailing bond of sympathy between Ulster unionists and the Conservative Party. Thus Conservatives have always been sensitive to traditional sentiment (for the Union, the British 'way of life'); to traditional purposes (law and order, opposition to terrorism); to traditional interests (the military, national security); and to traditional duties (protecting the lives and property of British citizens). It is too simple to dismiss these considerations as mere rhetoric, for rhetoric is also part of the reality of politics. However, while there are obvious similarities in perspective between British Conservatism and Ulster unionism – especially its formal reverence for the fact, status and durability of the United Kingdom – there are also clear differences of sentiment and commitment.

Before the First World War the cause of Ireland had preoccupied the Conservative leadership and had absorbed the energies of its brightest and best (and worst). The party's opposition to home rule had threatened to destroy the settled civilities of British parliamentary life even to the extent of provoking civil conflict. After that war the issue had lost its passionate intensity and no longer contradicted the proprieties of Conservative constitutionalism. It lingered, of course, but mainly on the wings of Conservative politics. The devolution of legislative authority over most domestic matters to a parliament in Belfast seemed to have achieved the best possible of all possible worlds – it removed the Irish question from British politics while satisfying the demand of the majority in Northern Ireland to remain within the Union. The partitionist settlement also salvaged Conservative self-respect: the party had done its duty for Ulster but had avoided the consequences of an intransigent position on Ireland. Thereafter, as George Boyce puts it, the Irish question 'was not what it had been between 1886 and 1922, an essential part of the education of a whole generation of British politicians'.[8]

Therefore, when the Ulster crisis forced its way back into British political life in the late 1960s most Conservatives had little or no feel for the problem. For most it was a fearful anachronism and a tiresome distraction from the business of government (in the 'real' Union of Great Britain). However, there remained those within the party who were unionist in the traditional sense. They constituted a relatively small number of MPs – never more than about thirty or so – though not without influence in the party at all levels. Whereas the first group has tended to give almost uncritical support to the policy of the leadership on Northern Ireland (whatever its details), the latter group has shown a willingness to dissent on principle.[9] This gap between principled unionism and pragmatic unionism (as far as Ulster is concerned), with the heavy bias in favour of the latter rather than the former, has underlined the distinction between the attitude of Ulster unionists and the generality of Conservative politicians. This distinction between principle and pragmatism was dramatised sharply at the time of the signing of the Anglo-Irish Agreement.

As Norton has pointed out, the Conservative Party has always taken pride in being a party of governance. 'By the manner in which it has governed, and by the policies it has pursued, the Conservative Party has managed to convey that it is a competent party of government.'[10] This governing idea at the heart of Conservative identity (most manifest, of course, when the party is engaged in what it takes to be normal activity; that is, when it is in office) is a strong pragmatic qualifier of issues of principle (like absolute fidelity to an unreformed Union). The justifications Conservative leaders made for the agreement may be boiled down to such pragmatic, governance-based assumptions. That only alienated unionists further. For unionists, of course, this was not just a pragmatic issue. It was and remains a defining issue of principle. As the governing party after 1979, the Conservatives encountered the requirements of government, which may be defined as the interplay between the ideological disposition of politicians and the bureaucratic rationalism of its officials. The Anglo-Irish Agreement was the product of that interplay and owes much to the influence of bureaucratic rationalism, albeit a bureaucratic rationalism informed by the assumptions of British political culture.[11] It may be useful at this point to put this bureaucratic rationalist/British political culture thesis in the context of arguments to be found in Fukuyama's *The End of History and the Last Man*.

Liberal rationalism and *thymos*

The proposition which everyone remembers in *The End of History and the Last Man* is Fukuyama's assertion that the defeat of communism means that there is no viable alternative to capitalist (liberal) democracy and that mankind has reached the endpoint of its ideological evolution. However, the real interest of Fukuyama's book lies elsewhere, in its discussion of the characteristics which together constitute the form taken by political modernity.

Very briefly – and simply – Fukuyama traces the triumph of liberal democracy to the successful reconciliation and synthesis of two competing visions of the political. The first, deriving from the liberalism of Hobbes and Locke, emphasises the centrality of self-interest and self-preservation and is dedicated to the arts of peace and trade in order to achieve the goal of material comfort. It seeks to modernise society through the taming of passion by reason, creating an order in which the rights of persons would find satisfactory inscription in the orderly conduct of public affairs. The second, termed *thymos*, or spiritedness, is the desire for recognition, glory and respect. It involves the assertion of the self or of the group against other selves and groups. It is (potentially) the root of conflict for its basis is honour, not interest, and therefore it is potentially beyond the scope of that rational compromise which the liberal takes to be self-evidently good for everyone. Hence, the *thymotic* character is associated in the liberal mind with fanaticism, the placing of principle before reason. *Thymotic* desire can take two distinct forms: *isothymia*, the desire for recognition of one's equality; and *megalothymia*, the desire for recognition of one's superiority. It is unnecessary to discuss precisely how Fukuyama believes capitalist democracy has successfully reconciled liberal rationalism and *thymotic* desire. I simply want to bank these ideas and to use them as a framework within which to approach the reasons informing the Conservative government's negotiation of the agreement.[12]

If one were seeking a term which would apply to the stated positions of successive British governments it would not be unionism; nor would it be nationalism. The appropriate term would possibly be *stabilism*; that is, the objective is to achieve stability in Northern Ireland and all else (to adopt the famous phrase of Peter Pulzer) is embellishment and detail. In other words, there is a tendency to understand the Northern Ireland problem in Hobbesian terms. The problem which ministers and officials seek to solve might be summed up thus: how can local politicians devise a rational and just compact among themselves and their communities in order to get out of a nasty and brutish state of nature and thus to secure the conditions of peace, putting behind them the fanaticism of historic disputes?

The two governments which were party to the Anglo-Irish Agreement, as well as those who subscribe to their endeavours, thought that they had a privileged position in envisaging the contours of such a just settlement because, unlike local politicians and their respective electorates, neither government was fully implicated in the passions of Northern Ireland. For all the difficulties presented by the weight of historical bag and baggage – Britain's role in Ireland and the ideological character of the Republic's constitution – the mindset of bureaucratic rationalism created a common ground upon which officials and ministers from Dublin and London could stand together and resist the residual calls on their attention of British unionism and Irish nationalism. That, at least, appeared to be the basis for equality of recognition and respect between governments. It is the manner in which the two governments have, since the 1980s, chosen to project their concerns about the crisis in Northern Ireland.

This approach understands the task of statecraft in Northern Ireland to be the transcendence of two mutually frustrating dogmas of denial. Stated simply, these two dogmas are: no first step *because* it is a step towards Irish unity – the unionist position – and no first step *unless* it is a step towards Irish unity – the nationalist/republican position. Ideally, the task would be to devise a formula which is capable of making the politics of dogmatic denial irrelevant. There would no longer be any need for negativity and frustration because everyone could be a winner. The formula might allow everyone to subscribe to the outlines of a settlement, permitting the communities there to engage constructively for the mutual benefit of everyone in Northern Ireland. In Fukuyama's terminology: institutional structures could be devised which might secure the liberal-rational goal of peace and stability by overcoming the destructive consequences of *megalothymia* – the desire to prove one's superiority – and transforming it into a positive *isothymia*, an acknowledgement of the equality of traditions. Some of the central political ideas informing this approach are easily identified; in particular, the prevailing idea of British policy in Northern Ireland has been that of balance.

The object of policy has been to create a 'balanced accommodation' of the contending parties in Northern Ireland. Essentially that is a claim to political virtue and rationality. This balance normally has been understood to mean the fashioning of an agreement which satisfies two mutually exclusive positions. It has been common, in other words, to propose that the nationalist aspiration to a united Ireland ought to be balanced against the unionist commitment to remain fully part of the United Kingdom.

It assumes a rational common good ultimately capable of being perceived by all participants. It's about building trust and mutual understanding. It is hoped that a balance of compromises can be arrived at to the mutual satisfaction of all sides. The parties in Northern Ireland might not like the compromises, but they ought to accept them in order to achieve an outcome with which their respective communities might be able to live. Ultimately, this approach is based on faith, a faith in the power of reason and argument to overcome what is understood to be irrational behaviour and violent fanaticism.

This liberal-rationalist approach is based on three interlocking assumptions which, if acted upon by all participants, should lead to a win–win situation. The first assumption is that a distinction can be made between symbolism and substance. Apparent symbolic defeats (e.g. for unionists, accepting some role for the Irish government in the management of the Ulster crisis) can bring substantial rewards; for example, political stability and the securing of Northern Ireland's position within the United Kingdom. Symbolic concessions by unionists, in other words, could mean the end of Northern Ireland's historic sense of instability and insecurity.

The second assumption is that politicians are capable of recognising the distinction between symbol and substance and are equally capable of acting on that distinction. The third assumption is that even though there might be a lot of wailing and gnashing of teeth, ultimately a deal can be cut on the basis of constitutional politicians accepting the value of substantial advantages even if they have to swallow a certain amount of distasteful symbolism. The universal advantage would be the isolation of the terrorists and the undermining of the support which has sustained them.

In short, it assumes that it is reasonable to envisage unionists swallowing some symbolic changes in Northern Ireland's place within the United Kingdom in order to secure the substance of Northern Ireland's place within the United Kingdom; and it assumes that nationalists can swallow the symbolism of Northern Ireland's continued Britishness in order to secure the substance of acknowledgement of their own tradition within Northern Ireland. This certainly would be an 'end of history' of sorts, an end of history in the sense of changing the pattern of mutual denial in Northern Ireland and ushering in a pattern of mutual recognition. Those who would hold this position – most British MPs and much of British public opinion – reckon that it is the sort of outcome which the majority of people in Northern Ireland wish to see.

In principle, then, such an approach may be read positively, in Fukuyama's own words, as 'a supremely rational act, in which the community as a whole deliberates on the nature of the constitution and set of laws that will govern its public life'. But as Fukuyama also goes on to say, 'one is frequently struck by the weakness of both reason and politics to achieve their ends, and for human beings to lose control of their lives, not just on a personal but on a political level'.[13] And if by 'losing control' we understand locally the inability of politics to make the required distinctions between symbol and substance, then experience would oblige us to believe that the result would be no different for a solution based on the best will of rationalistic purpose. The outcome is more likely to follow the pattern understood by Schmitt, a new dispensation for the struggle between friends and enemies. There is an eerie memory here of what Brian Faulkner once called 'necessary nonsense'. That phrase was Faulkner's way of trying to convince a sceptical unionist electorate in 1974 that the provisions of the Conservative government's commitment to a Council of Ireland, as provided for in the Sunningdale Agreement, were necessary symbolic concessions to Irish nationalism in order to secure substantial gains in practice.

The problem for Faulkner and his colleagues on the ill-fated executive of 1974 was that their electorate had very different 'ends' in view. Indeed, without too much exaggeration it is possible to understand Northern Ireland politics in terms of a distinct 'ism' (distinct, at any rate, within these islands): that of 'endism'. Put very simply, the single ideological coin of politics involves a nationalist sense of destiny, the end point of which is Irish unity and a unionist sense of the apocalypse, the end point of which is also Irish unity. Politics in this form is rarely (if ever) concerned with mutual recognition and stable accommodation. It is mainly about winning and losing in a struggle between friends and enemies, a struggle in which it is virtually impossible to tell the difference between symbolic issues and issues of substance, be those issues marches, anthems, flags or emblems, such as a Remembrance Day poppy. It is, in sum, the politics of communal assertion.

Thus unfolds a pessimistic understanding of what such a rationalistic strategy would create. Politics, in this view, are indeed about winning and losing, about victory and surrender, about mastery and humiliation. That, it is believed, is the true nature of the (Ulster) political. Real enemies have nothing to discuss. They can only manoeuvre. It is a world of conspiracy theories and manipulative stratagems, to such an extent that the possibilities for compromise or constructive opportunities – such as they may appear to those on the outside – are lost through politicians and officials being either too clever by half or being too paranoid for their own good. This is *thymos* or spiritedness with a vengeance. From a large menu of calculations, only one needs to be abstracted for our purposes.

For example, two key unionist assumptions have always been that the Irish state, never mind northern republicans, cannot accept fully the democratic legitimacy of Northern Ireland by satisfactory amendment (unionists would prefer the scrapping) of Articles 2 and 3 of its 1937 constitution (see below) – *isothymia* – and that there remains a powerful irredentist streak in southern Irish nationalism which has sustained the objectives of the IRA – *megalothymia*. For unionists, the obstacle to reason has been nationalist expectation itself which should be confronted head on by the British government. In other words, what unionists have sought – and what nationalists also seek – is what they also believe the other side is incapable of giving unless they are *forced* to give it up.

The Anglo-Irish Agreement, in terms of the benign rationalist thinking which informed it, was designed to change this style of politics – eventually. However, the powerful instinct which tells people that communal solidarity is ultimately essential (mobilising friends to challenge the enemy) if their culture is to be accorded full respect or even to survive has been traditionally more than a countervailing force to rationalist models of institutional accommodation or exhortations to respect the diversity of cultural and political beliefs. The business of definitive compromise, of the sort prescribed by bureaucratic rationalists and which we find in the justifications for the Anglo-Irish Agreement, has been interpreted consistently by political leaders as a threat to friends and to their own positions without ever satisfying the ambitions of the enemy. And in this political leaders generally reflect the deepest concerns of their respective electorates. Much of what happens and has happened in the political life of Northern Ireland may be gauged by that calculating rule of thumb. In other – Fukuyamian – words, the possibilities of politicians 'losing control' strike one more forcibly than the possibilities of the 'supremely rational political act' of reconciliation. With these notions in mind, let us return once more to the story of the agreement.

The bureaucratic rationalism of the Anglo-Irish Agreement

The avowed strategic purpose of the agreement was to encourage an attitudinal change in the cultures of unionism and nationalism in Northern Ireland and to foster the conditions for compromise such that their opposing identities and purposes could be accommodated within a balanced set of political institutions. The rationalism of the agreement lay in this. Yet it had reversed the priority of previous British initiatives by establishing a functioning 'Irish dimension' before attempting to establish some form of power-sharing devolution within Northern Ireland. It set up an Anglo-Irish Conference, the function of which was to provide the Irish government with a consultative role in the internal affairs of Northern Ireland and which would allow it to make recommendations for appointment to public bodies responsible for the administration of policy. This conference was to be serviced by a secretariat, stationed in Belfast, composed of both British and Irish civil servants, the duties of which were to oversee and to monitor the progress of conference decisions. It was also to assist in the drawing up of the agenda for conference meetings. The agreement acknowledged the right of the Irish government to 'put forward views and proposals on matters relating to Northern Ireland' and stressed that 'determined efforts' would be made by the British government to resolve any differences between itself and Dublin on these proposals. The provision for joint chairmanship indicated the equality of the two states, though the British government has never accepted, as ministers and officials would always repeat, that any of its sovereignty over Northern Ireland has been conceded.

On 'the modalities of bringing about devolution in Northern Ireland' and on proposals 'for major legislation and on major policy issues' the Irish government was recognised to have a major role to play. That role was not only to ensure equality of recognition for the nationalist 'ethos' but to act as a representative of the nationalist community. The text of the agreement was written in a bureaucratic style which served to conceal the significance of what the Conservative government had openly accepted: that the United Kingdom alone cannot determine adequately the welfare of a proportion of its own citizens. The expected quid pro quo has been Irish co-operation in the eradication of republican terrorism by security and judicial means, and its willingness to underwrite the main lines of British policy in the north. The purpose in this regard was not just for domestic legitimacy. It was also to legitimise British policy in Northern Ireland on a world stage.

The preamble to the agreement abounded in the language of rationalist optimism, especially the language of balance and symmetry. It proclaimed 'the need for continuing efforts to reconcile and to acknowledge the rights of the two major traditions that exist in Ireland'. Article 1, which claimed to define the status of Northern Ireland, made this plain. Both governments affirmed 'that any change in the status of Northern Ireland would only come about with the consent of the majority of the people of Northern Ireland' and both recognised that for the moment such a majority did not exist. But it did make provision that when such a majority should exist both governments 'will introduce and support in their respective Parliaments' legislation to give effect to a united Ireland. The symmetry implied in that formulation was equality of recognition for unionist and nationalist 'traditions'; and it corresponded neatly with the new symmetry of state involvement implied in the conference and the secretariat. Indeed, it was that symmetry, so finely rationalistic, which guaranteed the widespread support for the agreement in British and Irish public life, as well as in Europe and the United States. However, even within its own terms of reference, the agreement raised as many problems as it appeared to address. One is worthy of mention in the context of this chapter.

Not only the agreement but all Conservative policy statements on Northern Ireland had stressed the essential principle of democratic consent. However, the agreement itself was an infringement of that same principle. Unionists were neither involved in nor consulted about its structure or content. The justification for this which was most often cited – that there was no point consulting the unionists for they would not have consented anyway – simply confirmed its undemocratic status (in unionist eyes at least). Even if, after the fact, unionist leaders might have come to see some merit in the status guarantee of Article 1 of the agreement (which they did not, for the reasons we have already suggested) it would have been impossible for them to convince their electorate of its worth. Not only did the rationalism of the Conservative government appear to miscalculate the extent of unionist hostility to the agreement; it did not appear to understand the nature of that hostility. Unionists did not at all perceive a new structural symmetry in Anglo-Irish relations. They simply perceived a new *asymmetry* which seemed to provide for the privileged empowerment of the nationalist aspiration to unity at the expense of the democratic right of the unionist electorate to remain fully part of the UK. The 'enemies of Ulster' had won a victory and this only encouraged suspicion of political initiatives which should follow in the wake of the agreement rather than helping to defuse that suspicion. It heightened unionist fears of the Conservative government's willingness to consider dramatic changes in Northern Ireland's constitutional status. This was exactly the reverse of what Conservative supporters of the agreement claimed was the intention and precisely what its critics feared.

Conservative interests and the Anglo-Irish Agreement

If the bureaucratic-rationalist element in the agreement is manifest, what of the political interest of the Conservative leadership? The journalist John Whale had remarked perceptively on the occasion of Mrs Thatcher's election victory in May 1979 that her views of the Union were a bit like Old Testament theology: 'You find a strong threat of authoritarian changelessness, yet there is always a nevertheless. Both immobilists and advocates of change can find signs for their comfort'. Conservative orthodoxy, he suggested, has always been that Northern Ireland must stay part of the UK because a majority want it that way. Conservatives have never questioned this even in the days when Whitelaw 'was exploring the idea that the problem also had an Irish dimension'. Beyond that, however, the Conservatives have been pragmatic:

> Nevertheless, that very pragmatism allows the advocates of change to hope; because it also means that once a system is shown to be no longer workable, the Tories waste as little time as possible in going on reworking it. The Heath government changed its mind about many things besides Northern Ireland; and it would be no real surprise if the Thatcher government did the same.[14]

And the Thatcher government did do the same. The policy of the Conservative government confounded the expectations of Ulster unionist politicians. The unionist belief was that the new Conservative government would move towards regularising the peculiar, unresponsive parliamentary procedures of direct rule (the British dimension) and away from institutionalising any formal relationship with the government of the Irish Republic (the Irish dimension). The Conservative manifesto of 1979, with its stress upon local government reform, appeared to confirm those expectations. As it turned out, the Conservative government was to pursue a course of action quite the reverse of that proposed when the Tories were in opposition.

The developments which culminated in the Anglo-Irish Agreement of November 1985 had been set in train as early as 8 December 1980 when the British and Irish Prime Ministers met in the first Anglo-Irish summit in Dublin. The institutional arrangement established in its wake, the Anglo-Irish Council, was held by Thatcher not to involve any significant constitutional departure. As she put it in the House of Commons in 1982, no commitment existed on the part of the British government to consult with Dublin about Northern Ireland. That was purely a matter of domestic politics, a position she reaffirmed in 1984.[15]

Subsequent events and revelations show that the Prime Minister was accurate in her definition of the status quo but inaccurate in her suggestion as to the direction of government policy.

The most revealing assessment (insider and diplomatic) of the development of the agreement on the British side is to be found in the lecture by Sir David Goodall at Ampleforth College in November 1992. Goodall was one of the key British officials involved in the negotiation of the details of British–Irish proposals. As he indicated, Thatcher entered the negotiations determined not to compromise the Union and was primarily interested in finding ways to improve the security situation, especially in the area of cross-border co-operation between British and Irish forces. 'For this', argued Goodall, 'Mrs Thatcher was prepared to pay a price, but when the negotiations got seriously under way I do not believe she had any clear idea of what that price might be'.[16] Goodall claims that the intention of Garret Fitzgerald, on behalf of the Irish government, was to find a way of reconciling nationalists to the Union rather than breaking it. But: 'in Dr Fitzgerald's view this could only be done if the Republic were associated in some institutionalised way with the government of Northern Ireland, and if the institutions of law and order there – i.e. police and courts – were modified to make them more acceptable to the nationalist minority'.[17] In Goodall's opinion, once Thatcher had expressed a cautious interest in moving on this issue, Irish expectations about how far the United Kingdom government would go were quite unrealistic. The main thrust of the Dublin position was towards joint sovereignty over Northern Ireland, for which the Irish government was prepared to trade articles 2 and 3 of the Republic's constitution, articles which contain the so-called 'territorial claim' to the six counties. It remains Goodall's view that Fitzgerald finally got the message that Thatcher would not go that far after the famous 'Out, out, out' press conference in 1984 'and that they would be doing well to get as much out of the British as they eventually did'. And so emerged, according to Goodall, the 'central concept of the Agreement':

> firm and formal Irish acceptance of the Union (though without repeal of Articles 2 and 3 of the constitution) as a basis from which the Irish Government, on behalf of the minority in Northern Ireland, could be given a systematic and institutionalised influence on British decision-making there without any diminution of British sovereignty.[18]

Unionists, in their reaction to the final agreement, did not accept this concept nor any of its propositions.

In the House of Commons there was overwhelming Conservative Party support for the Anglo-Irish Agreement and acceptance of the reassurances given by Mrs Thatcher that it did not represent a 'sell out' of the unionists. There was and remained, however, an ambiguity in the *intellectual* Conservative response to that agreement. This ambiguity within the Conservative governing tradition may best be explored by abstracting and comparing the responses of Mrs Thatcher's two key supporters at that time: her Chancellor Nigel Lawson, who was not involved in the negotiating process; and her Foreign Secretary, Sir Geoffrey Howe, who was at the very heart of it.

Lawson's interpretation is very revealing of the Conservative governing style.

> The Agreement ... had been negotiated in total secrecy, largely by the Cabinet Secretary, Robert Armstrong. Not without cause, Margaret clearly regarded the Cabinet as far too leaky to be taken into her confidence. Geoffrey [Howe], as Foreign Secretary, was of course fully in the picture, as were Tom King, who had been appointed Northern Ireland Secretary in the reshuffle two months earlier, and his predecessor, Douglas Hurd. But with the possible exception of Michael Heseltine, then still Defence Secretary, the rest of us, so far as I am aware, knew nothing of it until it was presented to us for our approval, almost as a *fait accompli.*[19]

That the agreement, which represented such a profound reordering of the priorities of Conservative policy, should have been decided upon in this manner reveals much about the workings of the cabinet system under Mrs Thatcher and the prevailing attitude of senior politicians to Northern Ireland affairs. As Lawson recounts, he had 'considerable doubts about its wisdom' and 'indicated as much in Cabinet'. But he 'did not go so far as to oppose it'. Nor, he reports, did anyone else. Nevertheless, it is difficult to follow Lawson's logic even though one is compelled to accept his prescience.

He argues that the failure of previous grand initiatives had made him sceptical of optimistic rationalism in Irish affairs. 'I had no doubt', he goes on, 'that the Anglo-Irish Agreement would be a political liability, in the sense that the resulting alienation of the unionist majority would far outweigh any accretion of support from the republican minority, and I could not imagine any objective observer would believe otherwise'. The question, for Lawson, was whether the domestic 'political' cost would be outweighed by the 'military' benefits that might come from greater security co-operation with the Republic. He was sceptical at the time 'and the subsequent black comedy of attempts to persuade the Irish courts to extradite suspected terrorists did not make me any less sceptical'. Yet it is difficult, on the basis of that Conservative scepticism, to understand Lawson's conclusion that he 'was not sufficiently confident of where the balance of advantage lay to oppose the Agreement' in cabinet.[20] His memoirs show that he was clear about where the balance of advantage lay.

Lawson's view that the alienation of unionists would be the main result of the agreement was echoed later in Thatcher's plaintive cry to Fitzgerald: 'You've got the glory and I've got the problems'.[21]

Sir Geoffrey Howe, on the other hand, did not have the same practical doubts as Lawson, nor, indeed, the same theoretical concern about sovereignty as did his leader. She, argued Howe,

> had been concerned, for example, to maintain British sovereignty over the north. I had ceased thinking of that as a commodity which could or

should be measured and upheld in so many vertically designated packages. I was more concerned to provide for the interpenetration of influence between the several communities that have to share the British Isles together.[22]

Howe's concern, in other words, was to solve a problem and not to get hung up on principles or theories like 'sovereignty'. In basic outline here we have the difference between Conservative scepticism and Conservative pragmatism and an intimation of what was to occur later in the manifest divisions within the Conservative Party over Europe. Nevertheless, Howe remains convinced that 'there is no alternative' to the processes outlined in the agreement (an ironic reference to Mrs Thatcher's own phrase about the necessity of her economic reforms of the early 1980s). For him it was not the solution but the opening of a more hopeful and positive phase in Anglo-Irish relations which might create the conditions for movement within Northern Ireland and a tempering of the friend/enemy distinction.

What of Thatcher herself? She had originally been sceptical of the value of talks between officials of both governments since she 'did not think there was much to talk about' and disliked intensely the idea that the Irish government would bargain about security co-operation in return for political reforms in Northern Ireland.[23] 'It seemed to me that to withhold full co-operation to catch criminals and save lives because one wanted some political gain was fundamentally wrong. But the Irish side did not see it like that'.[24] For Thatcher, the 'acid test' of the agreement would be the question of security.[25] If the Prime Minister was dismayed by what she felt was her counterpart's, Garret Fitzgerald's, lack of realism in proposals for joint sovereignty, then her own suggestion that the border be redrawn also smacked of unreality. As official discussion continued throughout 1984 and 1985 it became clear that the dynamic of the process was coming from Dublin and that Irish proposals were skewing the frame of discussion in a direction the Prime Minister believed to be unacceptable. 'I found myself', she wrote, 'constantly toning down the commitments which were put before me in our own draft proposals, let alone being prepared to accept those emanating from Dublin'.[26]

The Prime Minister was clearly dismayed and personally hurt by the reaction of unionists to the agreement. For her, article 1 (the consent principle) ought to have satisfied their desire for constitutional security.

> I believed that this major concession by the Irish would reassure the unionists that the Union was not in doubt. I thought that given my well-known attitude towards Irish terrorism that they would have confidence in my intentions. I was wrong about that. But the unionists miscalculated too. The tactics which they used to oppose the agreement – a general strike, intimidation, flirting with civil disobedience – worsened the security situation and weakened their standing in the eyes of the rest of the United Kingdom.[27]

The distinction between Thatcher's view of Conservative constitutionalism and the unionists' populist variety is clearly enunciated in this passage.

Her instinct in this case (according to Fitzgerald) was to do something to placate unionist outrage, but the Irish government resisted this. Nevertheless, the Prime Minister promised, after discussion with James Molyneaux and Ian Paisley, the leaders of the Ulster Unionist and Democratic Unionist parties, to operate the agreement 'sensitively'.[28] And that meant evading the implementation of some of the more contentious objectives secretly arrived at in the discussions of 1984–5, notably on reform of the security and judicial system in Northern Ireland. The nationalist response to this was to accuse the British of bad faith. But such confusions were implicit in the very structure of the agreement.

Thatcher subsequently revised her view of the value of what she agreed to in 1985. The 'acid test' of security successes, she felt, had not been as positive as she had hoped.

> In dealing with Northern Ireland, successive governments have studiously refrained from security policies that might alienate the Irish Government and Irish nationalist opinion in Ulster, in the hope of winning their support against the IRA. The Anglo-Irish Agreement was squarely in that tradition. But I discovered the results of this approach to be disappointing. Our concessions alienated the unionists without gaining the level of security co-operation we had a right to expect. In the light of this experience it is surely time to consider an alternative approach.[29]

This admission was pounced upon by unionists as a retrospective admission of the failure of a misconceived policy and a justification for their own opposition to it. Unfortunately for unionists, this anti-Howe proposition carried with it no indication of what such an alternative to the agreement or its principles might look like.

Unionist reaction

Despite Thatcher's view that unionists should have put their trust in her constitutional bona fides their view was a simple one. What had been established was a framework which had a built-in and permanent capacity to develop irrespective of the attitudes of a single (and temporary) Prime Minister. They believed, to put it politely, that the Thatcher administration's Anglo-Irish policy put an ill-judged and single-minded purpose ahead of the constitutional 'legitimacy' of that policy. The agreement offended their notion of constitutional propriety and had overstepped the limits of acceptability. This is not at all peculiar to the Ulster unionist tradition. There are echoes of it in Scotland's fractious relationship with the Conservative government in the 1980s. The principle of parliamentary sovereignty, resorted to by the Conservatives to justify overriding local dissent, proclaims Britain to be a *unitary* state. This might be true for England, at a pinch for England and Wales. It was not and is not felt to be true in Scotland or Northern Ireland. The United Kingdom is for the Scots and the Northern Irish a *union* state, not a unitary state. And this implies important limits to what a government can or ought to do. In the unionist case it implies that meddling with the status of Northern Ireland without consent of the people there is not a prerogative of Westminster.

These considerations notwithstanding, the Anglo-Irish Agreement *was* signed and implemented over the heads of unionists and did place the people of Northern Ireland on a different footing from those in the rest of the United Kingdom. Consequently, there have been problems for unionists in remaining faithful to the fundamental wisdom of, in the words of Democratic Unionist Deputy Leader Peter Robinson, the Union, the whole Union and nothing but the Union.[30] This had obvious implications for the coherence of unionist politics.

For instance, James Molyneaux, leader of the Ulster Unionist Party and epitome of unionist constitutionalism, asserted that finding an alternative to the agreement would not involve any constitutional adjustment because 'Northern Ireland already has a constitution enshrined in statute, precedent and practice'. That, he argued, should be the 'solid foundation' upon which all else is to be built.[31] This was the familiar 'fact of the Union' argument. Unfortunately for Molyneaux, of course, the Anglo-Irish Agreement had already become part of the precedent and practice (though not the statute) upon which the government of Northern Ireland was based and thereby the potential, even the likely, benchmark for any future development. And so, believed unionists, this is how it would go if the policy assumptions of the agreement were not stopped in their tracks and reversed.

Unionist opposition to the Anglo-Irish Agreement also provoked a response of popular sovereignty, one embraced enthusiastically by the unashamedly populist DUP: the assertion of an absolute right to self-determination. This was the response which Thatcher thought to be outrageously misconceived and counterproductive. Again, there were obvious echoes of this attitude in Scotland. As Canon Kenyon Wright asked in a provocative address to the Scottish Convention, referring to Thatcher: 'What if that other single voice we all know so well responds by saying, "We say no, and we are the state"? Well, we say yes – and we are the people'.[32] And this in a convention which was in principle and intention avowedly non-separatist (as are unionists). In the Ulster case the reverse was true: unionists said no and Mrs Thatcher said yes. In both instances, of course, unionists and Scottish devolutionists were ignored.

The generality of unionist opinion attributed the Anglo-Irish Agreement to a design dedicated to the undoing of Northern Ireland's constitutional status. They saw it in Schmittian friend/enemy terms and not in benign Fukuyamian liberal/rationalist terms. The evidence for this accusation lay in the purpose informing the strategy of northern nationalism which was judged to be an attempt to maximise the advantage of nationalist friends against the unionist enemy, and a calculation that unionist isolation and demoralisation could be increased to such an extent that its 'veto' on moves towards Irish unity could be surmounted. For unionists, the British government appeared to have had no bottom line and the Irish government was interested not in accommodation but ultimately in the assimilation of Northern Ireland. The events which attended the signing of the agreement and the street protests and disturbances which followed may be read in the light of Schmitt's stark proposition that only a weak people will perish. Those who took to the streets were determined to make the point that if the British government was 'weak', the unionists were not. While few Protestants actually engaged in the disruption and many were appalled, like Mrs Thatcher herself, by the images of confrontation, the concern which that disruption represented did permeate widely and continues to do so today.

The challenge which faced unionists after November 1985 was, therefore, one of strategic political recovery. Their task had to be, first, to reaffirm the United Kingdom status of Northern Ireland which had appeared severely compromised by the concessions contained within, and by the language of, the agreement. This meant trying to remove those constitutional ambiguities which some understood to be the genius of the agreement. Second, unionists needed to redress the perceived imbalance of relationships by working towards some structure of government which would acknowledge, if not their majority control of policy development in Northern Ireland, at least the majority's right to determine the form of any relationship between Northern Ireland and the Republic of Ireland. This was understood to mean, in practice, trying to wrest the initiative away from unionist enemies, actual and potential. Third, unionists had now to confront the implication of the 'process' set out in article 1, namely the willingness of the British government to give effect to the ultimate wish for a united Ireland. To unionists, that commitment not only suggested the acceptance by London of the inevitability of Irish unity at some time in the future but, from its own point of view, the desirability of working closely with the Irish government to promote it. This may have been a mistaken interpretation (outraged *thymos* in the heat of the moment) but it did not appear to be entirely without substance. Not only had unionists to try to arrest this process but they had to rehabilitate their own position within the British political system. That was a difficult task and in the immediate aftermath of the signing of the agreement the prospects did not seem propitious. As Molyneaux was to state three years on:

> In mid-November, I had to make a stark personal choice between two alter-natives. Whether to accept that ten years' patient endeavour had been wiped out; or whether to pick myself up and start all over again. I decided upon the latter course in the week after the black weekend of the signing ceremony. That is why I told the great rally of over a quarter of a million people on 23 November 1985, to prepare themselves for the long, hard road to success.[33]

The contours of the unionist strategy which unfolded are relatively easy to map.

The one option which was not available to unionists at that time was to accept the invitation of article 4 of the agreement and the enticement of article 2(b). Together both provisions suggested that if unionists were to accept devolved government within the framework of the agreement which would secure 'wide-spread acceptance throughout the community' (i.e. power-sharing) then the scope of the Anglo-Irish Conference would be correspondingly reduced. Having vowed never to accept the provisions of the Hillsborough Accord, such a possibility was ruled out in advance by the outright rejection of the agreement by unionists. The agreement option of article 4 not being practical politics in 1985, two possible lines of policy offered themselves to unionist politicians.

The first position followed closely the impulse of the 'Ulster Says No' campaign and assumed that consistent and forthright refusal by unionists to accept its provisions would ultimately condemn the agreement to impotence. The form of the Hillsborough Treaty would probably remain but it would only have a minimal impact upon political life in Northern Ireland. There was also the assumption that definite limits existed to the potential for constructive statecraft between the British and Irish governments. Without unionist support the British government would be constrained in any move to fulfil those ambitions of nationalists which had been raised in 1985. Equally, most unionists were convinced that Dublin could not deliver on better security and cross-border legal co-operation, no matter how sympathetic British policy might be towards nationalist demands. It would be politic, in other words, to batten down the hatches and allow the agreement (rather than unionism) to self-destruct. In the meantime the important thing was to restore goodwill at Westminster and to strengthen all possible links within the parliamentary system. This was the position consistently defended by Enoch Powell and was the one with which Molyneaux, though not Paisley, had greatest sympathy.

Nevertheless, it was a position which involved real dangers for unionism. It depended on the assumption about the limits of the agreement being accurate and on the estimate of the lack of will on the part of British and Irish politicians being correct. Above all, it was a strategy which had, in the main, to rely on others or on favourable circumstances to rid unionists of the agreement. If the calculations proved to be mistaken, then there was no guarantee that some form of joint sovereignty might not be agreed between London and Dublin over the head (once more) of unionist objections. Ironically, resistance, passive or otherwise, might, in the end, entail acquiescence in the purposes of the Irish nationalist enemy.

The second possibility was, indeed, to try to negotiate an 'alternative to and a replacement of' the agreement. That was the phrase which appeared in the joint unionist manifesto for the general election of 1987, *To Put Right a Great Wrong*. From the moment the agreement had been signed there was a powerful tendency within both unionist parties which argued that saying no and hoping for the best was not good enough. This tendency felt that not only was the agreement humiliating to unionists but that this humiliation was immeasurably compounded by the assumption that unionist representatives did not have the ability to negotiate themselves out of it, did not have the ability to retrieve some *thymotic* self-respect by the exercise of atrophied political skills. It also tapped a very definite frustration within the unionist electorate that 'something' should be done to develop a positive alternative to sitting on the window-ledge of the Union as the deputy leader of the DUP, Peter Robinson, once described the position post-agreement.[34] By doing nothing, unionists might be able to restrain temporarily the drift towards Irish unity. But the longer term suggested only demoralisation and fatalism, confirmation that the spirit had gone out of unionism as a political idea. For, it was argued, it was contradictory to assert that the policy of the British government is to betray Ulster into a united Ireland while at the same time putting one's fate entirely in the hands and goodwill of a parliamentary system dominated by that policy.

However, this position was also fraught with all sorts of difficulties. Negotiating an alternative to and a replacement of the agreement would implicate unionists in the very logic of the relationships which the agreement embodied. Because the agreement had given the Irish government not only a place in the conference but a say in the 'modalities of bringing about devolution in Northern Ireland' unionists would have to engage directly with what their politics had always denied – that the Republic of Ireland should have a say in the internal affairs of Northern Ireland. The practicalities of negotiation would present the same sort of dangers which the operation of the agreement itself implied. For if unionists really did believe that the purpose of the agreement was to place them in the role of a permanent minority then they might find themselves in talks isolated and diplomatically bound by the British and Irish governments, by the SDLP and possibly, ultimately, by Sinn Féin. This is indeed how unionist critics of the talks which began in the spring of 1996 read the situation. They traced it back to what was already intimated in the Anglo-Irish Agreement, namely a strengthening of the Irish dimension in the affairs of Northern Ireland. That, according to these critics, would mean a worse fate for unionists than the Anglo-Irish Agreement itself.[35] That is precisely how they did react to the Belfast Agreement of 10 April 1998. Those unionists who supported the Belfast Agreement (tentatively a majority), of course, argue otherwise. But an assessment of the respective merits of either position goes beyond the scope of this chapter.

Conclusion

Therefore, in the years since the signing of the agreement this unionist conundrum has not been resolved. In the talks about the future of Northern Ireland which have taken place under a Conservative administration – in 1991, 1992 and 1996–7 – unionist politicians have been torn between the wisdom of placing constructive proposals on the table and the fear that such proposals will be taken as weakness and concession by the nationalist 'enemy'. This is also an intra-unionist struggle where those who seek to play a statesmanlike role, for example, the leader of the Ulster Unionist Party, David Trimble, are compelled to have regard for the certain attack of those other unionists who do not believe that it is possible to achieve an honourable settlement under the prevailing Anglo-Irish dispensation. Also in play is an ambivalent Anglo-Irish Agreement factor. On the one hand, the experience of the imposition of the Anglo-Irish Agreement, which is deeply seared in the minds of unionist politicians, is taken to be a lesson that unionism must not be seen to be reluctant to engage constructively in the task of 'finding a solution' to the Northern Ireland question. On the other hand, the experience of the imposition of the agreement has made unionist politicians more suspicious of the (now) joint Anglo-Irish proposals as to how that solution might be arrived at. These very difficult cross-currents make collective agreement among unionists exceedingly problematic.

The legacy of the Anglo-Irish Agreement has also posed difficult questions of logic for a Conservative Party which, under John Major in the 1990s, made much of its fidelity to the integrity of the United Kingdom in opposition to Labour's proposals for constitutional reform in Scotland and Wales. Major had rededicated the party to the traditional unionist cause. Addressing prospective parliamentary candidates in Glasgow on 22 February 1992 he stated:

> I believe that we should stand for the historic Union of the peoples of the United Kingdom. A Union in which our nations work together but each sustains and develops its rich and varied traditions. Let me tell you why. Because England and Scotland, Wales and Northern Ireland together are far greater than the sum of their parts [36]

What is it that is greater than the sum of the parts? It remained the familiar Conservative (and unionist) idea of the constitutional people, a people whose diverse traditions are formally united under the procedures of parliamentary democracy at Westminster.

In the last years of Major's government, and subsequently, the Conservatives proposed an old argument for England, Scotland and Wales which had currency at the time of the Irish home rule debates a century earlier. That argument, originally stated by unionist leader Sir Edward Carson, held that there was no halfway house between union and separation. In Scotland it proved a reasonably successful cry which stemmed the depletion of the Scottish Conservative vote in the general election of 1992. In sum, the Conservative position on Scottish and Welsh self-government was this: they can have separation if they want it; in the meantime, they can have no *self-determining* influence over their form of government.

In Northern Ireland, however, the Conservative position was that Northern Ireland could have a prescribed form of devolution/Irish dimension (there *is* a halfway house between union and separation). As critics were quick to point out, the Conservative principles governing the Union of Great Britain and Northern Ireland and the Union of England, Scotland and Wales had become manifestly inconsistent.[37] Equally, it may be concluded that, whatever the trajectory of Conservative policy on the Union, the relationship between British Conservatism and Ulster unionism has been changed utterly since 1985.

NOTES

1   C. Schmitt, *The Concept of the Political*, G. Schwab (trans.) (New Brunswick, N.J., 1976); F. Fukuyama, *The End of History and the Last Man* (New York, 1992).
2   Schmitt, *The Concept*, p. 27.

3 Ibid., p. 28.
4 Ibid., p. 29.
5 Ibid., p. 51.
6 See an interesting discussion of the possible conflict between the policy of a government and the responsibilities of the crown as guardian of the constitution in F. Mount, *The British Constitution Now* (London, 1992), pp. 93–112.
7 J. Stapleton, 'Law and state in English political thought since Dicey', *Durham Research Papers in Politics*, 5 (1993), p. 5.
8 D. George Boyce, *The Irish Question and British Politics 1886–1986* (Basingstoke and London, 1988), pp. 11–12.
9 See Arthur Aughey, 'Conservative Party policy and Northern Ireland', in B. Barton and P. Roche (eds), *The Northern Ireland Question: Perspectives and Policies* (Aldershot, 1994), pp. 121–51.
10 P. Norton, 'Introduction', in P. Norton (ed.), *The Conservative Party* (London, 1996), p. 11.
11 For an illustration of official attitudes see Brendan O'Leary, 'The Anglo-Irish Agreement: meanings, explanations, results and a defence', in Paul Teague (ed.), *Beyond the Rhetoric* (London, 1987), p. 24.
12 On the meanings of *thymos* see Fukuyama, *End of History*, pp. 143–211.
13 Ibid., p. 212.
14 John Whale, *Magill* (May, 1979).
15 T. Wilson, *Ulster: Conflict and Consent* (Oxford, 1989).
16 Sir D. Goodall, 'The Irish question, Headmaster's Lecture given at Ampleforth College, November 1992', *Ampleforth Journal*, 48, pt. 1 (January 1993), p. 120.
17 Ibid., p. 130.
18 Ibid. At a press conference at Chequers on 19 November 1984, following a meeting with the Irish Prime Minister, Thatcher ruled out Irish unification, confederation and joint authority. The Irish press chose to interpret this as a humiliation for the Irish government.
19 Nigel Lawson, *The View from No. 11* (London, 1992), p. 669.
20 Ibid., p. 670.
21 Garrett Fitzgerald, *All in a Life* (London, 1991), p. 570.
22 Geoffrey Howe, *Conflict of Loyalty* (London, 1995), pp. 426–7.
23 Margaret Thatcher, *The Downing Street Years* (London, 1993), p. 395.
24 Ibid., pp. 395–6.
25 Ibid., p. 397.
26 Ibid., p. 401.
27 Ibid., p. 402.
28 Arthur Aughey, *Under Siege: Ulster Unionism and the Anglo-Irish Agreement* (Belfast, 1989), p. 91.
29 Thatcher, *Downing Street Years*, p. 415.
30 *Belfast News-Letter*, 6 December 1985.
31 Ulster Unionist Party press release, 13 July 1992.
32 Quoted in A. Marr, *The Battle for Scotland* (Harmondsworth, 1992), p. 113.
33 James Molyneaux, speech to Friends of the Union, Westminster, 23 October 1988.
34 *Belfast News-Letter*, 18 November 1985.
35 See, for example, the arguments in Robert McCartney, *The McCartney Report on Consent* (Belfast, 1997).
36 Conservative Central Office, News Release, 22 February 1992.
37 Alex Salmond, 'A clean break and an amicable divorce', *Parliamentary Brief*, 3, 5 (1995), p. 35.

16 The Union

A concept in terminal decay?

Paul Bew

There is a battle currently going on for the soul of what remains of Irish unionism. The unionist community in Northern Ireland is split down the middle on the merits of the Belfast Agreement. The surprising feature of this debate is the absence of a historical dimension. The big political and economic facts of life favour the Ulster unionists: a very strong majority in Northern Ireland favours a Union which brings substantial material benefit. During his St Patrick's Day trip to the United States in 1994 Albert Reynolds openly admitted that Northern Ireland required the British subvention at the current level for many years to come. Presumably, it is partly in consequence of this insight that the Irish Premier also observed that he did not expect to see a united Ireland in his lifetime. Yet until recently, at least, unionism in Northern Ireland was clearly on the defensive and the tide of history appeared to favour the cause of Irish unity. In Harold McCusker's striking (if self-pitying) phrase, after the signing of the Anglo-Irish Agreement of 1985, Ulster unionism has been reduced in the eyes of its adherents to the status of an activity which can go on in private between two consenting adults. It is worth noting the changing language of successive Tory Secretaries of State for Northern Ireland: Tom King openly averred that he was a unionist; Sir Patrick Mayhew felt it safer to be a 'Northern Irelandist'.

How has it happened that unionism has come to be stripped of so many elements of its public respectability and credibility? At first sight, it is surprising. In many important respects the Union has historically been a success. From 1800 to 1921 it was compatible with substantial economic growth in Ireland – spectacular economic growth in the case of the north-east from the 1880s to 1920. It was compatible also with massive schemes of reforms of the spheres of landowner-ship, religious equality, education and social welfare which had the effect of making Ireland as a whole a heavily subsidised country on the eve of the Easter Rising of 1916; a country, too, which possessed a genuinely strong intellectual tradition in the scientific as well as the more literary pursuits. This was a strength across the board which compared well with the present marginality in science. There was a price, as Irish nationalists always insisted: a population of around 8 million on the eve of the horrendous tragedy of the famine had fallen to around 4 million.

But, as it happened – and contrary to every nationalist assumption – national self-government and nationalist economic and cultural policies proved to be no remedy. By 1956 one of the great leaders of the Easter Rising of 1916, Eamon de Valera, was presiding over a government with substantially higher rates of emigration than those which had characterised the last decades of the Union. With heavy irony, the population of 'Ireland unfree' (the six counties) had risen while that of independent Ireland had fallen. It had proved to be possible to create a subjectively more Gaelic and Catholic world but not increase the numbers of those (Pearse spoke wildly of 20–30 million) who wanted to enjoy it. Since then, the Republic, initially under the benign influence of its greatest Premier Sean Lemass (1959–66), has torn up the old Sinn Féin approach to national policy and has enjoyed much relative success. It remains the case, however, that, as Albert Reynolds has openly acknowledged, it cannot absorb the economic costs of the north and is indeed itself heavily dependent on assistance from the European Union.

Why then do those who defend the Union feel – quite rightly – that they are on the defensive? It all begins with Gladstone or, more precisely, to take the title of a pamphlet by a prominent Ulster Liberal Unionist, J.J. Shaw, *Mr Gladstone's Two Irish Policies: 1868–1886*. Mr Gladstone's first Irish policy was the policy of benign reform from above; he became the hero of many (perhaps a majority) of Ulster Presbyterians as he pursued the theme of equal treatment for all under the Union. Presbyterians in particular enthusiastically co-operated with Catholics in pursuit of religious equality and land reform from 1868 to 1885. As Shaw put it in his 1888 pamphlet: 'the policy seemed to us statesmanlike and liberal . . . It was to be carried out by bringing Irish law and Irish institutions into harmony with the interests and feelings of the great bulk of the Irish people'.[1] 'They have even now a profound belief in you', W. Hart Westcombe wrote in *The Irish Question: A Monograph in the Form of a Letter to the Prime Minister* in early 1886, 'but you will probably take a course one of these days which will disillusion them'.[2] Indeed so: Gladstone introduced his Home Rule Bill on 8 April 1886. The pressure forcing him in this direction had been immense. The violence associated with the Land League movement of 1879–82 had pushed him into the ugly decision of mass internment in 1881. In 1957 Conor Cruise O'Brien in a footnote with heavy meaning in *Parnell and his Party, 1880–90* called this decision a classic example of the self-defeating nature of the attempt to combine colonialism with democracy.[3] Gladstone agreed, and for this and for other more complex reasons – both positive and negative – decided to make a substantial concession to the Irish nationalist movement led by Parnell. So much was probably inevitable. What was not was Gladstone's dismissive treatment of Ulster Protestant and Presbyterian outrage – often led by his most enthusiastic erstwhile followers – as a mere outburst of crazed bigotry. Despite the advice of many of those close to him on the issue, in particular Ulster Liberal James (later Viscount) Bryce, he refused to exclude the north-east from his proposals. Ironically, in 1893 – and this has been widely ignored by his twentieth-century admirers – Gladstone was perceived to have accepted the case for exclusion, but by then it was too late. The prospect had opened up for Irish nationalism that a Liberal Prime Minister might place all of Ireland under a home rule parliament.

In reaction something starts to happen to the argument for the Union: it ceases to be a thesis (on the face of it a perfectly respectable one) that the future of Ireland as a whole would be a brighter one within the Union. It became, understandably, instead rather a more limited case for Ulster unionist self-determination, defended on the Gladstonian principle of the need to be responsive to popular local sentiment. In 1886 an 'Ulster loyalist' was already insisting: 'If an experiment in home rule must be tried in Ireland by the British public, then let it be tried where, perhaps, there may be a remote chance of its succeeding and where it has been asked for and let Ulster be excluded'.[4]

There was always the possibility of provoking a favourable English response for such an argument. Alfred Russell Wallace, co-discover, with Darwin, of the theory of natural selection, acknowledged the point with some force:

> Exactly the same Liberal principles which compel us to grant self-government to the great bulk of the Irish people forbid us to force these northern districts into a Union which is repulsive to them, and which will inevitably lead to extreme dissatisfaction and perhaps even to civil war.[5]

It is remarkable how little Sir Edward Carson says about the general case for the Union – which he profoundly believed in – during the third home rule crisis of 1912–14. Remarkable how often, he says instead, every argument which points towards special treatment for Irish nationalists is also an argument for special treatment for Ulster unionists. As the liberal unionist *Ballymoney Free Press* dolefully expressed it: 'The statement of unionist Ulster is that it merely wants to be let alone . . . Unfortunately since Satan entered the Garden of Eden, good people will not be let alone'.[6]

It was hardly an inspiring clarion call to outsiders. Yet, even at this level the argument had its merits and achieved cogent expression in the speeches of Bonar Law, Balfour and Chamberlain or in the writing of A.V. Dicey. There was much demagogy on the unionist side in the home rule crisis but the fact remains that Bonar Law was the first to articulate the principle of consent which still guides British and Irish policy. The sheer intellectual lustre of the unionist case is worth recalling: the University of Cambridge produced three Irish scientific knights, Sir George Stokes, Sir Robert Ball and Sir Joseph Larmour, to articulate the scientific community's opposition to home rule. In Oxford, Dicey's interventions in the Irish crisis are scrupulously restrained and lucid; the recently formed popular notion of Oxford academia urging on loyalist thugs in Belfast from the safety of their ivory towers is simply a caricature.[7] It all boils down, of course, to the relatively straightforward proposition: was the Asquith government right to propose (albeit half-heartedly) unilateral and substantive unwanted modification of a large community's membership within the UK?[8]

The prospect of partition loomed large in 1912–14. There was no good reason from *any* Irish point of view for not combining it with continued direct rule in the north; but London's hunger to disengage from a troubling and tedious island was becoming all too obvious and the prospect of two parliaments also loomed. Some began to worry about the fate of minority rights on the island. To counter this apprehension, as early as 1886 an optimistic theory of the future emerged to fill the intellectual vacuum. In a divided island both governments would have large minorities to accommodate – otherwise, retaliation would surely fall on one's own 'side', in the neighbouring polity. Ultimately Ulster unionists in 1921 did obtain their own parliament, but this was only achieved at a high price.

In the *Foundation of Northern Ireland* the Ulster unionist leader, David Trimble, wrote:

> There is a unionist myth about the Ulster crisis. It is that gallant Ulster took a stand, armed itself for the fight and its opponents in London backed down and its enemies in Ireland were defeated. Like myths generally, there is a kernel of truth to it and it says something important about the people who hold it. But the myth is not the whole story. The Covenant and the Volunteers were essential to demonstrate Ulster's will and Ulster's means to resist providing the backdrop to the political manoeuvres and negotiations in which the decisions were actually made. In those negotiations, unionists were realistic: they were not playing to the Gallery, but were seeking a result and had a realistic eye to what was possible. The unionist realism in knowing where to draw the line was matched by coolness and firmness in the crisis. Craig's skill in the post-war situation has not been fully recognised. His hand was weakened by war time; by British war-weariness; by republican violence and the communal disorder it provoked. But he kept his nerve. No longer could he be described as intransigent, especially not after he talked to de Valera, while the latter was still on the run and the willingness he later showed to confer with both Collins and Cosgrave.[9]

These are interesting comments. It is still not widely understood how 'high risk' the strategy pursued by Craig in 1921–2 was. He placed himself in the hands of that very faction of the British intelligence community led by Sir John Anderson in Dublin Castle and Basil Thomson of Scotland Yard which was determined to reach a compromise with the Sinn Féin leadership: a group which was determined to marginalise 'anti-terrorist' hardliners in the British state.[10] The underlying themes of the Craig–Collins discussions of 1922 – fair play for the nationalist majority in the north, co-operation, an 'all Ireland basis' and Dublin recognition of the Belfast parliament – are precisely the underlying themes of the Belfast Agreement reached in 1998.[11]

Perhaps unsurprisingly in this context, Craig came to believe that the hard-won local parliament would protect local unionist interests for ever against unwelcome outside intrusion. But this was far too optimistic an assessment. There was always an economic worm in the bud. Northern Ireland had passed its zenith of economic achievement; it became increasingly dependent on Treasury handouts, the existence of which Craig hid from the Ulster public as he sought to claim the benefits for his own parliament. Worse still – from London's point of view – the patriarchal Craig, attempting to ameliorate the harsh conditions of the

1930s, often sanctioned social expenditure which broke London Treasury guide-lines. In the thirties, too, a notably more sectarian and parochial tone began to inflect the rhetoric of senior Ulster unionists. In 1916 the unionists had been delighted to have as one of their prominent Westminster MPs the Catholic Sir Denis Henry. This style disappears; a Catholic unionist MP became unthinkable. In 1960 Basil Brooke MP still refused the advice of a majority of his parlia-mentary party to open up ordinary membership of the Unionist Party to Catho-lics. Devolution provided the perfect milieu for those unprepossessing Protestant *couches sociales* who, mesmerised by the great white parliament building at Stor-mont, felt that here was a plump chicken ready for the plucking by 'the right type'. Sir Wilfrid Spender, the able young English officer who had given up a highly promising military career because he was convinced of Ireland's strategic importance to London – then, as now, this was not a popular doctrine – spent nineteen years as a closet integrationist head of the Northern Irish civil service, wearily describing the devolved legislature as 'a factory of grievances'. The Whiggish Lord Charlemont, shortly after resigning from the Northern Ireland government, partly, it seems, as a result of the fatal decision to gerrymander Derry, aptly analysed the sectarian political culture of the 1930s in a letter to his friend General Hugh Montgomery.

> It's not entirely religious fervour – it's the gradual increase of pressure from independent organisations, leagues, socialism, all the political expressions of Ulster individualism. For the first ten years of self-government, the hurrah boys and their friends kept unionist MPs in their seats. But we are used to self-government now – this is the trend of present politics, and unless the Herodi-anism of the Protestant League can be out-Heroded, I, a supporter of the government, will lose my seat to a jackanapes, and with it, any chance of preferment.[12]

The benign theory of partition had not worked out. The Protestants fled the south in droves; those that stayed found in February 1934 that Fianna Fail was quite prepared (as were the Ulster unionists) to introduce new electoral arrange-ments which enhanced the dominant party's strength by destroying previous arrangements designed to protect minority interests.[13] Thousands of Donegal Protestants bitterly protested to Craig in Belfast – absolutely to no avail.[14] A settlement is a settlement is a settlement.

In the late thirties the regime inevitably became unpopular in Whitehall, where it was seen as a form of subsidised sectarianism. Such sentiments intensi-fied after the London rapprochement with de Valera embodied in the Anglo-Irish Treaty of 1938; this gave de Valera back the treaty ports and thus substantially limited the Allied war effort after 1940. The unionists were rescued only by Hitler and de Valera's insistence on a policy of neutrality. Interestingly, even in the aftermath of this sharp lesson, the London cabinet refused to accept the advice (from senior civil service sources) that reasons of national security implied that the UK had a selfish strategic interest in keeping Northern Ireland within the UK regardless of the wishes of a majority of its inhabitants; as Herbert Morrison made clear in public, the British government would not close the door on Irish unity if a majority in the north demanded it.[15] It is easy to see why: all Irish cabinets since the end of the Second World War have offered new strategic arrangements; for example, joining NATO, in exchange for Irish unity. In this sense the language of the Downing Street Declaration of 1993, or the Anglo-Irish Agreement of 1985, or the Sunningdale text of 1973 – all of which assume no selfish strategy or economic interest – is almost half a century old. No doubt it serves merely to pitch Britain's interest on a higher and more moral democratic plane.

Nevertheless, the war and its consequent gift to Ulster of the welfare state hugely strengthened the unionist regime and opened up a massive gap in living standards between north and south. The liberal Terence O'Neill made it clear in his memoirs that he assumed, when he took over as Premier in 1963, that the Northern Ireland Labour Party, not nationalism, was the main problem. *The* question of politics was why is Northern Ireland the least prosperous part of the UK? The issue of Irish unity was apparently marginalised. In consequence, O'Neill, desirous above all of 'stealing Labour's thunder' (his phrase) missed the moment in the early and mid-sixties when peaceful reform was a real possibility: the efforts to introduce reform *after* politics emerged on the streets in 1968 were doomed to failure.

Since the civil rights crisis, unionism has until recently been on the retreat. History, self-evidently, has not been on its side, but nor does it validate those 'Gladstonian' assumptions of men like Sir Robert Armstrong or Sir David Goodall who moved Mrs Thatcher to sign the Anglo-Irish Agreement. (A policy which, by the way, paid the merest lip-service to devolution, and thus – by heightening nationalist expectations and unionist fears – made it exceptionally difficult to achieve a devolved settlement over the next decade.) Its message is rather more equivocal but also rather more dark. Regional economic decline has reduced the influence of unionists to the point where Sir Patrick Mayhew – who in 1959 once eloquently explained to the Oxford Union that there were 'two nations' in Ireland now, in a not insignificant conceptual slippage – equally eloquently supported the Downing Street Declaration which is based on the existence of two rather different entities: 'the people of Ireland' and the 'people of Britain'. But the same provincial economic dependence which has dictated a decline in the bargaining power of the unionists has not had the same drastic effect on the concept of the Union. After all, Carson always defended the notion that the richer parts of the UK had a material responsibility towards Ireland – even the poorest parts of Mayo and Donegal. In current economic circumstances the Union remains a matter of material necessity for the people of Northern Ireland, all of them, and by implication 'the people of Ireland' as a whole. This much is not disputed by Albert Reynolds, but what of the interest of the rest of the UK?

In one of the few recent attempts by a senior figure in the British government to address unionist concerns, Sir Patrick Mayhew told the Irish Association in Dublin in May 1994:

Certainly unionists can sometimes be defensive and inclined to see them-selves as inhabiting an unsettled enclave in these islands. But there is another important side to unionism; the belief that all the different people of these two islands – English, Welsh, Scots and Irish, too – share far more than divides them, a belief that there is much value in their combined and various diversity as there is in their mutual conformity; a belief that in a democratic-ally established Union there is more strength to be found than in the sum of its constituent parts; and a belief, therefore, that all will gain from being freely associated within an entity that is a Union. These are political beliefs which, in their best and most inclusive form . . . are far from unique to the north-east of this island. They form an important part of the British Conservative tradition. They are the foundation of the United States of America. We see them reflected on the other side of the world, in the hopes and aspirations of President Mandela for a genuinely inclusive and democratic new South Africa, accommodating the diversity of all its people.[16]

The unionism which Sir Patrick Mayhew is here describing is the unionism which triumphed in the signing of the Good Friday Agreement. It lays great emphasis not just on the improved relations established by the agreement but sets great store by the increased east–west basis which is also promised. The emergence of devolution for Scotland and Wales has transformed the constitutional topography of the UK in a way that reduces the Northern Irish fear of devolution as an unwary second-class state which was widespread in the 1980s. Above all, it is a unionism – raised above the level of parochial and sectarian – which has a chance of attracting support throughout the United Kingdom. It is this point which internal critics fail to address but it remains the case that the prospects for any form of unionist politics – however modernised – in the circumstances of the United Kingdom remain uncertain. The choice bluntly is between an uncertain, problematical future and no future at all.

The Act of Union of 1800 had been intended to create a political forum where Irish grievances could be aired with relative freedom from sectarian influence. The Prime Minister, William Pitt, however, failed to persuade the King to grant that measure of Catholic emancipation which Pitt and his colleagues had been promising to Irish Catholics in the late 1790s. Pitt acknowledged ruefully: 'Ireland had long felt the narrow policy of Great Britain, . . . stained and perverted with selfish motives, [Britain] had treated her with partiality and neglect'.[17] In 1846 an outgoing Prime Minister, Sir Robert Peel, insisted:

I do not hesitate to say that in my opinion, there ought to be established between England and Ireland a complete equality in all civil, municipal and political rights . . . I mean there should be real, substantial equality in political and civil rights so that no person viewing Ireland with perfectly disinterested eyes should be enabled to say a different law is enacted for Ireland or, on account of some jealousy or suspicion, Ireland has curtailed and mutilated rights.[18]

All sections of the House of Commons – rather less impressed with other parts of Peel's speech – applauded this fine sentiment. But as the *Edinburgh Review* asked: 'What does it mean?' At the time of the famine (1846–50) nationalists were inclined to say very little. We do not have to believe that British policy was directed by the notion that God was punishing the Irish[19] to see that, inevitably, British rhetoric was condemned by a failure in practice to do more to prevent loss of the lives of a million United Kingdom citizens. As the *Cork Examiner* put it, on a heart-rending description of Skibbereen at the beginning of Black '47:

> A whole village is but the theatre of famine, disease, and death. One, two, three, four victims on one hovel! Old women turned into maniacs by hunger, and in their new-born ferocity, turning savagely on their own flesh and blood! And this in a Christian country – and under the proud banner of British sway! This on land united to England by a Union, considered as sacred as a holy covenant, so much so that the thought of severing it is regarded as a profanation, a sacrilege! Will no sound of woe penetrate the Cabinet or reach the heart of the Minister?[20]

At this moment Aubrey de Vere published, *English Misrule and Irish Misdeeds* (1848):[21] he argued that there were 'two Englands' – one a bad England which despised and humiliated Ireland and which could be seen in the indifferent response to the famine suffering; the other a 'good England' – 'noble, wise and strong' which sought to conciliate Ireland by measures of reform and justice. Aubrey de Vere lived to see the triumph of this 'good' England in Irish policy; indeed, he lived long enough to be irritated by the excesses of Gladstonian self-righteousness.[22]

Today, since the Downing Street Declaration of 1993, English Prime Ministers formally renounce what Pitt called 'selfish motives'. The Union survives only because it reflects the current will of the majority of the people of Northern Ireland; more than that, it survives on the basis of strict equality between nationalist and unionist in the province. Multicultural democracy can be characterised as an agreement to disagree (rather than consent on liberal values), civil and political rights for all, existence of a sphere common to all groups, state recognition of, and support for, the separate cultural communities and state neutrality (the state is neither with nor appropriated by any group). Such a project, the project of the Belfast Agreement, in a society bedevilled by historic ethnic tension is enormously complex and difficult; let us not forget elsewhere, in today's Europe, Germany denies citizenship to non-German residents settled as guest workers; Estonia in 1991 decided to deny citizenship to most non-Estonians, 40 per cent of the population. It has, therefore, to be underpinned by the clearest possible acceptance by nationalist Ireland that Northern Ireland is a legitimate part of the United Kingdom – and this is a key theme of the new international treaty which appends the Belfast Agreement. It is only such a recognition which allows David Trimble to talk so much as he has in recent speeches of a 'pluralist Parliament' for a 'pluralist people'. As Trimble has put it: 'When faced by either inclusivity or another generation scarred by self-defeating animosity, we chose inclusivity'.[23]

Fraught and difficult though this is, the Union has been finally stripped of any vestige of that exclusivism (indeed selfish motives and partiality) which attended its birth.

NOTES

1 This quotation is from the edition of Shaw's pamphlet to be found as *Ulster as It Is: A Review of the Development of the Catholic–Protestant Conflict in Belfast between Catholic Emancipation and the Home Rule Bill* (London, 1888), p. 43.
2 W. Hart Westcombe, *The Irish Question: A Monograph in the Form of a Letter to the Prime Minister* (London, 1885), p. 35.
3 Conor Cruise O'Brien, *Parnell and his Party, 1880–90* (Oxford, 1957), p. 55, fn. 3.
4 *Home Rule 1886: A Reprint from* The Times *of Articles and Letters* (London, 1886), p. 482.
5 See his essay in the pro-Gladstone collection of essays, Alfred Reid (ed.), *Ireland: A Book of Light on the Irish Problem* (London, 1886), p. 44.
6 *Ballymoney Free Press*, 8 May 1912.
7 Paul Bew, *Ideology and the Irish Question, 1912–16* (Oxford, 1994), pp. 52–5.
8 I have attempted to deal with this problem in ibid.
9 David Trimble, *The Foundation of Northern Ireland* (Lurgan, 1991), p. 31.
10 C.W. Ackerman, 'Ireland from the Scotland notebook', *Atlantic Monthly*, June (1922) pp. 608–10.
11 See, Paul Bew, *Irish Times*, 31 March 1997.
12 P. Bew, K. Darwin and G. Gillespie (eds), *Passion and Prejudice* (Belfast, 1992), p. 50.
13 See the neglected classic, Donal O'Sullivan, *The Irish Free State and its Senate* (London, 1940), pp. 415–18.
14 Denis Kennedy, *The Widening Gulf* (Belfast, 1988), is excellent on this.
15 M. Hughes, *Ireland Divided: The Roots of the Modern Irish Problem* (Cardiff, 1994), pp. 130–1.
16 Paul Bew and Gordon Gillespie, *The Northern Ireland Peace Process 1993–6* (London, 1996), p. 52.
17 Quoted in *Cork Examiner*, 14 January 1847.
18 *Edinburgh Review*, 89 (January 1849), p. 221.
19 Paul Bew, 'England's Willing Executioners', *Spectator*, 7 June 1997.
20 *Cork Examiner*, 6 September 1947.
21 Subtitled *Four Letters from Ireland Addressed to an English Member of Parliament* (London, 1848). The argument about the 'two Englands' is developed in the first letter.
22 W. Ward, *Aubrey de Vere: A Memoir* (London, 1904), pp. 312–57.
23 Paul Bew, 'Getting the Nobel Prize for Peace but no quiet', *Parliamentary Brief*, 5, 9 (March 1999), pp. 12–13.

Appendix

An Act for the Union of Great Britain and Ireland, 2 July 1800 (40 George III, c. 67)

Whereas in pursuance of His Majesty's most gracious recommendation to the two Houses of Parliament in Great Britain and Ireland respectively, to consider of such measures as might best tend to strengthen and consolidate the connection between the two kingdoms, the two Houses of the Parliament of Ireland have severally agreed and resolved, that in order to promote and secure the essential interests of Great Britain and Ireland, and to consolidate the strength, power, and resources of the British Empire, it will be advisable to concur in such measures as may best tend to unite the two Kingdoms of Great Britain and Ireland, into one Kingdom, in such manner, and on such terms and conditions, as may be established by the Acts of the respective Parliaments of Great Britain and Ireland.

And whereas in furtherance of the said Resolution, both Houses of the said two Parliaments respectively have likewise agreed upon certain Articles for effectuating and establishing the said purposes in the tenor following:

Article First. That it be the first Article of the Union of the Kingdoms of Great Britain and Ireland, that the said Kingdom of Great Britain and Ireland, shall upon the first day of January, which shall be in the year of our Lord 1801, and for ever, be united into one Kingdom by the name of *The United Kingdom of Great Britain and Ireland*; and that the royal style and titled appertaining to the Imperial Crown of the said United Kingdom and its dependencies, and also the ensigns, armorial flags, and banners thereof shall be such as His Majesty, by his Royal Proclamation under the Great Seal of the United Kingdom shall be pleased to appoint.

Article Second. That it be the second Article of Union, that the succession to the Imperial Crown of said United Kingdom, and of the dominions thereunto belonging, shall continue limited and settled in the same manner as the succession to the Imperial Crown of the said Kingdoms of Great Britain now stands limited and settled, according to the existing laws, and to the terms of Union between England and Scotland.

Article Third. That it be the third Article of Union, that the said United

Kingdom be represented in one and the same Parliament, to be stiled *The Parliament of the United Kingdom of Great Britain and Ireland.*

Article Fourth. That it be the fourth Article of Union that four Lords Spiritual of Ireland, by rotation of sessions, and twenty-eight Lords temporal of Ireland, elected for life by the peers of Ireland, shall be the number to sit and vote on the part of Ireland in the House of Lords of the Parliament of the United Kingdom, and one hundred commoners (two for each county of Ireland, two for the City of Dublin, two for the City of Cork, one for the University of Trinity College, and one for each of the thirty-one most considerable Cities, Towns, and Boroughs) be the number to sit and vote on the part of Ireland in the House of Commons of the Parliament of the United Kingdom . . .

Article Fifth. That it be the fifth article of Union, that the Churches of England and Ireland, as now by law established, be united into one Protestant Episcopal Church, to be called *The United Church of England and Ireland,* and that the doctrine, worship, discipline and government of the said United Church shall be, and shall remain in full force for ever, as the same are now by law established for the Church of England; and that the continuance and preservation of the said United Church, as the Established Church of England and Ireland, shall be deemed and taken to be an essential and fundamental part of the Union; and that in like manner the doctrine, worship, discipline and government of the Church of Scotland shall remain, and be preserved as the same are now established by law, and by the Acts for the Union of the two kingdoms of England and Scotland.

Article Sixth. That it be the sixth Article of Union, that His Majesty's subjects of Great Britain and Ireland shall, from and after the first day of January 1801, be entitled to the same privileges, and be on the same footing as to encouragements and bounties on like articles, being the growth, produce, or manufacture of either country respectively, and generally in respect of trade and navigation in all ports and places in the United Kingdom and its dependencies; and that in all treaties made by His Majesty, his heirs and successors, with any foreign power, His Majesty's subjects in Ireland shall have the same privileges and be on the same footing as his majesty's subjects of Great Britain . . .

Article Seventh. That it be the seventh Article of Union that the charge arising from the payment of the interest and the sinking fund for the reduction of the principal of the debt incurred in either kingdom before the Union shall continue to be separately defrayed by Great Britain and Ireland respectively, except as herein-after provided: That for the space of twenty years after the Union shall take place, the contribution of Great Britain and Ireland respectively towards the expenditure of the United Kingdom in each year shall be defrayed in the proportion of fifteen parts for Great Britain and two parts of Ireland: that at the expiration of the said twenty years the future expenditure of the United Kingdom (other than the interest and charges of the debt to which either country shall be separately liable) shall be defrayed in each proportion as the Parliament of the United Kingdom shall deem just and reasonable, upon a comparison of the real value of the exports and imports of the respective countries upon an average of the three years proceeding the period of revision, or on a comparison of the value of the quantities of the following articles consumed within the respective countries, on a similar average; viz. beer, spirits, sugar, wine, tea, tobacco and malt, or according to the aggregate proportion resulting from both these considerations combined; or on a comparison of the amount of income in each country, estimated from the produce for the same period of a general tax, if such shall have been imposed on the same descriptions of income in both countries; and that the Parliament of the United Kingdom shall afterwards proceed in like manner to revise and fix the said proportions according to the same rules, or any of them at periods not more distant than twenty years, nor less than seven years from each other; unless previous to any such period, the Parliament of the United Kingdom shall have declared as herein-after provided, that the expenditure of the United Kingdom shall be defrayed indiscriminately by equal taxes imposed on the like articles in both countries . . .

Article Eighth. That it be the eighth Article of Union, that all laws in force at the time of the Union, and all the courts of civil and ecclesiastical jurisdiction within the respective kingdoms, shall remain as now by law established within the same, subject only to such alterations and regulations from time to time as circumstances may appear to the Parliament of the United Kingdom to require; provided that all writs of error and appeals depending at the time of the Union, or hereafter to be brought, and which might now be finally decided by the House of Lords of either kingdom, shall from and after the Union be finally decided by the House of Lords of the United Kingdom; and provided that from and after the Union there shall remain in Ireland an Instance Court of Admiralty for the determination of causes civil and maritime only, and that the appeal from sentences of the said Court shall be to His Majesty's delegates in his Court of Chancery in that part of the United Kingdom called Ireland, and that all laws at present in force in either kingdom, which shall be contrary to any of the provisions which may be enacted by any Act for carrying these articles into effect, be from and after the Union repealed.

And whereas the said Articles having, by Address of the respective Houses of Parliament in Great Britain and Ireland been humbly laid before His Majesty, His Majesty has been graciously pleased to approve the same; and to recommend it to his two Houses of Parliament in Great Britain and Ireland, to consider of such measures as may be necessary for giving effect to the said Articles, in order to give full effect and validity to the same, be it enacted . . . that the said foregoing recited Articles each and every one of them, according to the true import and tenor thereof, be ratified, confirmed and approved, and be and they are hereby declared to be, the Articles of the Union of Great Britain and Ireland.

Index